D0085425

Refugees of Revolution

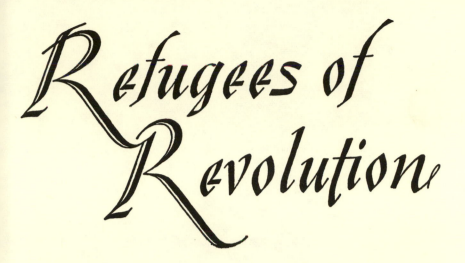

Refugees of Revolution

The German Forty-Eighters in America

by CARL WITTKE

GREENWOOD PRESS, PUBLISHERS
WESTPORT, CONNECTICUT

Copyright © 1952 by University of Pennsylvania Press

Reprinted by permission
of University of Pennsylvania Press

First Greenwood Reprinting 1970

SBN 8371-2988-5

PRINTED IN UNITED STATES OF AMERICA

PREFACE

THE GERMANS who came to the United States as a result of the tragic failure of the Revolutions of 1848 and 1849 were unique in the history of American immigration. Thanks to the political and cultural leadership of this small but exceedingly active group the total German immigration assumed unusual importance in the United States of a century ago.

The Forty-eighters included liberals, republicans, and radicals of every variety; men with university training and social standing, who were steeped in the intellectual tradition of Kant, Fichte, and Schiller; ardent and impractical reformers like Heinzen and Weitling; romantic, popular heroes like Hecker; noted physicians, inventors, jurists, and journalists. But the group also included many plain people, workers, farmers, clerks, and small businessmen, whose names have not been recorded in history. They too played their part in the movement to make Germany united and free, and emigrated to escape the consequences of their treason, or found the prevailing atmosphere so oppressive and economic conditions so uncertain that they resolved to build their future in a republic across the sea which promised both liberty and bread to the persecuted of every land.

The Forty-eighters, as this group of refugees is somewhat inaccurately known in United States history, were the cultural leaven and the spiritual yeast for the whole German element. They furnished the vitalizing intellectual transfusion which not only affected their fellow countrymen but influenced materially the political and social history of America during one of its most critical periods. The newcomers arrived at a time when all immigrants were on the defensive against American nativists, and they furnished the proud and aggressive leadership necessary to cope with such opposition. They were not the kind to surrender or become indifferent. They became genuinely excited about American issues, con-

v

vinced that they had a mission for the raw America of their day. Under their vigorous leadership, German-America experienced a cultural and political renaissance of unusual vitality, and the German element in the United States enjoyed its only "Hellenic Age."

I have tried to describe the total impact of the German Revolution upon America, as it affected both foreign and domestic affairs. Because one cannot appreciate the contributions of the Forty-eighters, or the internal conflicts precipitated among the Germans themselves by their aggressive and often tactless leadership, without understanding the nature of the German community in the United States at the time of their arrival, I have summarized briefly the German immigration before 1848. To illustrate the international character of European liberalism, I have noted the careers of a few Forty-eighters who were not of German origin, but belong in the same revolutionary tradition.

German Forty-eighters played a significant rôle in America for at least two decades. They figured prominently in the struggles over nativism and foreign policy; in the slavery controversy, the early labor movement, the rise of the Republican party, the Civil War, and post-war politics. Their influence was equally important in the cultural and intellectual progress of the period—in religion and its conflict with rationalism and free thought; in music, journalism, medicine, art, education, invention, the crafts and the professions, and in all the various societies and organizations in which German immigrants found an outlet for their gregarious instincts, and brought about the transit of their culture from the old world to the new. In short, I have attempted a history of the Forty-eighters with constant reference to the history of the whole German immigration, during the period when the influence of this remarkable group of refugees was at its zenith. I have also been concerned with the transformation of radical revolutionists into conservatives and ardent supporters of Bismarck and the Hohenzollerns, under the spell of the Franco-German War, and the Americanization process.

The files of the German language press from 1848 to 1875, and several German-American periodicals, are an indispensable source for a study of this kind. There is no other way to recapture the details of life in the German-American community of a century ago. It is here also that one finds the names of hundreds of Forty-eighters whose story has been completely overshadowed by the more glamorous, public careers of a

Schurz, Sigel, Kapp, Hecker, or Heinzen. If the list has become so long
as to constitute almost an encyclopedia of names, and the footnotes more
numerous than usual, my only justification is that it seems unlikely that
any one will cover such a mass of newspaper material soon again; that
I have written for serious scholars of the history of immigration as well
as other readers; and that it is important to establish the fact that the
Forty-eighter group was somewhat larger than is generally assumed, and
included the simple folk, as well as the "great names," who loved liberty
sufficiently to risk their lives in its defense.

My indebtedness to others is very great. Dr. Veit Valentin, supreme
authority on the Revolution of 1848, had hoped to write a history of the
Forty-eighters, when he came to America some years ago, himself a
refugee from German tyranny. His untimely death put an end to his
research when he had hardly got beyond the assembling of additional
data on the background of the German emigration. His widow made his
notes available to me, and I found them useful in reconstructing conditions in the German States immediately after the failure of the Revolution.

Through a generous grant from the Rockefeller Foundation, made
available by Dr. Luther H. Evans of the Library of Congress, for studies
in American History and Civilization, I was able to enlist the services of
Dr. Dora Edinger, historian and former co-worker of Dr. Valentin, to
read the *New Yorker Staatszeitung* and the *New Yorker Criminal
Zeitung und Belletristisches Journal* for the period from 1848 to the Civil
War. Dr. Russell P. Anderson, Director of the Western Reserve Historical
Society, made the files of the Cleveland *Wächter am Erie* available to me
under most favorable working conditions. I am indebted for similar
privileges with respect to the files of the Columbus *Westbote,* from 1848
to 1875, to Mr. John Marsh and Dr. James H. Rodabaugh of the Ohio
Archaeological and Historical Society. I must also again acknowledge
my obligation to those who helped me with materials in the preparation
of my earlier biographies of Heinzen and Weitling, which, in a sense,
were forerunners of the present work.

Mr. Wrayton E. Gardner of the Library of Western Reserve University
has been indefatigable in helping me with bibliographical details and in
procuring material from other libraries.

CONTENTS

Chapter 1 · *INTRODUCTION*

THE YEAR 1948 marked the hundredth anniversary of the popular uprisings which began in France early in 1848, and reverberated for a time through most of western Europe. For a few short months during the Revolution of 1848, liberalism was on the march against autocracy and reaction. National unification, individual freedom, greater economic opportunities, and popular self-government were the watchwords of a long-overdue revolt against the censorship, espionage, repression, militarism, and special privilege which marked the Age of Metternich. A new era of democracy and enlightenment seemed about to dawn throughout western Europe.

Unfortunately, to use once again the overworked phrase of George Trevelyan, 1848 was one of those turning points in human history when history failed to turn. The bright spring morning of revolution ended in another dark night of reaction, and the champions of liberalism and democracy, weakened by their own inability to agree on a program of action, were crushed by ruthless military power. The suppressed nationalities of Europe found themselves again under the heels of their exploiters and oppressors. As far as Germany was concerned, unification had to wait for a Chancellor whose policy of "blood and iron" eventually united the German states under the hegemony of the most militaristic and semi-feudal state within the whole imperial structure. For the German people, as well as for the rest of the world, the failure of the Revolution of 1848 had tragic consequences. Two World Wars have intervened in the meantime. They have been almost as disastrous for the victors as for the vanquished, and the Germans are still struggling with some of the same problems for which their forefathers took up arms against their hereditary, feudal rulers a century ago.

The centenary of 1848 aroused considerable interest in both Germany

1

and the United States. The noble experiment with the Weimar Republic had ended in a brutal Nazi dictatorship and World War II. Historians were tempted to review the recent march of events in the western world in terms of what had gone awry in 1848. The American Historical Association devoted the greater part of its annual meeting of 1948 to a reappraisal of 1848. Organizations like the Carl Schurz Memorial Foundation of Philadelphia planned special observances of the centenary, and the distinguished Chancellor of the University of Chicago flew to Frankfurt to deliver a challenging address on the events of 1848 and their bearing upon the problems of the present, in the hastily restored St. Paul's Church which . had housed the revolutionary dreamers a century ago. Berlin, occupied by the military forces of four victorious powers, and torn in two by a Russian blockade and the "cold war" between East and West, staged two rival celebrations, one before the ruins of the Reichstag, in the British sector, and sponsored by Social Democrats, the Christian Social Union, and the Liberal Democratic Party; the other, in the Russian sector, sponsored by Communists and their sympathizers, the Socialist Unity Party and the People's Congress for Unity and a Just Peace. All Berliners were given a holiday, and the *Berliner Zeitung* published the names of the victims of reaction who had died on the barricades of the Prussian capital on March 18, 1848. The Russian-sponsored celebration in the State Opera House opened with the playing of Beethoven's *Leonore Overture,* and was marked by several notable addresses and a public exhibition called "A Revolution and Its Precepts."[1] Despite an acute paper shortage and other difficulties of publication, numerous treatises dealing with the Revolution of 1848 appeared in Germany, and reflected not only the peculiar prejudices of the authors, but also the prevailing political sentiments of the particular sectors in which they were published.

The German Revolution of 1848 and 1849 is of special significance for the United States, for it touched off a large emigration to America. Although the primary cause of this immigration undoubtedly was economic, the disturbed political conditions of western Europe provided another powerful motive, and among the new arrivals were men, and some women, of substance, property, social standing, and excellent education, liberals and radicals and young intellectuals fresh from the universities, older and more seasoned agitators for political and social revolution, and patriots from every social class who had dreamed of unifying their fatherland on the basis of liberty, fraternity, and equality. It is with the history, problems, and contributions of these Forty-eighters, and particularly the political refugees among them, that this study is primarily concerned. They gave an intellectual, cultural, and political leadership to the German element in the United States which, for several decades, produced a cultural cohesion and a political and social influence unique in the history of American immigration.

It would be more accurate to speak of "Fiftyers" than "Forty-eighters," for most refugees came not in 1848 and 1849, but during the first half of the following decade. How many there were will never be known, and statistics depend largely on a definition of who was a "Forty-eighter." The mere counting of names is not the purpose of this study. Undoubtedly there were fewer than some enthusiastic German-American writers have claimed, and more than the "few thousand" whom Hansen recognizes in his study of the Atlantic migration.[2] Professor Zucker has suggested a "conservative estimate" of four thousand, but all such estimates include only the better-known among the new arrivals, and not the humble folk whose names do not appear in the newspapers. Economic factors may have been paramount in the decision of many artisans and peasants to make a new beginning in America, but the prevailing political climate in Germany was not without importance. On the other hand, it must be remembered that as time went on, and the veterans of 1848 gathered to celebrate the anniversaries of the Revolution, many a German-American who had raised neither sword nor musket, pen nor voice, in challenge of autocracy and reaction, and had emigrated solely for economic reasons, joined in the ceremonies and claimed the distinction of a "Forty-eighter," for no other reason than that he had come to the United States in the middle of the last century.

It is true that for the majority of German immigrants in the latter half of the nineteenth century the voyage to America represented if not an actual "flight from hunger," at any rate a deep desire to achieve greater economic freedom and security. Cheap homesteads and good wages in the "common man's utopia" across the sea attracted enterprising peasants and artisans. For such less articulate and less cultured fellow countrymen the political refugees among the Forty-eighters provided leadership at a time when conditions in America made their efforts both difficult and welcome.

For the purposes of this study, the term "Forty-eighter" is used in a limited sense, and applies only to those who in some way actually participated in the liberal movements and the Revolutions of 1848 and 1849, and left their homes because of a conflict with the established authorities, or because they realized that henceforth it would be either too dangerous or too intolerable to remain in a land in which a reactionary régime would be in the saddle for a long time to come. Usually even political refugees are moved to emigrate for a variety of reasons, among which economic considerations play a part. Basically, however, the cause of the departure of the Forty-eighters was their fundamental distrust of the governments in power. In the American Republic, whose Declaration of Independence and whose Constitution were well known to many of them, they hoped to find not only a new political freedom but an unhampered opportunity to exercise their talents.

There were many varieties of Forty-eighters. Not all conformed to the stereotype patterned on the career of Carl Schurz, the best known of the political refugees. Schurz will never lose his place of preëminence among the German political refugees. He became acclimated rapidly and completely, and played a distinguished rôle in American public life, and he has become a symbol for the large and diversified group who emigrated from Germany after the Revolution. Yet he was hardly typical of the group. He was younger than many of his fellow exiles, although most of the revolutionists were young men, and he came to America early enough in life to master the language of his adopted country, and to become equally eloquent in English and German. Furthermore, due to the substantial financial assistance which he received from the woman he married, Schurz never really experienced those critical years of poverty and unemployment which so terrified and embittered other refugees who found it difficult to become adjusted to a new environment and make a living for their families.

The Forty-eighters included men and women of many political complexions, from diverse economic and social groups. Among them were irrepressible radicals like Heinzen who never became completely adjusted to their new home; and extreme social reformers like Weitling, Sorge, and Weydemeyer who advocated a thoroughgoing social revolution according to their own plan for Utopia or the gospel of Karl Marx. Others belong to the forgotten thousands whose lives blended harmoniously into the American stream as they contributed their talents, great or small, to the building of America. Still others disappeared completely from sight after an unsuccessful struggle to gain a livelihood in a new land.

The revolutionary fire of 1848 and 1849 swept across all of western and central Europe, regardless of state boundaries, and the Revolution was an inter- and super-national phenomenon. The political refugees who came to the United States in the middle of the last century included not only German Forty-eighters, but Jewish liberals from Central Europe, Hungarians, Poles, Italians, Czechs, French, and representatives of other nationality groups. In the early days of their sojourn in America, these cosmopolitan liberals frequently coöperated to advance their common cause of human brotherhood and political liberty, and to give the movement an international character and significance.

FOOTNOTES

CHAPTER 1

1. Berlin *Tägliche Rundschau*, March 18, 1948.
2. Marcus L. Hansen: *The Atlantic Migration* (Cambridge, 1940) pp. 273-74. See also Marcus L. Hansen: "The Revolutions of 1848 and German Emigration" in *Journal of Economic and Business History*, II, 630-58.

Chapter 2 · *THE GERMAN ELEMENT BEFORE 1848*

THE GERMAN element in the United States before 1850 consisted primarily of the descendants of the Germans of the colonial period, and the more recent immigrants of the 1830's.

The German immigration to the American colonies really began with the eighteenth century, although there were isolated groups before that time along the seaboard, and in the middle Atlantic region. The political and economic collapse that followed the Thirty Years' War and recurring crop failures and famines in the Rhine Valley were primary causes of the German exodus in colonial times. Religious controversy, incident to the rise of numerous pietistic sects, and the intolerance of rulers and established churches toward dissenters, were other factors of importance. The promotional efforts of colonial land agents and the propaganda of ship companies also played their part in turning the immigrant tide from Germany toward America. By the time of the American Revolution, the German stock in the newly created United States probably totaled a quarter million.

By 1750, German farmers occupied a strip of land in New York known as the "German Flats" and extending for some twelve miles along the left bank of the Mohawk. Germantown was the distributing center for the colonial Germans in Pennsylvania, and from there the immigrant tide overflowed down the Valley of Virginia and through the mountain gaps into the South and West. In 1766, Benjamin Franklin estimated the Germans at one-third of the population of Pennsylvania, and by the outbreak of the Revolutionary War, the German population of the colony probably was between 110,000 and 125,000.

For the most part the colonial Germans were farmers, a simple rural

6

people, of good peasant stock. They knew how to locate good land and how to use it without depleting the soil, and they emphasized diversified farming. The large stone houses which rapidly supplanted their earlier pioneer dwellings still mark the Pennsylvania countryside. Even more impressive were the barns, built of stone and frame, and generally painted yellow or red, and to this day they identify a Pennsylvania German farming community. The Germans acquired herds of sleek and well-fed cattle and, in contrast with some of their Scotch-Irish and Irish neighbors, seemed to work harder and till their acres more intensively. They lived frugally, hauled their goods to market in huge Conestoga wagons which they developed, and manifested a deep-seated concern for material prosperity and adding new acres in each succeeding generation. Their thrift was so pronounced that they were accused, with considerable justification, of lacking interest in the finer things of life, and of being obsessed with the accumulation of material possessions to the point of avarice. The father generally exercised a stern, patriarchal authority over the entire family.

Religiously, the colonial Germans were divided into communicants of the established Lutheran and Reformed churches, and the sectarians, who belonged to a variety of religious sects representing strange religious experiments with new ways to attain salvation. The Mennonites, Dunkards, and Schwenkfelders are but a few of the best known of these German pietistic sects. A common strain of mysticism pervaded them all, and a desire to withdraw from the ways of the world and refuse to serve the state either in war or in politics.

From their native land these pioneers brought the folklore, superstitions, folk art, and customs of a simple peasant stock. The Pennsylvania German *hausfrau* made substantial contributions to American cookery. Customs from the Rhineland and Southern Germany have been preserved to this day and reflect the habits and culture of a hardworking, plain people who had always lived close to the soil. The skilled artisans who lived among them built implements and furniture which are highly prized collectors' items.

The intellectual and cultural level of such a people has been a matter of controversy. Some of their colonial contemporaries regarded the Pennsylvania Germans as utterly ignorant because they spoke a strange language and clung to strange beliefs, superstitions, and folk habits. The rate of illiteracy among them was high, and many German sects looked with disfavor upon all worldly forms of education and insisted that the training of their children must be rooted in the religious beliefs of their particular faith. Opposition to public schools was strong among the Pennsylvania Germans until the middle of the nineteenth century, and some of their descendants still insist on protecting their children from the contaminating effects of free public education. On the other hand, German papers, almanacs, and books were published in considerable numbers by early German printers of Pennsylvania, and the publications imported from abroad give additional evidence that the level of illiteracy could not have been as high as certain contemporary critics maintained.

It was this colonial group which developed that strange language known as "Pennsylvania Dutch," the oldest immigrant language still in daily use in the United States. Today it is the subject of serious study by scholars who see in it an historical and linguistic phenomenon of great importance. Several excellent anthologies of Pennsylvania German poetry and prose have been published in recent years, in an effort to keep the language alive as long as possible. Basically, it is a composite of dialects of the Upper Rhine, with an amazing addition of common English words, and a grammar and orthography all its own, and it has survived because of the early clannishness of the Pennsylvania Germans, the self-sufficiency and relative isolation of their farming communities, and the religious separatism nurtured by sectarian groups.

In contrast with the drab materialism of the early Pennsylvania German areas, most of these people, including the sectarians, had a great interest in, and love for, vocal and instrumental music. Pennsylvania German red earthenware is well known to students of American pottery. The peacock, dove, and tulip motifs appear on almost all examples of Pennsylvania German folk art, and its bedquilts, pottery and glassware, birth and marriage certificates, and sturdy chests, dressers, cupboards, tables, bedsteads, and chairs have become museum pieces of early American art.

This brief description of the characteristics of the "Pennsylvania Dutch" must suffice to characterize the early German element in America, although there were many variations within Pennsylvania itself, and still greater differences in other colonies. A sturdy, healthy, successful, plain people, their descendants have spread westward and southwestward throughout the United States, and northward into Canada. By the middle of the nineteenth century, however, the colonial German stock had lost most of its cultural and intellectual contacts with Europe. At the same time, their participation in American affairs, political or otherwise, was of minor importance. Germans who spoke and read "high German" regarded their strange *patois* with contempt. Almost completely cut off from the culture of their former fatherland, the Pennsylvania Germans also had avoided complete assimilation to the American pattern.[1]

The second important German group to come to America before the Revolution of 1848 came in greatest numbers after 1830. In general, they too were primarily motivated by the economic advantages which the United States could offer men and women who were willing to work to improve their status in life. America had good soil and cheap farms, and ship companies, railroads, land speculators, and western states eager for population tried to convince German peasants and artisans that opportunity beckoned from across the Atlantic. "America letters," written home by those already here, swelled the stream of immigration. The German farmer helped conquer the Mississippi Valley for agriculture, and German artisans, trained in the rigorous apprentice system of the old world, found a profitable market in America for their mechanical skills.

The majority of the immigrants of the 1830's and early 1840's were recruited from these two groups. A few seriously considered the possibility of planting German colonies in Texas, Wisconsin, and elsewhere, to preserve the German way of life in a strange environment, but such ventures in organized, coöperative colonization ended in failure. The archives of Dresden, Thuringia, Mecklenburg, and other German cities and provinces, moreover, reveal an eagerness to unload paupers and petty offenders upon the United States, and in many cases, pardons were granted on condition that the recipient leave at once and agree never to return. In some instances, local authorities provided clothing and other material assistance to speed the traveler on his way.[2]

Political unrest in the German states was a minor contributing cause of this pre-Forty-eighter immigration, but a major influence in the case of a small number of political radicals and refugees. The liberal movement in the Germany of the early nineteenth century and the spirit engendered by the War of Liberation against Napoleon lived on in the hearts of youthful German patriots, and particularly among the intellectuals in the universities, both faculty and students, and finally exploded in the two abortive German revolutions of 1830 and 1848. German *Turner* organizations, which did not become important in the United States until after the arrival of the Forty-eighters, originated in the days when Napoleon dominated Prussia, and were intended to make young Germans both strong and patriotic.

In 1817, Metternich and the reactionary princes launched an attack on the liberal ideas of the French Revolution, which continued to find expression in such incidents as the famous Wartburg Festival, a great student celebration to commemorate the Protestant Revolt and the fourth anniversary of the battle of Leipzig, which ended with a huge bonfire in which various symbols of tyranny, censorship, and oppression were tossed into the flames. The period of persecution which followed was known in Germany and Austria as the *Demagogenverfolgung*. A number of educated and liberal Germans, like Karl Follen and Francis Lieber, left for the United States. Follen became a teacher at Harvard, and was one of the early abolitionists and Unitarians. Lieber, who had fought as a lad against Napoleon and later in the Greek War of Liberation, became a distinguished publicist and scholar in the American academic world, particularly in the field of political science.[3]

In May 1832, students, burghers, craftsmen, farmers, and officials assembled in the ruins of the old castle at Hambach to listen to speeches about liberty and reform and the tyranny of petty princes. They paraded with black, red, and gold banners, the French tricolor and the flag of the Polish independence movement in a great demonstration which was both a joyous outing and a serious challenge to the established order. Like the earlier Wartburg Festival, the incident led to arrests and dismissals, especially in the Palatinate, and a more rigorous system of espionage, censorship, and police surveillance. Many participants in the demonstration had to bow their heads to the storm, but others came to New York, Philadelphia, St. Louis, Cincinnati, and to the prairie country of the West. Although the *Hambacher Fest* is but one incident in the tortuous history of liberalism in Germany, it is convincing evidence that the movement for reform persisted even in a police state.[4]

The number of liberal refugees who came to America in the 1830's is not unimpressive. Among the *Dreissiger* (the political refugees of the 1830's) were men like the Wesselhöfts of Philadelphia, and Gustav Körner, who escaped to the United States after being wounded in the

"Frankfurt Putsch" of 1833, and rose to political prominence in Illinois as a member of the early Republican party. Dr. Friedrich Adolph Wislizenus came to America, following the same foolhardy student uprising and after a round of fighting for the liberation of Italy. Educated as a physician in Switzerland, he began practicing in New York in 1835. Later he moved west, crossed the Rockies with an expedition of the St. Louis Fur Company, collected botanical and mineralogical specimens, and became a founder of the St. Louis Academy and president of the German Medical Society in that city.[5]

Karl Theodore Seidensticker, locked up "for life" in 1831, was pardoned in 1845 on condition that he leave for the United States. He became an editor and accountant in Philadelphia, and his son Oswald, a professor of German at the University of Pennsylvania.[6] Karl Minnigerode left Germany in the 1830's because of his liberal principles and became a pastor in Richmond, Virginia.[7] Friedrich Münch, philosopher, poet, journalist, and one of the most highly educated of the pre-Forty-eighters, settled as a farmer in Missouri and wrote voluminously for German-language papers under the name "Far West." Paul Follen led a group of German settlers to New Orleans in 1834. Friedrich Theodor Engelmann, who left Germany after the Revolution of 1830, grew grapes and fruit and made catawba wine on a farm near Belleville, Illinois. His son became a brigadier general in the Civil War, and a cousin practiced medicine in St. Louis.[8] George Bunsen came to Belleville in 1834, opened a model school, became superintendent of public schools in 1856, and founded the state normal school at Bloomington. His brother Gustav, who had fought for Polish independence in 1830, was killed during the Texas Revolution, and his stepson, Ferdinand Jakob Lindheimer, who had come with Bunsen in 1834, did distinguished work as a scientist on the flora of Texas.[9]

Hermann Ernst Ludewig, a prominent pre-Forty-eighter who arrived in 1842, practiced law in New York, and published bibliographies of American aboriginal languages. Anton Eichhoff was editor of the *St. Louis Zeitung*, Heinrich Roedter of the *Cincinnati Volksblatt*, and Wilhelm Weber of the St. Louis *Anzeiger des Westens*. Christian Kribben was a musician and a literary figure of early St. Louis; Maximilian Oertel, *bon vivant* and gifted editor, published the Catholic *Kirchenzeitung* for many years. Ernst Angelrodt, a former official in Tübingen, became a banker and businessman in Hermann, Missouri. Judge Johann Bernhard Stallo and Karl Rümelin were distinguished leaders of early Cincinnati's German element. Johann Andreas Wagener was outstanding in the German community of Charleston, South Carolina; Hermann von Ehrenberg, a radical student agitator of the 1830's, became a topographical engineer in the United States, and Friedrich Eckstein founded an Academy of Fine Arts in Cincinnati.[10]

More important than a catalogue of names is the influence which men of such caliber exercised upon the cultural level of the growing German communities in the United States. In 1832 the German immigration exceeded ten thousand; in 1834 it reached seventeen thousand; and by 1837 it totaled twenty-four thousand.

For several decades before the Forty-eighters arrived, Germans in the United States supported a number of singing societies and library and reading clubs, but such manifestations of cultural and intellectual interests were almost wholly limited to larger cities like New York, Philadelphia, St. Louis, Cincinnati, and Milwaukee. The first German church was organized in Louisville, Kentucky, in 1838, but a German monthly periodical which was started in 1840 survived only one year. Louisville's first singing society was organized in February 1848, just prior to the outbreak of the German Revolution.[11]

During the 1830's a number of new German newspapers appeared in the United States, and in some cases they were edited by political refugees. The *New Yorker Staatszeitung* began publishing in 1834. In the same general period belong such papers as the *Buffalo Weltbürger,* the *St. Louis Anzeiger des Westens,* the *Cincinnati Volksblatt,* the Columbus, Ohio, *Westbote,* and the Louisville *Beobachter am Ohio.* The Philadelphia *Freie Presse,* founded in 1847, remained influential for several decades. The *Lichtfreund* of Hermann, Missouri, one of the early papers edited and supported by rationalists, was founded in 1842, and under the able editorship of Eduard Mühl and Friedrich Münch managed to survive for a number of years. Dr. Samuel Ludvigh, a Hungarian refugee and freethinker identified with the German group, published *Der Wahrheitsverbreiter* in 1839, as well as a German campaign paper for Van Buren in 1840, before he founded his more famous *Die Fackel* in Baltimore, after his return from the Revolution of 1848.[12]

The German element before 1848 also found release for its surplus energies and gregarious instincts in the military and fire companies and political clubs popular in pre-Civil War days. There were German lodges of Masons and Druids; a small number of freethinking societies in communities like Hoboken, New York, and Milwaukee, closely integrated with radical sheets like the *Vernunftsgläubiger* (1838), the *Wahrheitsfreund* (1839), and the *Freisinniger Beobachter* (1837). Heinrich Scheib, a German rationalist, preached in the famous Zion's Church of Baltimore.[18] As early as 1836 Philadelphia had an organization for the support of German political refugees in Switzerland and London, and in 1840 Gutenberg celebrations were held in Philadelphia, Richmond, Cincinnati and other cities.[14]

Before 1848 Philadelphia supported a number of German churches, two German dailies, a German lecture series, a library, a singing society, and a rifle club, various beer gardens and German benevolent societies, and several small German bookshops. In 1847, on the Fourth of July, the Germans of Philadelphia staged a successful folk festival.[15] Cincinnati had similar organizations and, in addition, a patriotic society to aid persecuted liberals in Germany. In 1847, Cincinnati Germans sent $8,000 to the fatherland for relief purposes, and in the same year promoted a Goethe celebration at which Professor Calvin E. Stowe was the principal speaker.[16] The first German lager beer brewery was opened in Milwaukee in 1841, and three years later the city had its first German paper, the *Wiskonsin Banner*. German fire-fighting and military companies were active in the early 1840's, and Germans played an important rôle in the Democratic party. The first German elementary school was opened in Milwaukee in 1844; Schiller's *Kabale und Liebe* was presented by amateurs before 1848, and Ludwig's Garden dispensed beer, dancing, and free concerts since 1844. A German string quartet, organized in 1843 and later transformed into a Beethoven Society, attracted three hundred listeners to its first concert. German Lutherans and Catholics had several churches in Milwaukee by 1846, and its first freethinking society was founded in 1843 by Heinrich Ginal.[17]

Some German intellectuals of the 1830's, with more of a flair for the romantic than the practical, became "Latin Farmers," a title bestowed upon them by skeptical neighbors who discovered that the newcomers knew more about art, music, literature, Virgil, and Cicero than agriculture. Many such misfits lost their entire investment after years of toil and sacrifice. Some succeeded, and others moved in time into the cities to practice the professions and skills for which they were really fitted. Belleville, in St. Clair County, Illinois, one of the best-known "Latin" settlements, included such distinguished refugees of both 1830 and 1848 as the Körners, Engelmanns, Bunsens, Hilgards, and Heckers.

Politically, the German element belonged to the party of Jefferson and Jackson in the period before 1850, for neither the social and political philosophy of the Whigs, nor their name, appealed to the Germans. As early as the 1840's they shared the spoils of office; campaign literature was printed in German, and Germans occasionally were elected to local offices. In 1837, thirty-nine German leaders assembled at Pittsburgh to discuss ways and means to preserve the German language and its press in America, combat nativism, secure cheaper land for actual settlers, demand equal status for the German language with English, and promote a university on the German model and a normal school for the training of teachers of German. Steps to incorporate a German teachers' seminary were actually taken under the laws of the state of Pennsylvania, but the effort failed because of inadequate funds and the sharp rift between the liberal, free-thinking element and orthodox Protestants and Catholics.

Thus it is clear that intellectual and cultural activity among the Germans in America did not originate with the Forty-eighters. Actually the arrival of the self-confident, impatient, and aggressive reformers of 1848, who wanted to make the world over in a day, produced deep-seated antagonisms between the older and the newer leadership. Nevertheless, and despite outstanding leaders among the earlier immigration, the cultural and intellectual level of the German element as a whole had declined to a marked degree by 1850. The *New Yorker Staatszeitung* encountered great difficulties in the first few years after its establishment in 1834 because many readers resented its classical "high German" style, and preferred the vernacular.[18] In Milwaukee, Germans attended public dances in shirt sleeves and cavorted about with their hats on and with pipes in their mouths, for an admission fee of fifty cents, which always included free beer. The majority of the Germans in their daily conversations spoke a language that fell far short of the standards of Goethe and Kant. Many both spoke and wrote an ungrammatical, unidiomatic German, badly corrupted by English terms and inflections into a curious "German-American" tongue. German servant girls shed their language as quickly as their old-fashioned European costumes, and insisted upon using English, however wretched their command of the new language might be, while young German businessmen and artisans were forced to use English in their daily dealings with the public. The corruption of an immigrant language is evidence that the Americanization process is proceeding naturally, but to intellectuals, recently arrived from Europe, it indicated a deplorable cultural deterioration and petrification.

In general, the German element was not highly regarded before the Civil War, and its own lack of self-respect did not improve the situation. Although the ability of individual Germans was readily recognized, Germans as a class were referred to as "damned Dutch," and German farmers, artisans, innkeepers, and small businessmen were considered inferior to the average American. German observers from abroad bemoaned the fact that their countrymen in the United States were reduced to the same low intellectual level as the Irish, the only noticeable difference being that whereas the Irishman was always represented with a whiskey bottle, the beer mug and the pipe were the symbols for the Germans. Books and newspapers were regarded as superfluous baggage in many German homes, and the language of ordinary intercourse often was so extraordinarily coarse that conversations frequently ended with the well-known phrase from Götz von Berlichingen. Politically the Germans were accused of blindly following their ward heelers like voting cattle, bought by free beer on election day.[19] German newspapers, with a few notable exceptions, were poorly edited, made up with scissors and paste-pot, contained little intellectual food, and often were written in a style that became progressively more corrupt with the infiltration of English words and American slang.

It may be that the percentage of university men among the immigrants of the 1830's was as high as in the 1850's, but these earlier "knights of the spirit" had fewer newcomers to lead than the Forty-eighters who impressed their talents upon the heavy German immigration of the 1850's. The older leadership, moreover, maintained a far closer connection with the descendants of the colonial German stock and the church groups than the Forty-eighters.[20]

After due recognition of the achievements of the German element in the United States before the middle of the last century,[21] and of the high caliber of some of its leaders, the fact remains that the Forty-eighters introduced the most powerful political and cultural leaven that has ever affected the German group in America.

FOOTNOTES

CHAPTER 2

1. The literature on the colonial Germans, and especially the Pennsylvania group, is large and still growing. For further details, see Albert B. Faust: *The German Element in the United States* (New York, 1909) Vol. I; Jesse L. Rosenberger: *The Pennsylvania Germans* (Chicago, 1923); C. Henry Smith: *The Mennonite Immigration to Pennsylvania* (Norristown, 1929); James O. Knauss: *Social Conditions Among the Pennsylvania Germans in the Eighteenth Century* (Lancaster, 1922); *The Pennsylvania Germans*, edited by Ralph Wood (Princeton, 1942); Earl F. Robacker: *Pennsylvania German Literature* (Philadelphia, 1943); Walter A. Knittle: *Early Eighteenth Century Palatine Emigration* (Philadelphia, 1937); Heinz Kloss: *Levendiche Schtimme aus Pennsilveni* (Stuttgart and New York, 1929); Frances Lichten: *Folk Art of Rural Pennsylvania* (New York, 1946); and Carl Wittke: *We Who Built America, the Saga of the Immigrant* (New York, 1939), Ch. VI, pp. 66-97.

2. See also Eduard Delius: *Einige Worte über das Hochland in Süd-Carolina für Auswanderer nach Amerika gerichtet* (Bremen, 1841).

3. See Frank Freidel: *Francis Lieber, Nineteenth Century Liberal* (Baton Rouge, 1947).

4. "Das Hambacher Fest," in *Der Deutsche Pionier* (Cincinnati) XIV, No. 3 (June, 1882) pp. 110-13.

5. Harry B. Weiss: *The Pioneer Century of American Entomology* (New Brunswick, N. J., 1936) pp. 231-32.

6. Hermann Julius Rütenick: *Berühmte Deutsche Vorkämpfer für Fortschritt, Freiheit und Friede in Nord Amerika von 1626 bis 1880* (Cleveland, 1881) pp. 208-9. Hereafter cited as Rütenick: *Deutsche Vorkämpfer*.

7. Friedrich Kapp: *Aus und Über Amerika, Thatsachen und Erlebnisse* (Berlin, 1876) II, p. 374. Hereafter cited as Kapp: *Aus und über Amerika*.

8. Rütenick: *Deutsche Vorkämpfer*, pp. 166-74.

9. *Ibid.*, pp. 178-81.

10. See Rütenick: *Deutsche Vorkämpfer*, p. 177; also Franz Köhler: *Geschichte und Zustände der Deutschen in Amerika* (Cincinnati, 1847) and Gustav Körner: *Das Deutsche Element in den Vereinigten Staaten von Nord Amerika* (Cincinnati, 1880) *passim*.

11. See L. Stierlein: *Der Staat Kentucky und die Stadt Louisville mit besonderer Berücksichtigung des deutschen Elements* (Louisville, 1873) pp. 67-105. Hereafter cited as Stierlin: *Kentucky*.

12. See Dieter Cunz: *The Maryland Germans, A History* (Princeton, 1948) pp. 261-62; *New Yorker Staatszeitung*, Aug. 21, 1849; and Cleveland *Wächter am Erie*, June 6, 1867. Hereafter cited as Cunz: *Maryland Germans*.

13. Cunz: *Maryland Germans*, p. 270.

14. See Hermann Schuricht: *Geschichte der Deutschen Schulbestrebungen in Amerika* (Leipzig, 1884) pp. 38-53.

15. C. F. Huch: "Die Deutschen in Philadelphia ums Jahr 1847," in *Mitteilungen des Deutschen Pionier Vereins von Philadelphia*, (1910), XVII, pp. 13-21, and by the same author, a similar article in *Deutsch-Amerikanische Geschichtsblätter, Jahrbuch der Deutsch-Amerikanischen historischen Gesellschaft von Illinois*. (Chicago, 1910) X, No. 4, pp. 233-40. Hereafter cited as *Deutsch-Amerikanische Geschichtsblätter*.

16. Emil Klauprecht: *Deutsche Chronik in der Geschichte des Ohio Thales und seiner Hauptstadt Cincinnati* (Cincinnati, n.d.) pp. 177-79.

17. Bayrd Still: *Milwaukee, The History of a City* (Madison, 1948) pp. 65, 68, 72-79, 87, 89, 92, and 126; Wilhelm Hense-Jensen and Ernst Bruncken: *Wisconsin's Deutsch-Amerikaner bis zum Schluss des neunzehnten Jahrhunderts* (Milwaukee, 1900) and Rudolf H. Koss: *Milwaukee* (Milwaukee, 1871) *passim.* See also Irmgard Erhorn: *Die deutsche Einwanderung der Dreissiger und Achtundvierziger in die Vereinigten Staaten und ihre Stellung zur nordamerikanischen Politik* (Hamburg, 1937) pp. 16-31.

18. *New Yorker Staatszeitung*, April 14, 1858.

19. See Heinrich Börnstein: *Fünfundsiebzig Jahre in der Alten und Neuen Welt. Memoiren eines Unbedeutenden* (Leipzig, 1881) 2 vols., II, pp. 199-205. Hereafter referred to as Börnstein: *Memoiren.*

20. Heinz Kloss: *Um die Einigung des Deutschamerikanertums* (Berlin, 1937) pp. 216-17. Kloss has little sympathy for the Forty-eighters, holds them responsible for the factional divisions among the German-Americans, and thinks they used their German language and culture only as a means of spreading their "cosmopolitan" ideas of freedom, p. 219.

21. See further on this matter, Heinrich A. Rattermann: "Das deutsche Element in den Vereinigten Staaten von Nord Amerika vor 1848," in *Der Deutsche Pionier*, XII, No. 4 (July, 1880) pp. 148-58, and No. 6 (Sept., 1880) pp. 233-39. For a biographical sketch of this remarkably gifted German-American, see Sister Mary Edmund Spanheimer: *Heinrich Arnim Rattermann, German-American Author, Poet and Historian, 1832-1923* (Catholic University, Washington, 1937).

Chapter 3 · *THE REVOLUTION*
OF 1848-1849

T HE REVOLUTION which began in Paris in February 1848 and swept through most of western Europe upset thrones in many lands, both great and small, for the revolt against autocratic authority and feudal privilege represented a belated sprouting of seeds sowed by the French Revolution and scattered over Europe during the Napoleonic Era. To their leaders, the uprisings symbolized a triumph of the rationalism of the Enlightenment and a realization of the dreams of poets and intellectuals who championed a cosmopolitan humanitarianism based on natural law and the inalienable rights of man which transcended all national and racial boundaries. The Revolution of 1848 has been called the last great international movement,[1] and its German phase was but part of a contagious, ideological revolution which started in Paris in 1848, and had as its objective the overthrow of the system of legitimacy and reaction which had become fastened upon most of western Europe after the final defeat of the Great Napoleon.

In France, the revolution against the government of Louis Philippe began when a Paris crowd insisted upon celebrating Washington's birthday on February 22, although the government refused to sanction the demonstration. The Bourgeois Monarchy was overthrown with surprising speed, as diverse groups united to destroy the old régime. Republicans and socialists, old-line imperialists who hoped for the return of the glories of the Napoleonic Empire, and strange breeds of reformers, social revolutionists, and Utopian dreamers coöperated at the outset, only to fall apart when it became necessary to evolve a positive program. In June, Paris workingmen rose a second time against a revolutionary government which had failed to give them bread and jobs. In the end, Prince Louis

Napoleon Bonaparte, trading upon the magic of a great name and the memories of his great uncle, was elected president of the Second French Republic. On December 2, 1851, through a military conspiracy, and on the anniversary of the Battle of Austerlitz, his well-known *coup d'état* ended in the proclamation of the New Empire, with himself as Emperor.

In the Austro-Hungarian Empire which was the seat of Metternich's power, the revolution was significantly affected by the aspirations of Hungarians, Bohemians, Italians, and other suppressed nationality groups of the Habsburg state. Louis Kossuth led the Hungarian uprising. His reputation as a sincere liberal, his genuine devotion to the popular cause, and his unexcelled and fiery eloquence made him an effective leader. He advocated not only political and constitutional reforms, but also tried to lift the feudal burdens which landed aristocrats still imposed upon the peasant class. In Vienna, street fighting by workers and students forced Metternich to decamp for England, and for a brief moment it looked as though genuine reforms would be enacted in both Austria and Hungary. Liberal constitutions were promulgated in both countries, including a bill of rights which granted freedom of speech, press, and religion. Revolution broke out also among the Bohemians in Prague, and a Pan Slavic Congress was convened in that ancient city to give a cosmopolitan label to the movement for reform.

Without pursuing the progress of events in greater detail, it need only be added that the various nationality groups within the Empire soon were in furious disagreement; Prague was captured by an imperial army, and Vienna surrendered after a fierce bombardment. Parliament was dismissed and the constitution repudiated, and large numbers of revolutionists went to jail or into exile. Substantially the same results occurred in Hungary, except that eventually Hungarians fought not only with Austrians, but against Slavs as well. The Czar of Russia sent his armies to restore the Habsburg power, and Kossuth fled, first to England and then to the United States, to appeal unsuccessfully for funds to revive the revolution.

In Italy, revolts broke out in many small states and cities of the Peninsula; the Pope fled from the Eternal City, and for a short period Mazzini and Garibaldi were in control of Rome. In northern Italy, Italians fought to drive the Austrians out of Lombardy and Venetia, as well as to gain greater popular rights. In the end, Austrian armies were victorious, reaction swept the Italian states, and the Pope was restored to his throne by the French troops of Louis Napoleon.

Ireland, Denmark, England, Switzerland, Poland, Belgium, and the Netherlands experienced similar agitations for greater individual liberty and popular government, although in some cases moderate concessions were obtained without resort to arms. England, industrially the most advanced, and Russia, the most backward nation in Europe, escaped revolution altogether. Our major concern is with the revolutions in Germany, but it is well to remember that the movement was international in character, and that political refugees to the United States after 1848 included representatives of many European groups.

The Germany of the early nineteenth century was but a geographical expression. Absolutism reigned in most of the German states, generally unchecked by representative institutions or popular participation in government. In a land of many quarreling states, the spirit of nationalism had been at low ebb for several decades. The German Confederation which followed from the Congress of Vienna was a weak, loose union of sovereign states, and the Diet which met at Frankfurt under the presidency of Austria, a meeting place for ambassadors who were the mouthpieces of kings and princes who could not themselves come to this "center of inertia." Prussia vied with Austria for control of the Confederation, and both powers hated anything remotely resembling the liberal, democratic ideas planted in Europe by the French Revolution.

The Vienna revolution of March 13, 1848, was followed by peasant uprisings in Württemberg and Baden. Excited peasants marched on the castles of their feudal princes, refused to pay their feudal dues, and drove out the governing bureaucracy. All along the Rhineland men took up arms, and thrones were hastily abandoned by their royal occupants, in the wake of the advancing patriot army, or were salvaged by ignominious surrender to the demands of the revolutionaries. On March 18, a mob in the courtyard of Berlin forced the King of Prussia to promise a constitution and a parliament. Fighting broke out between the military and the mob, barricades appeared in the streets, and the shooting ended only when the Prussian King yielded to the demands of the mob and agreed to withdraw his troops from the city.

Revolutionary liberals called a national assembly, and on May 18 the

Frankfurt Parliament convened amid high enthusiasm and optimistic predictions of national unification and reform. Of 831 representatives, elected by a wide, democratic suffrage, 569 were university men, and the great majority belonged to the bourgeois class. From the outset, the work of the Parliament was seriously handicapped by the old quarrel between Austria and Prussia for hegemony over the German states, by the trouble with the Danes over Schleswig, and by a sharp division over whether Austria should be excluded from a new federal state. Archduke John of Austria finally was chosen president of the projected federation. A simple-minded man of sixty-six, his only claim to democracy was the fact that he had lost his status at the Habsburg court by marrying a postmaster's daughter.

The Frankfurt Parliament fought bitterly over the form of government appropriate for a united Germany. Radicals wanted a republic and no further truck with kings and princes; others favored a moderate, constitutional monarchy, with a hereditary royal house. When it finally was resolved to proceed with plans for a federated empire, the imperial crown was offered to Frederick William of Prussia, who by this time had re-gained control of Berlin by the use of the army. Firmly convinced of the divine right of Hohenzollerns to rule, he spurned a crown "picked up from the gutter" from the hands of the representatives of the people. The division on this critical issue had been close in the Frankfurt Parliament, 290 members favoring the invitation to the Prussian King, and 248 abstaining from voting. The monarch's refusal to assume leadership of a unified Germany which many believed eventually might develop into a more democratic state meant the end of the Parliament's influence, and it already was at low ebb. Moderate liberals returned to their homes. A democratic minority of some hundred and fifty members met as a rump parliament in Stuttgart. The people rose a second time in rebellion, but rebels and rump Parliament were easily dispersed by the military. The Stuttgart Parliament could not survive the pressures exerted by Württemberg, Austria, and Prussia, and the popular uprisings of May 1849 in Saxony, Baden, and the Bavarian Palatinate were suppressed by Prussian troops. Although considerable progress had been made in some German states toward the correction of old abuses, particularly the old feudal obligations, and the revolutionary movement therefore cannot be dismissed as a total failure, Germany sank back into reaction, and remained disunited until 1871. It is not too much to say that the German people have not yet recovered from the wounds they suffered in 1848.

A large number of American Forty-eighters were leaders in these popular demonstrations against the monarchy and the old autocratic order. Some belonged to local diets or the Frankfurt Parliament; others were publicists and editors, and some commanded troops in the field. Friedrich Hecker led the *putsch* in Baden in 1848 and returned from the United States in 1849 to lead a second futile revolt. Carl Schurz achieved fame as a revolutionist through the jail delivery by which he helped rescue his old professor, who had been imprisoned as a dangerous revolutionary agitator. Karl Heinzen, Gustav Struve, and Fritz Anneke belonged to the extreme republicans, and August Willich and Wilhelm Weitling were early German communists. Lorenz Brentano represented the moderates, whom extreme republicans considered traitors to their cause. Amand Gögg and Joseph Fickler were revolutionary publicists.

The German Revolution was not lacking in spirit, ideals or examples of personal bravery, but it had few practical weapons with which to combat an established order supported by standing armies. Popular demonstrations were numerous and spirited, and members of the Turner movement, revolutionary clubs, worker's organizations, and student groups played leading rôles in them. There was much parading and singing, drinking and speech-making, and bombastic proclamations were issued by the dozen. The demonstrations had more of the appearance of a picnic or outing than a serious military operation. Ludwig Blenker's troops, for example, celebrated Pentecost in Worms in 1849 for several days, with an abundant supply of good wine, rather than proceed promptly to the more serious business in hand. Veit Valentin described the Revolution as something romantic and easy-going, "a comfortable, pleasant anarchy." The revolutionary levies lacked arms, food, and equipment. Many patriots carried nothing more deadly than scythes, threshing flails, and antiquated shooting irons into the battle against professional soldiers, and many of their officers knew little about military tactics, and had received their commissions by the votes of their own men in democratic elections.[2]

For Germany, the Revolution was a futile and belated effort to catch up with the spirit of 1789, a battle between the ideology of the French Revolution as opposed to agrarian feudalism, a union of altar and throne, and the police state. In many respects, it was a "revolution of intellectuals," "the product of a moral idea," and "born at least as much of hopes as of discontents."[3] The philosophy of liberalism was widely disseminated among students, Turner, and certain portions of the urban population, and had found noble expression in the literary writings of Ludwig Börne, Heinrich Heine, Moses Hess, and Karl Gutzkow, and in the poems of Anastasius Grün, von Fallersleben, Ferdinand Freiligrath, "the Trumpeter of Revolution," and Georg Herwegh. It is significant that fifty years after the French Revolution the ideas of democracy and personal liberty evidently still flourished among a large segment of the German people, and after a generation of suppression exploded in revolution.

The bourgeois element desired greater political power. This substantial and enlightened urban middle class hated the petty persecution and espionage of the police state, and wanted a constitution to restrain the arbitrary powers of the ruler and guarantee greater participation for the middle class in the formulation of political and economic policy. The middle class also wanted a united country for patriotic reasons, and to abolish irritating tariff barriers between many petty states and establish a sound national currency, good for business. Both the commercial and the industrial bourgeoisie opposed the feudal class structure and both demanded legal guarantees of basic individual rights, as a protection against absolute monarchy.

The Parliament which debated so long and eloquently in St. Paul's Church in Frankfurt failed in large measure because of the moderate tactics of the bourgeois element and the inner contradictions and conflicts from which this class suffered. Its representatives, supported frequently by the intellectuals, too often took flight from practical reality into the realm of theory and dreams, and proclaimed the form of democracy without understanding how to make it function in practice. The bourgeois wanted no Jacobin Revolution to uproot the whole social and economic order. They were satisfied with moderate economic reforms, national unity, equal social status with the feudal nobility, freedom of the press, speech, assembly, and religion, trial by jury, and a better educational system, to insure orderly progress and avoid social revolution. The middle class had little difficulty in combining forces with the peasantry against the army, the bureaucracy, and the feudal nobility, but it had little in common with the emerging proletariat. The Frankfurt "Parliament of Professors" spoke for the discontented masses, but it had no program on which all classes could unite. Peasants were not interested in the theoretical questions of the intellectuals, and wanted only to be released from the feudal burdens upon their farms. The workers of the cities, still inarticulate and unprepared for major political action, had no clear program, and were handicapped by the inexperience of their leaders.

The Frankfurt Parliament spent most of the summer and fall of 1848 in hammering out a bill of rights—"the interior decoration" for a new national house which was never completed.[4] Copies of the American Declaration of Independence and the United States Constitution were much in evidence in German liberal circles during these years, and some American newspapers regarded the German Revolution as a logical extension of 1776 into Europe.[5]

Many writers have ridiculed the Frankfurt Parliament as an assembly of starry-eyed professors and academicians, and as late as 1911 the German historian, Hermann Oncken, referred to the "negligible minority" who failed in their attempt "to impose an artificial republic on the German people." It is true that three-fourths of the members of the revolutionary parliament were former university students and fifty-seven were schoolmasters and forty-nine university professors, probably "the most highly educated parliament in constitutional history."[6] Its roster included men of the highest ethical and moral standards, as well as opportunists and compromisers, but the genuine devotion of the majority to the old liberal ideal of personal freedom cannot be questioned. Professors, students, and writers marched arm in arm with craftsmen and peasants in the great popular demonstrations which ushered in the Revolution. The Frankfurt Parliament had both brains and ideals, but lacked practical experience. While idealists at Frankfurt made speeches about the *Völkerfrühling,* the old guard planned their destruction with Machiavellian cynicism. The Parliament, functioning within the framework of classical liberalism, brought about few fundamental economic or political reforms. Nevertheless some of its principles, so eloquently and sincerely espoused by liberals and republicans at Frankfurt, reappeared in the constitutions of the individual states, and were destined to be reborn in the short-lived constitution of the Weimar Republic after World War I.

The common man of Germany in 1848 was motivated primarily by economics and not by the theories of philosophers and professors. By the 1840's Germany was in the early stages of her industrial revolution, and old-time craftsmen were being displaced by machines and the factory system. The principles of laissez-faire economics had superseded the controls and benevolences of the old guild system, and labor unions had not yet developed to voice the grievances of the new working class. As railroads were threatening the old wagoners, so machines were beginning to deprive skilled craftsmen of their livelihood. By 1848 the city proletariat had emerged as a new factor in the national economy. Vienna and Berlin had populations over four hundred thousand; Hamburg and Breslau over one hundred thousand; and Munich, Dresden, Cologne, and Königsberg were approaching one hundred thousand. The early weeks of the Revolution were marked by the smashing of machines by irate and unemployed workers in several parts of Germany.

The disruption of the old economy by the industrial revolution was aggravated by a series of crop failures and a period of high prices and unemployment. The potato rot struck disastrously at the most important staple food for the masses of Central Europe, and in the two years after July 1845 potato prices rose 425%, wheat 250%, and barley approximately 300%. Many peasant proprietors still had to deliver part of their harvests to the landlord or the church. Hunger riots occurred in a number of German cities. Food was scarce, prices were rising, and unemployment increasing, because of the introduction of labor-saving machinery, and the competition which infant German industries encountered from more advanced countries like England and Belgium. The years immediately preceding 1848 were marked by serious labor disturbances in Silesia, Saxony, Austria, and Bohemia, and by bread and potato riots in Berlin, Stuttgart, Ulm, and elsewhere. To add to the miseries of the people, the winter of 1847-48 was unusually severe. These were the economic conditions which started the heavy flow of immigrants to the United States in 1847 and 1848, and to a lesser degree to Latin America and especially Brazil. The immigrant tide abated in 1849, the year which marked the triumph of reaction, only to rise again in the 1850's.

The economic and social conditions of the German peasant and laborer explain the common man's interest in reforms, and account for the faith of a growing minority in the new gospel of communism. Though relatively inarticulate, the common people swelled the ranks of the revolutionary forces, and eventually many joined the better-known political refugees in a huge migration to other lands. For communists like Wilhelm Weitling, the formation of a workers' international to include the whole human race, rather than the political unification of Germany, was the main issue. Karl Marx returned to the Continent from England, and with Friedrich Engels published the *Neue Rheinische Zeitung* in Cologne. The Frankfurt Parliament received many petitions from German workingmen. When the Revolution failed, radical labor leaders bitterly accused the liberals of deserting them, while the latter retorted that it was the orthodox communists who had refused to coöperate.[7]

Bourgeois liberals were terrified by the haunting specter of radicalism and communism which seemed to foreshadow a revolt of the masses against law and order. For the first time, an industrial proletariat had raised its head in Germany as a political force, and workers had fought shoulder to shoulder with students on the barricades of Vienna and Berlin. A recent scholar has observed that "Germany's 1789 came over fifty years too late, at a time when new forces and portents of class conflicts made a classical liberal revolution impossible east of the Rhine."[8]

One other factor in connection with the Revolution is important. In the interplay between the nationalistic aspirations of minority groups and the struggle for constitutional reform and individual rights, the forces of nationalism finally triumphed over the ideology of liberalism. The rights of ethnic minorities were debated vigorously in and out of the Frankfurt Parliament, but Germans were unwilling to grant independence and equal privileges to Poles and Czechs; the Magyars to the Poles; and the Czechs to the Ruthenians. When the Frankfurt Parliament, after eloquent tributes to Poland's valiant struggle for liberty, finally voted that that nation should be restored without endangering "German interests," it became clear that nationalism had triumphed over liberalism. In an assembly of academicians and theoreticians, humanitarianism failed to transcend the claims of racial, religious, or national boundaries.

The Revolution of 1848 was the first German revolution to come from the people since the Peasant Revolt of Martin Luther's day, and it ended with tragic results for Germany and the rest of the world. Well-to-do bourgeoisie compromised with kings and princes; Turner and students dissipated their effectiveness in a fantastic romanticism which looked back to the Middle Ages instead of forward; peasants and petite bourgeoisie made a second appeal to arms in 1849 when it already was too late, and the workers were still too unorganized to assume leadership in a democratic movement for extensive social reforms.[9] In the words of Ricarda Huch, "the short day of the Revolution began in a fiery red dawn and ended in storms and rain."[10] Nevertheless, this was essentially a humane revolution. No one was guillotined; there was no wholesale confiscation of property, and no political tribunals were set up for mass trials. Outwardly, at least, 1848 was primarily a political revolt, supported by high ideals of pure humanitarianism, and in the words of Professor Valentin, its most distinguished historian, "a humane revolution is necessarily a semi-revolution."

Immediately after the collapse of the rebellion, ten thousand political refugees sought asylum in Switzerland. Others remained in Germany, harassed by the authorities and subject to arrest, and joined the heavy stream of emigration from the fatherland at a later date. When diplomatic pressures from neighboring powers forced Switzerland to weaken in its policy of giving hospitality to political offenders, many left for England, long a haven for the persecuted of many lands, and eventually a large portion of the exiles crossed the Atlantic to America.[11]

FOOTNOTES

CHAPTER 3

1. See Georg Smolka: "Die Deutsche Revolution, 1848," in *Frankfurter Hefte, Zeitschrift für Kultur und Politik* III, No. 5 (May, 1948) pp. 401-14.
2. See also Carl Wittke: *Against the Current, The Life of Karl Heinzen* (Chicago, 1945) Chapter IV—"Revolution in Practice." Cited hereafter as Wittke: *Heinzen*.
3. See L. B. Namier: *1848: The Revolution of the Intellectuals* (London, 1944) p. 4.
4. Hans Rothfels: "1848—One Hundred Years After" in *The Journal of Modern History*, XX (Dec., 1948) No. 4, pp. 291-319. See also the excellent article by Sigmund Neumann: "The Structure and Strategy of Revolution: 1848 and 1849" in *The Journal of Politics* II, pp. 532-44.
5. Arthur James May: *Contemporary American Opinion of the Mid-Century Revolutions in Central Europe* (Philadelphia, 1927) pp. 10-11, 22.
6. Rothfels—*loc. cit.*, p. 310.
7. On this point, see *New Yorker Staatszeitung*, April 7, May 24, 1849; Aug. 29, 1850; March 6, 1852; *Die Republik der Arbeiter* (New York) May 1, 1852; and "Die Arbeiterfrage im Frankfurter Parlament," in *Die Neue Zeit* (Stuttgart, 1883) I, pp. 38-46. As evidence to prove that the proletariat was more interested in food than a free press, may be cited—"Was geht uns die Pressfreiheit an? Pressfreiheit ist es die wir verlangen."
8. Oscar J. Hammen: "Economic and Social Factors in the Prussian Rhineland in 1848," in *The American Historical Review*, LIV, No. 4 (July, 1949) p. 840. The entire article covers pp. 825-40. See also Alfred Mensel: *Die deutsche Revolution von 1848* (Berlin, 1948).

28   REFUGEES OF REVOLUTION

This study is specially interesting because it is "published by license of the Soviet-Military Administration of Germany."

9. See Alexander Abusch: *Der Irrweg einer Nation* (Berlin, 1947) pp. 89-104.

10. Ricarda Huch: *Alte und neue Götter* (Berlin, 1930) p. 506.

11. For additional references for the German Revolution of 1848-49, see Veit Valentin: *Geschichte der deutschen Revolution von 1848-49*—2 vols. (Berlin, 1930) which is unsurpassed; Ulrich Stephan Allers: *The Concept of Empire in German Romanticism and Its Influence on the National Assembly at Frankfurt, 1848-1849* (Washington, 1948); Charles W. Dahlinger: *The German Revolution of 1849* (New York, 1903); Ferdinand Schreyer: *Geschichte der Revolution in Baden, 1848-49* (Darmstadt, 1909); Otto Wiltberger: *Die deutschen politischen Flüchtlinge in Strassburg von 1830-1849* (Berlin, 1910); Paul Neitzke: *Die deutschen politischen Flüchtlinge in der Schweitz, 1848-49* (Charlottenburg, 1926); Dieter Cunz: "The Forty-eighter Collection at the University of Bern"—in *The American-German Review*, XV, No. 1 (Oct., 1948) pp. 4-5; Ernst Kaeber: *Berlin 1848* (Berlin, 1948) which concentrates on the role of the workers in the Prussian capital; Herbert Arthur Strauss: *Staat, Bürger, Mensch—Die Debatten der deutschen Nationalversammlung 1848/49 über die Grundrechte* (Aarau 1946); and Arnold Whitridge: *Men in Crisis, The Revolutions of 1848* (New York, 1949).

Among the many memoirs and reminiscences by participants may be mentioned: Friedrich Hecker: *Die Erhebung des Volkes in Baden für die deutsche Republik im Frühjahr 1848* (Basel, 1848); Gustav Struve: *Geschichte der drei Volkserhebung in Baden* (Bern, 1849); Johann Philip Becker and Christian Esselen: *Geschichte der süddeutschen Mai-Revolution des Jahres 1849* (Geneva, 1849); and Franz Sigel: *Denkwürdigkeiten aus den Jahren 1848-49* (Mannheim, 1902) and the *Reminiscences of Carl Schurz*, 3 vols. (New York, 1906-8); also Frederick Bancroft, editor, *Speeches, Correspondence and Political Papers of Carl Schurz* (New York, 1913).

Chapter 4 · THE RESPONSE
FROM AMERICA

O N MARCH 18, 1848, the steamer *Cambria* docked in New York with the startling news that Louis Philippe was in flight and Paris in revolution. With the same boat came a letter from London from Freiligrath to his friend Heinzen, editor of the *Deutsche Schnellpost* in New York, in which the poet wrote excitedly: "The newspapers you will receive with this steamer will tell you everything. The bomb has exploded! Paris, Europe is in flames." Enclosed with the letter was a poem, dashed off as Freiligrath watched the reports from the Continent posted by the London papers. It began with the line, "Im Hochland fiel der erste Schuss," and was a vigorous call to action by liberals everywhere. Heinzen published the poem in his paper, and it was copied by the *New Yorker Staatszeitung* and other German-language newspapers, and read at German-American mass meetings, hastily called to celebrate "the liberation of Europe." Freiligrath's poem stimulated dozens of versifiers to send less distinguished efforts to their favorite German-language paper. What such literary effusions lacked in poetic quality they made up in revolutionary fervor.[1]

German-Americans had been mildly interested in German unification and reform before 1848. On March 12, 1844, for example, a German Society, organized at the Astor House in New York, adopted the black-red-gold emblem of the German liberals as its official colors, and its members met periodically to drink toasts to "a free and united Germany."[2] When well-known German political agitators, such as Karl Heinzen, came to the United States several months before the Revolution, part of the German press hailed the arrival of such "authorities in revolution" as a major event in German-American relations. New York Germans drank

29

the health of the inveterate enemy of the Prussian bureaucracy, and at a banquet in his honor Heinzen urged the Germans in America to join their brethren in the fatherland in a "great army of the spirit," to free those still in chains. In Philadelphia, Heinzen was welcomed with a parade and a serenade by the German singers.[3] Several weeks before the arrival of the *Cambria,* leading Germans in New York had met in Columbia Hall to prepare resolutions calling upon the German people to revolt.

News of the uprising in the German states swept like wildfire through the German-American group. "France is free. Revolution in Bavaria," read the headlines in the Columbus, Ohio, *Westbote* of March 24, 1848, whose circulation jumped twenty per cent immediately. Two weeks later the editor predicted that the Revolution was more than "a straw fire," that the German people would break the chains of censorship and tyranny, and all of western Europe would become democratic.[4] For several weeks the "glorious news" proved so exciting that German-language editors lacked words sufficiently strong to express their satisfaction with what was happening in Europe. The *New Yorker Staatszeitung* eagerly awaited the arrival of each steamer, and its excellent reports of the march of events were copied by German papers in the interior. Such news items carried date lines from Königsberg, Breslau, Dresden, Leipzig, Berlin, Munich, and many cities of the Rhineland, and editors featured the accounts of special correspondents. "The divine right kings are trembling in their shoes," commented the *Staatszeitung* on April 1, 1848, "the day of liberty is dawning all over Europe and we are entering upon great days, fraught with destiny." Germans were admonished to show no mercy for their former rulers, and many Americans regarded the Revolution as a belated fulfillment of the promise of 1776.[5]

In the larger cities revolutionary clubs were organized among the Germans to raise money for arms for the revolutionists, and to support political refugees and their families who had been forced to flee to France or Switzerland. The more optimistic predicted a sizable war chest and planned to publish revolutionary tracts for distribution by special commissioners in Germany. Determined that the Revolution must not fail for lack of money or effective propaganda, several German-American papers featured addresses from "The Republicans of Germany to the People of the United States," and reprinted appeals from such popular revolutionary heroes as Friedrich Hecker.[6] Reports of events in Germany filtered through to such remote villages of the United States as the little pietistic, communistic settlement of Zoar in rural Ohio,[7] and in Louisville, Kentucky, a little struggling German weekly became a daily "because of the excitement about events in the old fatherland" and the demand by the Germans of Louisville for late news each morning.[8]

The small group of German radicals already in the United States planned to return to Germany immediately, and suddenly became centers of attraction for German patriotic rallies. They were provided frequently with funds to promote the revolution on their return to Europe, and with resolutions of sympathy and support. Heinzen started for Liverpool, on the return voyage of the *Cambria,* with some $400 of his own money, of which nearly half was borrowed, which he planned to pay back by free advertising in his *Deutsche Schnellpost.* Additional amounts had been contributed by German-American sympathizers, and he was plagued to the end of his days by critics who accused him of wasting funds intended for the Revolution in extravagant living.[9]

Hermann Kriege, a sincere young idealist whom Marx denounced on several occasions for deviating from the party line, edited the *Volkstribun* in New York before the Revolution, as an organ for land and labor reforms. He immediately returned to Europe as the representative of a German-American revolutionary society. Wilhelm Weitling, Utopian communist and labor organizer, traveling about in America in the interest of his various reforms when news of the Revolution reached New York, abandoned his plans for an *Arbeiterbund* and social insurance to hurry back to Germany, and in a farewell address in Philadelphia promised to help establish a German Republic superior to that of the United States. He took part in democratic congresses in Berlin with little effect on their proceedings, distributed revolutionary pamphlets in Frankfurt and Heidelberg, and published a paper in Berlin to advocate his social theories. Francis Lieber, an outstanding representative of the older German intelligentsia in America, wept for joy as he announced the Revolution to his college class in South Carolina, and promptly sailed for home, only to return bitterly disillusioned and genuinely homesick and convinced that matters would have turned out differently had he arrived in time to be elected to the Frankfurt Parliament. His son Oscar fought with the rebels in the streets of Berlin on his father's birthday and in the very street where he was born. Karl Zeuner, who had escaped a ten-year prison sentence by immigration to the United States, returned to Germany from Cincinnati, and was enthusiastically received in his native city of Butzbach. Resolutions prepared by the "German Democrats of North America" were read in the Frankfurt Parliament amid wild applause. A German book publisher was arrested for circulating resolutions from Philadelphia Germans addressed to their blood brothers in Germany,[10] and as late as 1853, a German-American woman, traveling in Heidelberg with a package of revolutionary literature, was seized for disseminating dangerous doctrine from America.[11]

Within a week of the arrival of the *Cambria* with news of the Paris Revolution, a mass meeting was planned in New York to appeal for men and money,[12] and agents of various German governments dutifully reported to their royal masters that American "demagogues and workers" were plotting to make Germany a republic, and that the more respectable New York German merchant class looked with extreme disfavor on such a challenge to law and order. A preliminary meeting in New York to plan a great public demonstration was so largely attended by Germans, French, Irish, and Americans that the hall could not accommodate the crowd. In passionate oratorical flights, and with tears streaming down their cheeks, spokesmen for the Germans and the French of New York sang the "Marseillaise" and demanded that the Rhine frontier between these historic enemies be abolished. Kriege, Dowiat, and Försch spoke on this occasion, and the committee on arrangements included Heinzen, about to take off for Germany, and Ivan Tyssowski, a Polish refugee who had been dictator of Cracow before coming to New York, where he earned a living as a journalist and gave fencing lessons to Americans who had money for such nonessentials.

The great *Revolutionsfest* itself took place in New York a week later, ushered in with a hundred-gun salute, and a requiem mass in the French church for those who had fallen on the barricades of Paris. French, Germans, Irish, Italians, English, Swiss, Poles, and Americans marched in a parade, hours long, down Broadway and to the park, where a speaker's stand had been erected. A triumphal chariot, drawn by four white horses and decorated with the colors of the participating nationality groups featured the procession. At the ceremonies which followed the parade the mayor presided, and Jakob Uhl, owner of the *New Yorker Staatszeitung,* made the opening address. Fourteen speakers, using four different languages, and including Albert Brisbane, Hermann Kriege, and Tyssowski, harangued the enthusiastic crowd. Congratulatory resolutions, addressed to the French people, were read in English, French, and German, and Germans were urged to return to the fatherland to help transform it into a "sister republic" of France. One notable resolution closed with the sentence, "When the black-red-and-gold flutters proudly beside the Star Spangled Banner, and the spirit of George Washington watches over them both, then Germans on both sides of the Atlantic will cry in their hearts, God bless Germany."[13] The underlying theme of the meeting was the thought that the whole world must be made free, regardless of racial and national distinctions. The celebration ended past midnight, with songs and fireworks and the shooting of rockets from the balcony of the City Hall. It led to the organization of a German revolutionary society, which met periodically thereafter, to listen to patriotic songs by German singers, and to dispatch new exhortations to Germany. Its members wrote to friends and relatives in the homeland to urge the establishment of a German republic, and emphasized that moderate reform and a constitutional monarchy would not suffice. Propagandists for a German republic became so outspoken that the New York *Journal of Commerce* warned both Germans and Irish that they had no right to use the United States for military expeditions and plots against foreign nations with which the government was at peace. The society, however, continued to appeal for funds to send volunteers to Europe in squads of twenty-four, with equipment estimated at $200 per man.

On May 8, the German societies of New York met again to honor the heroes who had lost their lives in the Revolution. This time all political banners were excluded from their solemn procession, and a memorial service attracted a crowd of nearly one hundred thousand from various national groups. German singing societies, bands, lodges, and workers' organizations joined with Italian, French, Polish, Swiss, and Jewish societies in a parade whose central feature was a catafalque, bearing an urn with the inscription "Liberty."

At a May festival in New York, a German orator demanded a union of all mankind into a common brotherhood, born "out of the black of the night, the red blood of the martyrs, and the golden promise of liberty."[14] Germans meeting in the Shakespeare Hotel, owned by Eugen Lievre and destined to become a rendezvous for political refugees, resolved in June

1849 to create an "American legion" to fight for a German republic, to prove that "America has not forgotten Montgomery, Lafayette, Kosciusko, Pulaski, von Steuben and DeKalb."[15] When an epidemic of cholera prevented a Fourth of July parade, German, Hungarian, French, Italian, and Polish "proletarians" met in a "great feast of brotherhood," to display battle flags of the Mexican War, and to collect $111 for the Revolution.[16] A financial report of the Revolutionary Society of New York in August 1849 indicated that $256 had been disbursed for travel expenses for eighteen men, presumably on their way to Europe.[17] As the plight of political refugees in the Swiss cantons became steadily worse, organizations like the New York *Liederkranz* planned benefit concerts for their relief.[18] Public demonstrations in other cities lacked the international character of the celebrations in New York City, but there was hardly an American community of any size where the German Revolution did not prompt similar expressions of sympathy and support.

In April 1848 the steamer *Washington* left New York harbor, bedecked from stem to stern with the black-red-gold colors of the German Revolution, and bearing "An Address of the German Brethren in the Free Union of America to the German People," signed by hundreds of Germans from Philadelphia,[19] to be read in the Frankfurt Parliament. Such distinguished representatives of the German immigration of the 1830's as Dr. Georg Seidensticker and L. A. Wollenweber were among the sponsors of Philadelphia's various demonstrations. On April 24, 1848, a crowd gathered in Independence Square to felicitate the new French Republic and listen to speeches in English, German, French, Spanish, and Italian. Ten Germans spoke from a platform draped in the revolutionary colors; the band played the "Marseillaise," a singing society sang the famous revolutionary song, and the crowd cheered the American, the French, and the future German Republic. The *Freiheitsverein* of Philadelphia sent $318.50 to the American Consul in Basel for the support of political refugees, and Hecker societies and workers' clubs gave balls and concerts to raise additional funds.

In Baltimore, the city farthest south to receive many Forty-eighters, the mayor, Senator Reverdy Johnson, and General Sam Houston addressed a "German Patriotic Meeting" early in 1848.[20] In Louisville, a German "Patriotic Society" gave a concert in Odd Fellows Hall for the benefit of German political refugees; a Louisville tavern keeper renamed his "Frankfurter Hof" the "Deutsche Republik," and a newly organized *Liederkranz* gave its first public performance for the benefit of the family of Robert Blum, "victim of the Habsburgs."[21] Milwaukee celebrated on April 17, 1848, with an added attraction of burning a king in effigy and inviting a Catholic priest to discourse on the sufferings of the Irish in their struggle for freedom. The day's ceremonies, in which Germans, Irish, French, Scotch, and Scandinavians joined, ended with fireworks and the organization of a "three cent society," to which each member promised to contribute that amount weekly for the Revolution. A benefit concert in the Congregational church by the newly organized Milwaukee *Musikverein* netted $51.02.[22]

The Germans of Cincinnati, after one month of effort, collected a war chest of only $183, but the women promised a hand-embroidered red-black-and-gold flag to the first German state to become a republic,[23] an amateur German theatre company gave benefit performances, special collections were made in the churches, and a bazaar was opened on January 12, 1849, to raise funds for the Revolution.[24] In Detroit, Germans and French together organized a "liberty society."[25] In Pittsburgh, Germans met at the Court House to plan for the support of the victims of the German Revolution.[26] In St. Louis, French, Italians, Poles, Irish, Americans, and Germans participated in a great demonstration in April 1848, and German military companies and singing societies, marching alongside Irish Catholic organizations, brought the day's festivities to a close with an impressive torchlight procession. In Charleston, South Carolina, the Germans postponed their celebration until the Fourth of July, when they presented revolutionary colors to German merchant ships in the harbor, and invited their captains and crews to join in the local parade.[27]

Gustav Körner, distinguished intellectual of the older immigration, and a leader of the "Grays" in the later controversies with the "Greens," made a notable address to his fellow Germans in the "Latin settlement" of Belleville, Illinois, in January 1849, and several hundred copies were sent to Germany.[28] The resolutions voted on this occasion will suffice as a final illustration of the attitude of liberal Germans toward the Revolution. "Thousands of miles separate us from Germany," they began, and continue, "Years have passed since we bade our native soil the last fond adieu, but neither distance nor time have weakened the love we bear to the land of our youth. . . . We do know German affairs, for they have driven us hitherwards. We know what is possible, for we see accomplished here what we wish for you. We are no better than you are, but our laws and institutions are better than yours. . . . Only through liberty comes union such as Germany needs." The resolutions closed with a call to action against the "inhuman cruelties of a drunken, soldiery" and "a drunken King," and admonished kinsmen across the water to demand a republic.[29] Although a large part of the German element, especially in the farming areas, was relatively unmoved by the exciting news from Europe, the resolutions and demonstrations of sympathy and support described above originated with German immigrants who had lived in America for a number of years before the Forty-eighters arrived.

Friedrich Hecker was regarded as "the hero of 1848" both here and abroad. A lawyer from Mannheim and a member of the legislature of Baden, he led the uprising of 1848, and retained his tremendous popularity even after he fled to Switzerland and to the United States. In 1849 he returned to Europe only to find that the new appeal to arms which he had been summoned to lead had been suppressed before his ship docked on the European Continent. Hecker was a romantic revolutionist, a great maker of phrases, an eloquent orator in English, French, or German, and a man who never outgrew some of the characteristics of German student life. Although not a radical in the sense that Heinzen, Willich, Anneke, Struve, or Weitling were radicals, workers, soldiers, students, and Turner sang the "Hecker Lied" at their convivial gatherings; poems commemorated Hecker's sacrifices for the liberty of his countrymen; men wore "Hecker hats" and decorated the walls of their homes with pictures of their hero. In Philadelphia, F. W. Thomas sold many copies of a lithograph portraying Hecker in the costume of a revolutionary captain, wearing a Tyrolean hat, and armed with gun, saber, and pistols, and the Hecker cult grew to fantastic proportions on both sides of the Atlantic.

As soon as the American consul in Basel reported in 1848 that Hecker was en route to America, the editor of the *New Yorker Staatszeitung* began to drum up support for a public reception and reprinted long accounts of the Revolution prepared by Hecker with the aid of Franz Sigel, Möglich, and others, which had appeared in Switzerland.[30] Hecker arrived in New York from Southampton on October 5, 1848, "a proud day in the history of the Germans and the future German Republic." Welcomed as "the most distinguished representative of republican principles in Germany," he was escorted to the City Hall by a committee of the

City Council and representatives of the German colony, and greeted by the mayor while a crowd of twenty thousand cheered. Hecker replied graciously in English, and after listening to another address of welcome in German, proceeded to the Shakespeare Hotel on the corner of Duane and William streets, where the owner dispensed credit, food, and lodging to refugees unable to pay. At a mass meeting in Tammany Hall, sponsored by leaders of the German community, Hecker explained that he had come to observe a truly republican government in operation and to prepare himself for a second revolution, and he made frequent references to the fact that the Frankfurt Parliament was greatly interested in the American constitutional system. At the close of the exercises, the honored guest was escorted to his hotel by German military companies and members of the French Democratic Society.[31]

Hecker's receptions in Newark and Philadelphia moved him to tears. Thousands of Germans had assembled at the wharf on Walnut Street in the latter city to escort him to the Franklin Hotel, to a dinner arranged by the Philadelphia *Arbeiterverein*. The thinly veiled attacks of the sponsors on aristocrats here and abroad offended Hecker, however, who complained that the whole occasion lacked dignity. A formal reception at the City Hall followed, and Hecker spoke at the Chinese Museum, and attended a performance of a German theatre company before moving on to Baltimore. By October 22 he was in Cincinnati, where a tavern had been named in his honor. Nine days later he arrived in St. Louis. Hecker continued to appeal for funds to rearm the Germans, though he grew weary of parades, torchlight processions, banquets and other demonstrations. In Pittsburgh, Baltimore, Cincinnati, Louisville, and Indianapolis he disappointed and offended many of his countrymen by vetoing their plans and speaking too briefly to satisfy the crowds.[32]

In January 1849, Hecker agreed to leave Belleville, where he had isolated himself, to make the main address at a huge meeting in St. Louis for the formation of a permanent revolutionary society. Here he expressed the conclusion that "the German fatherland now lives on in the Far West," rather than in Europe, and that genuine republicanism could expect support henceforth only from America.[33] Shortly thereafter, Hecker answered a call of the People's Government of Baden to lead a new appeal to arms. He was disappointed by the meager financial support which he received in America, and irritated by accusations that he used funds intended for the Revolution to buy a farm in St. Clair County, Illinois. When the Germans of New York planned a rousing farewell, he refused to accept the honor unless he could be assured that German-Americans with the means to do so henceforth would contribute to his cause.

Hecker sailed on the *Cambria* on June 27, 1849, accompanied by several friends, including Thomas Mayne Reid, veteran of the Mexican War, novelist, and writer of juvenile fiction, several Polish and Hungarian officers, H. R. Schöninger, and Hermann Gritzner, a member of the left at Frankfurt and a commander of revolutionary troops in 1848. On his arrival in Europe, Hecker learned that the rebellion had collapsed a second time. For a time he toyed with the thought of going to Hungary to aid the Hungarian revolutionaries, but returned to America instead and settled permanently in Illinois. Everywhere in Europe he had been under police surveillance and he had counted the days when he would be back in "the great free country" which he had seen for the first time less than a year ago.

Although speeches, parades, and resolutions were plentiful in 1848, financial contributions from German-Americans were not, and the *New Yorker Staatszeitung* contrasted the niggardliness of the Germans with the sacrifices Irishmen made for the liberation of their native land. Moreover, as the Philadelphia *Freie Zeitung* had pointed out, German workers, with little to give, were more generous than the well-to-do, and middle-class German merchants regarded revolutionary changes of any kind with suspicion.[34] Enthusiasm could not be sustained at the high level of the spring of 1848, and saner counsels restrained hot-heads who wanted to continue the revolution from an American base of operations. Sober, successful bourgeois Germans with money to give refused to support volunteers and adventurers itching to fight. A mass meeting protesting the execution of Robert Blum, the most prominent martyr of 1848, netted a ridiculously small sum for the Revolution. Moreover, certain German religious journals, and Bishop Hughes's Catholic *Freeman's Journal* opposed revolution on principle. Catholic opposition wrecked the plan to give Garibaldi an official welcome in New York, and Archbishop Hughes denounced the Kossuth excitement of 1850 and 1851 in unequivocal terms.[35] A correspondent of the *New Yorker Staatszeitung,* writing from Philadelphia, berated the German middle class for its lack of republican principles and for regarding the leaders of the Revolution as irresponsible communists who wanted to destroy private property.[36] The cause was further weakened by bitter factional quarrels which divided even the most devoted friends of republicanism among the German element in the United States.[37]

For several years the German-language press continued to report the progress of the liberal movement in Germany with keenest interest. The *Staatszeitung* of New York summarized the comments of leading newspapers in Germany, and printed reports by special correspondents from important Central European cities. The editor quoted Hecker's *Volksfreund,* published in Rheinfelden, and called attention to such brochures as Gustav Siegmund's "Prussia, Revolution and Democracy," in which Herwegh's brother-in-law, and Julius Fröbel, and Arnold Ruge predicted Russia's destiny to become a democracy. Smaller papers copied the metropolitan press for interested readers in the provinces. In general, the German-American press revealed a remarkably keen understanding of the clash of interest groups in the Frankfurt Parliament, and gave intelligent appraisals of the attitude of peasants, workers, bourgeois, feudal landholders, and other classes.

The tangled military situation, as the rebels took the field under Sigel, Blenker, Hecker, Fenner von Fenneberg, and Louis Mieroslawski, their Polish commander-in-chief, was described in the American German-language press in considerable detail, as well as the capture, arrest, and subsequent fate of leading German radicals. The coverage was so extensive that the names of many Forty-eighters and their rôle in the Revolution were well known to German-Americans before they set foot upon American soil.[38] For twenty-five cents the *New Yorker Staatszeitung* sold caricatures of the Austrian Emperor, Metternich, Louis Philippe, the King of Bavaria, and other symbols of the old order. In time, however, as the early enthusiasm died down, newspaper comment became more critical of the failure of the Revolution to achieve substantial results, the attitude of the United States Government toward it, and the factional divisions in the Frankfurt Parliament between republicans who desired a federal structure on the American model and those who advocated a replica of the French Republic.

James Buchanan reported that the Revolution of 1848 was hailed "with one universal burst of enthusiasm," and Henry Wadsworth Longfellow spoke for most of his countrymen when he said, "So long as a king is left upon his throne there will be no justice on the earth."[39] No voice, either German or American, was raised on behalf of kings or the *status quo*, however much the indecision at Frankfurt, and the futile efforts to compromise with kings and princes disappointed and angered leaders of the German group in the United States. The German-language press debated whether Germany was ready for a republic, or when she might be,[40] and compared the Frankfurt Parliament unfavorably with the American Constitutional Convention of 1787. The editor of the Columbus *Westbote*, disgusted with the temporizing tactics of the Frankfurt group, concluded that Christ himself could not have freed the German people, but would have been crucified a second time,[41] and concluded that the differences between the blessings of America and the tyranny of Europe were irreconcilable. Occasionally European papers, like the Westphalian *Volksfreund*, took notice of criticisms by the American press and of "America letters" written by German farmers and laborers in the United States, but the discussion usually ended with the comment that "Germany is not America," that Germans have never known liberty, and could not be expected to achieve it immediately. Others believed that unification would come only as the result of a foreign war, presumably with Russia.[42]

The attitude of the American Government in Washington, and of "old man Taylor," the President, was vigorously criticized in German-American circles. A resolution of sympathy for the German Revolution was pigeon-holed in the Committee on Foreign Relations of the House of Representatives. Spokesmen for the German element resented such strict neutrality, urged the sale of American vessels to a "German Central Government," to protect German commerce and immobilize the Danish Navy during the controversy between Denmark and Prussia over Schleswig, and suggested that German ships be manned temporarily by American seamen, under American naval officers.[43]

With the final failure of the Revolution in 1849, interest shifted to the fate of political prisoners caught in the dragnet of the military and the police, and the ten thousand political refugees who found asylum in other countries, notably Switzerland. For a half-dozen years after 1849, the German-language press in America reported the experiences of Hecker, Zitz, Fickler, Tiedemann, Sigel, Blenker, Germain Metternich, Adolph Rösler von Oels, Willich, Struve, and other Forty-eighters. Treason trials were adequately covered in the American press, and the censorship of such radical publications as the *Neue Rheinische Zeitung* of Marx and

Engels[44] duly noted. The *Deutsche Schnellpost* of New York reported daily on the arrival of refugees, and the *New Yorker Staatszeitung* urged the United States Government to grant passports for political refugees and remove legal barriers to their entry. As hundreds of refugees and other immigrants awaited passage money and food at Havre, German-Americans were urged to contribute to their relief. A special organization in New York "for the aid of the political refugees of 1848-49" watched over new arrivals when they landed, and furnished transportation inland; and similar groups were organized in St. Louis, Cleveland, Cincinnati, Boston, Rochester, Milwaukee, Pittsburgh, Hartford, Augusta (Georgia), and elsewhere.[45]

FOOTNOTES

CHAPTER 4

1. See, for example, *New Yorker Staatszeitung*, April 22, May 13, 20, June 10, Nov. 4, 11, 1848; Jan. 20, June 16, July 14, 1849; Aug. 3, Dec. 3, 1850; Jan. 26, 1853.
By 1851, the German singing societies of Baltimore were singing a variation of Arndt's famous poem,—

> "Was ist des Deutschen Vaterland?
> Wie heisst sein theures Heimatland?
> Es heisst nun Amerika
> Des Deutschen Heimat ist jetzt da."

New Yorker Staatszeitung, June 6, 1851.
2. See Hermann Schuricht: *Geschichte der Deutschen Schulbestrebungen in Amerika* (Leipzig, 1884) p. 39.
3. Wittke: *Heinzen*, pp. 53-57.
4. *Der Westbote* (Columbus, Ohio) April 7, 1848. Cited hereafter as *Westbote*.
5. See *New Yorker Staatszeitung*, March 25, April 1, 15, May 1, 1848.
6. See on these points, *Ibid.*, June 10, 1848; Jan. 13, Feb. 17, 1849; and *Westbote*, Oct. 6, 1848.
7. Edgar B. Nixon: "The Zoar Society: Applicants for Membership," in *The Ohio Archaeological and Historical Quarterly*, XLV, pp. 343-44.
8. L. Stierlin: *Kentucky*, p. 107.
9. Wittke: *Heinzen*, pp. 59-60.
10. *New Yorker Staatszeitung*, March 3, 1849.
11. On these matters, see *New Yorker Staatszeitung*, April 29, July 15, Aug. 5, Sept. 23, 1848; April 2, 1853; C. F. Huch: "Die Deutschamerikaner und die deutsche Revolution" in *Mitteilungen des Deutschen Pionier Vereins von Philadelphia* XVII (1910) pp. 23-25; Freidel: *Francis Lieber* pp. 244-47; and Carl Wittke—*The Utopian Communist: The Life of Wilhelm Weitling, Nineteenth Century Reformer* (Baton Rouge, 1950). Hereafter cited as Wittke: *Weitling*.
12. See also Philipp Wagner: *Ein Achtundvierziger* (Brooklyn, 1882) p. 163.
13. *New Yorker Staatszeitung*, March 25; also April 8, April 22, 1848; and *Westbote*, April 14, 1848.
14. *New Yorker Staatszeitung*, April 22, 29, May 13, June 10, 1848.

15. *Ibid.*, June 30, 1849.
16. *Ibid.*, July 7, 1848.
17. *Ibid.*, Aug. 18, 1849.
18. *Ibid.*, Dec. 9, 1848; June 2, 7, 22, 1849.
19. Edmund A. Thomaser: "Achtzehnhundredvierziger Macht—als im Lenz das Eis gekracht," in *Staats-Herold Almanach* (New York, 1948) p. 42.
20. Cunz: *Maryland Germans*, pp. 270-71 and *New Yorker Staatszeitung*, June 17, 1848.
21. Stierlin: *Kentucky*, pp. 112-14, and appendix, p. 13.
22. See Still: *Milwaukee*, p. 115; and Koss: *Milwaukee*, pp. 263-65.
23. *Westbote*, April 14, 1848.
24. See T. S. Baker: "Young Germany in America," in *Americana-Germanica* (Philadelphia) I, 73-74.
25. *New Yorker Staatszeitung*, April 29, 1848.
26. *Der Deutsche Pionier* (Cincinnati) III, No. 4 (June, 1871) pp. 101-2, quoting the *Pittsburger Courier* of May 3, 1848.
27. *New Yorker Staatszeitung*, May 6, July 15, 1848; also June 16, 1849.
28. Evarts B. Greene: "Gustav Koerner, a Typical German American Leader," in *Deutsch-Amerikanische Geschichtsblätter* VII (April, 1907) pp. 76-83.
29. See *Memoirs of Gustav Koerner, 1809-1896*, edited by Thomas I. McCormack (Cedar Rapids, Iowa, 1909) I, 533-40. Cited hereafter as Koerner: *Memoirs*.
30. *New Yorker Staatszeitung*, Sept. 22, 23, 1848.
31. *New Yorker Staatszeitung*, Oct. 7, 14, 21, 1848.
32. *Westbote*, Oct. 27, Nov. 11, 1848.
33. *New Yorker Staatszeitung*, Feb. 17, 1849.
34. See C. F. Huch: "Die Deutschamerikaner und die deutsche Revolution," in *Mitteilungen des Deutschen Pionier Vereins von Philadelphia*, XVII (1910), 25-33; and an article by the same author on the same subject, in *Deutsch-Amerikanische Geschichtsblätter*, XI (January, 1911), 37-47.
35. Merle Curti: "The Impact of the Revolutions of 1848 on American Thought" in *Proceedings of the American Philosophical Society*, Vol. 93, No. 3 (June, 1949) p. 213.
36. *New Yorker Staatszeitung*, April 21, 1849.
37. See on these points, *New Yorker Staatszeitung*, April 22, Dec. 16, 1848; Jan. 1, Feb. 10, June 1, 1849.
38. For examples of the reporting of the German Revolution, see *New Yorker Staatszeitung*, March 10, April 11, May 13, 20, 27, 29, June 17, July 15, 22, 29, Sept. 9, Oct. 28, 1848; April 7, June 7, July 15, 1849; Jan. 26, March 23, 1850.
39. Quoted in Merle Curti: *loc. cit.*, p. 211.
40. *New Yorker Staatszeitung*, April 18, 1848; July 6, 1848.
41. *Westbote*, Jan. 2, 1852; also June 9, 15, 1849.
42. *New Yorker Staatszeitung*, Jan. 13, March 24, April 14, 1849.
43. *Ibid.*, Feb. 17, March 9, April 14, June 27, 1849.
44. See *Ibid.*, Aug. 5, Sept. 23, Dec. 18, 1848; Jan. 6, 13, 20, and July 31, 1849; April 6, 1850; March 24, 28, 1853.
45. See for details, *New Yorker Staatszeitung*, July 29, 1848; Aug. 4, 25, Oct. 27, Nov. 10, Dec. 14, 22, 1849; Feb. 2, 21, March 2, May 25, 1850; May 15, 1851; and *Westbote*, Dec. 7, 1849.

Chapter 5 · THE GREAT MIGRATION

THE DECADE of the 1850's produced a net immigration larger in relation to the existing population than any other decade in American history, and the excess of arrivals over departures totaled about 12% of the population of 1850.[1] While the total foreign-born population increased 84.4% during the decade, the German-born population increased 118.6%. In states like Wisconsin, the increase among the German element was 225.4%, as compared with a total increase of all foreign-born in that state of only 154.4%.

Reviewing the total German immigration by years (and subject to some inaccuracies in computation) we find that in 1847, 82,473 Germans entered the United States; in 1848, 62,684, and in 1849, 63,148. After 1850, the totals mounted rapidly until they reached 152,106 in 1852, 150,094 in 1853, and 229,562 in 1854. Although the totals continued large, the German immigration began to decrease in 1855 and continued to do so until after the Civil War.

Reports from such sources as the German Society of New York confirm the fact that 1854 marked the peak of the German immigration before the Civil War. Friedrich Kapp, a Forty-eighter who became a member of the Immigration Commission of New York, estimated the total German influx from 1845 to 1854 at slightly over a quarter million, and concluded that each immigrant represented a total financial and economic asset to the United States of at least $500.[2] Other sources fixed the average capital of the German immigrants who came in 1855 at $61.18 per capita.[3]

As suggested in an earlier chapter, much of the German immigration consisted of discontented, hard-pressed workers and farmers. An examination of the evidence from both sides of the Atlantic indicates that in many cases it is impossible to divorce economic causes entirely from the discontent resulting from prevailing political conditions. The complete failure of the Revolution stimulated many to take the final step, after having weighed the arguments in favor of a change of scene for a long time. Confusion and disillusionment were in the air, and many Germans after 1848 were oppressed by a sense of defeat, frustration, and despair. Such psychological factors affected men and women who had no specific political reason to emigrate and had not actually clashed with the authorities in 1848 and 1849. Local and state governments encouraged the dissatisfied, the trouble-makers, the agitators, the failures, and the paupers to leave, and aided them in making a speedy exit. The governmental policy to do a little blood-letting for the good of the state originated in part from the events of 1848, and prospective emigrants, eager to improve their economic status, and aware of a republic across the sea where men could find jobs and breathe air that was free, were rather easily persuaded. Thus it becomes difficult to separate political refugees, the real Forty-eighters, from the rest of the German immigration.

The evidence from American and German sources proves conclusively that the bulk of the immigrants who came from Germany after 1848 belonged to the farming class. Figures for Baden for the period from 1850 to 1855, indicate that farmers constituted 50.7% of the immigration, and artisans 26%, and that the remainder represented various categories, from unskilled laborers to teachers and artists. The pressure to leave Baden was so heavy that when a society to furnish information and assistance to prospective immigrants was organized in that state in 1849, it received three thousand applications in a few days. A government commission on emigration and several private groups in Baden provided data on climate, working conditions, and travel costs to the United States, and answered inquiries about the condition of the soil, the availability of doctors, schools, and churches, the status of the Indian menace, and "the cost of a block-house." The archives of the German states for the period immediately following the Revolution reveal that whole villages and parishes were practically dissolved in southern and western Germany, and that nearly all the able-bodied seemed eager to leave.

In Schönau, a parish in Baden, 369 out of a population of 2,919 indicated their desire to emigrate. In St. Blasien, the number was 976 out of a total of 4,089, and in certain parishes the percentages ran much higher. Government and private agencies provided funds to help the poor and the undesirable to depart, and in the local records, beside the name of many immigrants, stands the notation "the cost was paid by the parish." Such financial assistance usually included money for travel and gifts of food and clothing. Occasionally funds were sent directly from Baden to German societies in England or the United States to aid penniless arrivals during their first critical weeks in a new country.

In the fall of 1850, the government of Baden began a systematic campaign to get rid of political offenders. On March 21, 1851, the Minister of the Interior requested information from the Minister of War on the number of prisoners still confined at Rastatt, a key point in the uprisings of 1848, and data on their fitness for emigration. Democratic papers still were subject to severe censorship, and were frequently suppressed; and citizens who wore anything red were regarded with suspicion. Soldiers were quartered in private homes.[4] In many cases an offender or a prisoner was pardoned on condition that he leave the kingdom, with the understanding that he would have to serve his complete term should he ever return. Official records reveal that along with men of character, integrity, and property, thieves, vagabonds, petty offenders, beggars, and mothers of illegitimate children were shipped off in considerable numbers to the United States. The musty archives record a story of defeat and hope, of initiative and shiftlessness, of profound human tragedy and frustration. American consuls protested to the German authorities for dumping undesirables upon the United States, and forcing American consular offices to assume responsibility for the human flotsam which congregated at the ports of embarkation. In a few instances, immigrants were shipped back to Europe from New York, or allowed to disembark only on condition that they leave immediately for the West.

What has been said about Baden can be repeated for Saxony, Mecklenburg, Hanover, Niederhessen, Stettin, Mainz, and other German provinces and cities. The Frankfurt Parliament had discussed ways and means for the protection and support of immigrants, and societies in Cologne, Darmstadt, Düsseldorf, Stuttgart, and elsewhere wrestled with the problem.[5] In Munich, as late as 1853, the police were still picking up men and boys wearing "Hecker hats," and in the same year, raids by the Berlin police resulted in the arrest of forty persons suspected of new conspiracies against the government.[6] The Bavarian Archives record as the most common reasons for emigration in 1849 and 1850, the "hope for better subsistence" and "dissatisfaction with political conditions."

A correspondent of the Columbus *Westbote* reported that many who left Southwestern Germany belonged to neither the laboring nor the peasant class, but were substantial citizens eager to escape petty persecution by the government, or anxious to leave before another revolutionary crisis, and reports from Berlin told the same story. The *Louisiana Staatszeitung,* spokesman for the German element in New Orleans and vicinity, commented that the only future for Germans in Europe was in jail or the poor house.[7]

In Hesse-Kassel, minor offenders were released on condition that they depart for America, and in the same area agents from California were permitted to recruit young women for dance and entertainment halls for western mining towns. The shady traffic developed into such a scandal that the Germans of San Francisco took steps to end the disgraceful practice.[8] In Leipzig, several organizations helped paupers and petty offenders to get to New York,[9] and as late as 1866 the *Pittsburger Volksblatt* complained that Württemberg still was using the United States as a dumping ground for criminals.[10]

Among the 1,150 persons who left Niederhessen in 1852 there was a retired lieutenant of the army, a barber, a seminary student, a rag-picker, wood-carver, merchant, schoolteacher, musician, basket-maker, and a number of bankers, farmers, carpenters, millwrights, and other artisans, and such local lists are fairly typical for other areas. The lists almost always included the names of students who had exhausted the opportunities offered by several German universities and no longer were acceptable to any.[11] In 1852, the *New Yorker Staatszeitung* reported that twenty thousand persons were prepared to leave Hessen; that many others were getting ready to emigrate from Schleswig and Thuringia, and that political refugees in considerable numbers had congregated at the port of Hamburg.[12]

German official policy vacillated with reference to the great drainage of population to America, and varied from state to state. The Emigration Society of Leipzig urged the government of Saxony to insist that immigrants travel in German ships, and proposed an agreement with the United States whereby newcomers could acquire land on easy terms, settle in compact groups, and continue to trade with the mother country, apparently on the theory that if emigration could not be prevented it might at least be made profitable to the mother country.[13] The journal of a national immigration society in Frankfurt suggested in 1850 that emigration be used "to raise the culture of the United States," and since most Germans then in America had come "with few exceptions from the lowest levels," represented "the poorest and most ignorant portion of the German people," spoke a corrupted German, and knew nothing of German history, the society advocated free passage for doctors, lawyers, teachers, preachers, painters, engineers, and architects, to enrich the intellectual and cultural life of pioneer America.[14] Prussia, with abundant space in her eastern provinces, was torn between the desire to get rid of disgruntled subjects and the need for farmers to till her vacant land. Prussian bureaucrats maintained that emigration should be directed by the government to countries where Germans could preserve their cultural unity. Why continue to send hard-working Germans to build up American man power? "In North America," according to a report in the Prussian state archives in 1849, "German immigrants become Anglo-Americans in the second generation. Therefore we want to find a new area where the German nationality can be preserved."[15]

Emigration from Germany, as well as other parts of Europe was also stimulated artificially by those who profited from the immigrant business. Bremen and Hamburg, Germany's leading ports, found the immigrant traffic so remunerative that they vigorously opposed all efforts to discourage emigration. The commercial interests of Havre, London, and Liverpool maintained agencies in Germany to recruit prospective immigrants, and thousands of Germans were transported across the English Channel to London and Liverpool before proceeding across the Atlantic. American states like Wisconsin, eager for population, carried on an active propaganda in Germany.[16] The brochures of Friedrich Münch, an early German settler in Missouri, circulated in Germany during the 1850's, along with less reliable publications, such as that of the "German Society of Minnesota," which set forth the advantages of that state.[17] In Stettin, a pamphlet inviting Germans to join Cabet's French Icarian colony in Nauvoo, Illinois, was prominently displayed in the taverns.

Governments were almost powerless to counteract such propaganda. In 1853 the city of Marburg tried to prohibit agents from soliciting emigrants, and the city fathers were particularly irritated because several political refugees had returned after a short stay in the United States to persuade their countrymen to follow their example. Steamship companies and land companies distributed advertising, which was frequently misleading. An agent of the Pennsylvania Railroad sold tickets in Bremen in 1856, and a publication issued in Saxony described the advantages of Texas, Virginia, and California. Americans able to speak German made the rounds of the taverns in the winter months to boost America, and as late as 1873 Otto von Corvin, known as the "betrayer of Rastatt" ever since he surrendered that key point to the King of Prussia in 1848, distributed maps and immigration propaganda for Minnesota at the World's Fair in Vienna.[18]

Some German authorities hoped to divert emigrants from the United States to Latin America. In the late 1840's, the Prussian Society for the Mosquito Coast, the Stuttgarter Society for Chile, a colonization society for Southern Brazil with headquarters in Hamburg, and a society for Western Australia were active along these lines. A Prussian prince was interested in promoting a German immigrant colony on the Mosquito Coast in Central America, and was surprised to encounter opposition from a "pack of English vagabonds and swindlers." A Prussian consul reported on the advantages of Guatemala, and German merchants stressed the attractions of Nicaragua. Friedrich Gerstäcker, novelist and world traveler, was subsidized to report on conditions in both North and South America, and Emperor Dom Pedro of Brazil promised a friendly reception for Germans who would settle in his country.[19]

Early in 1849 the German-American press reported that families from all parts of the fatherland were leaving for political reasons, reactionaries because they "feared a war," and democrats because they "were bitter" over the outcome of the uprisings of 1848.[20] In an interview with the press, a recent arrival in Philadelphia explained that he had come to the United States because he was convinced that "liberty would not be won in Germany within the lifetime of any one now living." German refugees who found temporary asylum in France after 1848 feared they would be transported to Algiers, and preferred America to Africa. Others found their welcome wearing thin in Switzerland and "turned their eyes and hearts toward America," fearful that the German and Austrian governments would force their extradition by the Swiss government. An editorial in the *Frankfurt Journal* of 1850 reported that France and Sardinia would no longer honor the passports of refugees. From Mannheim came reports that refugees from Strassburg and the Palatinate were assembling their belongings for the trans-Atlantic voyage, and the reminiscences of a Palatine revolutionist published in the *New Yorker Staats-zeitung* described how he "crossed the Rhine into Alsace and from there proceeded via Havre to America."[21] A patriot executed by a firing squad in Mannheim enjoined the mother of his children to take them to America, for "it is better to die there than here," and a correspondent from Thuringia wrote, "In the background, in the minds of all immigrants, is the thought that Germany is ruined."[22]

Every large German-American community acquired its quota of new immigrants, and among them were prominent ex-revolutionaries. Newspapers reported their arrival, and explained that their sentences had been abbreviated, or that they had been pardoned outright on condition that they leave at once. Among the newcomers were some who had served prison terms. Many simple-minded artisans or peasants who had joined the soldiery during the excitement of 1848 and 1849 had been convicted of high treason and condemned to from eight to twenty years in a military prison. At Heidelberg a judge inquired of eighteen rebels whether they preferred immigration to America to serving out their sentences, and when they chose the former, offered them money for the journey. A document prepared by Veit Zöller, listing the names of 181 persons from many cities and towns who were held in jail at Zweibrücken as a result of the uprising in 1849, and giving occupations, religion, and length of sentence, indicates that of the group (a few names are undecipherable) 90 were Protestants, 46 Catholics, and 36 either had no church connection or listed themselves as "free thinkers." The age limits of the prisoners were eighteen to sixty-four, but the great majority were under forty, and over half were under thirty-five. Among the arrested suspects were ten government clerks, five burgomasters of little villages, six students, seven schoolteachers, two physicians, three ministers, one veterinarian, one actor, and two notaries. Nineteen were in some way engaged in business, five were innkeepers, eleven were farmers, and nine were day laborers. The list included representatives of more than thirty crafts and specialized occupations. Some had been held in confinement for just a few weeks, others for a longer period, but none for more than six months. Such lists illustrate the appeal which revolution made to men in all walks of life. A correspondent from Mainz, watching the departure of emigrants from Baden and Rhenish Bavaria, commented, "They depart without experiencing the least pain of farewell, because of present political conditions."[23]

Irritating police regulations and the snooping of meddling bureaucrats convinced many who were not actually involved in the Revolution that political progress was impossible in Germany. "We know people," wrote a correspondent of the *New Yorker Staatszeitung* from Baden in 1852, "who left 5,000 to 8,000 gulden to the government just so they might be permitted to regain possession and control over their remaining property. . . . All the reactionaries are pouncing upon the property of the revolutionaries, and the officials are becoming wealthy through sucking the life blood of the people."[24] The people of Hesse and Thuringia complained specifically of government interference with their political rights and their religious liberty. Several German states prohibited the circulation of German-language papers published in the United States, and in 1853 a physician in Altenburg was recommitted to prison for helping political offenders to escape to America.[25] Ludwig von Baumbach, a former member of the Hessian Diet and the Frankfurt Parliament, sold his estates several years after the Revolution and settled on a farm in Ohio so that his children might be reared in an atmosphere of liberty and freedom. The records of Darmstadt show that 116 soldiers deserted between May and October 1852 and emigrated to America, and sailors from the fleet frequently adopted a similar course.[26] "Despotism drives the friends of liberty into foreign lands," wrote a German from Switzerland in 1852, "and capital disposes of the proletariat by sending them across the ocean also."[27]

The multiplication of evidence of this kind indicates that political reaction was a more important factor in explaining German emigration during the middle nineteenth century than some writers have appreciated. Six years after the Revolution an editorial in the *New Yorker Staatszeitung* observed, "Whoever lived through 1848 must agree that 1849 was not an accident nor even a defeat, but that it merely brought to public view a chronic malady. . . . It may be that liberty is finished in Europe for a century, and . . . will have to be reintroduced some day from across the Atlantic. In the meantime, all democrats may have to make the long trek to Havre, Antwerp and Liverpool."[28]

Thousands embarked in Hamburg and Bremen, or Havre, Antwerp, Rotterdam, or Liverpool. Many left without permits or passports or other papers, and managed somehow to avoid the police. Some were rowed to the ship's side to evade the law. Inspection at Bremen and Hamburg was lax, despite the fact that special halls were built to house the thousands who streamed through these cities on their way to America. Many came with the huge wagon trains which hauled freight to the North Sea, and spent their meager resources before they reached the point of embarkation. From north and central Germany the usual route followed the Elbe and the Weser to Hamburg and Bremen. For those who came from the Upper Rhine country, Havre was the most convenient port. Hundreds came down the Rhine in little boats. Others took the road from Strassburg, which was crowded with long files of carts, drawn by underfed beasts, and filled with the women and children and the few belongings which emigrants were determined to rescue from the European debacle. Littell's *Living Age* likened this great human caravan to "a convoy of wounded, the relics of some battlefield."[29] Still others traveled in the cotton wagons which returned empty to northern France from the textile factories of Alsace. With these caravans, emigrants proceeded to Paris, and thence by boat down the Seine to Havre. When the Strassburg-Paris railroad was opened, it provided quicker connections with the French port.

Mainz was a principal rendezvous for emigrants from South Germany and Switzerland. At least ten agents worked in the city in the early 1850's to direct the stream to the particular port of embarkation for which they solicited business, and a huge market in Mainz sold food and clothing to prospective emigrants. Here also were provided the facilities for exchanging familiar money for strange new currencies, and spending a last few convivial hours with the tavern keepers. In 1851 it was estimated that thirty thousand immigrants passed through the port of Havre annually. Frequently the crowds were so large that hundreds camped in the streets. "The streets were thronged with emigrants, chiefly South Germans, Alsatians and Swiss," wrote a German in 1851 who was on his way to America. In the spring of the year, the city looked more like a German than a French community. There were German shops and taverns, and German "immigrant runners" who swooped down on their innocent victims, like "a horde of parasites," and were paid on a per capita basis, depending upon how many they could defraud. Many of their victims had been in Havre for weeks without accomplishing their departure from Europe.[30] The clergy tried to alleviate the miseries of this mass of stranded humanity, and social agencies, such as the *Société havroise de secours pour les emigrants allemands,* did a limited amount of relief work among them.

Immigration at all times requires stout hearts and strong bodies, and an extraordinary amount of determination. Some did not survive the ordeals of the 1850's, and many more suffered psychologically and physically from their experience. Many a Forty-eighter cursed the day he left his native fireside, however poor it may have been. Immigrant ships of the middle nineteenth century offered few improvements over those of a century earlier as far as the comforts of their human cargo were concerned, as immigrants and their families traveled on vessels which had hauled cotton and tobacco to Europe, and whose owners divided the hold, by hastily constructed thin partitions, into steerage space to carry human freight on their return voyages to Baltimore or New Orleans.

The horrors and dangers of the ocean voyage in the typical immigrant ships of a century ago have been described in scores of reminiscences and travel accounts. In many cases such accounts are exaggerations. Yet many give a true picture of human beings packed like herring in a steerage that was little better than a black hole. Immigrants were frequently robbed before they left their homeland, robbed again on shipboard, and then shamelessly exploited on arriving at their destination. The food aboard spoiled quickly; the water supply was inadequate; and although travel accommodations usually stipulated "all meals, but without meat and butter," many passengers sold their extra trousers, mufflers, watches, and other belongings on the way over to provide their families with adequate food. Many contracted diseases on the voyage and landed in a hospital as soon as they debarked in New York.[31] The newspapers of the 1850's are full of indictments of the immigrant traffic and of statistics revealing the high mortality rate among the newcomers, and the "many German beggars in the streets of New York."[32] The offices of the Immigration Commission on Canal Street were piled high with chests and trunks, sacks and baskets, filled with "the possessions of poor immigrants whose bodies rest on the bottom of the sea."[33]

The opportunities for exploiting and defrauding the immigrant were almost without limit. Graft and bribery fed on the immigrant traffic on both sides of the ocean. American railroad agents sold tickets in Frankfurt and other German cities. Occasionally an unscrupulous American consul collected improper fees, or accepted commissions from business houses and hotels for referring immigrants to them. The sea voyage safely passed, the immigrant was likely to run into beasts of prey in human form who pounced upon their victim on his arrival, and exploited his ignorance of American conditions and his inability to speak English. Ports like New York were infested with "runners" and "shoulder-hitters" paid by truckers, railroads, hotels, and boarding houses to lure innocent victims into their clutches. Runners, in addition to a salary, usually were paid on a commission basis. When the Erie Railroad tried to get along without them it discovered that competitors were diverting its passenger business to their roads. Ship captains sometimes sold permits to runners for $50 to $100, guaranteeing them the monopoly right to exploit their passengers.

Immigrants usually stayed for awhile in the port where their ship docked. Some stayed too long, and depleted their remaining assets until they were reduced to the level of beggars or objects of public charity. Others were fortunate enough to find employment at once. When immigrants finally started inland, they usually bought their tickets at a "booking office," where they were frequently overcharged, or received tickets which would carry them only part way. The handling of baggage lent itself to fraud and exploitation, and emigrant trains were notoriously bad, overcrowded, hot and smelly. Passengers were packed into freight cars or antiquated coaches, and sometimes had to sleep on the floor, and as "foreigners and dutchmen," traveled more like animals in a cattle car.

A common route for immigrants going west by water took them by steamboat up the Hudson, then across the 350-mile Erie Canal with its eighty-four locks, on "line boats" that traveled at a top speed of three miles per hour, and for which the fare usually was one cent a mile. At Buffalo, deck passage to Detroit could be bought on a lake steamer for $3.00, and from Detroit immigrants frequently traveled farther up and down the lakes, to Chicago or Milwaukee. Steamboat explosions were numerous, and added to the hazards of the trip. Several of the worst disasters occurred on the lakes and on the Mississippi in the 1850's. Finally, it must be added that some of the worst swindlers and the most unscrupulous runners and operators of taverns and immigrant boarding houses were the countrymen of the new arrivals, who knew their language and enough of their background to win their confidence, and used their advantage to rob and exploit their blood brothers.[34]

These were some of the conditions which immigrants of every nationality encountered in the 1850's. The superior education and social standing of the Forty-eighters did not shield them from such unhappy experiences, and some found it more difficult to adjust to them than their humbler brethren. Many Forty-eighters came over in steerage and landed in New York without visible means of support, and a large number never left the ports where they disembarked. Others fanned out over the country, on farms and into the cities of the West, such as St. Louis, Milwaukee, Cincinnati, and Chicago, and as far south as New Orleans and Texas.

The plight of the immigrant did not leave Americans entirely unmoved, and sincere efforts were made to do relief work among the newcomers and help them find employment. Organizations for this purpose were formed among the Germans already here, and some enlisted the support of kind-hearted native Americans. The *Deutsche Gesellschaft* of New York was one of the largest, oldest, and most active of these immigrant aid societies. Dating back in its origin to a much earlier period, it was stimulated to renewed activity by the heavy German influx after 1848. It raised funds by various devices, including lotteries by which the fancy needlework of German ladies was sold at a good price. Immigrants from Schleswig-Holstein living in New York organized their own society to aid the veterans and refugees of the war between Prussia and Denmark.

The reports of the German Society of New York throw light on the whole question of immigration. In 1852, the Society had receipts of $11,047 and disbursed $9,204. It found jobs for 5,956 persons during that year, on farms, in trades, and in private homes. In the preceding year it distributed $7,498 among 6,613 persons—certainly not a high per capita contribution! The monthly reports of the organization indicate the volume of immigration, and show that in June 1852, 22,339 Germans landed in New York, and that the great majority moved on into the West. Two hundred were entirely destitute and became temporary charges of the Society. Both German and American consuls coöperated with the organization's relief work.

By 1853, the membership of the New York Society had declined to 501, and many were delinquent in their dues. Factional quarrels forced a reorganization, and for a time the Society considered employing a paid director, a post for which Friedrich Kapp was quick to apply. Kapp's law firm of Kapp, Zitz, and Fröbel offered its services to immigrants for the purchase of travel tickets, and the transfer of funds between Europe and America.[35] Other leading Forty-eighters, such as Sigismund Kaufmann, Joseph Fickler, and Oswald Ottendörfer, were greatly interested in the activities of the Society, which included furnishing medical and nursing service for newly arrived immigrants and Germans who had been in the United States less than five years and could not speak English. The friction over the internal management of the Society is of no concern for our present purpose, but it is interesting to point out that the organization received only lukewarm support from the *New Yorker Staatszeitung,* and the *New Yorker Criminal Zeitung und Belletristisches Journal* and the *New Yorker Abendzeitung* were openly hostile.

The German Society of New York was the best-known but not the only relief organization. Baltimore, in the 1850's, had a *Deutscher Hilfsverein.* Chicago's German Aid Society, directed primarily against immigrant runners, was formed in 1854 after a particularly tragic railroad accident. Among its supporters in later years were Dr. Ernst Schmidt, a radical Forty-eighter; George Schneider, a prominent refugee journalist and politician; and Fritz Baumann, a well-known German architect, who was a friend and admirer of Karl Heinzen. The Chicago Society employed a full-time agent to meet immigrants on their arrival in the city and to protect them from exploitation.[36] In Cincinnati, a German Catholic Immigrant Society offered protection to the newcomers and tried to give them sound counsel. In Philadelphia, the German National Society for the Protection of the Immigrants in North America was chartered by the state and had at its head a highly respected pastor of the German Reformed Church. The St. Louis German Emigrant Aid Society held a charter from the Missouri legislature and was primarily concerned with immigrants who came up the Mississippi on river boats from New Orleans. In the year 1848-49, 9,000 German immigrants arrived in St. Louis; in 1849-50 there were 14,403; the next year only 10,715, and in 1851-52, 12,624. The St. Louis Society was especially exercised over the brutal treatment of immigrants on river steamers, and reported that as many as twenty to thirty passengers had died on a single voyage and been buried along the banks of the Mississippi. In March 1855, the St. Louis organization found jobs for 283 workers on the railroads, 192 farm and factory laborers, 121 woodchoppers and unskilled workmen, 163 female domestics, 35 artisans, one teacher, six store- and barkeepers, and apprenticed thirteen young immigrants to masters who would teach them their business or trade.[37]

Such private charities and benevolent societies helped many to find their first jobs, and offered them sound and honest advice. But the critical psychological readjustment from one country to another, from one language to another, and from one cultural pattern to another, was largely a task which the immigrant had to face by himself, as he struggled to find new roots for his uprooted life.

FOOTNOTES

CHAPTER 5

1. P. K. Whelpton: "A History of Population Growth in the United States," in *Scientific Monthly*, Oct. 1948, pp. 277-88.

2. Friedrich Kapp: *Aus und über Amerika* (Berlin, 1876).

3. *Westbote*, Feb. 29, 1856; and report of the Deutsche Gesellschaft von New York in *New Yorker Staatszeitung*, Feb. 25, 1856.

4. *Westbote*, Jan. 25, 1850.

5. See Georg Leibbrandt and Fritz Dickmann: *Auswanderungsakten des Deutschen Bundestages (1817-1866) und der Frankfurter Reichsministerien (1848-1849)* (Stuttgart, 1932) pp. 69-77; also Oscar Canstatt: *Die deutsche Auswanderung, Auswanderer-fürsorge und Auswandererziele* (Berlin 1901) pp. 36, 71, and especially Ch. VI and VIII; and Hildegard Rosenthal: *Die Auswanderung aus Sachsen im 19. Jahrhundert, 1815-71* (Stuttgart 1931) pp. 26, 48, 50.

6. *Westbote*, May 6, 1853.

7. Cited in *Westbote*, July 1, 1853; *see also* June 3, 1853; April 13, 1849.

8. E. von Philippovich: *Auswanderung und Auswanderungspolitik in Deutschland* (Leipzig, 1892) *passim*, and *New Yorker Staatszeitung*, Sept. 17, 1859.

9. Ray A. Billington: *The Protestant Crusade, 1800-1860* (New York, 1938) p. 36.

10. Cited in Cleveland *Wächter am Erie*, Nov. 8, 1866.

11. Many of these details were gathered from the German Archives by the late Veit Valentin, but never published, and were made available to me by his widow.

12. March 13, April 8, 1852.

13. Leibbrandt and Dickmann: *op. cit.*, p. 32.

14. *Der Deutsche Auswanderer—Zeitschrift zur Kentniss des Deutschen Elements in Allen Ländern der Erde* (Frankfurt, March 9, 1850).

15. *Preussische Geheime Staats Archiv*, VI, No. 11, Oct. 23, 1849.

16. Theodore C. Blegen: "The Competition of the Northwestern States for Immigrants," in *The Wisconsin Magazine of History*, III (1919-20) 3-29.

17. *New Yorker Staatszeitung*, May 7, 1859.

18. *Wächter am Erie*, July 30, 1873.

19. See Emilio Willems: *A Aculturcão dos Alemães no Brasil* (Sao Paulo, 1946); also

Albert Hoerll: "Die Deutschen Kolonisten in Chile," in *Deutsche Arbeit in Chile*, edited by Ernst Maier (Santiago de Chile, 1910) I, pp. 21-25, 35.

20. *New Yorker Staatszeitung*, April 7, 1849.

21. For details, see *New Yorker Staatszeitung*, May 12, Aug. 4, 9, 11, Sept. 15, 22, 1849.

22. *Ibid.*, Oct. 9, 1849; May 18, June 15, 1850.

23. See also *New Yorker Staatszeitung*, Aug. 7, Oct. 2, 1851; Jan. 5, 1852. The *Verzeichniss der wegen Hochverraths in dem Verwahrungs—Hause zu Zweibrücken verwahrten Personen*, was made available to me by my colleague, Professor Hippolyte Gruener, whose maternal grandfather, Christian Kern, was No. 97 on the list.

24. *New Yorker Staatszeitung*, May 3, 1852.

25. *Ibid.*, May 11, 1852; Dec. 14, 1853.

26. *New Yorker Staatszeitung*, June 14, 1852; also *New Yorker Criminal Zeitung*, July 16, 1858. The *New Yorker Criminal Zeitung* was known as the *New Yorker Criminal Zeitung und Belletristisches Journal*, and the *New Yorker Belletristisches Journal*, and some of its supplements, for a time, as *Intelligenz-Blatt der New Yorker Criminal Zeitung*. It ran from 1852 to 1907, and will be cited hereafter as *Belletristisches Journal*.

27. *New Yorker Staatszeitung*, July 16, 1852.

28. June 14, 1854.

29. Quoted in J. B. McMaster: *History of the People of the United States* (New York, 1914) VII, p. 222.

30. Diary of Leopold Grüner, of Hohenzollern-Sigmaringen, 1851, made available to me by Professor Hippolyte Gruener.

31. For further details, see Wittke: *We Who Built America* (N. Y. 1939) Ch. VII; Kapp: *Aus und über Amerika*, I, pp. 199-242; Oscar Canstatt: *Die Deutsche Auswanderung* (Berlin 1901) pp. 151 *et seq.*; and *Denkschrift des Berliner Zentralvereins für die deutsche Auswanderung und Kolonisation* (March 1854).

32. See *New Yorker Staatszeitung*, Dec. 2, 1853, and F. J. Egenter: *Amerika ohne Schminke* (Zurich 1857) p. 21.

33. Egenter: *op. cit.*, pp. 96-100.

34. See *New Yorker Staatszeitung*, July 25, Aug. 18, 24, Nov. 2, 1854, for a particularly notorious case involving the firm of Richmüller and Löscher.

35. *New Yorker Staatszeitung*, June 29, 1850; June 2, Oct. 2, 1851; *Belletristisches Journal*, March 30, 1855.

36. A. J. Townsend: "The Germans of Chicago," *Jahrbuch der Deutsch-Amerikanischen Historischen Gesellschaft von Illinois*, XXXII, p. 20. Hereafter cited as Townsend: *The Germans of Chicago*.

37. J. Thomas Scharf: *St. Louis, History of St. Louis City and County* (Philadelphia 1883) p. 1764. Cited hereafter as Scharf: *St. Louis*.

Chapter 6 · UPROOTED LIVES

As the political refugees of 1848 came up New York harbor after weeks of weary travel, on steamers that required at least two weeks to cross the ocean, or on sailing vessels that took much longer, their hearts must have beat faster with a flood of conflicting emotions. There was sadness and a deep sense of loss for a fatherland which had forced them into exile, and high hopes and great expectations for the land of Jefferson, Franklin, and Washington. As the immigrant ships came up the harbor their passengers' first impressions of America were the Marine Hospital, the green stretches of Staten Island still spotted with forest growths, the tower of Sandy Hook lighthouse, the high steeple of old Trinity Church, the attractive New Jersey shore to the left, and the harbor itself, full of steam and sailing vessels.

"These new argonauts seeking the golden fleece of liberty," as the Forty-eighters were described by one of their own group, included men of character, ability, and spirit who were fitted by education and experience to lead their fellow German immigrants. Their efforts to breathe a new spirit of liberty into a decaying Germany had lost them home, property, jobs, and social position. In an America without kings and princes, petty bureaucrats, state police, state church, or censorship, they were prepared to try again to make a living and to expound their theories of reform.

Perhaps the Germans in America would have experienced a significant cultural renaissance without the help of the Forty-eighters, for by the middle of the last century they had gained a firm footing in their new home, and were rapidly emerging from the pioneer stage into comfortable, middle-class respectability with some time for leisure. The nativist agitation of the 1850's made them more determined to preserve their language and defend their culture against narrow-minded nativists, and thus a crisis in assimilation occurred which retarded the normal Americanization process and fastened a hyphen upon German-Americans which did not disappear until World War I. To overcome any feeling of inferiority, Germans loudly proclaimed the superiority of their own culture, and founded societies, schools, and newspapers to insure its survival.

The Forty-eighters arrived at a time when the German group was on the defensive and needed leadership. Acting as a "spiritual yeast" to leaven the mass of their countrymen, they resolved to stir them up to a better appreciation of their potentialities for spiritual and cultural progress. Even their severest critics admit that the refugees infused new life into the German-American group and for the first time gave them aggressive political leadership. Ernst Bruncken, a writer not too sympathetic with the claims of the newcomers, nevertheless admitted that "during the short period of their ascendency they modified profoundly the life and attitude of the German element, and thereby the character of the American people."[1] Hitherto an army without officers, and recruited largely from men who made their living on the farm or in the workshop, the Germans were transformed into an articulate force marshaled by a high command of singular audacity and ability.[2]

The newcomers included doctors of philosophy, graduates in theology, law, and philology; students whose academic careers had been interrupted by the Revolution; state officials who had lost their posts; students, lovers and practitioners of science and the arts, foresters, economists; men who knew their Greek and Latin but could not drive a nail or practice a trade; intellectuals who could describe in detail what the ancient Romans wore but lacked the funds necessary to buy decent clothes for themselves; men who could discourse on metaphysics but whose boots were without soles—in short, able, educated, sincere enthusiasts for world reform, starry-eyed intellectuals and budding professional men who "had learned everything except what would be useful to them in America."

Their recent European experience had not dampened their zeal for storming the heavens of reform. Though deeply impressed by the philosophy of Jefferson, and thrilled to be in a land without kings or feudal lords, they nevertheless felt that the United States needed their attention if it was to attain the ideal of their dreams.[3] To realize that goal, the republic had to be reconstructed on political, social, and religious lines; the influence of Puritans, Sabbatarians, and prohibitionists superseded by the graciousness and the joys of Continental living; American democracy expanded along socialistic lines; and music, art, and the theatre nurtured in the barren atmosphere of a raw frontier.

The new arrivals immediately precipitated heated divisions of opinion among the Germans themselves, and German Catholics and German Lutherans gave them a cold reception. Their blunt, impolite manners, their pettiness in debate, and their hypercritical attitude toward most things American and German-American did not help matters. The intellectuals among the Forty-eighters included many who were both immodest and extremely intolerant of the opinions of others, and they labeled as reactionaries, compromisers, and cowards all those with whom they happened to disagree. Some found it difficult or impossible to shed the drinking habits of their student days. Others were especially inconsiderate of their elders, particularly in matters of religion, and the total group had the usual quota of crooks and fools.

Yet these newcomers had come to stay, and they had the capacity and the spirit to become excited about issues. They had high aspirations for the German element in America and, having set their sights high, they refused to compromise. They would convert the cultural wilderness of America into a blooming garden and build cities and farms and homes. Eventually an extraordinarily large proportion of them fought to preserve the Union which had seemed so imperfect on their arrival. They had sacrificed for an idea in Germany, and they were prepared to tackle American problems with equal courage. The best of them battled with pen and speech and all the weapons of the mind, and with deep conviction. Hundreds went to pieces in the bitter struggle for their daily bread. Some were romantics who loved to play the rôle of the martyr in America as they had loved to play it abroad, and had little to offer except their reminiscences as professional revolutionaries and soldiers of fortune. But when the "storm and stress" period of the Forty-eighter immigration finally passed, most of these frustrated idealists settled down to become peaceful, useful, law-abiding and sometimes distinguished Americans. They "brought a flood of spring sunshine" into the life of America, and no immigrant group before or after them manifested the enthusiasm and the spirit of these erstwhile revolutionists, and no group left such a deep impression upon German-American culture. During the period of their ascendency, the Germans in the United States enjoyed what has been referred to as their "Hellenic Age."[4]

The "German type" of the 1850's, in the minds of native-born Americans, derived largely from their experience with the Forty-eighters. Most of them had large beards or heavy mustaches which marked them off from the clean-shaven faces of average Americans. The German refugees wore caps or soft, slouch felt hats, in contrast with the high, stiff hats popular in the United States at the time. It was not long before papers like the Cleveland *Plain Dealer* regularly referred to the Forty-eighters as "hair-lipped Germans and red republicans." In the early years of their American experience political refugees, erstwhile professors, doctors, lawyers, theologians, and other German university men, met regularly at favorite taverns or lager-beer saloons in Milwaukee, St. Louis, New York and elsewhere, at a special "Stammtisch" or "Kneiptisch," to debate, sing, and drink furiously, after the fashion of their student or army days. The most interesting company frequently could be found in the saloons, where the discussions ranged over an amazingly wide variety of political and social questions, on such a high intellectual level that the debates attracted many listeners. Some of the regular participants on such occasions were "the terror of German saloonkeepers," for they were opinionated and violent, loud and gesticulating, and ready to discourse on the most impracticable plans for world reform. Some refused to go to work, "until the right to work had been guaranteed to all men" by government decree! These were the "bums of the revolution," as they were labeled by their fellow countrymen, the ill-adjusted who regarded manual labor as beneath their dignity and their talents. In the end, they too could not escape the fatal choice between work and starvation.

The Forty-eighters washed ashore in the United States by the Revolution were an interesting and curious collection of individuals from every walk of life. In a list of over three hundred names prepared by Professor Zucker, and including only the more prominent for whom biographical data was easily obtainable, we find 74 became journalists in the United States, 67 served in the Civil War, 37 were physicians, 25 teachers, 25 Turner or physical education experts, 22 lawyers, 21 businessmen, 16 authors, 12 farmers, 11 musicians, 11 became diplomats, 9 were engineers, 9 ministers of the gospel, 8 published poetry, 7 were innkeepers,

7 became members of legislative bodies, 6 were jewelers, 5 bankers, 5 pharmacists, and 5 leaders of rationalist societies. Such figures indicate the variety of professions and occupations which Forty-eighters followed in the United States. Refugees advertised in the German press for employment as private tutors in foreign languages and music, and at least one of their number, Dr. Karl Schramm, offered to perform weddings, baptisms, and burials at reasonable rates, as well as give instruction in English and music.[5]

The names of the most famous among the political refugees appeared frequently in the German language newspapers. One finds many references to Hugo Wesendonck, a former member of the German diet who went into business in the United States; Hans Reimer Claussen, hero of the Schleswig-Holstein affair and a leftist at Frankfurt, who practiced law in Iowa; Maximilian Beck, captured at Rastatt; Franz Sigel and Ludwig Blenker who fought again in the Union Army; Professor Anton Füster, a member of the Vienna Academic Legion in 1848, who taught school in the United States; Joseph Fickler, liberal Catholic journalist of Constance; Fenner von Fenneberg who commanded a people's army in the Rhenish Palatinate; Karl Theodor Bayerhoffer, full professor at Marburg, radical pamphleteer and member of the Hessian Diet, who settled on a farm in Wisconsin; Gottlieb Kellner, a radical social democrat of Kassel, who edited the Philadelphia *Demokrat* and directed an adult evening school; and Wilhelm Loewe aus Calbe, a member of the Rump Parliament in Stuttgart who practiced medicine in New York.

Equally well known to German-American readers were such leaders as Lorenz Brentano, once a minister of the revolutionary government in Baden, who rose to the editorship of the *Illinois Staatszeitung* after unsuccessful ventures in farming and brewing, and served in both the Illinois legislature and the United States Congress. Jakob Müller, member of the provisional government of the Palatinate in 1849, became Lieutenant-governor of Ohio. Hermann Raster, a student of history and political science at Leipzig and Berlin, and an ardent revolutionist in 1848, edited the *Buffalo Demokrat,* the *Illinois Staatszeitung,* and the *New Yorker Abendzeitung,* contributed to *Appleton's Encyclopedia,* and was collector of internal revenue in Chicago, and a member of its school and library boards. Reinhold Solger, with a Ph.D. from Greifswald, came with Kossuth to America and achieved distinction as a scholar, journalist, and lecturer. Baltimore's Forty-eighters included Dr. Adolph Wiesner, a native of Prague who took part in both the Austrian and German Revolutions; Adelbert J. Volck of Augsburg who taught dental surgery in Baltimore; the journalists Wilhelm Rapp, August Becker, and Carl Heinrich Schnauffer; and prominent German pedagogues such as Wilhelm Müller and Friedrich Knapp.[6]

Hermann Joseph Aloys Körner, a student of Hegel and a theologian of freethinking principles, who emphasized the social gospel and was charged in 1848 with "political agitation in the schools," got his first job as a teacher of drawing through the help of William Cullen Bryant, taught art in the New York public schools for twenty-six years, and left a bibliography of twelve publications and a two-volume autobiography. Franz Joseph Pabisch, D.D. and LL.D., who shouted "Down with Metternich!" as a member of the Vienna mob, directed a Catholic seminary in Cincinnati, and published in the fields of church history, canon law, and botany, and was something of a painter.[7] Heinrich Börnstein, once president of the *Société des Democrats Allemands* in Paris, and one of the originators of Herwegh's "German legion" which marched from Paris to help the German revolutionists, arrived in New Orleans in 1849, with twenty-four chests and trunks, and enough clothes and shoes to last him for several years. He became a leading journalist, politician, and theatre director in St. Louis. Friedrich Kapp tried the wine business, tutoring, translating, and newspaper work before becoming a successful German lawyer in New York City, a publisher of historical and biographical works, and a commissioner of immigration.[8] Carl Schurz did not expect "mountains of gold" in America, but relied on vigorous and uninterrupted application to assure success. He taught himself English by reading the Philadelphia *Ledger,* English novels and masterpieces, and translating the *Letters of Junius* back and forth from English to German; and his rise on the escalator of public favor was so rapid that it carried him into the President's Cabinet and the United States Senate.[9]

Men of such caliber stand out as intellectual giants in the history of German immigration. There were other hundreds of plain people who worked in trades or small businesses, or on farms, and made a reasonable success of their lives. In this category of Forty-eighters belong artisans like Adam Best, a simple cooper of Cincinnati; Charles Rauch, a tailor's apprentice who owned a restaurant in St. Paul, and was a member of its city council; John Murer, a carpenter who became a justice of the peace in Buffalo; and Joseph Fränkle, who became a stonemason in Cincinnati, where he died in 1860. Captain Adam Schumacher, a millwright's son from Heidelberg, fought with Sigel at Waghäusel, worked as a shoemaker in Cincinnati, fought again with the Ninth Ohio Volunteers in the Civil War, and ended his career as a saloonkeeper.[10] Alois Derleth, a choir director and actor in Germany before 1848, was the manager of the Tyrolean House in St. Louis.[11] Joseph Fickler took over the Shakespeare Hotel in New York from Eugen Lievre and boarded refugees for seventy-five cents a day or four dollars a week.[12] A former tribune of the people in Silesia ran a beer hall in a suburb of St. Louis. In Philadelphia, a third-class inn was managed by a former head of the provisional government of Rhenish Bavaria. Franz Wutschl, a Viennese revolutionist, operated the Vienna Legionair restaurant in New York, and a compatriot owned the Fortress Rastatt.[13] Max Weber, a veteran of the revolution in Baden and a brilliant soldier in the American Civil War, was a hotelkeeper in New York. Gustav Struve lived for a time with a Philadelphia tavern keeper who had lost a son in the battle of Waghäusel, and S. L. Kapff, a South German radical, operated a saloon in Hoboken, and in 1853 was arrested for violating the Sunday closing ordinance.[14] When Kapp made a tour of German hotels and taverns with Zitz, Fröbel, and Weitling in 1850, he found them so filled with political refugees that he resolved not to live in any of them lest he never learn English.[15]

The difficulties of finding employment in a new country were great, and men highly trained for academic careers were forced to take work of any kind, however menial. German musicians sought posts as organists, or gave music lessons, although handicapped by their inability to use English fluently. Artists occasionally got commissions to paint portraits in the larger cities. But with the possible exception of medical doctors, German professors and university men found little opportunity to practice their professions during their early years in America. Scores of highly gifted men, thoroughly grounded in science, philosophy, and literature, perished in their lonely struggle for subsistence, while the character of others disintegrated so rapidly that they lost all self-respect, or sought solace in the lethal stupor of the whisky bottle and went down to forgotten graves. "Learned professors, writers and artists," wrote one of the more successful Forty-eighters, "men who were at home in every branch of learning, were forced to support themselves . . . by making cigars, acting as waiters or house-servants, boot-blacks or street sweepers . . ."[16]

Heinzen, finding it impossible to feed himself by lecturing, gilded wooden frames at three dollars a week, and lived with his family in a garret room in Hoboken, before he began his brilliant but unprofitable career as a crusading journalist. Willich worked as a carpenter. Heinrich Hammermeister, a dramatic singer whose property was confiscated in Berlin, made cigars in New York, and had to be buried at the expense of his fellow actors in 1860.[17] Karl Schleicher, who had commanded a company of sharpshooters in Stuttgart in 1848-49, made a miserable living in the United States as a soap maker, a hunter, and a manufacturer of fireworks, and lived his last four years on public charity. He died at ninety-five in Sauk City, Wisconsin.[18] Joseph Rudolph, a Vienna revolutionary well trained in the Latin classics, made shoe polish which he peddled in hand-baskets, then paid ten dollars to learn how to make cigars, and manufactured them at ten cents a hundred. With two others, he lived in an attic room for three dollars a month, and relied for food mainly on the free lunches dispensed at that time with a nickel glass of beer. In spite of such an inauspicious beginning, he was the owner of a furniture store in Chicago when he retired in 1885.[19]

Ferdinand Behlendorff, a native of Dresden, who studied law at Leipzig and fought in the Saxon Revolution of 1849, earned seventy-five cents a day carrying bricks and mortar at Cape Girardeau, Missouri, worked for farmers in the vicinity, and in his leisure hours read Prescott's *Conquest of Mexico*. He became an officer in the Civil War, and deputy collector of customs in Chicago.[20] Wilhelm Stängel, a law student at Jena, worked as a house and sign painter in Louisville.[21] Fritz Anneke was a manual laborer on the Chicago and Galena Railroad before becoming state librarian in Madison, Wisconsin.[22] Ernst Violand, a native of Lemberg, who was educated in a Jesuit college, and condemned to death during the Revolution, wrapped cigars in New York in 1850 and later combined his cigar business in Peoria, Illinois, with lecturing, writing for the newspapers, and making stump speeches for the Republican party.[23] Karl Graf, a former teacher in Kaiserslautern, worked in Cincinnati as a day laborer, surveyor, and lacquerer before he obtained a teaching position in the public schools.[24] Leopold von Gilsa, a Prussian ex-army officer and later a colonel of the 41st New York Regiment, played the piano in saloons on the Bowery. Dr. M. E. Lilienthal, rabbi of a New York synagogue, encountered a refugee on the streets who asked for a bite of bread in German, French, English, and Italian.[25] Börnstein met a bartender in a second-class hotel who was a former professor of philology,[26] and the *New York Tribune* reported the harrowing experiences of a former German judge whose wife died in an insane asylum after a hopeless struggle to feed five hungry mouths; of a German merchant who picked wool with his wife from morning until night for twenty cents a day; and of a former German postal employee who made match boxes in New York and pawned his few possessions to procure food for his hungry family.[27]

Such experiences reveal the tragedy of men who found freedom in the United States, but no bread; of scholars able to quote Homer, but forced to work with pick and shovel as day laborers on canals and railroads; of accomplished musicians who became piano tuners and "beer fiddlers"; of Ph.D.'s who worked as porters and house painters; of mathematicians who painted signs for stores, and of German dancing teachers who masqueraded as French in order to attract a more fashionable clientele.[28] In the eyes of most native Americans they were "Dutchmen," and generally "damned Dutchmen."

Although history still is written without much reference to the female half of the race, something should be said about the women in the Forty-eighter immigration. Obviously wives and mothers shared the hardships, depression, and cultural isolation of husbands and sons in a strange land, but unfortunately very few recorded their experiences anywhere except in the sacrifices they made for their men. We know that Elisabeth Tschech, daughter of the man who tried to assassinate the King of Prussia, fled by way of Belgium, Holland and England to the United States, and made her living in New York with sewing and needlework, and as a domestic servant.[29] The widow of the martyred Robert Blum spent some time in America visiting her son, and lived for a short period, quite unhappily, in the North American Phalanx at Red Bank, New Jersey.[30] Amalia Struve, who had served a prison term, followed her husband into exile, assisted him materially in his literary and journalistic labors, and published two volumes of reminiscences of the Revolution under her own name. The most famous of the women Forty-eighters, however, was

Mathilde Franziske Giesler-Anneke. Born a Catholic, married at nineteen to her first husband and speedily divorced, after a most unhappy experience, she became a freethinker, a radical, and an advocate of equal rights for women. During the Revolution she rode into battle with Fritz Anneke, her second husband. A poet and a playwright, she moved in circles in Cologne which gave her contacts with such celebrities as Marx, Gottfried Kinkel, Engels, and Freiligrath, and in the United States she became the founder of a woman's journal, a lecturer on woman suffrage, and the director of a well-known girls' school in Milwaukee.[31]

The number of Forty-eighters who died within a few years of their arrival in America was surprisingly large, and in many cases death was directly attributable to lack of proper food and housing. Wilhelm Rothacker, editor of the *Turnzeitung,* died of tuberculosis in Cincinnati in 1859 at the age of thirty-one, and the German press appealed for support for his destitute wife and four children. Among his works, published in 1860, were poems in praise of liberty and an essay on Patrick Henry.[32] Gottlieb Rau, a merchant who had been sentenced for his participation in workers' congresses, died in New York one year after his arrival. Florian Mördes, a former official in Baden, died in Peach Creek, Texas, in 1850. Heinrich Hoff, publisher of radical literature in Mannheim and an intimate friend of Hecker, died a pauper in a New York hospital in 1852. Fenner von Fenneberg was committed to an asylum for the insane in 1858, and left a wife and two children utterly without means.[33] Carl Steinmetz of Durlach, Baden, and Franz Geigel, both of whom had been sentenced to death in 1849, died within less than four years of their arrival in the United States.[34] Carl Heinrich Schnauffer, one of the most gifted literary figures among the Forty-eighter immigration, died of typhoid in Baltimore at the age of thirty-one.[35] Joseph Mühlebach, a former burgomaster in Baden who preferred perpetual exile to six years in jail, died in New York in 1858. Franz Joseph Reich, a comrade of Hecker, died at forty-six.[36] Franz Schmidt von Löwenberg, a member of the Frankfurt Parliament and a champion of rationalism, died in 1853 in Cuba where he had opened a school.[37] Theodor Dietsch, another veteran of 1848 and a former member of the city government of Arneberg, died in Cincinnati in 1857, as editor of the *Deutsche Republikaner,* leaving a widow and three children completely destitute. Heinrich Loose, champion of the working class and founder of freethinking congregations in Silesia and the Palatinate, taught school in Williamsburg, New York, and Milwaukee, edited a labor paper in the latter city, and died sick and insane in the poorhouse.

Four other specific cases involving men of genuine promise must complete this gruesome record of hardship and early death in the land of freedom. Hermann Kriege, devoted disciple of Ludwig Feuerbach, and a tireless reformer on two continents, died penniless and insane at the age of thirty, after a short journalistic career in New York and Chicago, and was buried from the offices of the *New Yorker Staatszeitung,* wrapped, according to his wish, in an American flag. Among his works were biographies of Thomas Paine and "The Fathers of the Republic."[38] Rösler von Oels, who had demanded the abolition of the monarchy and the nobility in the Frankfurt Parliament, and was known as "the imperial canary" because he generally wore a bright yellow suit and had a red beard, operated a school in New York, moved to Milwaukee, and published a Whig campaign paper in Quincy, Illinois, in 1852, in the interests of Scott's candidacy for the presidency. When the Whigs lost the election and the paper folded, the editor was abandoned by the politicians and left to starve. The evidence indicates that he died of delirium tremens, for he turned too often to the flowing bowl to forget his troubles. When he died, German papers printed the now familiar appeals for aid for his family.[39]

Christian Esselen was one of the noblest and most honest of the Fortyeighters. Well trained in philosophy and the classics at Freiburg, Heidelberg, and Berlin, and a sincere young idealist, he had been a student friend of Friedrich Kapp, and had known Marx and Bakunin. A genuine friend of labor, he regarded the Frankfurt Parliament as ultraconservative. After the revolution Esselen fled to Switzerland, where he was protected and influenced by Albert Galeer, a teacher whose home in Geneva was the asylum for many homeless refugees. In 1852 Esselen, at the age of twenty-nine, came to the United States. Here he published his *Atlantis,* dedicated to the emancipation of the human mind and to the spread of liberalism throughout the world. Struggling against tremendous odds, but refusing to compromise his high principles as an editor, Esselen managed to keep his paper alive for six years by moving it about from Detroit to Milwaukee to Chicago to Dubuque to Cleveland to Buffalo to New York. Though driven by poverty from city to city, he did not abandon his faith in the United States as the world's last hope for liberty. He became an ardent abolitionist, and was deeply depressed by Buchanan's election in 1856. He championed free public schools and called upon his fellow Germans to make their best cultural contribution to their new fatherland. Desperately homesick and ruined by the panic of 1857, he too tried to drown his sorrow in alcohol, and the gifted journalist, novelist, and playwright, died in a mental hospital on Blackwell's Island at the age of thirty-six.[40]

Eduard Pelz, the son of a Saxon innkeeper, had been apprenticed to a bookseller, and worked in a bookshop in Copenhagen. At the age of twenty-four he was able to open his own shop in Breslau, where he published small treatises and did lithographing. From 1836 to 1839 he was in the book business in St. Petersburg, Russia, and upon his return to Germany published a series of "Petersburg Sketches." Deeply interested in the sufferings of the Silesian weavers, he issued a number of pamphlets which won for him the title of the "Silesian O'Connell," and led to his arrest on charges of inciting the weavers to insurrection. In 1847, after completing a *Life of Peter the Great,* Pelz sold his property in Silesia and moved to Leipzig. The next year he was drawn into the Revolution in Stuttgart, was elected to the Frankfurt Assembly, edited a radical paper, and made numerous public addresses. Driven out by the reaction, he came to the United States in steerage in 1850, and lost his remaining resources in an unhappy publishing venture in New York. While his daughter did embroidery work on shirts to keep herself and her father from starving, Pelz tried his hand as a correspondent for European papers, as a secretary for a land company, and worked as a clerk in a law office. Somehow he managed to survive the crisis in his affairs, and with his interest in writing undiminished. After the death of his wife, he returned to Germany, where he died in 1876.[41]

The list of suicides among the Forty-eighters included Harro Harring, a strange and romantic megalomaniac whose checkered career in many lands ended in self-destruction in London.[42] It included also Georg Richard Hoffmann, a Bavarian revolutionist who taught music and directed the German singers of Louisville;[43] Julius Minding, a German physician who published scientific and political tracts, poems, and a tragedy, *Sixtus V,* which was performed in Germany. One year after landing in New York he gave up the struggle, and was buried at the expense of the Prussian Consul.[44] Moritz Goetz of Coblenz, journalist and teacher, committed suicide when his last funds had been exhausted.[45] Heinrich Waldemar Wagner, who spent ten years in a Saxon jail following the rebellion in Dresden, came to the United States in 1859, where he made a wretched living as a tavernkeeper in New York. A suicide note addressed to the *New Yorker Staatszeitung* contained his last five dollars to pay for publication of his death notice and transmission of two copies of the paper to Dresden.[46]

Unfortunately the Revolution also disgorged its crop of swindlers and impostors upon the United States. Such men traded on their alleged revolutionary records, and in most cases were unemployed vagabonds who entertained American audiences with fantastic tales of their exploits for German freedom in order to get free meals and easy living. The German language newspapers frequently carried announcements warning against swindlers and exposing their spurious claims to fame.[47] In 1851 the St. Louis *Tribune* reported that several individuals from Landau, who actually had betrayed the patriots in 1849, were en route to America, and it advised all Germans "to greet such creatures with the universal contempt and scorn which they deserve."[48] The *New Yorker Criminal Zeitung und Belletristisches Journal* exposed a Berlin dealer in ribbons who posed in America as a Ph.D.,[49] and the *New Yorker Staatszeitung* of April 15, 1858, reported at length on the activities of an impostor from Cologne, pointing out that "for years the title of political refugee has been usurped by sharpers of every kind."

For some years after 1848, German communities in the United States also suffered from a spy mania. Alleged spies, presumably in the pay of the German governments to report on the activities of political refugees in this country, were exposed in the public press. Perhaps the worst example of the spy hysteria was the case of a Dr. Junghanns of Cincinnati, who was accused of masquerading as an ardent democrat, spying for the Prussian government, and betraying Joseph Fickler to the authorities in 1849. Although Junghanns emphatically denied the charges in a statement in the *New Yorker Criminal Zeitung und Belletristisches Journal* of July 1, 1853, a mob of Cincinnati Germans, estimated between six hundred and a thousand, made a noisy demonstration before his residence and burned the suspect in effigy, whereupon Junghanns fled into the Kentucky hills and was never heard of again.[50]

The first years in America were bound to produce disillusionment for transplanted and uprooted revolutionaries. The United States turned out to be a land of strange contrasts—devotion to the principles of Jefferson and Jackson and unbounded personal liberty, and several million black men held as slaves; excessive drinking and a fanatical campaign to make the nation bone dry through so-called "temperance laws"; much talk at election time about ascertaining "the will of the people," and political campaigns controlled by bosses and party machines; freedom of religion guaranteed in the Constitution, and an intolerant fundamentalism expressed in blue laws which violated every concept of personal liberty as the continental European understood the term.

One Forty-eighter wrote about "the naked, grim life of America," full of deceit and hypocrisy, devoid of sentiment and primarily lived for public show, with showmen in the pulpits, and "square-headed sectarians and temperance fanatics trying to dictate how people should live," and "politics a matter of machine work and plunder, without any higher ideals" and carried on solely for the personal profit of professional politicians. He looked in vain for one real university in America, and found that all education was on a very mediocre level.[51] Other critics ridiculed the American habit of chewing and spitting tobacco, sitting for hours in chairs that rocked, putting feet on the table, feeding on pies, pork and beans instead of sausage and sauerkraut, going to "human bull fights" (pugilism), entertaining ladies by letting them ravage sweets at confectionaries, drinking toasts at banquets in water or cups of tea, wearing "standing collars" and frock coats and being completely preoccupied with "business." They berated the low artistic and musical tastes of Americans, who were said to prefer "Yankee Doodle" to Beethoven, and if the latter were unavoidable, asked for the Pastoral Symphony because it suggested a thunderstorm.[52]

Obviously such criticisms were exaggerated and often unfair. But in a period of disillusionment and homesickness, many refugees have been unfair to the people who have given them hospitality. The Forty-eighters had not yet learned that there was not one America, but many. With their "heads full of hollow theories about liberty," and ignorant of the language and American conditions, their first impressions of the new republic proved disappointing, and instead of waiting until they knew America better, they proceeded at once to act as its critics, "teachers and reformers."[53]

Most refugees got their first glimpse of the land of their hopes and dreams in New York, a dirty, crowded city in 1850, dusty in summer and bogging down in mud after each rain. Cattle still were driven down its main thoroughfares, beggars and prostitutes infested the streets, saloons did business on almost every corner, and Italian hurdy-gurdy men furnished musical diversions for the people. Everybody seemed to be in a hurry. Gentlemen tossed off their "eye-openers" at the bar to rush out into the streets; people ran to dinner tables, piled high with plates of food which they consumed in complete silence—"not to enjoy it but to feed the machine."[54] Everything seemed to operate for profit, whether it was religion, politics, medicine, fortune-telling, astrology, or spiritualism. The high crime rate, and the advertisements of astrologers and clairvoyants in the newspapers amazed and shocked the more intelligent German immigrants. "Loafers" and "loungers" hung around the barrooms, smoked and drank and spat tobacco juice like virtuosi, wore their hats over their left ears and hanging down their necks, followed the parades, ran to fires with volunteer fire companies, and preyed upon and insulted immigrants whom they called "damned Dutchmen."[55] On election days the riffraff of the city took over the polls. Americans seemed to have no interest in theory or ideologies, including the theoretical bases for their own democracy, and sacrificed "emotion and the sunny heights of reason" to materialism, utilitarianism, and ruthless competition for the almighty dollar. Even the faces of native Americans suggested "an arithmetic table," and their eyes "an unpaid bill."[56]

Esselen pointed out that the United States was hardly beyond its pioneer stage, and gave due credit to the energy, enterprise, persistence, eagerness, and generosity of the American people. What the United States needed, according to this observer, was time to borrow, develop, and assimilate the cultural treasures of Europe. In turn, she would compensate the old world with her liberal ideas and her priceless republicanism. Julius Fröbel, author of fifteen letters written in 1858 about America for Leipzig papers, emphasized that the United States had no room for dreamers or romantic weaklings, but offered great rewards to those who were willing to work. He advised men whose major loves were beer, cigars, and music to remain at home, for they would not easily adjust to a new land teeming with energy and "business."

Thus, as with all immigrants, two forces were at work upon the German

Forty-eighters—a disintegrating force and an integrating force, the force that breaks down and the force that preserves the unity of an immigrant group. For a time these two forces conflicted, and each prevented the operation of the other. Even the most successful Forty-eighters had their months and years of trial and frustration. Many were completely integrated into American life; others, like Heinzen, that "uncompromising Cato," lived a life of frustration to the end. Even Kapp found little to praise in the United States of 1850 except its superior political system.[57] "We are wanderers, sojourning in brick and frame houses," wrote another in a melancholy vein,[58] and even Schurz referred to his feeling of "desolation" and "forlornness" as he wandered about New York during the first months of his residence in America. Francis Lieber nearly twenty years earlier had summarized his reactions in the sentence, "I cannot say I have homesickness for Germany, but for Europe, for science and art."[59]

The friction and misunderstanding which developed between the old and the new German leadership, between "Grays" and "Greens," did not improve the lot of the newcomers or their early attitude toward America. For a number of years German-American affairs were seriously affected by the bad blood engendered between those who came before and those who came after 1848. The Forty-eighters regarded the older leadership as ineffective, and most of their journals as positively disgraceful. A fierce war broke out among the journalists, the "Greens" denying any cultural progress by the "Grays"; the latter denouncing the "Greens" as inexperienced, radical hot-heads who were completely ignorant of American conditions. The "Greens" referred to their predecessors as reactionaries, and the latter retaliated by advising would-be world reformers to settle down, earn a living, and acquire citizenship before embarking on schemes to revolutionize the American way of life.

The *New Yorker Staatszeitung,* leading organ of the older group, and the employer of several Forty-eighters on its staff, denied the right of mere "guests" and "strangers" to criticize the United States, and insisted that "many a mechanic knows more about American politics than the intellectuals." Esselen replied in the *Atlantis* that only he is a "stranger" who fails to grasp the genius, the institutions, and the historic mission of the American people, and contended that Germans should not be asked to give up the culture of their fatherland or abandon their hopes for the eventual political emancipation of the German people.[60] Forty-eighters maintained that all was barren in the United States before they came, and that the renaissance in the cultural life of the German-American group dated specifically from their arrival. In politics, the newcomers referred with contempt to the "Grays" as voting cattle, who condoned human slavery. They criticized Germans who were satisfied with the petty jobs of policeman or constable, distributed by cheap American politicians who called them "Charley" and "John" on election day. In short, the "Greens" announced their determination to infuse Anglo-American civilization with a "Germanizing process," and to revive the cultural and intellectual interests of their older fellow countrymen.

"Grays" and "Greens" attacked each other as fiercely as bigoted nativists attacked all the foreign born. The Columbus *Westbote,* a vehicle of opinion for the older German immigration, admitted that the earlier group was not "learned in books," but insisted that it had succeeded and prospered in the rugged battle for existence in a new country. Although devoted to the country which had given them their opportunity, older immigrants had been so busy making an honest living that they had no time for theories or to complain of American institutions. The editor concluded that civilizations and cities are built and forests cleared by work, not philosophical theories, and repeated the familiar charges against the newcomers, including a sarcastic reference to military records which seemed to consist largely of boastful talk in the taverns. Nevertheless, the *Westbote* hoped for a reconciliation of "Grays" and "Greens," to enhance respect for the German element as a whole.[61]

The relentless force of Americanization and common sacrifices on the battlefields of the Civil War eventually healed the breach between these contending factions. Though some Forty-eighters proved obstinate and difficult to assimilate into the American pattern, the task was accomplished in due time. America became their fatherland, as it has of other men determined to remain free. "Only a year ago," wrote Dr. Anton Füster shortly after the Revolution to Joseph Goldmark, distinguished Jewish Forty-eighter from Vienna, "we were reverently singing the German national anthem. Now it sounds different. What is the German fatherland? Is it Austria? No, I was forced to flee from there. Is it Prussia? No. There I was arrested. Is it Saxony? No. There warrants were issued against me. Is it the free city of Hamburg? No. There I was driven out by the police. Where is the German fatherland? In England and America!

Only in those lands is there a safe and honorable refuge for Germans whose love of liberty and honor has not been silenced by Russo-Prussian-Austrian bayonets."[62]

FOOTNOTES

CHAPTER 6

1. See Ernst Bruncken: "German Political Refugees, 1815-1860," in *Deutsch-Amerikanische Geschichtsblätter* IV (1904).

2. See also John A. Hawgood: *The Tragedy of German-America* (New York, 1940) Ch. VIII; and Marcus L. Hansen: *The Immigrant in American History* (Cambridge 1940) pp. 135-36.

3. See a speech by Friedrich Hassaurek, in *Wächter am Erie* (Cleveland, May 28, 1875).

4. See Gustav Struve: *Diesseits und Jenseits des Ozeans* (Coburg, 1863); Jakob Mueller: *Aus den Erinnerungen eines Achtundvierzigers* (Cleveland, 1896); and Daniel Hertle: *Die Deutschen in Nordamerika und der Freiheitskampf in Missouri* (Chicago, 1865) pp. 19-21.

5. *New Yorker Staatszeitung*, Oct. 13, 1848; *Belletristisches Journal*, March 30, 1850. See especially, A. E. Zucker: "Biographical Dictionary of the Forty-eighters," in *The Forty-eighters, Political Refugees of the German Revolution of 1848*, edited by A. E. Zucker (New York, 1950) pp. 269-357. Hereafter cited as Zucker, *Forty-eighters*.

6. Dieter Cunz: "The Baltimore Germans in the Year 1848"—in *The American-German Review*, X, pp. 30-33.

7. *Der Deutsche Pionier*, XI No. 11 (Feb. 1880) pp. 410-20.

8. Edith Lenel: *Friedrich Kapp* (Leipzig, 1935).

9. Claude Fuess: *Carl Schurz, Reformer* (New York, 1932) p. 42; *Intimate Letters of Carl Schurz*, translated and edited by Joseph Schafer (Madison, 1928) p. 108; and Chester V. Easum: *The Americanization of Carl Schurz* (Chicago, 1929). For biographical sketches of other Forty-eighters, see *Berühmte Deutsche Vorkämpfer für Fortschritt, Freiheit und Friede in Nord-Amerika, von 1626 bis 1888. Einhundert und fünfzig Biographien* (Cleveland 1891). Hereafter cited as *Berühmte Deutsche Vorkämpfer*.

10. *Der Deutsche Pionier*, X, No. 11 (Feb. 1879) p. 451.

11. *New Yorker Staatszeitung*, Jan. 30, 1860.

12. *Ibid.*, Jan. 8, 1855.

13. *Ibid.*, Jan. 8, 1852; see also Hermann Joseph Aloys Körner: *Lebenskämpfe in der alten und neuen Welt, Eine Selbstbiographie* (New York, 1865).

14. *Belletristisches Journal*, Sept. 23, 1853.

15. For other references to less prominent Forty-eighters, see *Der Deutsche Pionier*, XV (No. 6) Sept. 1883, p. 254, for Johann Wieser; *Ibid.* (No. 10) Jan. 1884, p. 419, for Bernhard Ehrhard; *Ibid.* No. 7 (Oct. 1883) p. 302, for Franz Bauer, a soap-maker; and *Deutsch-Amerikanische Geschichtsblätter*, I (Jan. 1901) p. 23, for Ernst Violand, Theobald Pfeiffer, Emil Gillig, Friedrich Tritschler and Franz König, all of Peoria, Illinois; and Koss: *Milwaukee* (Milwaukee 1871) pp. 315-17; August P. Richter: *Geschichte der Stadt Davenport und das County Scott* (Davenport, Iowa 1917) pp. 392-94; hereafter cited as Richter: *Davenport*.

16. Quoted from Börnstein's memoirs in Schuricht: *Geschichte der deutschen Schulbestrebungen* (Leipzig 1884) p. 55.

17. *New Yorker Staatszeitung*, Feb. 2, 1860.

18. *Der Deutsche Pionier*, XIV, No. 3 (June 1882) p. 116.

19. Joseph Rudolph: "Kurzer Lebensabriss eines achtundvierziger politischen Flüchtlings" in *Deutsch-Amerikanische Geschichtsblätter*, VII, No. 2, April 1907, pp. 89-96; No. 3 (July 1907) pp. 139-42; No. 4 (Oct. 1907) pp. 152-54; and VIII (1908) pp. 21-80.

20. "Recollections of a Forty-eighter" by Major Ferdinand Behlendorff, *Ibid.* XV, pp. 310-51.
21. Stierlin: *Kentucky* pp. 119-20.
22. Koss: *Milwaukee*, pp. 318-19.
23. Letter of Ernst Violand, Dec. 4, 1873, in *Wächter am Erie*, Jan. 12, 1876.
24. *Der Deutsche Pionier*, XVII, No. 2 (1886) p. 133.
25. *New Yorker Staatszeitung*, July 23, 1850.
26. Börnstein: *Memoiren* II, p. 204.
27. Quoted in *Westbote*, Nov. 15, 1849.
28. See Eduard Pelz: *Kompass für Auswanderer nach den Vereinigten Staaten Nordamerikas mit besonderer Richtung auf die Landung im Hafen von New York* (Kassel, 1853) 2nd Ed., p. 38.
29. *Westbote*, May 16, 1851.
30. *Wächter am Erie*, Oct. 17, 1867.
31. See Anna Blos: *Die Frauen der Deutschen Revolution von 1848* (Dresden, 1928) and Henriette M. Heinzen and Hertha Anneke Sanne: *Biographical Notes in Commemoration of Fritz Anneke and Mathilde Franziske Anneke,* manuscript volumes in the State Historical Society Library of Wisconsin (Madison, 1940).
32. *New Yorker Staatszeitung*, Dec. 1, 1859; *Belletristisches Journal*, Dec. 2, 1859.
33. See *Westbote*, April 8, 1858.
34. *Wächter am Erie*, Aug. 9, 1852; July 20, 1853.
35. A. E. Zucker: "Carl Heinrich Schnauffer"—in *24th Report of the Society for the History of the Germans in Maryland* (1939) pp. 2-8.
36. *New Yorker Staatszeitung*, May 14, 1859.
37. *Wächter am Erie*, April 27, 1853.
38. *New Yorker Staatszeitung*, Jan. 3, 16, 1851; see also *Aüsgewählte Briefe von und an Ludwig Feuerbach,* edited by Wilhelm Bolin (Leipzig, 1904) I, pp. 84-85; II, pp. 143-45; p. 167.
39. See *New Yorker Staatszeitung*, Aug. 24, 1855; *Belletristisches Journal*, Aug. 24, 1855; *New Yorker Handelszeitung*, Aug. 22, 1855; and *Der Deutsche Pionier*, VII, No. 1 (March 1875) p. 20.
40. See Esselen's *Atlantis* (Sept. 1855) III (N.S.) pp. 166 and 178; *Westbote,* May 26, 1859; *New Yorker Staatszeitung*, May 19, 1859; Koss: *Milwaukee*, pp. 425-26.
41. *Der Deutsche Pionier*, VIII, No. 6 (Sept. 1876) pp. 213-27.
42. *Wächter am Erie*, June 10, 1870.
43. *Der Deutsche Pionier*, XI, No. 3 (June 1879) p. 92.
44. *Wächter am Erie*, Dec. 30, 1874.
45. *Der Deutsche Pionier*, XV, No. 1 (April 1883) pp. 3-7.
46. *Wächter am Erie*, July 30, 1874.
47. *Belletristisches Journal*, May 26, 1854; *New Yorker Staatszeitung*, Jan. 20, 1851.
48. Quoted in *Westbote*, March 21, 1851.
49. Nov. 9, 1860.
50. *New Yorker Staatszeitung*, July 19, 1853; *Belletristisches Journal*, June 17, July 22, 29, 1853; *Westbote*, July 20, 1853; see also *Wächter am Erie*, Aug. 10, 1853; *New Yorker Staatszeitung*, June 3, 1852, Oct. 13, 1860.
51. Philipp Wagner: *Ein Achtundvierziger* (Brooklyn 1882) pp. 261-63.
52. See *Atlantische Studien* (Göttingen, 1853-57) IV, pp. 23-25.
53. See Ludwig von Baumbach: *Neue Briefe aus den Vereinigten Staaten von Nord Amerika in die Heimat* (Kassel, 1856) pp. 72-73.
54. Wagner: *op cit.*, pp. 163-64.
55. *Atlantische Studien*, II, p. 23, 24; I, pp. 161-69.
56. *Atlantis*, Aug. 1855, III (N.S.) pp. 86-91. For other descriptions, favorable and unfavorable, see *Atlantische Studien*, I, pp. 50-58, 95-109, 186-94; *Die Republik der Arbeiter*

(New York) April 26, June 14, 1851; Oct. 14, 1854; July 21, 1855; Moritz Wagner and Karl von Scherzer: *Reisen in Nordamerika,* (Leipzig, 1854) I, Ch. VIII; and Friedrich Gerstäcker: "Wie ist es denn nun eigentlich in Amerika" (Leipzig 1849) 127 pp.

57. Kapp to Feuerbach, Jan. 28, 1851, in Lenel: *Kapp,* pp. 81-83.

58. *Atlantische Studien,* II, p. 86.

59. Freidel: *Lieber,* p. 112.

60. *New Yorker Staatszeitung,* Aug. 17, 1853; Feb. 28, May 10, 1854; and *Atlantis,* Aug. 1855, III (N.S.) pp. 108-11; see also, Carl Daniel Adolf Douai: *Land und Leute in der Union* (Berlin 1864) pp. 55-57, 205.

61. *Westbote,* May 20, 1853; June 23, 1854; May 25, 1855, quoting *San Antonio Zeitung* of Dec. 17, 1852. See also, Daniel Hertle: *Die Deutschen in Nordamerika und der Freiheitskampf in Missouri* (Chicago 1865) p. 22; Wilhelm Hense-Jensen and Ernst Bruncken: *Wisconsin's Deutsch-Amerikaner bis zum Schluss des neunzehnten Jahrhunderts* (Milwaukee 1900) I, pp. 134-35. Hereafter cited as Hense-Jensen and Bruncken: *Wisconsin's Deutsch-Amerikaner.*

62. Josephine Goldmark: *Pilgrims of '48* (New Haven, 1930) pp. 165-66. The tragedies of 1848-49 produced scores of poems dealing with immigration. See, for example, Justinus Kerner's "Auswanderers Heimweh" (1851); and Ernst Moritz Arndt, "Aus Frankfurt weg!" (May 1849); "Die deutschen auswandernden Krieger" (1851); and "Nachklang aus 1848-49" (1853) in Ernst Moritz Arndt; *Gedichte* (Berlin, 1860) pp. 566, 576, and 586; also *Amerika im Deutschen Gedicht,* by Max Rohrer (Stuttgart, 1848).

Chapter 7 · NON-GERMAN FORTY-EIGHTERS

WHEN WESTERN Europe exploded into revolution in 1848, all the liberal forces west of Russia hailed the occasion as the beginning of a new springtime in the life of the nations and the bright new dawn after a long night of reaction. When that springtime ended in a killing frost, political refugees from many lands scattered to the far corners of the western world, and particularly to the United States. The majority of that revolutionary immigration was German, but other political exiles from western and central Europe made their way to Latin America, into the Near East, to Belgium and Holland, or across the border into France to find temporary but uncertain asylum in a nation whose republicanism was destined to change soon into another Napoleonic dictatorship.

Switzerland and England, the most democratic countries in Europe, attracted most of the refugees who remained on the Continent. Thousands of Germans, and smaller numbers from other nationalities, found at least temporary asylum in the Swiss cantons. In many cases they became a relief problem for the local communities, and the Swiss state was subjected to heavy diplomatic pressures from powerful neighbors for their extradition. England, with her historic appreciation of freedom of speech, served as a halfway house for many refugees whose ultimate destiny was America. For a time the center of the European revolution was in London, for Marx, Kinkel, Mazzini, Ruge, and others congregated there to plot new upheavals and to quarrel vehemently about minor details of their programs for world reform. Although London offered the refugees little bread it did guarantee freedom of speech and of the press. The London refugee colony of the middle of the last century was one of the most interesting international groups ever assembled anywhere. It represented all shades of radicalism and cosmopolitanism. Whether the exiles were German, French, Poles, Italians, Hungarians, or Czechs, they had one common background—their unsuccessful encounter with monarchical institutions on the Continent.

The same cosmopolitan internationalism which characterized many of the reformers of 1848 also distinguished many Forty-eighters who came to the United States, and their number included many nationality groups. Generally speaking, no sharp national cleavages divided the newcomers, for they all belonged to the revolutionary tradition of 1848, which included not only a program of national reforms, but a philosophy of progress, critical radicalism, republicanism, and a cosmopolitanism which disregarded state boundaries. For a short time after 1848, Garibaldi, Lamartine, Ledru-Rollin, Kossuth, and Gottfried Kinkel were residents of New York.

Some of the most prominent Forty-eighters ended their days in the British Isles. Karl Heinrich Schaible of Offenburg, for example, became a professor in the Royal Military Academy, and Eugen Oswald a teacher in the school of the Royal Navy at Greenwich. Johann Ronge founded a humanistic congregation in England, after the pattern of the free congregations promoted by German Forty-eighters in the United States. Graf Oscar von Reichenbach distinguished himself as a scientist in England, and Hermann Müller, who had served a seven-year sentence in a German jail after the revolution, wrote significant historical works on ancient Greece which were well received by the British people. Marx, Engels, Karl Blind, the Socialist, Karl Schapper, a member of revolutionary clubs in Paris before 1848, Arnold Ruge, prominent Neo-Hegelian and former professor at Halle, Gottfried Kinkel, formerly of the faculty at Bonn, and other well-known radicals and reformers remained in England for many years and made a living in various ways, but particularly as teachers and journalists. Ferdinand Freiligrath was an accountant in London for years before he finally decided to return to Germany.

Periodically the American press spread the rumor that such distinguished German literary figures as Ruge, Freiligrath, and von Hoffmannsthal were on their way to New York. It was reported that Ludwig Feuerbach, philosopher of materialism and enemy of organized religion, and Mazzini, the Italian liberator, would soon be in the United States. Garibaldi actually made candles for a time on Staten Island, and his little shop has become one of the historic monuments of New York. There was a cosmopolitan, one-world flavor about these revolutionists, and the early public demonstrations in America in support of revolution were international gatherings which voiced the aspirations of several nationality groups. The welcome to Kossuth the Hungarian and Kinkel the German in the 1850's, as both traveled about to raise funds for a new revolution, was by no means limited to representatives of their own groups, and on several occasions Kossuth made special appeals to the Germans.

It is important to remember that student uprisings had occurred not only in Vienna and Berlin but also in Prague and Budapest, and that Mieroslawski fought for both Polish and German freedom, and was wounded in a similar struggle in Sicily. The prominent Polish revolutionary refugee, Ivan Tyssowski was associated with Karl Heinzen in New York as co-editor of the *Deutsche Schnellpost*. When Appolonia Jazella, a heroine of the Polish risings, arrived in New York in 1849 with a group of Hungarian refugees, she was serenaded by a German singing society.[1] In 1853 Major Joseph Jerzmanowski and other Polish refugees in New York petitioned Jefferson Davis, the Secretary of War, for authorization to recruit a Polish Corps for the American army.[2] Poles, Austrians, and Germans claim Albin Francis Schoepf, born near Cracow, whose mother was a Pole and whose father an official of the Austrian government. Schoepf deserted from the Austrian army in 1848 to join a Polish legion organized to help the Hungarian revolutionists. Eventually he escaped to the United States by way of Turkey, and became a member of the coast survey and the patent office, and a brigadier general in the Civil War.[3] Joseph Karge and Wladimir Krzyzanowski had similar experiences. The former, a native of Posen who was educated in German and French universities, was wounded in 1848 and came to New York in 1851, opened a private school, served in the Civil War, and taught languages at Princeton for more than twenty years.[4] Krzyzanowski, a native of Prussian Poland, became a civil engineer in the United States, an active Republican, and an officer in the Union Army; and when he died in 1887, Carl Schurz delivered his funeral oration.[5] The so-called German regiments of the Civil War contained a number of Poles, and the Garibaldi Guards of New York included Polish, Hungarian, and Italian veterans of 1848. Their first colonel was Frederick George Utassy, an Hungarian.[6]

Dr. Franz A. von Moschzisker, a native of Lemberg, Galicia, was trained in the school for cadets of Vienna for the Austrian army, but in 1848 joined the Hungarian Legion. Imprisoned for his part in the Revolution, he managed to escape with his family to England, where he studied English and medicine, became a professor of modern languages at King's College, London, and published a history of German literature. In 1852, Moschzisker arrived in the United States, and after a short practice in New York and Philadelphia, became a well-known eye specialist in Baltimore, and the author of a book on the ear.[7]

Perhaps the most interesting of this Polish-American group was the radical agitator Adam Gurowski. Born in Kalisz, Poland, in 1805, he had studied under Hegel, served a prison sentence in Poland, and later was an agent for the republican movement in Paris. In 1835 he published *La Verité sur la Russie,* a treatise advocating Pan Slavism. He returned to Russia, fled again in 1848, and came to the United States in 1849, where he received an appointment to the Harvard faculty in 1851. His tenure proved brief and troublesome to the college administration, however, and Gurowski left Cambridge to work for Greeley on the *New York Tribune.* During the Civil War he was one of a curious group of self-constituted advisers on international affairs in Washington. He lasted but a short time in his "confidential position," and thereafter became a violent critic of the Lincoln and Johnson administrations, lingering on in Washington, a bizarre and annoying figure, until his death in 1866.[8]

The small Italian community of New York City was deeply interested in the events of 1848, and New York already had its *Società di Unione e Benevolenze Italiana* for the help of needy Italian immigrants. On January 20, 1851, a musical entertainment was arranged in Tripler Hall for the benefit of Italian political refugees and the New York *Daily Tribune* urged all to go who had "a soul for Italian music and a heart for Italian freedom." A Committee of Italian Political Refugees was organized in 1851, and the American *chargé d'affaires* in Rome helped young Italian political prisoners finance their passage to the United States. In the spring of 1853, eighty-four exiles, followers of Mazzini in Lombardy, arrived in New York on the Sardinian frigate *San Giovanni.* Three months later, twenty-five refugees arrived from the Papal States, and in 1856 another small group who had been prisoners of the Austrians in 1849. Mayor Fernando Wood protested to President Pierce that the influx of refugees was bringing in undesirables, and the American consul in Turin reported that the newcomers were "ripe for violent changes in every social order."

Probably the most stormy figure among the Italian refugees who came to America after 1848 was the notorious Father Allesandro Gavazzi. The *New York Tribune* welcomed the hero of the Italian liberal movement, when he arrived in the spring of 1853, as "the herald of freedom" and described his persecution at the hands of the papal police. The Society of Friends of Civil and Religious Liberty gave him a public reception in the Broadway Tabernacle. Presently Gavazzi renounced both the priesthood and his Catholic faith, and began lecturing on political and religious freedom. Serious riots resulted from his exhortations, and the erstwhile priest became a key figure in the bitter nativist and anti-Catholic agitation of the 1850's. American Catholics accused Gavazzi of deliberately inciting their Protestant neighbors to violence. When Gaetano Bedini, the papal nuncio, arrived in New York in the midst of the nativist excitement, Italian and German refugees of 1848 joined to denounce this "wolf in sheep's clothing," and the *L'Eco d'Italia* referred to that "abominable butcher" who shared responsibility for the bloody reaction which followed 1848.[9]

A considerable number of Czechs had immigrated to the United States by 1850, because of the failure of the revolutions of 1848 and 1849, and others continued to arrive throughout the early 1850's. The group that settled in the old Commercial Street area of Cleveland were radicals and freethinkers, closely affiliated with the German radical group. Carl Adam, a Forty-eighter from Prague, directed the singing society of the Cleveland German freethinkers. Racine, Wisconsin, received so many Czech political refugees in the 1850's that it was known as the "Czech Bethlehem." The first Bohemian paper in the United States was published there in 1860. Other Czech Forty-eighters settled in New York City, or scattered into the agricultural states of the upper Mississippi Valley.

The most colorful group among the non-German Forty-eighters undoubtedly were the Hungarians. When Louis Kossuth arrived in America to work for Hungarian independence, he found several hundred Hungarian Forty-eighters already here. Others came with the "Magyar Demosthenes" or arrived in the early 1850's. According to one not too reliable account, Austrian spies reported to Vienna that 158 Hungarian revolutionary exiles had settled in the United States by the fall of 1851; 69 in New York, 21 in Chicago, 6 in St. Louis, 4 in Albany, and the remainder in the West and South. Such figures could have included only the most prominent Hungarian exiles. It is known that Hungarian Forty-eighters settled in St. Louis, New Orleans, and the larger cities of the East; that several appeared in San Francisco during the gold rush; and that efforts were made to establish farm colonies in Iowa, Texas, and New Jersey. Intermingled with the Hungarians to such an extent that accurate differentiation becomes impossible were Poles, Jews, and South Slavs who had participated in the Hungarian revolution, or had studied at the University of Budapest, whose traditions of academic freedom attracted a cosmopolitan student body.

Laszlo Ujhazy was the most famous Hungarian Forty-eighter. The defender of the fortress of Komarom took out his first papers for American citizenship two weeks after his arrival in New York in 1849, and with a group of Hungarian officers developed romantic ideas about establishing a colony of Hungarian "Latin Farmers" somewhere in the West. After a royal welcome in New York, a delegation was sent to Washington to seek the aid of Congress. Americans by this time were quite "Hungarian conscious," and the party of refugees was welcomed on its way to Washington, with serenades and torchlight processions, and Ujhazy addressed an audience in Independence Square, Philadelphia, in German. The Hungarian Count and his colorful retinue dined at the White House, were welcomed by the President to this "natural asylum of the oppressed from every clime," and heard Senators Cass and Seward urge Congress to grant the emigrés adequate acres from the public domain.

Eventually Ujhazy and some of his followers bought twelve sections of land in Decatur County, Iowa, and named their colony New Buda. The United States government established a postoffice in the little community and appointed its founder the first postmaster. Before long the colony of refugees and Magyar aristocrats had a large log "castle" but not much else, and their agricultural methods greatly amused their frontier neighbors. The population of New Buda probably never exceeded seventy-five, but its inhabitants maintained contact with Kossuth and other leaders in Hungarian affairs. George Pomutz, who became an officer in the Civil War and an American consul, promoted the settlement by advertising its lots as far east as New Jersey, but could not save the community. Ujhazy after the death of his wife moved to Sirmezo, Texas.[10]

Hungarian intellectuals and bureaucrats were no more successful as

"Latin Farmers" than their German counterparts. Yet the little settlement of New Buda contained some interesting characters, including the poet, Paul Kerenji; Ignatius Hainer, a professor who tried farming and then went back to teaching at the University of Missouri; and Frank Varga, once a judge of Kossuth's military court and now a farmer in Iowa, who had left London with $2,250 in cash. Other prominent Hungarians in Iowa were Stephen Radnich, who farmed there for half a century, and Nicholas Fejervary who made a fortune in real estate in Davenport, and left an old people's home to the community. His daughter gave the city Fejervary Park. Julian Kune became a successful operator on the Chicago Board of Trade, and John Xantus, who started in America as a ditch-digger, railroad hand, and hospital steward, later did notable work as an ornithologist. Xantus was typical of scores of European naturalists who came to America around the middle of the last century. Something of a Baron Münchhausen who knew how to adorn a tale, much of which was plagiarism or pure invention, he nevertheless collected twenty-four boxes of *naturalia* in Southern California for the Smithsonian Institution, and later shipped another forty-three boxes from Mexico.

Lazarus Meszaros, a gifted linguist, a general in the Hungarian revolutionary army, and a member of the Hungarian Academy of Science, settled with several of his comrades on a farm in New Jersey. When their farm buildings were destroyed by fire, he taught German in a school on Long Island. Miklos Percel (Perezel) and Kornell Fornet also took up farming. The community in Scott County, Iowa, and in Davenport itself, included Felix Spelletick, a former law student at Budapest, who fled to Iowa in 1851, and Theodore Rombauer, an engineer who had supported Kossuth, and is generally classified as a German-Hungarian. After a short and unprofitable experience on a farm, he moved into Davenport, where he gave lessons in German, French, and English.[11]

The Hungarian Forty-eighters of Boston included a Protestant minister, several former army officers, and Karoly Zerdahelji, a musician. Colonel Eugen Arthur Kozlay, who came with Kossuth, worked as an engineer in New York and served in the Civil War with the 54th New York Volunteers.[12] Anthony Vallas, a former teacher of mathematics in Budapest, returned to teaching in Louisiana. Alexander Kocsis, an anthropologist, settled in New Orleans. Charles Kornis Tothvarady founded a journal for Hungarian exiles in America. Adolf Gyurman, former editor of Kossuth's official organ for the Hungarian republic, edited a German paper in New York in 1852, and Louis Schlessinger, a veteran of the revolution, became a filibusterer in Nicaragua and a coffee planter in Guatemala. Anthony Poleski, a former lieutenant of Hussars and one of the revolutionists of 1848, made his home in Chicago in 1850.[13]

Georg vom Amsberg, though born in Hildesheim, became colonel of a Hungarian regiment in 1848-49 and fought under General Henry Dembinski in the Hungarian Revolution. He served nine of a sixteen-year prison sentence, settled in New York City, was a riding master in Hoboken, and colonel of the 45th New York during the Civil War. Albert Anselm, claimed by both Germans and Hungarians, organized volunteer regiments in St. Louis among these two groups in the opening months of the Civil War. Major General Julius H. Stahel, another source of controversy between German and Hungarian writers, and a veteran of Kossuth's army, published the *Deutsche Illustrierte Familien Blätter* and did other literary work in the German language in New York. According to Hungarian scholars, he had changed his name in London from Szamvald to Stahel. After his Civil War service, he was American consul in Yokohama and Shanghai. Other Hungarian refugees, such as George Pomutz, Philip Figyelmessy, and Alexander Ashboth also were rewarded in later years, in recognition of the political importance of their nationality group, by appointments to consular or minor diplomatic posts.

Michael Heilprin, a Jew born under Russian rule in Poland, and one of the great linguists of modern times, deserves special mention. He took part in the Hungarian revolution, as secretary of its literary bureau, and in 1849 followed the Hungarian revolutionary army from place to place, and finally escaped to Paris. Six months later he returned to Hungary and apparently was permitted to teach school without molestation. Eventually he went to London, where he met Kossuth again, and in 1856 he arrived in the United States with letters of introduction from the great Hungarian patriot. Here Heilprin worked for more than twenty years for *Appleton's Cyclopedia* and the *Nation,* and published his scholarly work on the *Historical Poetry of the Ancient Hebrews*. His son Angelo, born in Hungary, and brought to the United States as a small boy, became a well-known scientist and Arctic explorer.[14]

Dr. Arthur Wadgymar, born in Czakaturen, Hungary, was a surgeon in the Hungarian army during the revolution of 1848-49, a doctor in the

Dutch Navy from 1850 to 1852, and a soldier in the Crimean War. He became professor of chemistry and botany in the St. Louis College of Pharmacy, and later in the Humboldt Medical College of the same city, and published several scientific papers on *Trichina spiralis*. In 1873 he moved to Texas,[15] and did considerable work in the field of entomology. Originally the Hungarian intelligentsia were so closely identified, culturally and politically, with the German element in the United States that an accurate differentiation of the two nationality groups is extremely difficult.

The same problem arises with reference to the Jews among the Forty-eighter immigration. In 1849 there were about fifty thousand Jews in the United States, of whom nearly fourteen thousand lived in New York City. Part of the rapid growth of the American Jewish population during 1849 and later was due to the failure of the revolutionary movements in Central Europe, for which Jews both here and abroad had entertained high hopes. Isaac Mayer Wise was so certain of the outcome of the revolution that he planned leaving Albany to return to Austria. The failure of the uprisings in Central Europe were particularly disappointing to Jews, and still more discouraging was the Hungarian anti-Semitism which Kossuth found it impossible to control.

A substantial number of Jews participated in the Revolution in 1848 and 1849. Some were German Jews, others subjects of the Austro-Hungarian Empire, and some had lived for a time in France. In almost every case they were ardent patriots, completely identified with the political and national units to which they owed allegiance, and fully integrated with the cultural life of their respective communities. These facts deserve emphasis, for many reformers and revolutionists in 1848, despite high-sounding phrases about the rights of man, were not without anti-Semitic prejudices. There had been anti-Jewish incidents and riots during the revolution in Baden, Franconia, Hessen, Posen, Prague, and Pressburg, Hungary, and in Germany Jews still suffered from legal disabilities, although educational opportunities were generally open to them without discrimination.

The strong liberal tradition of many German Jews found expression before 1848 in the writings of Heinrich Heine, Moses Hess, ardent apostle of the working class and prophet of Utopia, Ludwig Börne, Gabriel Riesser, and others. Jewish students took part in the radical agitation at the University of Berlin, and there were twenty Jewish casualties on the Berlin barricades in 1848. Memorial services for the victims of the Prussian military were conducted by Catholic, Protestant, and Jewish clergymen.[16] Jews were members of the Frankfurt *Vorparlament,* and five had seats in the Frankfurt Parliament. Eduard von Simson was its president, Riesser its vice-president, and Dr. Maximilian Reinganum one of its most radical members and an ardent protagonist of Jewish rights. Another member was the Jewish poet, Moritz Hartmann from Bohemia, a leftist who led the republicans in the rump parliament of Stuttgart. Jews also sat in the state diets. Some published radical journals, and some were rationalists and freethinkers who had discarded orthodox Jewry to become agnostics and enemies of all organized churches.

Professor Bertram W. Korn found twenty-six bona fide Jewish Forty-eighters who came to the United States after the Revolution. His figures err on the side of cautious conservatism. Most men in his list, with the exception of Joseph Goldmark and Abraham Jacobi, were young students in 1848. Jewish Forty-eighters, like most Jews in every period of our history, settled in the larger cities. Several were active in the politics of early San Francisco. In 1856, Gabriel Riesser, while on a visit to America, was honored by Jewish Forty-eighters at several banquets. Weil von Gernsbach, also known as Weil von Bühl, was a veteran of the Baden revolution, who tried to win the Jewish vote for Stephen A. Douglas in 1860. Sigismund Kaufmann, a power in the *Turnvereine,* was a Republican elector for Lincoln. August Bondi, who at fourteen belonged to the Vienna student corps of 1848, settled in St. Louis, went with John Brown into "bloody Kansas," and served three years in the Union Army.[17] Benjamin Szold, another veteran of the Vienna Revolution, became a rabbi, championed Negro education in Baltimore, and published a memorial essay in German in 1879, honoring the philosopher Moses Mendelssohn on the hundred and fiftieth anniversary of his birth. The rabbi's daughter was one of the early American champions of Zionism, and the founder of Hadassah.[18]

There were at least four Jewish rabbis among the Forty-eighters. In addition to Szold, they include Samuel Kalisch, a radical journalist prosecuted by the Prussian government; Henry Hochheimer, a soldier; and Adolph Heubsch. All four were active in rabbinical work in the United States. Max Cohnheim, a former contributor to the Berlin *Kladderadatsch,* edited the *New York Humorist* in 1859, and wrote plays for the German theatre. Ernst Christian Friedrich Blume, a German Jewish tanner pressed into the service of the Russian Army in Odessa, worked for the liberation of Poland in 1848, and later settled in Baltimore.[19] The Goldmark, Wehle, and Brandeis families left Hamburg in 1849 for the United States, with possessions which included two grand pianos, amateur paintings, chests of music and books—twenty-seven boxes in all. These highly cultured Austrian and Bohemian Jews made their way from New York to Cincinnati and Louisville. Each was successful in his own field of work, and several became distinguished.

Isidor Busch, publisher of revolutionary tracts in Vienna, arrived in New York in January 1849, opened a book store, and began publishing a German-Jewish weekly known as *Israels Herold* on March 30, 1849. His style was too literary and philosophical to attract sufficient readers, and the editor too liberal to win the support of the orthodox, and his journal expired in three months. Discouraged by his New York experiences, Busch moved west to St. Louis, opened a grocery and became an authority on the growing of grapes. An extreme abolitionist, he served three terms in the Missouri state legislature, and was an aide to General Frémont. He was an active promoter of the B'nai B'rith Order, and president of the German Immigration Society of St. Louis. The most distinguished German Jewish Forty-eighter was Abraham Jacobi, one of the early giants in the history of medicine in the United States.

Not all Jews who came to the United States during the period of the Forty-eighter immigration played such important rôles. The group included many plain people. Apparently hundreds of Jews in Prague and Budapest wanted to emigrate to America, and steamship lines advised them of the sailing time of vessels to New York, Baltimore, New Orleans, and Galveston. In June 1848 a number of young Jews left Bremen for America. Most of them were craftsmen and small businessmen from Hungary, Bohemia, Galicia, and Moravia. The following year about four hundred Jews left Prague. Their letters indicate that they not only sought greater economic advantages, but freedom and religious toleration in a country where "the man comes first, then religion and the state and all else."[20]

The cultural assimilation of Germans and German Jews in the United States is attested by the fact that Jewish Forty-eighters, whatever the country of their origin, became part of the German-American community, and were accepted as fellow champions of the republican traditions of 1848. Jews moved in the same cultural milieu with Germans in the United States throughout most of the nineteenth century. They belonged to German *Turnvereine,* and several Jewish Turner were prominent leaders of these gymnastic societies and vigorously advocated their radical programs. Jews belonged to German-American literary clubs, and generously supported the German theatre. They were a majority of the German Orpheus singing society in New York, in 1855. The New York *Arion* excluded Jews for a short time from its musical activities but soon recanted and opened membership to German Jews as readily as to all others interested in cultivating German music in America. In the decade before the Civil War, conventions of Jewish organizations conducted their business in the German language.[21]

Brief mention must also be made of the Irish political exiles who made their way to America a century ago. With many Irishmen rebellion against the British had become chronic, and there was an abortive uprising in Ireland in the glorious year of revolution, as there had been on earlier occasions when Continental Europe was in crisis. With unwarranted optimism, Irish patriots in 1848 toyed with a proposal to recruit a brigade of their American countrymen for service in the Emerald Isle. In the early 1850's, prominent Irish refugees joined the international brotherhood of revolutionists in New York and other eastern centers who had dedicated themselves to the cause of liberty and republicanism throughout the western world.

Perhaps the most prominent of these Irish Forty-eighters was Thomas Francis Meagher, a choleric, romantic son of Erin who became a Union officer during the Civil War, and died years later under somewhat mysterious circumstances in Montana, where he closed a turbulent and frustrated career as acting governor of the new territory. Meagher had gone to Paris shortly after the outbreak of the French Revolution of 1848 to extend the felicitations of the Irish people, had been brought to trial for treason for his foolhardy ventures in Ireland, and deported, along with other Irish political prisoners, to Van Diemen's Land.

In the spring of 1852, Meagher arrived in New York. He was escorted from the dock by enthusiastic Irish-Americans for a grand reception in Brooklyn; the Meagher Club of New York presented him with beautifully bound copies of Sparks' *Life of Washington* and Bancroft's *History of the United States*, and Meagher spent his first months in America attending receptions and dinners and listening to toasts and serenades honoring him as the living symbol of Irish revolution. The eloquent Irishman lectured to large audiences in many places on such subjects as "Ireland in '48" and "Young Ireland, or Irish Politics in 1848," and his only critics seem to have been some of the Catholic clergy who were offended when Meagher identified his cause with that of Kossuth and Mazzini whom the hierarchy considered unbelievers and enemies of the established order.[22]

FOOTNOTES

CHAPTER 7

1. *Westbote*, Dec. 28, 1849.
2. Miecislaus Haiman: *Polish Past in America, 1608-1865* (Chicago, 1939) p. 39.
3. *Ibid.*, pp. 129-33. Wilhelm Kaufmann, in his volume *Die Deutschen im Amerikanischen Bürgerkrieg, 1861-65* (Munich, 1911) claims Schoepf as a German.
4. Haiman: *op. cit.*, pp. 123-28.
5. *Ibid.*, pp. 118-23.
6. *Ibid.*, p. 110.
7. *Der Deutsche Pionier*, XII, No. 9 (Dec. 1880) pp. 357-58.
8. *Dictionary of American Biography*, and LeRoy H. Fischer: "Lincoln's Gadfly—Adam Gurowski," in *The Mississippi Valley Historical Review*, XXXVI (Dec. 1949) No. 3, pp. 415-34.
9. See Howard R. Marraro: "Italians in New York in the Eighteen Fifties" in *New York History*, XXX, No. 3 (July 1948) pp. 279-85; No. 2 (April 1949) pp. 181-203.
10. See Lillian M. Wilson: "Some Hungarian Patriots in Iowa," in *The Iowa Journal of History and Politics*, XI, pp. 479-516; and Emil Lengyel: *Americans from Hungary* (New York, 1948) pp. 47-64.
11. For other names, see Richter: *Geschichte der Stadt Davenport*, Ch. 39, pp. 416-42; and *New Yorker Staatszeitung*, Nov. 28, 1855. For the career of Xantus, see Henry Miller Madden: *Xantus: Hungarian Naturalist in the Pioneer West* (Burlingame, Calif., 1949).
12. *Der Deutsche Pionier*, XV, No. 10 (Jan. 1884) p. 421.
13. Bessie L. Pierce: *History of Chicago*, II (New York, 1940) p. 22.
14. Gustav Pollok: *Michael Heilprin and His Sons* (New York, 1912).
15. S. W. Geiser: "Notes on Some Workers in Texas Entomology 1839-1880"—in *Field and Laboratory*, XVI, No. 1 (Jan. 1947) p. 40.
16. Adolf Köber: "Jews in the Revolution of 1848 in Germany," in *Jewish Social Studies*, X (April, 1948) pp. 135-64.
17. *Autobiography of August Bondi* (Galesburg, Ill., 1910).
18. Cunz: *The Maryland Germans*, p. 331.
19. *Wächter am Erie*, April 13, 1870.
20. See Leopold Kompert: "To America! A 48'ers Call to Freedom" in *Commentary* (New York) March 1949, VII, No. 3, pp. 273-77; *New Yorker Staatszeitung*, March 24, 1849; and Guido Kisch: "The Revolution of 1848 and the Jewish On to America Movement," in *Publications of the American Jewish Historical Society*, No. XXXVIII, Part 3

(March 1949) pp. 185-234; and Bertram W. Korn: "American Jewish Life a Century Ago," in *Yearbook LIX, The Central Conference of American Rabbis* (Philadelphia, 1949) pp. 3-32.

21. *New Yorker Staatszeitung,* Nov. 2, 1855; and Rudolf Glanz: *Jews in Relation to the Cultural Milieu of the Germans in America up to the Eighteen Eighties* (New York, 1947).

22. See Robert G. Athearn: *Thomas Francis Meagher: An Irish Revolutionary in America* (Boulder, Colorado, 1949) especially Chs. II-IV.

Chapter 8 · *"GERMAN FENIANISM"*

I<small>T HAS BEEN</small> a characteristic of political refugees to cling to the hope that some day they could return to their native land and renew the struggle for the causes whose defeat had sent them into exile. During the first years of their residence in a new land they are often torn between earning a living and striking root in new soil, and the desire to go home to all the things which they were forced to leave behind. "I can find neither rest nor peace in America," wrote one of the Forty-eighters; "this world is not our world." Though unusually successful and highly regarded by his fellow Americans, the writer, Friedrich Kapp, could not shake off the "demon thought" which turned his eyes and heart constantly toward the fatherland, and after nearly two decades he returned to Germany to end his days in the land of his youth.[1]

If this was the experience of a man of Kapp's ability and success, it requires little imagination to understand the conflict of emotions that tore the souls òf men to whom America was less kind and generous. "No one in Germany will understand," wrote another of the veterans of 1848, "how hard it is for a refugee to leave for America. The younger men say 'we shall come back, at the first call.' But the more experienced can only smile in sadness. The thin threads that stretch across the ocean will snap all too quickly in the crisp American air."[2] In later years, some Germans talked about being "citizens of two worlds," but actually few people ever are. Many refugees, for years after they had been transplanted from the old world to the new, were like men without a country, rejected by Europe, and not yet accepted by America.

Wherever leading Forty-eighters congregated, whether in London, Zurich, or New York, their discussions during the first years of their exile turned to planning a second German revolution, and ways and means to provide the men and money necessary to insure its success. The later

1840's and the early 1850's were what Friedrich Hassaurek, a youthful refugee from Vienna, once called "the period of German Fenianism," for it was during these years that the more radical German Forty-eighters tried to influence the United States in favor of a second republican uprising in Germany, in the manner of Irish-Americans, who used America in the days of the Fenian movement as a fulcrum, and their political power as a force, to compel England to grant independence to Ireland.

As suggested in the preceding chapter, some of the most ardent German Forty-eighters remained in London, and were part of a colorful and turbulent colony of political refugees from Poland, Hungary, Italy, France, and the German states. They wanted to be near what they called "the revolutionary terrain." From London Amand Gögg, Gottfried Kinkel, Franz Sigel, Arnold Ruge, Karl Marx, and others issued directions to their followers in the United States. The young Schurz was a member of the committee of German refugees who welcomed Kossuth to London in 1851. For many years after the interest of the Germans in America in another European revolution had died out, and the Forty-eighters no longer responded to the propaganda of the exiles in London, that irrepressible coterie of dreamers and bitter-enders continued to plot for another revolution.

In the spring of 1853, German-American papers carried appeals from Gögg and Ruge's "People's League," asking American republicans for financial assistance and reminding Germans that "the European world is moved by a lever which has its fulcrum in Paris," and therefore Germany could be liberated only by restoring republicanism in France.[3] Johann Ronge, a relative of Schurz by marriage, and chairman of the German People's League of London, urged the Germans in America to raise military forces for a second revolution, and demanded that voters use their influence to compel the government in Washington to abandon neutrality for a more friendly attitude toward European revolutions.[4] Arnold Ruge, with a philosopher's delusion about the power of his own subject to sway the world, predicted that salvation would come by way of Spain, whose students, steeped in German philosophy, would provide the spark for a general European revolution.[5] August Willich, "a red republican," whose red hair and full beard made him a picturesque figure, moved among his disciples in London like a second savior, making plans to organize "the men of principle," who sat at his feet in the beer halls, and whom he would lead across the Channel for another attack on monarchy and special privilege.[6]

As the months lengthened into years, and hopes for a second revolution grew ever dimmer, the London group shrank in size and lost many of its leaders to America. Sympathizers in Germany and the United States ceased sending money to support agitators whose profession had become making a revolution instead of a living. Louis Napoleon's *coup d'état* killed the Second French Republic and was a blow to the dreamers about a republican Europe which even the most sanguine could not ignore. Dictatorship in Paris meant that counter-revolution, not republicanism, was on the march. Hungary, Austria, and Prussia sank back into a period of reaction dominated by army, censor, and hangman, and the Russian Czar, determined that Central Europe must be "saved from chaos," kept a watchful eye on his western neighbors. The most optimistic champions of revolution could not ignore the significance of these portentous events. Wilhelm Weitling had hailed the new Napoleon as "the heir of Louis Blanc," who would rid France of the "humbuggery" of endless democratic debate, prepare the way for the downfall of the bourgeoisie and initiate reforms which would benefit workers and peasants. But by 1852, he and other misguided radicals knew better. Napoleon had become not only a dictator, but "a brainless adventurer" and an "imperial fool."[7] As the French dictator settled more securely on his throne, the plight of German refugees in London became more hopeless, but an irreconcilable minority continued to look longingly toward the United States and hope for a miracle from across the sea.

The 1850's witnessed vigorous patriotic movements among the Irish, Hungarians, Poles, and Italians in the United States. Each group hoped to use America as a base of operations against reaction in the fatherland. The Germans were no exception, and among the Forty-eighters found able leaders who boldly appealed in the German-language press for volunteers to liberate Germany.[8] In the spring of 1849, an offer of substantial financial rewards for the assassination of the rulers of the German states and the murder of Napoleon[9] seems to have been made, and Heinzen argued eloquently for tyrannicide "as the chief means of historical progress."

In 1852, a Forty-eighter from Baden reported that ships lay ready at New Orleans to transport German immigrants to Europe for a second revolution.[10] When war broke out between Turkey and Russia, German, Polish, and Hungarian veterans of 1848 seized the opportunity to return to the Continent to fight for liberty. Willich, now a resident of the United States, but ready on a moment's notice to unsheathe his sword in a new war of liberation, urged his fellow Forty-eighters and their friends to organize local committees throughout the nation, register with him in New York, and await the signal to strike a new blow for freedom in Europe.[11] A Turkish Immigration Society was organized to help the Turks against the Russians; various refugee groups made plans for volunteer corps, and the German Turner of New York arranged a concert to defray the expenses of a new foreign legion. Radical German editors stubbornly maintained that such military expeditions would violate neither the American Constitution nor the neutrality laws, and insisted that anyone who had his first citizenship papers should receive full protection from the American government, even if he engaged in war against a nation with which the United States was at peace. A few of the more restless veterans of 1848, tired of waiting for new adventures in Europe, joined American filibusterers in Nicaragua.[12]

For a half-dozen years after 1848, the radical German element in the United States supported fantastic plans to send men and money to Germany. A group in Louisville, in 1850, predicted the date for the new uprising for the following spring, and recommended organizing a regiment of mounted artillery to be sent across the ocean at a moment's notice. Two years later, the Germans of Louisville still were sponsoring picnics and sharpshooting tournaments to provide the sinews of war for another attack upon the kings and princes of Germany.[13] Weitling preached the imminence of complete revolution;[14] the Turner collected defense funds for communists on trial in Cologne and elsewhere, and Gustav Struve, in a passionate address dedicating the new red flag of the New York *Social Turnverein,* was confident that the banner soon would be unfurled overseas in a great battle for liberty.[15] German refugees in Philadelphia spurred German revolutionary societies to renewed activity, and the president of the local committee in Cincinnati advised target practice.[16] A military commission, headed by Willich and other Forty-eighters, was organized in New York to enlist veterans of recent European revolutions, regardless of nationality, to plan a military library, and to recruit engineers, architects, and surveyors.[17] Each Sunday, in the Shakespeare

Hotel, militia companies were briefed for foreign service. The Cleveland *Plain Dealer* reported in 1851 that 150 Cleveland Germans were ready to leave for Germany for an uprising scheduled for the following spring.[18]

Such activities may be ridiculed as fantastic and impracticable or denounced as violations of American neutrality. The majority of the Germans in the United States did not approve such madcap plans, and papers like the *New Yorker Staatszeitung* warned against "revolutionary quacks" who wanted American men and American dollars for foolhardy ventures. It is significant, nevertheless, that a half-dozen years after 1848 such proposals still appealed to the radical fringe of political refugees from several European countries.[19]

When Louis Kossuth arrived in New York for a tour of the United States on behalf of Hungarian independence, the enthusiasm of many German refugees reached fever pitch, for to them the distinguished Hungarian was revolution incarnate. The Germans responded to the "Kossuth craze" with more fervor than any other group. They came to his meetings in large numbers and bought his bonds; and his reception was so cordial that it led Kossuth to overestimate the importance of the German vote in the political campaign of 1852. French, Italian, and Irish republicans joined in the demonstrations of sympathy for the Hungarian revolution.

Kossuth arrived on the U. S. S. *Mississippi* on December 5, 1851. His party, which included his wife and children, a sizable retinue of Hungarians, and some Italian refugees, totaled fifty-eight persons. As his ship approached Staten Island, shore batteries fired salutes, bands played, and a crowd of two-hundred-thousand shouted to the Hungarian liberator from the Battery. After a parade into the city, Kossuth listened to speeches in German, Spanish, Italian, and English, and delegations from other cities delivered messages of welcome from American and foreign-born groups. Twenty thousand persons attended a mass meeting in New York, and when Kossuth spoke at Plymouth Church for an admission charge of five dollars a person, he was able to raise $12,000.

The "Kossuth craze" literally swept the country and found expression in strange ways, as the Hungarian leader traveled about with his retinue of liveried servants, secretaries, and guards. In New York, his sympathizers organized an "Association of Nations" to stimulate revolutions against all despots in Europe; in far-off Little Rock, Arkansas, "The

Central Southern Association to Promote the Cause of Liberty in Europe" had the same objective. Kossuth was received at the White House and in the halls of Congress, and was the guest of honor at a Congressional banquet. Sumner called him a "living Wallace, a living Tell"; the *New York Times* likened him to "Epaminandos, the last Greek of European annals," and Webster observed that "the world has waited for nearly nineteen hundred years to see his like."[20] A Baptist minister in New York compared Kossuth's tour with the Second Coming of Christ. Large crowds in Louisville, Cincinnati, and other cities urged the immediate recognition of Hungarian independence. Meantime, Hungarian Loan Certificates, payable to the bearer on demand one year after the establishment of an independent Hungarian government, were made available to anyone ready to implement his passion for revolution with good American dollars.[21]

Despite the enthusiasm of the crowds, Kossuth encountered many difficulties. A furious debate broke out in Congress over American intervention in European affairs. Webster sobered sufficiently to offer Kossuth "sympathy, personal respect and kindness, but no departure from our established policy." Henry Clay had pleaded fervently against involvement "in the tangled web of European politics," and urged that we "keep our lamp burning brightly on this Western shore, as a light to all nations," but not "hazard its utter extinction amid the ruins of fallen and falling republics in Europe." Radicals tried to commit Kossuth to abolitionism and socialism, and he parried both issues as long as he could. When he finally declared his opposition to the program of communist radicals, men like Weitling, who originally had supported him, denounced him as a reformer who thought only in terms of narrow national and political frontiers, and was unconcerned with justice for the working class.[22] Heinzen, irritated because Kossuth would not commit himself on abolitionism and socialism, concluded that "the morning star of the revolution" had become the "brilliant evening star of the reaction." The abolitionist agitation, rapidly moving toward a bloody climax, was a source of continual embarrassment, and Southerners became suspicious of Kossuth's campaign because it had the support of prominent abolitionists.

Probably the greatest hostility came from the hierarchy of the Catholic Church. It was not difficult to portray Kossuth, a European trained in the tradition of rationalism and the Age of the Enlightenment, as a symbol of nonconforming Protestantism and an anti-clerical agnostic, and some of his speeches in America supported such conclusions. Bishop Hughes called him a "humbug." Orestes A. Brownson, a restless character who finally sought peace in the Catholic fold, referred to Kossuth as "one of the most dangerous characters now living." The Catholic *Freeman's Journal*, organ of the New York diocese, denounced the Hungarian patriot as "a demagogue," "a tyrant and an enemy of Christianity," and described his followers as "vipers too pestiferous and disgusting to be longer endured in society." The *National Intelligencer*, a conservative non-Catholic Whig paper, likened Kossuth's activities to Paine's diabolical *Age of Reason*— "kindred emanations of dangerous minds and . . . heresies fatal to the established truth."[23]

Such attacks only endeared the Hungarian to the rationalists among the German Forty-eighters. Kossuth's popularity among native Americans diminished rapidly after the first few weeks of excitement, his reception in New York and Washington on his second visit was cool indeed, and no one came to see him off when he sailed for Europe in July 1852. Only the Germans in the larger cities of the East and the Middle West continued to support his program.

In Philadelphia, Kossuth was welcomed with a torchlight parade led by German Turner and including many German organizations from dramatic clubs, workers' societies, and military companies to German singers, who marched in a blinding snowstorm, and forced the indisposed Hungarian hero to listen to the address of welcome in his bedroom.[24] In Baltimore, Schnauffer, an ardent young Forty-eighter, introduced Kossuth as a leader of the Germans. German lodges contributed to the Kossuth National Loan; and newspapers like the *New Yorker Staatszeitung* and the Columbus *Westbote,* organs of the older German immigration, welcomed the Hungarian hero as eagerly as the radical Forty-eighters. A "Ladies Association for the Friends of Hungary" collected over a thousand dollars; the Germans of Louisville contributed fifteen hundred dollars after Kossuth spoke in English at the Court House and in a hall used for the auctioning of tobacco, and in German in an American church, for an admission fee of one dollar.[25] In Columbus, German grenadiers, an artillery company, the Turner, members of the city council and the state legislature escorted Kossuth to the Ohio capitol. German butchers mounted on heavy delivery horses brought up the rear of this curious procession. The day's festivities, which began with a salute by German artillery drawn up at the depot, ended with official greetings from the Governor, several speeches, and a midnight serenade by the Columbus *Männerchor* at the Neil House, forcing the tired hero to appear once more on the balcony of the hotel to make another speech in German.[26]

By the time Kossuth's strenuous tour came to an end, the famous Hungarian was low in spirit and had suffered many disappointments. He had not handled his interviews on American public questions too dexterously, but he still had faith in the German element. In his last address before a German audience in the Tabernacle in New York he pleaded with his listeners to persuade the American government to abandon its policy of isolation, and he followed this extraordinary speech with a secret circular letter to various German societies urging them to influence the United States government to assume a larger role in world affairs.

The backbone of German support for Kossuth was scores of little revolutionary societies *(Revolutionsvereine)* founded by Forty-eighters in many localities, and with central headquarters in Philadelphia. Although their propaganda for revolution attracted considerable attention in the German-language press, their influence was negligible as far as the course of American politics was concerned. Sometimes such societies operated in an atmosphere of mystery, plots and counter-plots, which extended across the sea to the refugee group in London. Although many Forty-eighters became involved in programs for world revolution, Schurz and Hecker kept aloof from such impracticable measures, and the latter completely ignored all communications from the *Revolutionsvereine*.[27]

Gottfried Kinkel, the "German Kossuth," came to America from London to dramatize the appeal for a second German Revolution. He was a sensitive, lovable, sincere person, a former professor at Bonn, with the soul of a poet. He had carried a gun as a private in 1848, and had been wounded, captured, and sentenced to life imprisonment. His dramatic liberation from behind Prussian prison bars by Carl Schurz, on whom Kinkel had had great influence, made both men heroic figures in the international revolutionary movement. Kinkel began his tour of the United States three months before Kossuth arrived. Their objectives and tactics were essentially the same, although Kinkel was less well known in America, and his appeal was greatly handicapped by the factional strife which divided German refugees here and abroad. In London the Kinkel faction, supported by Willich, Schurz, and others, had resolved to raise two million dollars for another German revolution; but another group, including Gögg, Ruge, Fickler, and Franz Sigel, emphasized propaganda techniques rather than money, and planned an educational campaign for world revolution. Before his arrival, Kinkel had contributed to German-American papers, and appealed for funds. When he landed in New York in September 1851 to begin the grand tour, he was accompanied by a secretary, George Hillgärtner, a Heidelberg lawyer who had escaped to Switzerland and England after a death sentence, and who later was identified with several leading German-American newspapers.

In New York, Kinkel stirred a convention of Turner from eastern and midwestern cities to a frenzy by telling them that "the hour of revolution is at hand, and Germany expects every Turner to do his duty."[28] In Philadelphia, he spoke to five thousand people in the Chinese Museum, where Dr. Heinrich Tiedemann, Hecker's brother-in-law, a veteran of the Baden Revolution and a close friend of Schurz, presided. Tiedemann was so captivated by the German professor that he accompanied him on his lecture tour and became treasurer of his revolutionary fund. In Baltimore, between $1,200 and $1,500 were pledged at a single meeting. Cincinnati greeted Kinkel with a torchlight procession from the Turner Hall, speeches by the mayor and others, and pledges of $2,600. In Cleveland, Jakob Müller, a Forty-eighter, acted as secretary of Kinkel's finance committee. A bazaar sponsored by Cleveland Germans yielded four hundred dollars "toward the overthrow of the thrones and despotism of Europe, and the upraising of such noble men as Kossuth, Mazzini and Kinkel."[29] In Milwaukee, Kinkel addressed several German groups and lectured to the *Arbeiterverein* on the status of the laborer in Europe. Milwaukee Germans produced the usual parades, music, artillery fire, and torchlights appropriate to the occasion, and the women raised over three hundred dollars at a bazaar.[30] Virtually the same program was repeated in Chicago, where, according to one account, $7,700 were subscribed to the German National Loan.[31] On his way to New Orleans, early in 1852, Kinkel spoke in English and German at the Louisville Court House, and spent several convivial hours at the favorite tavern of the Louisville Forty-eighters.[32] In Natchez, the ladies organized an auxiliary to support the German revolution.[33]

Kinkel was a speaker of great ability and personal charm, but his greatest success seems to have been with workers' and women's groups. Although greeted by large crowds, like his Hungarian contemporary, he quickly discovered how fleeting fame can be and how difficult it was to sustain enthusiasm for another European revolution. Kinkel also became involved in some of the political issues that divided the American people. When a Negro group in Cleveland resolved to support the German National Loan, and a local German society thanked the Negroes for their help, Kinkel was branded by part of the press as an abolitionist.[34] The Whig *Ohio State Journal* regarded him as an "infidel" and "a representative of unbelieving Germany."[35] Extreme radicals, like Weitling, ridiculed "the nebulous German republic of the professors," claimed that German workers had been shabbily treated by republican reformers, and demanded a communist revolution, instead of empty phrases about liberty and nationalism.[36] Börnstein of the *Anzeiger des Westens,* though personally friendly to Kinkel, opposed his impractical ideas, and debated with him for five hours before a German audience in St. Louis which each speaker was permitted to address no less than four times.[37]

Such experiences were discouraging to a romantic idealist, but the widening rift among German revolutionary groups proved far more distressing. The controversy finally revolved around Kinkel and his chief rival, Amand Gögg. Gögg came to the United States to represent the extreme left wing, or the "red republicans" of the German emigré colony in London. His main appeal was for the organization of a nation-wide "German-American Revolutionary League," whose objective should be revolutionary propaganda. Gögg advocated the distribution of revolutionary literature among Germans here and abroad, and concentrated upon a campaign of education to win support for an American policy of coöperation with the revolutionary elements of Europe. In some respects, Gögg's program was more like Kossuth's plan for an international revolution than Kinkel's. But whereas the latter sold bonds for a new German revolution, Gögg proposed to collect dues of five cents a month to finance his propaganda. Gögg expounded his program to large audiences, and organized affiliates of his *Revolutionsbund* in Boston, Erie, New York, Buffalo, Philadelphia, Baltimore, Washington, Reading, Pittsburgh, Harrisburg, Allegheny, Wheeling, Columbus, Cincinnati, Dayton, St. Louis, Louisville, Peoria, Chicago, Milwaukee, Detroit, Richmond, and other cities.[38]

The battle between Kinkel's *Revolutionsverein,* organized in London to raise funds for an armed revolt, and Gögg's *Agitationsverein,* with headquarters also in England, and of which his *Revolutionsbund* was the American counterpart, became extremely bitter. Gögg's group insisted that the way to overthrow the German princes was by secret propaganda; Kinkel believed in the imminence of a new military conflict between republicans and reactionaries. Fortunately their only weapon was newspaper invective. When a number of German organizations, in the hope of ending the controversy, called a congress in Philadelphia in January 1852, Kinkel would have no part in its proceedings. Fifteen organizations, including the Turner, participated, an *Amerikanischer Revolutionsbund für Europa* was formed, according to Gögg's proposals; Philadelphia was made the headquarters of the new society; and Fickler and Gögg solemnly declared the *Agitationsverein* of London dissolved.

Not to be outdone, Kinkel convened his own congress in Cincinnati, to underwrite and guaranty his national loan. Although Hecker, Kapp, Tiedemann, Anneke, Rothacker, Struve, Caspar Butz, and other prominent Forty-eighters assured Kinkel of their moral support, only eight delegates appeared. The sponsor made a detailed report of his visits to twenty-two cities, whereupon the Cincinnati congress repudiated its Philadelphia rival, and asked Kinkel to continue his activities. Such assemblies did little except widen the rift between the two contending factions. Each bombarded the German societies with its speakers, and the whole controversy was thoroughly aired in the German-language press, with a superabundance of invective.

A second and final congress of the *Revolutionsbund* met at Wheeling from September 19 to September 22, 1852. Called by the Philadelphia group, it was completely under the influence of the more radical supporters of Gögg. Sixteen delegates attended, including prominent Forty-eighters such as Müller of Cleveland and Wilhelm Rothacker, and claimed to speak for 1,112 revolutionary societies in more than a dozen American cities. Dr. Konradin Homburg of Indianapolis, who had been in the United States since 1824, presided. Letters from Kossuth, Mazzini, Gögg, and Ledru Rollin were read. In their effort to restore harmony, the delegates testified to the sincerity of both Kinkel and Gögg, and endorsed Kossuth's loan as well, and recommended that the Turner, eager to fight for a "red republic," begin drilling at once. The congress created the usual committees; sent an inquiry to Franklin Pierce to find out what he thought about American intervention in Europe, and received no reply from the President; advocated free trade, tariff and postal agreements with European nations; demanded that all standing armies be dissolved; made pronouncements on marriage, slavery, and the defects of the American Constitution; and decided to distribute the speeches of Gögg and Kossuth abroad.[39]

The major concern of the congress, however, was how to arouse the United States to an understanding of its destiny to build a world republic, with America at the center. The curious idea found its most eloquent and fantastic expression in a speech by Karl Goepp, the substance of which was later incorporated in a book entitled *The New Rome,* with Theodore Pösche as co-author, which the congress resolved to circulate in several languages.

Goepp, a native of Silesia, had been in the United States since 1834. His father was a prominent member of the Moravian Church at Bethlehem. The son was an ardent Free Soiler and, in the 1860's, a law partner of Friedrich Kapp, but he was not a Forty-eighter. Pösche had studied philosophy and theology in Saxony in preparation for the ministry. A fiery orator, he had led a one-day revolt at the University of Halle, and then had fled into South Germany and eventually to London, to join the colony of foreign refugees. A sixteen-year prison sentence hung over his head in Germany. In 1852 Pösche came to America, and settled in Philadelphia as a schoolteacher, marrying the daughter of Eduard Pelz, the Forty-eighter who had championed the cause of the Silesian weavers. In 1858 Pösche became headmaster of a private school in St. Louis, and later a statistician in the Census Bureau and the Bureau of Internal Revenue. He had been in trouble with the German police because of a manuscript entitled *Das Neue Rom,* and when he discovered that Goepp had produced a somewhat similar pamphlet entitled *E pluribus unum,* the two men decided to collaborate on a book, which Pösche wrote first in German, and Goepp translated into English.

In his speech to the Wheeling congress, Goepp demanded "an empire not of conquest and of subjugation, not of inheritance, not of international frictions and hatreds, but of fraternity, of equality and of freedom," and he implored the United States "to fulfill its destiny and out of many worlds create a single one." In the book, *The New Rome,* published by

Putnam in 1853, "as a map of the future of mankind," the authors contended that the United States must become for the modern world that "orbis terrarum" which Rome had been for the ancient world, for "America is the crucible" in which European, Asiatic, and African nationalities and customs are melted into unity. Goepp and Pösche believed the British Empire eventually would find "its real centre" in the United States, and that Russia alone would resist the American march toward world domination. They predicted a final struggle between these two giants, with the United States emerging victorious, and envisaged, as the result of that last great struggle for power, a universal state based on freedom, brotherhood, and equality, and with the United States at its controlling center.[40]

The Wheeling congress, fully persuaded by Goepp's thesis, prepared a manifesto to all democratically minded Europeans. This extraordinary document stressed the "historical necessity" of the American Union to expand until it included all the states of Europe, so that "by the annexation of the civilized world to America" the national motto, *E pluribus unum* would encompass the earth. As Rome had absorbed the ancient world, the national states of Europe must be dissolved "in the universality of the American character." After Cuba, Canada and Mexico had been absorbed, the American republic would use its overwhelming power to build "one world," end the conflict of competing sovereignties, and establish a universal republic. The delegates at Wheeling resolved to educate the American people to an understanding of their historic mission, and Europeans to an acceptance of this solution of their problems. As further evidence of its intentions, the congress changed its name to "Volksbund für die alte und neue Welt."

Forty-eighters like Hecker and Hassaurek branded such a program as fantastic, absurd, and impractical, and many "Grays" considered it the work of cranks. Nevertheless such resolutions merely restated, in more extreme terms, the hopes and desires of many immigrants who would have liked to use the United States to reform and liberate western Europe. The United States in the 1850's had a "Young America" group comparable in many respects to the "Young Italy" and "Young Germany" movements in Europe, and the "Young America" wing of the Democratic party was quite vocal in the campaign of 1852. While Whigs and Southern Democrats continued to advocate American isolation, and warned against becoming involved in a war on "mistaken humanitarian grounds," others, including Stephen A. Douglas, bombastically defied the crowned heads of Europe and called upon the United States to "interpose both her moral and her physical power" in the great struggle between despotism and liberty, reaction and republicanism. Such appeals fitted into the American gospel of progress and expansionism, and American idealism was supported by the promise of new markets for American goods and an outlet for the American missionary spirit.[41] Parke Godwin of the *New York Post,* for example, chided Americans for their failure to make a greater impression on the rest of the world, and called upon them to play a global rôle, stop aggression and support republican movements everywhere, preach a positive, dynamic liberalism, and if war came, boldly accept the sacrifices involved in "a glorious struggle for liberty, justice and humanity."[42]

Such arguments coincided beautifully with the ideals of radical German exiles, and their missionary zeal for a second great European struggle of liberation found a hearing even in conservative, older German newspapers.[43] Radicals of this type repeatedly appealed to the government to abandon its "narrow neutrality" and proclaim the destiny of the United States to convert all the Americas from the Arctic to Cape Horn into a great republic and extend the blessings of democracy to Europe. Esselen envisaged a federation of Europe with Germany at the center of a new brotherhood of nations, and branded American neutrality as a "base, common egotism," which isolated the United States from the common interests of mankind and thwarted its destiny. "Neutrality is a political mask," commented the *Atlantis,* in a tirade against a narrow national patriotism, "which permits republican nations to become the executioners of liberty in other lands."[44] Heinzen would have extended the Monroe Doctrine to the world. He could see only "an irreconcilable contest between republican and despotic governments," and therefore wanted the United States to break off diplomatic relations with all monarchical governments, ship war materials to Hungarian, Italian, and other revolutionary groups, emancipate Europe, and lay the foundations for an ultimate Congress of the Peoples of the World.[45] Many resolutions adopted by German groups during Kossuth's visit to the United States demanded a similar foreign policy, and stressed the moral obligation of the United States to break the chains of reaction which held Europe in bondage.

To all who challenged such extreme proposals, radical Forty-eighters replied that they would control enough of the German vote in 1852 to force the new administration to adopt the new foreign policy. Before the Democratic Convention of 1852, a number of German organizations made their interventionist demands known to the politicians and demanded a policy of "active sympathy in the international relations of Europe."[46] The Cleveland *Wächter am Erie,* edited by a young Forty-eighter, repeatedly referred to the struggle between democracy and reaction, progress and retrogression, for control of the world; regarded it as inevitable; and argued that because the Czar of Russia was ready to intervene on behalf of European autocrats, the United States must not stand idly by and watch Europe become "cossack."[47]

As controversies multiplied over the arrest of German-Americans who returned with their first American papers to the fatherland, or were pressed into military service on their arrival, or had their property confiscated, the German press, both radical and conservative, argued vociferously for a bolder American policy toward the German tyrants. German-language newspapers advocated special pacts of friendship with Switzerland and the recall of the American minister to Berlin, and insisted that in the event of another German revolution the United States government must secure full belligerent status for German-Americans who might return to the fatherland to fight.[48]

Kinkel's plea for two million dollars for a second revolution netted less than ten thousand dollars in actual cash after expenses for travel and printing had been deducted. It is impossible to compile accurate figures. The German patriot was honored by parades, serenades, fairs, and bazaars, but sold few bonds for the new German Republic. It is difficult to discover what actually became of the Kinkel fund, though Kinkel himself was scrupulously honest and constantly sought instructions as to what he should do with the small balance in hand when he returned to London to make a living by tutoring and lectures on America. Reports of his fund-raising activities had appeared regularly in German-American papers. They did not always agree in detail, but they reveal that the most generous contributions came from Cincinnati, New Orleans, Baltimore, Cleveland, and St. Louis.[49] The administrators of the small amount that was left, after the plan for a German National Loan was officially abandoned, repeatedly sought instructions and received a variety of conflicting proposals, ranging from a plan to start a paper for the German exiles in London, to giving the money to needy political refugees, printing propaganda for circulation in Europe, and fitting out a German volunteer corps to fight with Garibaldi in Italy. Here in America, Detroiters wanted their money back to invest in a German school; Pittsburghers asked that it be returned to the original donors.[50]

Amand Gögg's rival organization had raised exactly $36.07 in the five months following adjournment of the Congress of Wheeling, an amount hardly adequate "to overthrow the German princes." Gögg himself came back to the United States in 1872, as a traveling salesman for a wine business which he inherited from his father in Baden, and lectured in English, French, and German about his latest plan to save the world. Always a propagandist and a pacifist at heart, he advocated "A League of Freedom and Peace" for the disarmament and the republicanization of Europe.[51]

By 1853, the point of view of many extreme revolutionaries among the Forty-eighters had begun to change. Another revolution was not just around the corner, and it became clear that political refugees had to shift their sights from Europe to America and settle down to making a living, for they were likely to remain in the United States for a long time. Schurz, "tired of the futile doings of the refugees," wrote to Kinkel from Philadelphia in 1853, "Your agitation and Kossuth's and the Revolutionary Confederation have so used up the enthusiasm for transatlantic affairs, and the European events since 1851 have made the Americans so distrustful that the people must be given rest and quiet to recover from their chagrin and disappointment. . . . If the Americans have hitherto had not much use for the German revolution, no one is to blame for that but the Germans here. . . ."[52] Börnstein referred to the fiasco at Wheeling as the "dying rocket" of the "Greens" and the closing episode in "the German-American period of Revolution."[53] The *Westbote,* more impatient and less kind, caricatured Gögg's activities in a cartoon depicting a huge barrel with a heavy German beard sticking out of the bung-hole, and entitled "A Revolution in the Palatinate from 100,000 seidel beer."[54] Hecker admonished his fellow Forty-eighters to abandon their dreams of Utopia and their "sickly yearning" for revolution, and the *New Yorker Staatszeitung* reminded its readers that they were now citizens of the United States, and had no further political obligation to Germany.[55]

In due time, the period of storm and stress passed. Even the most ardent radicals admitted the hopelessness of their cause, and the sanest among them sensed the unfavorable reaction of Americans toward foreigners who would sacrifice the resources of their new home for the benefit of a former fatherland. Of greater significance, however, was the fact that the energy of the Forty-eighters, formerly spent in making revolution, was channeled rather easily into various reform movements in the United States. The chronic organizers and agitators turned to reforming America. Christian Esselen stated the case in his usual pungent manner. In an appeal to his fellow exiles, he urged radicals who were waiting impatiently for another revolution in Europe to concentrate on the fight for greater liberty and humanitarianism in the United States. "We believe," he wrote, "that the best preparation for the revolution is to remain fresh and healthy in body and spirit, and to prepare and condition ourselves for the coming struggle for liberty in Europe by taking part in the battle for freedom here. To do that, more than propaganda and national loans are needed. We must not look upon ourselves as refugees in America. This nation is not our land of exile. Here one can fight as vigorously as in Europe for our highest and most sacred ideals, and the battle for the realization of those ideals is rightly ours." Esselen referred to the United States as "the great school of politics," a laboratory and a training ground for Europeans, where they could learn about universal suffrage, popular sovereignty, and free public education, and he appealed to Forty-eighters to cease complaining and devote their energies to the building of a better America.[56]

FOOTNOTES

CHAPTER 8

1. Friedrich Kapp: *Aus und Über Amerika* (Berlin, 1876) I, p. 301.
2. *New York Staatszeitung*, July 13, 1850.
3. *Wächter am Erie*, March 12, 1853.
4. *New Yorker Staatszeitung*, Dec. 16, 1853.
5. *Ibid.*, June 22, 1854.
6. Gustav Mayer: *Friedrich Engels* (New York, 1936) p. 133; Philipp Wagner: *Ein Achtundvierziger* (Brooklyn, 1882) pp. 181-83.
7. *Die Republik der Arbeiter*, Jan. 3, April 3, Nov. 20, 1852; Jan. 8, 1853.
8. *New Yorker Staatszeitung*, April 28, 1849.
9. *Westbote*, April 6, 1849.
10. *Belletristisches Journal*, May 28, 1852.
11. *Wächter am Erie*, Nov. 22, 1853.

12. See *New Yorker Staatszeitung*, Oct. 20, Dec. 15, 23, 24, 1853; Feb. 3, April 11, 1854; Jan. 25, April 17, May 1, 1856; *Belletristisches Journal*, Oct. 23, 1857.

13. Stierlin: *Kentucky*, pp. 118 and 137.

14. *Die Republik der Arbeiter*, June 28, 1851.

15. *New Yorker Staatszeitung*, Aug. 23, 1851.

16. *Ibid.*, Nov. 29, 1851; March 5, 6, 1852.

17. *Ibid.*, Oct. 24, 1853; Jan. 2, 1854.

18. *Cleveland Plain Dealer*, Nov. 18, 1851.

19. See also, Robert Ernst: *Immigrant Life in New York City, 1825-1863* (New York, 1949) p. 178.

20. John W. Oliver: "Louis Kossuth's Appeal to the Middle West—1852," in *The Mississippi Valley Historical Review*, XIV (March 1928) pp. 481-95.

21. See J. B. McMaster: *History of the People of the United States*, VIII, pp. 146-57; Ray A. Billington: *The Protestant Crusade, 1800-1860* (New York, 1938) pp. 330-34; and Andor Leffler: "Kossuth Comes to Cleveland," in *The Ohio Archaeological and Historical Quarterly* (July 1947) Vol. LVI, pp. 1-16.

22. *Die Republik der Arbeiter*, Feb. 14, 28, 1852.

23. See Billington, *op. cit.*, pp. 330-34.

24. C. F. Huch: "Kossuth und die Deutschamerikaner" in *Mitteilungen des Deutschen Pionier Vereins von Philadelphia*, XVIII (1910) pp. 19-21.

25. Stierlin: *Kentucky*, pp. 136-37.

26. *Westbote*, Feb. 6, 1852.

27. See also, *Intimate Letters of Carl Schurz*, edit. by Joseph Schafer (Madison, 1928) p. 117.

28. *New Yorker Staatszeitung*, Oct. 2, 1851.

29. Cleveland *Daily True Democrat*, Nov. 21, 1851.

30. Koss: *Milwaukee*, pp. 347-49; 369.

31. Bessie L. Pierce: *History of Chicago* (New York, 1940) I, pp. 27-28.

32. Stierlin: *Kentucky*, pp. 135-36.

33. *New Yorker Staatszeitung*, Feb. 13, 1852.

34. *New Yorker Staatszeitung*, Feb. 21, 1852.

35. *Westbote*, Nov. 28, 1851.

36. *Die Republik der Arbeiter*, June 21, 1851.

37. Börnstein: *Memoiren* II, pp. 124-34.

38. *New Yorker Staatszeitung*, Feb. 11, June 3, 18, July 13, 1852; *Westbote*, March 18, 26, 1852.

39. See *Der Deutsche Pionier*, VIII, pp. 90-97, 155-59; and C. F. Huth: "Revolutionsvereine und Anleihen," in *Mitteilungen des Deutschen Pionier-Vereins von Philadelphia*, XVIII (1910) pp. 1-19; and *Wächter am Erie*, Sept. 25, 1852.

40. See Eduard Schläger: "Der Wheelinger Congress im September 1852," in *Der Deutsche Pionier*, VIII, No. 3 (Jan. 1876) pp. 90-97.

Schläger was the presiding officer at Wheeling. See also Theodore Poesche and Charles Goepp: *The New Rome, or The United States of the World* (New York, 1853); Julius Goebel, Jr.: "A Political Prophecy of the Forty-eighters in America," in *Deutsch-Amerikanische Geschichtsblätter* (Chicago, 1912) XII, pp. 462-98; T. S. Baker: "Young Germany in America," in *Americana-Germanica*, I, pp. 87-94; *New Yorker Staatszeitung*, Sept. 30, 1852.

41. Merle E. Curti: "Young America," in *The American Historical Review* (Oct. 1926) XXXII, pp. 34-55.

42. Quoted in Merle Curti: "The Reputation of America Overseas," in *American Quarterly*, I, No. 1 (Spring 1949) pp. 81-82.

43. See *Westbote*, Oct. 31, 1851; *New Yorker Staatszeitung*, Nov. 11, 1856.

44. *Atlantis* (June 1855) II, p. 446; and III, N.S. (Sept. 1855) p. 183.

45. Wittke: *Heinzen*, pp. 257, 258, 265.

46. Cleveland *Daily True Democrat,* July 21, 1852.

47. *Wächter am Erie,* Aug. 9, 14, 1852.

48. See *New Yorker Staatszeitung,* June 12, 1849; March 30, 1850; Feb. 13, March 26, 1852; Nov. 3, 1853; *Belletristisches Journal,* March 24, 1854; March 21, 1856.

49. See *Wächter am Erie,* Nov. 24, 1852; *Die Republik der Arbeiter,* Nov. 27, 1852; Pierce: *History of Chicago,* II, pp. 27-28.

50. See, e.g., *New Yorker Staatszeitung,* Feb. 1, 9, 1853; Aug. 27, 1852; Nov. 25, 1852; *Belletristisches Journal,* July 27, 1860; *Wächter am Erie,* Aug. 1, 1860; *Westbote,* Nov. 26, 1852.

51. *Wächter am Erie,* Feb. 24, May 11, 1872.

52. Joseph Schafer: *Intimate Letters of Carl Schurz,* pp. 113-14; 119-21; 364.

53. Börnstein: *Memoiren,* II, p. 150.

54. *Westbote,* April 22, 1853.

55. March 18, 1852; June 22, 1852; Jan. 19, 1854.

56. *Atlantis* (June, 1855) N.S. II, pp. 413-18.

Chapter 9 · "*LATIN FARMERS*"

EVERY IMMIGRATION to America has included men and women who dreamed of building a Utopia on the prairies of Mid-America. In the spirit of Rousseau's "free and noble savage" they entertained romantic but unrealistic notions about carving a home out of the primeval forest, where they might live according to their heart's desire and a social pattern of their own choosing. Others dreamed of establishing in the New World a replica of their old fatherland, stripped of its faults, where they could preserve the customs, language, and traditions of their people, and hand them down, uncorrupted, to their descendants. Very few conceived of a state within a state, politically separated from the rest of the United States, although many would have preferred a cultural and spiritual isolation.

Among the Forty-eighters there were impractical dreamers about an America which existed only in the writings of poets and travelers whose souls had been moved by the romance of America's streams and mountains and the solitude of her unbroken prairies, to ecstasies about an unspoiled Garden of Eden across the sea. Men of education and culture, with a zeal for liberty, were peculiarly susceptible to such fictional accounts about the United States in the Storm and Stress period when young Germans worshiped Nature and Primitive Man, à la Rousseau. James Fenimore Cooper's books enjoyed phenomenal popularity in Germany for a century, and German literature of the early nineteenth century contained many allusions to America. Some were quite uncomplimentary, to be sure, and focused attention on the hypocrisy and materialism of American civilization, but others pictured the United States as an ideal country where "the New Germany" would find freedom from censorship, standing armies, social castes, secret police, and prying bureaucrats.[1]

The immigration of young Forty-eighters, intellectuals and frustrated revolutionaries, with more than the normal dose of Teutonic *Weltschmerz,* and radicals disillusioned with reactionary and decaying Europe, included its small quota of those who sought balm for their wounded spirits in America's forests and prairies. Lawyers, professors, and doctors, forced into political exile, hoped to realize in the open spaces of America the individual liberty for which they had fought. In the Mississippi Valley, land was cheap. Relatively few of the newcomers had the faintest notion of the practical obstacles encountered when books were exchanged for plows, and the learned professions for pioneer farming, yet a number of immigrants of the post-revolutionary years embarked on the great adventure. These were the men whom their American neighbors called "Latin farmers," partly in amazement and partly in derision, for they knew much about the classics and the book-learning of the universities, but practically nothing of the art of farming in a frontier society.

There were German Latin farmers in America before the Forty-eighters came. Actually a smaller percentage of Forty-eighters turned to the land than during the earlier nineteenth-century German immigration. The earlier arrivals included Friedrich Münch, who worked with axe and plow in Missouri. A German professor who settled in the same state in the 1830's cut his first corn with the sword which his brother had wielded in 1813 in the Napoleonic wars, and reported meetings with others of his kind whose "songs of liberation of the years 1817 and 1818 made the primeval forests of Missouri ring."[2] The German settlement at Belleville, St. Clair County, Illinois, was the best known of the "Latin settlements" of the refugees of the Revolution of 1830, and the *Belleviller Zeitung* was already well established when it welcomed Hecker and his fellow revolutionists to the community in 1848.

Although the number of Latin farmers was relatively small among the Forty-eighters, some interesting types were found among these later arrivals. Although trained for the professions, the refugees embarked with courage and enthusiasm on a project intended to rehabilitate their frustrated lives and their personal fortunes. Many failed, and lost their investment to their hired hands. Others recovered their equilibrium quickly enough and drifted back into the cities while there was still time to find more practical and congenial ways of making a living.

"It sounds so good, so idyllic," wrote Kapp in 1853 in an article published in Göttingen, "to read in Europe about the blockhouse on the lonely prairie."[3] Actually most refugees found their experiences with farming under frontier conditions both stultifying and unrewarding. "The romantic West" proved to be rich in land and scenery, but short of nearly everything else. In an article in the unfriendly *Atlantische Studien,* the writer referred to the freedom of the prairie, except from weather and disease, and "the living death" to which talented intellectuals were condemned when they had to perform hard manual labor which any day laborer could do twice as well and with half the effort. The spiritual rebirth, the regeneration of the individual, à la Faust, which many expected from the frontier, turned into a dull routine of plowing, occasional conversations with boring neighbors who had little interest in cultural or intellectual matters, and an almost unbearable loneliness which even the whisky jug could do little to dispel.

German immigrants complained that the American farmer was a "frosty, taciturn, unmannerly individual," who sat glum and silent in the taverns, advanced solemnly, at regular intervals, to the bar to down another whisky, and then relapsed into silence.[4] The Latin farmer admitted that he enjoyed complete freedom and independence, and that the government was extraordinarily liberal, but such advantages were more than offset by long hours of physical drudgery, a serious shortage of capital, and complete isolation from kindred spirits. "If we only had such simple European diversions as a casino and a bowling alley," was a complaint heard frequently in the farm country of the Middle West. Whenever a group of refugees happened to settle in the same neighborhood, they foregathered, with pathetic eagerness and regularity, to spend the evening with the flowing bowl and in singing German student songs.[5] A German farmer in Indiana complained about the American farm diet, and contrasted the habits of American farm women with those of his spouse to the great disadvantage of the former, but he suffered the crowning blow when neighbors mistook the little German "Garten Haus" which he had built on his premises, for a bird sanctuary.[6]

The recorded tales about Latin farmers are numerous. One of these intellectuals, to the utter amazement of his neighbors, made a chemical and microscopic analysis of the soil before he began digging holes for fence posts. Another, a musician, was seen milking his cows in a dress suit. Others spent much of their time hunting game, and ended in

bankruptcy, or were forced to hire out as day laborers at fifty cents a day.[7]
There is the story of a Latin farmer who settled with his wife in Michigan, and left a record of his five years on the farm. He had been an officer in the Austrian army and had joined the revolutionists in 1848.
In Michigan, he built a small frame house in the midst of the forest and succeeded, after much effort, in clearing twelve acres in a tract of eighty acres. His house had no lawn around it, and a plain board served as a sidewalk. A small vegetable garden, a cow and a few chickens were the farmer's main sources of support. Though always dressed in torn clothing and a red shirt, his neighbors referred to the German farmer as a man of distinguished bearing. The furniture in his house was typically German, and on the wall hung a Tyrolean hat, several maps, and two guns. Though a man of some means when he arrived in the United States, the farm was heavily mortgaged at 10 per cent, and the owner did all the work himself. Apparently the man and his wife, who once had known the cultural delights of Vienna and the art centers of Italy, bore their lot with stoic equanimity. Their only diversions from the daily monotony were spending Sundays in the woods, picking berries, or visiting a German farmer in the neighborhood. Very rarely friends dropped in for a game of whist, and were received with the graciousness of the old world salon, though the refreshments fell far short of European standards.[8]

Friedrich Kapp, after a tour of the West, which included Illinois, Wisconsin, and Texas, recorded his impressions of the Mississippi Valley region in an article written in 1852 but not published until 1876, after his return to Germany. After all proper allowance for exaggerations, emphasis on the dramatic and the unusual, and the author's intention to make America less attractive to German immigrants, Kapp's account of the life of the Latin Farmers is revealing. In one of his most interesting passages he wrote of fellow countrymen and former companions in revolution whom he found in the woods and prairies—"a little professor of philosophy who spent far more of his life with Hegel's dialectic than in milking cows" and "whose fine white hands were too delicate for hard steel pens." They had become hard and gnarled from plowing and clearing the forest. "Not far away," the account continued, lived "the ambitious, political intriguer, who sought a career on the parliamentary rostrum and in the diplomatic salon, and who spent more time at the opera and the club than in forest or field," and had just shipped his first consignment of pork to New York. Still another, "a booted pretender of heroism and martyrdom, with an impudent, deceitful lawyer's mouth," declaimed to trees and fields how the world had ignored his talents, and played "the role of the stern Cato in his smock." "All these fragments and remnants of the Palatine, Baden and Saxon uprising," Kapp concluded, "these law-givers, dictators, provisional governors and regents, ministers, civil commissioners, triumvirs, generals and staff officers—in what forests and blockhouses have they found asylum, where have they settled and where are they living out their monotonous lives? They wished it so, and they are disintegrating of and by themselves."[9]

Johann Michael Scheffelt, a German farmer and brewer, who lost his property because of his activity in the legislature of Baden and the Parliament of Frankfurt, settled on a farm near Buffalo in 1849, and died within four years of his arrival in the United States.[10] Emil Rothe, a native of Silesia who had studied law in several universities and was a leader in the revolution in Breslau, came to New York in 1849, and bought a small farm and orchard near West Hoboken, New Jersey, where he planted peach trees and tried to raise vegetables and tobacco. Unsuccessful in the East, he tried again in Wisconsin, where his farming venture proved equally discouraging. Like many others, he eventually returned to the practice of law, became the publisher of the *Watertown Weltbürger,* and after the Civil War edited a German paper in Cincinnati, and was elected the first president of its German Literary Club.[11] Lorenz Brentano, temporary head of the provisional government of Baden in 1849, spent nine years on a farm near Kalamazoo, Michigan, and then, like Rothe, moved to the city to resume his practice and to enter the field of journalism.

There was a substantial number of Latin Farmers among Wisconsin's Forty-eighters. Here land was fertile and cheap, heavily wooded and well supplied with water, and railroad and steamship lines recruited immigrants for the state, and a state commissioner of immigration maintained offices in New York. Among the settlers along Lake Michigan, north of Milwaukee, there was a former burgomaster of Meiningen, to whose farm the Germans of the city came in considerable numbers during the hunting season to shoot game. We have an account of a bearded German doctor who lived on a farm near Milwaukee, drove to the city twice a week in an old upholstered buggy brought from Berlin, performed well

on the violin, and had his bookshelves well stocked with Goethe and
other German authors.[12]

Karl Theodor Bayerhoffer, freethinker and professor of philosophy at
Marburg, who fled to Switzerland after 1848, farmed near Monroe, Wisconsin, for seventeen years, and then moved to the prairie in Illinois.
Here he lectured to his farmer neighbors, contributed to Harris' *Journal
of Speculative Philosophy,* and published a treatise on "The Nature of
the Universe, and the Laws of Humanism, Represented from the Standpoint of Reason." He also was a frequent contributor to German newspapers on such subjects as labor and women's rights, and engaged in
violent arguments with Heinzen about communism and socialism.[13] Hans
Balatka was a farmer in Wisconsin before he moved to Milwaukee to
pursue a career as a musician and director of orchestras and choruses.
Sheboygan County attracted a number of Latin Farmers. Carl von Brause,
a freethinking rebel from the Palatinate, lived in Manitowoc and built
a home in what was known as "Phantom Hollow." Wilhelm Wagner,
who lost his pastorate in 1849, and escaped a jail sentence by crossing
the border into Switzerland, arrived in New York in 1851 and bought
120 acres west of Monroe, Wisconsin, where he lived with a friend in a
primitive little blockhouse.[14] The Milwaukee *Gradaus,* in 1858, described
German farming communities in Wisconsin where stumps still stood
in the village street, but where discussions in the taverns were on a high
intellectual level, and singing societies rehearsed regularly. It was not an
uncommon experience when travelers stopped to water their horses at
a farmer's house in the German areas of Wisconsin to find the owner
playing a piano, or to be greeted by a bespectacled farmer who could
quote Latin.[15]

Wilhelm Laer, trained for the legal profession in Germany, tried farming in Southern Ohio, and gave lectures in the Shakespeare Hotel in
New York on "The Attitude of the Farmer toward the Social Question."[16]
A group of Latin farmers in Wood County, Ohio, which included professional men involved in the German Revolution, failed in their efforts
to maintain a quasi-communistic community.[17] Ludwig von Baumbach,
an author of ability, farmed in Ohio before moving to Milwaukee.[18]
Eduard Rapp, who had been director of a school in Germany and an
active participant in the Revolution, spent his first ten years in the United
States on a farm in Cuyahoga County, Ohio.[19] Karl Tafel, the son of a

court official in Stuttgart, and a student at Tübingen, left for America after the Revolution. In Cincinnati, in 1849, he met the daughter of Ferdinand Friedrich Autenreich of Stuttgart, and the two were married. Although trained as an apothecary, Tafel decided to try his hand at farming. He and a theological student from Esslingen bought adjoining plots of heavily forested and uncleared land, about twelve miles from Sandusky on the Portage River, and into this Ohio wilderness Tafel took his bride in the dead of winter, 1851. Their carriage became stuck in the muddy road, and the pair completed their bridal journey to their new home in a manure wagon. On their arrival, they found their little one-room house filled with smoke and chickens, which had come through a broken window. There were several Germans from Esslingen in the neighborhood, and one had a piano. In typical Latin farmer fashion, Tafel worked in the fields, in dress coat and top hat, and met with neighbors as often as possible to sing German student songs. Before the end of the first year, Tafel sold his place and moved to Indiana for a second attempt at farming, and with little more success. During the Civil War, he took his family to Louisville, where he became a successful pharmacist, the profession for which he had been trained.[20]

Johann Friedrich Gottlob Lange, a native of Halle, a freethinker and a veteran of the fighting in Berlin in 1848, after several unsuccessful ventures in New York and Milwaukee, settled on a farm near Bloomington, Illinois.[21] A number of Forty-eighters were absorbed into the older German Latin settlement in Belleville, where Hecker, "the Romantic of the Revolution," found new thrills like Cincinnatus of old in following the plow, breeding fine horses and cattle, and making excellent wine. Some of his fellow refugees referred to him as "a handsome ruin," but Hecker ignored the disparaging comments of "the little Dantons and Robespierres," refused to become embroiled in their "fruitless journalistic bouts," and urged his countrymen to forget the past and settle down to hard labor as he had done. On numerous occasions, vagabonds and frauds, posing as political exiles, sought the hospitality of his farm and consumed his substance.[22] Hecker loved to be photographed as the modern Cincinnatus at the plow, and his picture appeared on the front page of the German edition of *Leslie's Weekly,* but even the most famous of the Latin Farmers could not balance his budget from farming alone. On several occasions he abandoned his bucolic retirement for extended lecture tours or political campaigns. In his spare time, he published a biographical sketch of Thomas Paine and a German translation of his *Rights of Man,* and lectured throughout the country, for an admission charge of fifty cents, on such topics as "Lincoln and Cromwell"; "Our Republic, Its Critics and Opponents"; "Woman's Rights Movement" (which he opposed); "The Culture of the Aztecs"; "American Railroad Monopolies"; and "A Summer in the Rockies."[23]

Six veteran officers from the Schleswig-Holstein crisis of 1848 settled on the Iowa prairie, and built a large house near Davenport, where the group apparently spent more time in argumentation, hunting, singing, and convivial drinking than in the cultivation of the soil. Needless to add, their venture ended in failure. One of the partners moved to a farm in Missouri, and later served in the Civil War and in the Nebraska legislature. Another became a deputy county surveyor, and still another edited a German paper in New Orleans. A number of veterans of the Danish War worked as day laborers on Iowa farms. Carl Rotteck, a veteran of the Baden Revolution, tried farming in Iowa before turning to journalism. Jacob Kroeger, a Lutheran minister involved in the Revolution, alternated farming in Iowa with preaching in Wheeling. Albert Wolff, a Forty-eighter from Brunswick, and a former student of theology at Göttingen, who was arrested in Dresden in 1849 for street fighting, settled in Minnesota in 1852. After two years of futile struggle on a farm in Carver County, Minnesota, Wolff moved to St. Paul to edit a German paper. Franz Bacherl, a Bavarian dramatist, came later than most Forty-eighters, although for the same reasons, and with his daughter lived in a sod house in Nebraska before moving to Columbus, Nebraska, where he became a schoolteacher.[24]

Texas attracted a surprisingly large number of Forty-eighters. Although, as a rule, immigrants shunned the South, German colonization societies had manifested an interest in this area before 1848, and Texas was known to many Germans before the political refugees of 1848 began to settle there. Communities such as Sisterdale and New Braunfels retain a strong German cultural flavor in this day. Börne, Texas, was founded by Forty-eighter Latin farmers and named after Ludwig Börne, the German patriot and writer; and Blum Hill, settled in 1855, bore the name of Robert Blum, the martyr of 1848. Washington County, whose population was greatly augmented by German refugees after 1848, had one farming community known as Latium and another known as Berlin.[25]

Eduard Degener, son of a Brunswick banker and a member of the Frankfurt Parliament, settled on a farm in New Braunfels in 1850. He was the first German to represent Texas in the United States Congress, sat in one of the Texas constitutional conventions, and lost two sons in the Union Army during the Civil War.[26] Julius Dresel, a native Rhinelander, son of a well-to-do wine merchant, and a student of history and literature at Heidelberg, was another political exile on a farm near New Braunfels, where he wrote essays, poems, and sonnets whose main theme was homesickness for Germany. Oskar von Roggenbucke, a major who resigned his commission in the Prussian army in 1848, lived on a farm near Comfort, Texas.[27] Lieutenant Leopold Biesele, a veteran of the revolution in Baden, came to Texas with his bride in 1850, and built his blockhouse on a nine-acre farm. Unlike most Latin Farmers, he prospered and gradually increased his holdings to five hundred acres. Florian Mördes, another veteran of the Baden uprising, settled near New Braunfels. After his death, his widow returned to Vienna and married Julius Fröbel.[28]

In 1852, in Sisterdale, German farmers came from a thirty-mile radius to meetings of a Freethinkers' Society, to sit under a clump of trees and listen to rationalist disputations and lectures on St. Simon and Fourier.[29] *Der Republikaner,* a German weekly, was published in Börne as late as the 1880's.[30] In Comal County, German farmers supported an agricultural and horticultural society as early as 1852, and imported trees and shrubs from abroad. A *Reform Verein* met regularly in Fredericksburg, at least as early as 1854, to discuss agricultural problems and to subscribe for publications in that field.[31]

Such items suggest the persistence of intellectual activity and cultural interests even among the primitive conditions of a raw Texas frontier. A member of the American boundary commission which drew the Mexican-United States boundary encountered a Texas German who had been a professor of natural history, spoke English well, and had a library of two thousand volumes in a house which had no glass in its windows, and beds stuffed with straw.[32] Ernst Kapp, a Ph.D. from Bonn, and a political refugee, spent sixteen years on a fifty-acre farm in Texas before returning to Germany in 1865, was president of the "Freier Verein" of Sisterdale in 1853, cleared the forest with his own hands, learned cabinet-making and the blacksmith trade and how to build wagons, and is remembered as one of the early geographers of Texas. In 1850, he wrote his brother: "Books and cultural means we have plenty. If I appear at this time to think only of cattle, corn, fence-rails and similar interests, I do not forget . . . the spiritual that lies in material things, as cultural matériel . . ."[33]

Frederick Olmsted, famous traveler whose references to the Forty-eighters whom he encountered on the farms of Texas have been frequently quoted, described houses of Latin farmers, who had "Madonnas on log walls," drank "coffee in tin cups upon Dresden saucers," played the piano well, and had bookcases "half-filled with classics, half with sweet potatoes."[34] After supper, neighbors for miles around gathered at these frontier homes to play the piano, listen to German classical music, waltz with their women, and sing the songs of their student days.

"In Texas," wrote Fröbel, "I have met former German farmers, officers and professors following the oxen and the plow, and I have found them unwilling to exchange their present occupation for their former positions." Their fortitude elicited his profound admiration, and he concluded that despite, or perhaps because of, incredible hardships, they had grown in moral stature.[35] The careers of many political refugees who were foolhardy enough to believe that no special skill was required to succeed as a farmer had no such happy ending, but wherever Latin farmers settled, they were an object of curiosity for their neighbors, and a cultural leaven for the American frontier.

FOOTNOTES

Chapter 9

1. Carl Wittke, "The America Theme in Continental European Literatures," in *Mississippi Valley Historical Review*, XXVIII, No. 1 (June, 1941) pp. 3-26.

2. See Gert Göbel: *Länger als ein Menschenleben in Missouri* (St. Louis, 1877).

3. Edith Lenel: *Friedrich Kapp*, pp. 75-76.

4. Wagner and Scherzer: *Reisen in Nord Amerika*, II, pp. 424-25.

5. *Atlantische Studien* (Göttingen, 1853) I, p. 44.

6. *Ibid.*, I, pp. 47-48.

7. Richter: *Geschichte der Stadt Davenport*, p. 567.

8. *Der Deutsche Pionier*, XI, No. 6 (Sept. 1879) pp. 214-16.

9. See Friedrich Kapp: *Aus und über Amerika* (Berlin 1876) I, pp. 291-306.

10. *Wächter am Erie*, Nov. 24, 1853, *Westbote*, Dec. 2, 1853.

11. Heinrich A. Rattermann: "Die Erinnerung an Emil Rothe," in *Deutsch-Amerikanische Geschichtsblätter*, XI (Oct. 1911) No. 4, pp. 222-40.

12. Wagner and Scherzer: *Reisen in Nord Amerika*, II, pp. 122-23.

13. W. A. Fritsch: "Karl Theodor Bayerhoffer," in *Americana Germanica*, V, pp. 19-25.

14. *Deutsch-Amerikanische Geschichtsblätter* IV (April 1904) pp. 5-19.

15. *Westbote*, Aug. 5, 1858. See also, William Whyte: "Chronicles of Early Watertown" in *Wisconsin Magazine of History*, IV (1920-21) pp. 287-314; and Joseph Schafer: "The Yankee and Teuton in Wisconsin," *Ibid.*, VII (1923-24) pp. 3-21.

16. *New Yorker Staatszeitung*, April 18, 1853.

17. *Der Deutsche Pionier*, XV, No. 8 (Nov. 1883) p. 312.

18. *Ibid.*, XV, No. 9 (Dec. 1883) pp. 355-56.

19. *Ibid.*, XV, No. 6 (Sept. 1883) p. 255.

20. See "Latin Farmers in Northwestern Ohio," edited by Leonard Koester, in *Northwest Ohio Quarterly* (Summer 1949) XXI, No. 3, pp. 113-19.

21. *Deutsch-Amerikanische Geschichtsblätter*, II (Oct. 1902) pp. 39-40.

22. *New Yorker Staatszeitung*, Oct. 12, 1858; *Westbote*, Dec. 30, 1852.

23. See *Westbote*, March 23, 1849; Dec. 20, 1850; *Wächter am Erie*, Aug. 24, 1871; March 5, 1873; Nov. 12, 1874; March 1, 1875.

24. *Wächter am Erie*, March 24, 1869.

25. See R. L. Biesele: *The History of the German Settlements in Texas, 1831-1861* (Austin, 1930) pp. 56-57, 60, 63. Hereafter cited Biesele: *Germans in Texas*.

26. *Der Deutsche Pionier*, II, No. 1 (March 1870) pp. 10-11; Rütenick: *Deutsche Vorkämpfer*, pp. 287-89.

27. *Der Deutsche Pionier*, XV, No. 8 (Nov. 1883) p. 335.

28. Amand Gögg: *Ueberseeische Reisen* (Zurich 1888) pp. 136-37.

29. Kapp: *Aus und über Amerika*, I, p. 287.

30. Gögg: *op. cit.*, p. 141.

31. Biesele: *Germans in Texas*, p. 208-9.

32. *Westbote*, Nov. 29, 1850.

33. Quoted in S. W. Geiser: "Dr. Ernst Kapp, Early Geographer in Texas," in *Field and Laboratory* (Jan. 1946) XIV, No. 1, pp. 16-31.

34. Frederick L. Olmsted: *A Journey through Texas; or a Saddle Trip on the Southwestern Frontier* (New York, 1857) p. 430.

35. Julius Fröbel: *Die Deutsche Auswanderung und ihre Culturhistorische Bedeutung* (Leipzig, 1858) p. 16.

Chapter 10 · *FREETHINKERS AND*
PERSONAL LIBERTY

THE GERMAN immigration of the middle nineteenth century included large numbers of Lutherans and Catholics and smaller groups of other denominations, and among the Forty-eighters there were many who had affiliated actively with organized religion in the fatherland, and continued their church connections in the United States. But the group which attracted the greatest attention, and provoked the heated controversies of the 1850's, was composed of the intellectual radicals who described themselves as rationalists, materialists, and freethinkers. The hostility and concern which they aroused among older Americans, and especially among church people and members of the clergy, was one basic reason for the nativist desire to restrict immigration from Europe in the decade preceding the Civil War.

The German rationalist revolt against supernaturalism, clericalism, and dogmatism stemmed from the writings of such well-known figures in the history of philosophy as Hegel, Feuerbach, Bruno Bauer, and Arnold Ruge, and produced a radical movement which reverberated through Protestant and Catholic ranks alike. It found its most vigorous expression in the *Freimännervereine* (free men's societies) and *Freie Gemeinde* (free congregations) organized first in Germany and later imported into the United States. Their principles varied from agnosticism to avowed atheism, and from militant anticlericalism to more moderate programs which have a certain similarity with the more liberal Protestant faiths of the present day, such as Unitarianism, Universalism, liberal Congregationalism, or the community churches which profess no specific creed. The rationalist revolt of the German freethinkers never penetrated the German masses, here or abroad, to the point where it became part of the life and spirit of the German people, but in the United States the radicals of the German immigration were strong enough to challenge the long-venerated traditions and tenets of American Puritanism.

There were a few German freethinking societies and congregations in the larger American cities in the early 1840's, and certain leaders of the German immigration of the 1830's were identified with the rationalist movement. But its greatest stimulus and support came from the refugees of 1848, many of whom combined political and economic radicalism with a materialist philosophy which opposed all theological systems, creeds, dogmas, supernaturalism, and revelation, and regarded church rituals as unworthy of intelligent, thinking men. The fact that the church in Germany generally had supported the police state and the throne, and had helped to crush the Revolution, was a major factor in the violent anti-clerical attitude of many Forty-eighters. In America the rationalist movement infiltrated the Turner societies, and furnished scores of able journalists whose papers, however short-lived, disseminated the radical doctrines among German readers, and alarmed Americans by the belligerence and tactlessness with which they challenged sacred religious and social customs of the Republic. The extreme anti-clerical wing of the Forty-eighters made friendly relations of the Germans as a whole with their American neighbors more difficult, and produced bitter divisions among the Germans themselves. Freethinking journals like the *Antipfaff* of St. Louis were as rabid in their attacks on Lutherans as they were against Roman Catholics.[1]

To describe precisely the views of the Forty-eighter rationalist group is most difficult, for some were avowed atheists, others deists, or humanists, and still others expounded a rather vague pantheism. Some were out-and-out materialists, others favored organizations similar to the present-day Ethical Culture Society, and believed one could foster the good life without special reference to a creator. In the heat of battle, all were labeled "infidels" and "atheists," and neither Americans nor Germans made nice distinctions. It is a mistake to say German radicals were indifferent to religion; they were too much concerned with it. Many Forty-eighters devoted far more time and energy to religious questions than their American neighbors devoted to their churches.

The rationalist tradition derived from Lucretius, Descartes, Bacon, and Spinoza, and Forty-eighters heard it debated in the universities during their study of Kant, Hegel, Fichte, Schilling, and Lessing. They read Ludwig Feuerbach's attacks on all supernatural religion, and many were impressed with David Strauss's stress on Christianity as a social gospel, stripped of all revelation, dogma, and creed. In the field of science, Karl Vogt, Jakob Moleschott, Ludwig Büchner, and Alexander von Humboldt were their teachers, and in their books they found the scientific basis for their philosophy of materialism. Many Forty-eighters regarded themselves as the heirs of the "Enlightenment," and the apostles of historic rationalism. In the United States they volunteered for a German-American *Kulturkampf* against Puritanism which would confront "the dogmas of priestcraft" with their enlightened humanism.

Freethinkers believed in the potentialities of man. They asked for no intervention from a supernatural force. They accepted all the implications of the concept of evolution, the perfectibility of man, and "enlightened progress," along the road of philosophy and reason, and the more extreme hoped to build the new order "on the ruins" of Christianity. They stressed man's duty to question, investigate, and doubt what he could not understand, and believed with Heinzen, one of the most consistent of the group, that "not faith, but doubt . . . is the divining rod of truth."[2]

Christian Esselen defined his philosophy as "the practice of truth." He admitted that, like the marbles of ancient Greece or the verse of Homer, Christianity would remain a part of human culture, but he foresaw the time when it would be studied in the universities as present-day men learn from their professors about Plato, Socrates, Confucius, and Mohammed. He rejected dogma, authority, faith, and a personal God, and denounced every form of spiritual tyranny over the minds of men by priests and religions.[3] Others advocated a religion of humanism to transcend the divisive forces of nationalities, states, churches, and social groups, and make men brothers of one human family, living in a social order of liberty, equality, and fraternity. The ultimate philosophical goal of the humanists was harmony—harmony between rulers and ruled, capital and labor, rich and poor, the superstitious and the emancipated thinker, the rational approach to social problems, and a universal empire of eternal peace.

Eduard Schröter, an honest and noble spirit who was one of the most active leaders of the German freethinkers, defined his position as follows:

"The freethinker has a book of revelation older than the Bible, Koran, Vedas, Zendavesta. It is the book of Nature and of World History. It belongs to no sect, but is free for all. In it mankind learns to read; from it man draws all knowledge that leads him to happiness in the heaven on this earth. . . . All that is required is to make a proper use of his five senses and to use his Human Reason, to study Nature and its laws and to serve it; to analyze everything—all events—in their natural source and origin, and in their natural activity." Although Schröter's humanism acknowledged an infallible creator, mankind was to be completely emancipated from "popes, fathers of the church, saints, the Bible, papal bulls and encyclicals."[4]

Heinzen's views represent another variety of the philosophy of the freethinkers. He was the most logical champion of materialism, and his violent encounters with fellow radicals forced him to define his position with unusual care and clarity. Though born a Catholic, Heinzen rejected not only transcendentalism in every form, but all suggestion of a "will to create." All that is, he contended, is the result of natural processes, and what men call "spirit" stems from man's nervous and physiological structure. He regarded psychology as a purely experimental science based on physiology, and rejected metaphysics altogether. He emphasized the laws of nature, the eternity of the universe, the inevitability of never-ending change, man as the product of his environment, and mind the highest function of matter. Heinzen's faith was in science, and he believed that "a microscope or a new chemical element can upset a whole philosophical system." In history he found no divine process, only a law of change and progress. Heinzen regarded man's moral sense as a product of his material environment, and the human spirit, like everything else in the universe, a product of materialistic evolution. He used the word "God" only in the sense that "God is the world, and the world is God," and admitted that his mind could not grasp the concept of eternity. By leaving a wide margin of choice to the human will, he introduced a measure of idealism into his materialist doctrines. Heinzen opposed every form of religious cosmogony, and attacked all organized religion and churches with savage vigor, reserving his sharpest blasts, however, for the Catholic hierarchy. Since the "self-conscious mind" of man was for him the acme of life, and the basis for man's freedom and rational processes,

Heinzen believed all religions founded on faith and authority must be destroyed.

Having disposed of God, religion, and priests with Olympian invective, Heinzen, like other so-called freethinkers, proceeded to enunciate his own stern code of personal conduct, based on the search for truth, beauty, justice, and human happiness. He described human love as "the most beautiful relation in life," and he urged men to strive for harmony with themselves and their fellows, in a spirit of liberty and truth. Happiness was not a matter of selfish indulgence of the senses, but depended upon a severe code of ethics and morals. He admitted that he knew radicals with less honor and principle than "popes and despots." He denounced vice and self-indulgence, and in one of his best lectures remarked, "The coarse atheist ranting in the beer house against religion, and believing that in this cheap way he is initiated into true human society," is as bad as the religious fanatic with his miracles and prayer wheels.[5]

Men of such positive views did not feel intellectually at home in an America which some described as a "primeval forest of churches and dogma." They resolved to turn the light of German art, science, and philosophy on the dark night of American Puritanism, and refused to compromise with American bigotry. They would remold their adopted country according to the enlightened European pattern, and end the "materialism and corruption" of the United States. A German observer wrote in 1853 that in America, "the dictates of the Bible and the creed of the New Testament have not yet been superseded by philosophical and socialistic schools and critiques." Here every church and sect violently opposed "the newer German philosophy"; the term "infidel" was applied alike to Jew, Turk, pagan, philosopher, atheist, and socialist; and the "tyranny of public custom and morals" was "enforced by a legion of priests." Gentlemen were expected to belong to a church, medieval oaths were imposed in the courts, legislative bodies opened their sessions with prayer, proclamations bristled with references to the deity, and blue laws took the joy out of Sunday.[6] Freedom of religion, in short, seemed to mean only freedom for religious sects and denominations to carry on their special form of idolatry, leaving no place for the "honest infidel."

Heinzen labored to plant the leaven of radicalism in the American body politic, shake the Germans out of their mental lethargy, and provide the necessary antidote "for the intellecutal knownothingism" of the

United States.[7] Hassaurek and Kapp made no distinction between simple Christianity and the theology and traditions of Puritanism, and regarded both as rank hypocrisy. The sudden craze for spiritualism and "spirit rappings," papers like the New York *Spiritual Telegraph,* and the advertisements of mediums and clairvoyants, confirmed the need for enlightenment and intellectual emancipation. "If the choice is between Puritanism and Catholicism, the latter is the more human and liberal," wrote the Forty-eighter who edited the Cleveland *Wächter am Erie.*[8] American Puritanism, Esselen insisted, is a "darker force" than in Cromwell's day, for it opposes not only the Catholic Church, but all philosophy, natural science, and progress, and anything else which it chooses to label as "unbelief."[9] For the dissemination of their message of emancipation and enlightenment, German freethinkers resorted to the lecture platform, the German language press, the publication of pamphlets and books, and the organization of free men's societies and freethinking congregations, which they hoped eventually to unite in a national body to meet annually in national convention.

The German immigration, ever since 1815, had included opponents of the sectarian spirit prevailing in the United States. Gustave Körner, in his well-known volume on the German element before 1848, described German freethinking groups in Philadelphia with their own "free thought" papers, such as J. G. Wesselhöft's *Alt und Neue Welt* (1834), L. A. Wollenweber's *Der Freisinnige* (The Free Thinker) (1838), and Samuel Ludvigh and F. W. Thomas' *Der Wahrheitssucher* (The Truth Seeker) (1839). New York had a *Vernunftsgläubiger* (Rationalist) as early as 1838, and Friedrich Münch contributed regularly to Eduard Mühl's *Lichtfreund* (Friend of Light) in Hermann, Missouri. There were several free congregations in Milwaukee before 1848, of which perhaps the best known was Heinrich Ginal's "Die der Wahrheit geweihte Halle" (The Hall dedicated to Truth), an organization founded by the former Lutheran pastor in Philadelphia.[10] The famous *Zions Gemeinde* of Baltimore represented the same tradition during the pastorate of Heinrich Scheib. Johann Bernhard Stallo, an immigrant of 1839 and a leader of the Cincinnati Germans, was active in the legal battle to keep Bible reading and hymn singing out of the public schools. In New York a "free Catholic" congregation, founded in 1846 by a former Franciscan, braved the relentless opposition of Bishop Hughes.

The *Freimännervereine,* organized by refugees of the German Revolution of 1848, were both more radical and more numerous than these earlier prototypes. We cannot be sure where the Forty-eighters established their first freethinking society, but one of the earliest was the organization in Cincinnati, promoted by Friedrich Hassaurek, who edited the violently anticlerical *Hochwächter,* in which he combated not only orthodoxies and hierarchies, but also the indifference and stupidity of his fellow Germans. In 1852 he engaged in public debates with Wilhelm Nast, the founder of German Methodism, and the following year argued for eight nights with a Methodist minister about the morality and rationality of Christianity, in a hall overflowing with German listeners.[11] The next year the Cincinnati *Freimännerverein* was able to provide its own hall, promote a series of evening and Sunday lectures and debates, support a singing and dramatic section, a mutual insurance society, and a special auxiliary for women.

The Cleveland *Freimännerbund,* organized in the early 1850's, had a membership of two hundred,[12] and supported a gymnastic program similar to that of the Turner, dramatic entertainments, and a German-English school. At least twice each week the members assembled for debating, and the organization celebrated the anniversaries of the birthday of Thomas Paine, and the death of Robert Blum, with great ceremony. St. Louis had a similar organization in 1851. A Milwaukee society was founded in June 1852 or 1853, probably following a lecture by Hassaurek, and within a year merged with the Workers' Educational and Reading Club. Peter Engelmann was its first president and Hans Balatka acted as secretary. In 1854 Bernhard Domschke, another political refugee, came from Boston to direct its program.

The *Freie Gemeinde* of Sauk City, Wisconsin, was incorporated in 1852, and the next year began meeting in its own building, built on land deeded by Agoston Haraszthy, a Hungarian humanist and freethinker who departed for California in 1849. Sauk City was a "freethinkers' heaven"; the congregation had a healthy growth under Eduard Schröter, its "speaker" for more than thirty years, and his *Humanist* circulated among twenty similar organizations. Leaders of free thought, like Franz Sigel, Heinzen, and Robert G. Ingersoll, spoke in the hall at Sauk City, and members buried their dead in a special "freethinkers' cemetery" in an adjoining village.[13] Schröter's congregation welcomed all who wished to unite "in truth and love," including Jews, Protestants, and Catholics. An orthodox Jew, commenting on conditions in Wisconsin in 1856, complained that so many Jews "became a prey to the Atheists."[14]

In New York, Rudolf Dulon, Karl Schramm, and Franz Schmitt, another veteran of the Frankfurt Parliament, were pioneers among the German freethinkers. Dulon, who had been a pastor in Bremen and Magdeburg, and especially active in organizing educational societies for workers, published several radical sheets in 1848, and was arrested in Hanover in 1851. Two years later he arrived in New York, where his name already was well known to the German group. He delivered public lectures at the Shakespeare Hotel and elsewhere, and edited a paper whose pantheistic leanings aroused the opposition of several journalists who were atheists.[15] About 150 responded to Dulon's call for the organization of a free congregation, with Joseph Fickler as president. Dulon proved to be a tactless and dictatorial leader, however, and resigned after a year of factional strife.[16]

Nikolaus Schmitt, another veteran of the Frankfurt Parliament, was the first president of the free congregation in Philadelphia. The "Society of Free Men" of New Orleans was organized in 1853, and in the fall of 1855 a *Humanitäts Gemeinde* began meeting in the Odd Fellows Hall in the Crescent City, whose total German population at the time was approximately fifteen thousand. Professor Anton Füster, a Catholic refugee of the Vienna Revolution, was the first speaker of the Boston group.[17] In Buffalo, the leader of the free congregation published the anticlerical *Morgenröthe* (The Dawn).[18] Other societies were formed among the Germans of Indianapolis, Sandusky, Louisville, Toledo, Columbus, Detroit, Massillon, Chicago, Albany, Evansville, Pittsburgh, Baltimore, St. Louis, and Hermann, Missouri. German soldiers had their own "chaplains of atheism"[19] in the Civil War, and Gögg found traces of the influence of freethinking Forty-eighters in Texas as late as the 1880's.[20]

Leaders of German freethinking societies and congregations were known as "speakers" *(Sprecher)*. Some received a modest salary, others were unpaid. Among them were men of questionable training and character, clerical vagabonds expelled from regular congregations here or abroad, who tried to make a living by affiliating with the rationalists in the United States. The movement was never strong enough to support schools to train its own speakers, and therefore had to recruit from any available source. As a result, several organizations were victimized by ex-preachers who had left their former churches for reasons that were not reassuring, and a few revealed too great love for the bottle and the gambling table. Characters of such questionable background helped bring the whole rationalist movement into disrepute among church people.[21] On the other hand, many able and high-minded theologians had severed their regular church connections because of honest conflicts over dogmas and creeds, and were men of character, integrity, devotion, and keen intelligence.

Schröter, a seceder from both the Catholic and the Lutheran churches, and an exile since 1850, definitely belonged to the latter group. With tremendous energy, he labored in many sections of the United States to breathe new life into the rationalist movement, and at Sauk City he supplemented his meager salary of $150 a year as speaker by long hours on a farm. Alexander Loos, a native of Silesia, had studied theology in Breslau and been a village pastor and speaker of two free congregations in Germany. In 1852 he found the repressive atmosphere of Prussia intolerable and lost his last clerical post because of his liberal views. After a short interval as a teacher of languages and music, he became speaker of a free congregation in Philadelphia, and served the group with distinction for many years. Four years before his death in 1877, he published an English translation of Ludwig Büchner's *Materialism, Its History and Influence on Society*. Carl Lüdeking, a student of theology who attacked the German state church, came to America in 1851, and was appointed speaker of the free congregation in St. Louis. Here he conducted a progressive school, wrote extensively for Turner publications, and fought courageously for the rights of women. In 1869 he was a delegate to the congress of freethinkers in Naples.

In many respects, the most successful of the German "speakers" was Friedrich Schünemann-Pott. Born in Hamburg in 1826, reared in Holstein, and working as a baker's apprentice until a teacher persuaded his father that the young man's talents deserved greater opportunities, he finally was able to study theology at Marburg, and became an ardent follower of Feuerbach and David Strauss. In 1848 he clashed with the authorities because of his liberal sermons and was imprisoned for *lèse majesté*. Saved from deportation by Baron Ernst von Pott, who adopted him and gave him his name, Schünemann-Pott, as he was known hereafter, came to the United States in 1854. With his background as a leader of the rationalist movement and the founder of several free congregations in Germany, he had little difficulty in being chosen speaker of a similar group in Philadelphia. From that center he exercised a significant influence on the whole movement throughout the United States. He was a brilliant lecturer, and traveled widely. For twenty-one years he edited the *Blätter für freies religiöses Leben*. In addition to regular Sunday meetings, Schünemann-Pott's Philadelphia group maintained a singing society, a reading club, a library, a dramatic society, and a "free Sunday school." The congregation survived long enough to celebrate its fiftieth anniversary in its own hall, but in 1907 the group sold its property and combined with the *Sozialistische Liedertafel*. Joseph M. Reichard, a member of the Parliament of 1848, was its vice-president for many years.

The rise of freethinking organizations led to several attempts to unite the radical Germans in state or national congresses or federations. A call issued in 1853 by the Milwaukee *Arbeiter Bildungs und Leseverein*, the freethinker group, and August Willich's radical Turner club, to form a "league of free men," attracted delegates from twenty-three societies in Wisconsin. A central committee divided into five sections, with Forty-eighters as chairmen, dealt with civil rights, education, physical training, art, and mutual insurance societies.[22] The organization arranged a celebration of the birthday of Thomas Paine in January 1854, and publicized a platform which included, in addition to the familiar denunciations of dogma and ecclesiasticism, vigorous attacks on nativists and temperance fanatics, strong approval of the aims of organized labor, and free homesteads. Although launched with high hopes, the state federation of Wisconsin proved short-lived, and a similar attempt, originating in Texas, ended in complete failure.[23]

In 1854, in response to a call from Cleveland and Sandusky, representatives of radical German societies from Toledo, Sandusky, Massillon, Dayton, Hamilton, Akron, Columbus, and Cleveland met in the "Free Men's Hall" of Cincinnati. The delegates included Jakob Müller, Cleveland Forty-eighter, and Friedrich August Hobelmann, one of the most radical of the radicals. The "Platform of the Free Germans of Ohio" opposed the reading of the Bible and the recital of prayers in public schools and legislative bodies, and denounced legal oaths and Sunday closing laws. In addition, the group was strongly anti-slavery; called for the repeal of the fugitive slave law of 1850; favored free homesteads to be distributed regardless of color or citizenship; and advocated a new foreign policy, a ten-hour day, a mechanics lien law, public education, progressive inheritance taxes, and the abolition of capital punishment.[24] Five years later a "League of Free Congregations in North America" was organized by Schünemann-Pott, and in the same decade conventions were called in Indiana, Illinois, and Texas, but none achieved great success. Heinzen's League of Radicals, meeting in Philadelphia in 1876, attracted a handful of delegates from freethinking organizations, including the ever-faithful Schröter of Sauk City, but the League's last meeting, held in 1879, was attended by only twenty delegates,[25] although radical German groups continued to be active for a while longer. In 1908 Milwaukee still was listed as the headquarters of the "League of Free Congregations and Free-thinking Societies," but membership had declined to seven organizations and less than a thousand individuals.

The energies of most radicals were drained off into the political controversies of the Civil War Era, the abolitionist crusade, and the problems of reconstruction. The halls of the freethinkers in Cincinnati and St. Louis had to be sold, and factional strife wrecked other groups. Heinzen regarded the program of the Ohio Germans as too conservative, and labor leaders like Weitling considered the activities of freethinking societies as "mere recreation for capitalists" which diverted attention from more important issues. Schröter hated the communists; Hassaurek objected to paid speakers. Thus, although freethinkers, Turner, and other breeds of radicals agreed as to their prime objective, they never were able to coöperate harmoniously. Moreover, as an Ohio editor observed cynically in 1858, it was difficult to sustain interest in solely intellectual causes, without beer and cards.[26]

Freethinking societies believed freethinking churches fostered a new ecclesiasticism. A writer in 1853 pointed out that atheism had developed a priesthood no better than "the Dominicans of the Inquisition," ready to persecute those who deviated however slightly from their own brand of orthodox radicalism.[27] Some groups were victimized by dilettantes and charlatans, or suffered from the rapid turnover in leadership because of inadequate salaries. Speakers drifted into journalism, or back into regular pulpits. Moreover the radical program was largely negative—opposition to ecclesiastics—and agreement on positive issues was difficult to obtain. Yet many ideas first advocated in America by European radicals gradually became acceptable to a growing number of Americans, as the success of independent congregations, the Unitarians, the Ethical Culture movement, and the general decline of the Puritanism of earlier days abundantly testify, although there is no necessarily causal connection. In Davenport, Iowa, German Forty-eighters joined the Unitarian Society, and many of their descendants still belong to that liberal group.[28]

In their heyday, freethinking societies were interested in many activities. They founded rental libraries for the dissemination of radical literature, supported dozens of little journals, published tracts and books, and sponsored public lectures on an amazing variety of subjects. In 1871 the Conference of Freethinkers, desiring a textbook for its Sunday schools, commissioned the Swiss, H. M. Kottinger, to write the catechism of humanitarianism, known as *Leitfaden für den Unterricht in den Sonntags-Schulen freier Gemeinden,* and it was adopted and used from coast to coast.[29] Somewhat earlier, the Rev. E. W. Lindensmith published his *Kleiner Katechismus für Achtundvierziger Schnautzer* in Cleveland.

The Sunday lectures usually were held in halls decorated with banners and portraits, and in the absence of an altar, the speaker addressed his listeners from behind a table banked with flowers. No organ or instrumental music was permitted, and if the congregation sang at all, it used special songs about liberty, reason, brotherhood, and the dignity of man. The lecture series in Milwaukee, in 1853, included discourses on the ancient Greeks, geology, optics, comets, music, "The Relation of Theology and Natural Science," and "Jesus Regarded from the Political Standpoint," and the society was keenly interested in labor and political problems, including socialism. In 1853, the celebration of Paine's birthday attracted over six hundred persons of all nationalities in Milwaukee. The organization also sponsored social events, including the German May Festival. In Cleveland, the freethinkers permitted women to attend their meetings.[30] Great efforts were made to arouse an appreciation of Thomas Paine, his *Age of Reason* and *The Rights of Man,* and German radicals were convinced that the great patriot was neglected because priests objected to his religious views.[31] The freethinkers enthusiastically supported public education, and established interesting educational experiments known as "schools for free men," in St. Louis, Columbus, New York, and other cities, where they applied new theories of considerable pedagogical significance.

Unfortunately, as far as their American neighbors were concerned, the constructive program of freethinking Forty-eighters was almost completely overshadowed by the violence of their anti-clerical attacks. In the German-American *Kulturkampf* between "humanism and priestcraft" both sides were unnecessarily belligerent and frequently unfair. Friedrich Fratny's Milwaukee *Volksfreund,* for example, recommended that all Jesuits be hanged as traitors to the Republic. The attacks on Catholic papers like the Milwaukee *Flugblätter* of the 1850's were as vile and pornographic about the confessional, alleged priestly intrigues, and the immoralities of convents and nunneries as the most sensational anti-Catholic publications in the heyday of Knownothingism. Domschke, otherwise fairly balanced and scholarly, referred to Irishmen as "American Croats," "our natural enemies, not because they are Irishmen, but because they are the truest guards of the Papacy."[32] There were Forty-eighters who "out-knownothinged" the Knownothings in their anti-Catholic prejudices, and actually welcomed nativist attacks on Catholicism, on the theory that after the Catholic church had been disposed of, "there is time to attack Protestantism."[33] August Willich attacked the Roman Church in scurrilous terms; Kapp referred to the churches as *Pfaffenkasten* ("priest boxes"); and the St. Louis *Anzeiger des Westens* was perpetually exercised about the machinations of the Jesuits. Profane parodies of Scripture published in rationalist journals, and the unrestrained mockery of the sacred rituals of church people, indicated that the new rationalism was in danger of becoming a new form of bigotry.[34]

Cremation, still regarded by most Americans with horror, but specially favored by German radicals, became a source of violent controversy between freethinkers and church people, and the former's insistence upon their right to dispose of their dead in any way they wished provoked numerous public protests against what Americans described as "non-Christian burial." On one occasion, when the "Christian" neighbors of an "infidel" refused to help a sick man during a long illness, and apparently gloated over his sufferings as divine punishment for his unbelief, the Cleveland *Freimännerbund* voted him a weekly allowance.[35] In Cincinnati, the burial of the speaker of the *Freie Gemeinde,* a political refugee of Baden who had left the Catholic Church, provoked a storm in the public press. The corpse, inadvertently buried in a Catholic cemetery, was first removed by Catholics for reinterment in an unconsecrated spot, and then reburied by radicals according to their own ritual. A similar incident in Milwaukee attracted wide attention in the German-language press.[36]

Disturbances of this kind caused American journals such as the *North American Review* to express alarm about the "atheists or radicals" among the educated Germans, and to deplore the "irreligious influence of thousands of German infidels."[37] The Cleveland *Plain Dealer* referred regularly to "hair lipped, infidel red Republicans" and to Hassaurek as "horserack and infidel."[38] The *New York Tribune* regarded "skepticism and materialism" as one of the "bad effects of the German immigration," while the *Journal of Commerce* denounced "recently imported infidels" who indulged in orgies of drunkenness, published "devilish German papers," and desecrated the American sabbath.[39] In Louisville, a committee of Presbyterians resolved to "save the Germans," make them good Americans, and "through the various Christian churches make them into true Christians."[40] As late as 1866 the author of a pamphlet on Lawrence College, in Wisconsin, expressed alarm about "the flood of rationalism" from Europe, referred to the "beer-fogged skepticism" of the radical freethinkers, and appealed to enlightened Christians to unite against their unwholesome influence.[41]

The anticlericalism of the extremists provoked several outbreaks of violence. In St. Louis a German mass meeting resolved to march against a Jesuit monastery where a German was said to be held against his wishes, but fortunately the more stable element persuaded the hotheads to leave the matter to the law.[42] Other incidents, sensationally reported in the press, cannot be verified, but without question the worst disturbance occurred in Cincinnati, during the visit of the papal nuncio, Archbishop Gaetano Bedini, in 1853.

To radical Forty-eighters the name Bedini was anathema, not only because of his high position as a prince of the church, but because they believed he had played a major rôle in suppressing the revolutions in Italy in 1848 and supporting the Austrian reaction, and he was specifically charged with responsibility for one of the executions in Bologna in 1849. When the Roman Curia resolved to send Bedini to the United States, violent demonstrations against the nuncio were probably unavoidable, in view of the many political refugees, including several prominent Italians, who had found asylum in America. Honored by church and state, Bedini made his way across the United States to Cincinnati, where the *Hochwächter,* owned by Hassaurek, already had alerted its readers in a fiery editorial, entitled "Thus far and no farther." The editorial, written by Hobelmann, a refugee who had published the *Frühlingsboten* in Bremen, reviewed Bedini's career, and called upon the freethinkers of Cincinnati to demonstrate against the "Bloodhound of Bologna." On Christmas day the *Freimännerverein* of Cincinnati, eight hundred to a thousand strong, marched on the residence of the archbishop where the nuncio was a guest, carrying banners and transparencies inscribed with "Down with Bedini," "No Papacy," and "Liberty, Equality, Fraternity."[43] Strangely enough, the Turner had refused to join the procession. Arriving before the archbishop's residence, the paraders set up a terrific noise, and exhibited an effigy of the nuncio, strung up on a gallows. Suddenly a squad of heavily armed policemen arrived on the scene. According to the German version of the incident, Irish police provoked a fight. Shots were fired, one man was killed, others injured, and a number were arrested, including innocent bystanders, whereupon the crowd beat a hasty retreat. Hassaurek, regarded as a prime instigator of the trouble, was arrested the next day. His *Hochwächter* insisted that the police provoked the shooting and cited the presence of two hundred women in the parade to prove its peaceful intent. When Archbishop Purcell offered a contribution for the injured, the *Freimännerverein* spurned his gift with another violent attack on Jesuitism.[44]

Reports of the incident spread through the German-language press, and anti-Bedini meetings were held in Milwaukee and other cities; Louisville raised a defense fund for the Germans under arrest,[45] and an effigy of Bedini was carried through the streets and finally dumped into barrels of burning tar.[46] The *New Yorker Staatszeitung* characterized the mayor of Cincinnati as the "tool of the priests" and held him responsible for ordering out the police, though it seems that he was out of the city at the time of the disturbance.[47] Conservative papers like the *Westbote* denounced the incident as the work of wild extremists, and were particularly incensed because the demonstration had been planned for the Christmas season.[48] It is interesting to note that in the end all prosecutions were dropped, and some five thousand nativists later burned Bedini in effigy without police interference.

Such demonstrations led to strong reactions among German church people. The Old Lutherans of Illinois, Michigan, Missouri, and other states were deeply offended, regarded the radical Forty-eighters as a menace to both church and state, and insisted that the preservation of Lutheranism was synonymous with the preservation of German culture in America. Philipp Schaff, in 1855, referred sarcastically to the "so-called educated immigrants, many of whom were floated over by the unsuccessful revolutions of the year 1848 and 1849 . . ." He detested rabid atheists and agnostics who undermined religious faith with science and education, and excoriated freethinking Forty-eighters as misguided and vicious individuals who were "not only estranged . . . from all Christianity and the Church, but even from all higher morality, and deserve rather to be called the pioneers of heathenism and a new barbarism than of civilization." "This godless German-American pest," he concluded, as manifested "in so many scurrilous political newspapers and tippling houses in all the larger cities," could only bring "reproach and shame" upon the whole German element.[49]

In Milwaukee and elsewhere in Wisconsin, freethinkers and German Catholics locked horns in furious encounters. On the side of the radicals were the freethinking societies, such lodges as the Sons of Hermann, Schröter's *Humanist,* Fratny's *Volksfreund* and Schoeffler's *Banner;* on the side of the church were Bishop John Martin Henni, the Catholic hierarchy, and the Milwaukee *Seebote*.[50] When a Catholic paper in New York attacked the prominent revolutionary Germain Metternich as a "plain murderer,"[51] the *New Yorker Staatszeitung* appealed for funds to enable him to sue for libel. Ernst Violand and Carl Preussner, veterans of the Vienna revolution, and the former a renegade from Catholicism, were attacked as atheists.[52] A Detroit priest berated local German societies from his pulpit and denied the sacraments to parishioners who consorted with them.[53] In Cincinnati, the *Wahrheitsfreund* (Friend of Truth) founded by Father Henni, and probably the first German Catholic paper in the United States, attacked refugees "who sought to unite the holy cause of freedom with enmity toward the church."[54] Another Catholic writer, in the *Central Blatt and Social Justice,* referred to the "scorn and contempt" which refugees heaped upon men who "had remained untouched by what they pleased to call 'the great ideas of the time,' " obviously a reference to the unorthodox materialism of Moleschott and Büchner, the philosophy of Hegel, Feuerbach, and Strauss, and the radicalism of Weitling and Marx. "No other Catholic immigrants," the writer continued, "were so bitterly attacked by men of their own blood after coming to this country as those of the German tongue" and "only the German priest who had knowledge of the inroads upon the Catholic faith in the fatherland could appreciate the dangerous situation that resulted from the arrival of the Forty-eighters."[55] A Catholic missionary priest, reporting from Wisconsin to an archbishop in Vienna in 1852, referred to "the rotten elements" which had "stolen into this country" since 1848, and to the "followers of Hecker and Kossuth" as "most annoying and disgusting to Catholics."[56]

The Catholic leadership launched a vigorous counter-attack, built new parishes among the German Catholics, and provided them with German priests,[57] and their efforts were especially successful in the rural areas of Wisconsin and other midwestern states. The church helped newly arrived immigrants, and established additional parochial schools. In Louisville, the Catholics founded *Der Adler* to neutralize the "destructive tendencies" of Forty-eighters and their kind.[58] In St. Louis, the Jesuit, Father P. Martin Seidel, issued the weekly *Katholisches Sonntagsblatt,* later known as the *Herold des Glaubens,* to hold the line against Börnstein's radical *Anzeiger des Westens.* In Milwaukee, Dr. Joseph Salzmann started the *Seebote,* and attacked liberals and freethinkers as maliciously and tactlessly as the worst blasts against the Catholics from the radical *Banner* or *Volksfreund.* Salzmann referred regularly to Eduard Schröter as the "Wormser-Sauhirte."[59] Bishop Henni refused permission for a performance in St. Mary's Church of Haydn's *Creation* by the *Milwaukee Musikverein,* because the director and many members were freethinkers.

Franz Saler founded the German Catholic *Kalender, Hinkende Bote am Mississippi* in St. Louis in 1855, because devout Catholics regarded the more famous *Lehrer hinkende Bote* as an anti-Catholic almanac. Catholic Church papers were established in Buffalo, New York, Baltimore, Chicago, and Racine, and benevolent societies were organized to counteract the influence of German lodges. The *Central Verein* of German Roman Catholic Beneficial Societies, founded in Baltimore in 1855, included twenty-nine local groups in 1860, and expanded rapidly thereafter.

It advocated parochial schools, functioned as a mutual insurance society, and found homes for newly arrived immigrants. In summarizing the effects of the agitation of the freethinkers among the Forty-eighters, whom she regarded as "a destructive influence" and a "great power for agnosticism," a Catholic student of the period concluded that "the Providence of God utilized the irreligion of the Forty-eighter anti-clericals as a means to hasten a great Catholic cause."[60] However that may be, the rationalism of the Forty-eighters drove a sharp wedge between church and non-church people, and created a division among the German group which had political and other repercussions for several decades.

Regardless of their differences about religion, there was one issue on which the Germans united. They all opposed legislation to make Sunday a "day of gloom." The clash between the Continental Sunday, and the controversy over the right to drink beer whenever and wherever one wished, became an issue of fundamental personal liberty for the entire German element, and Forty-eighters were among the most vocal opponents of temperance legislation and blue laws.

In 1839 Michael Chevalier had written, "Nothing is . . . more melancholy than the seventh day in this country; after such a Sunday the Labour of Monday is a delightful pastime."[61] "The Americans have arranged matters . . . so that the rest of Sunday is the rest of the tomb," commented Karl Theodor Griessinger, a revolutionary of 1848, after five years in the United States. "Everywhere," he continued, "you will find pleasure places closed, restaurants, theatres, shops shut tight, all means of communication halted, all the streets empty, the whole city a cemetery. . . . On no other day, at no other hour, does the German feel more deeply that he is a stranger in a strange land, and always will remain a foreigner. . . . Six days shalt thou labor in the sweat of thy brow, and on the seventh shalt thou drink lager to thine heart's content, but secretly, and by theft, like a thief in the night . . ."[62] Frederika Bremer, a Scandinavian, made similar comments during her visit to the Northwest in 1850.[63] In New York, police broke up a party of French and Germans who were drinking wine and playing whist on Sunday,[64] and in Williamsburg, a group of Turner, called "Hecker Boys," were arrested for singing on the Sabbath.[65] When he kept his Shakespeare Hotel open on Sunday, Eugen Lievre was charged with operating a disorderly house.[66] In St. Louis, where the Germans advertised their Sunday recreations in Börnstein's paper, the editor was summoned before a jury concerned with enforcing Sunday legislation, and when he refused to testify under oath, was held in contempt of court.[67] In Cleveland, German Turner, doing their setting-up exercises in the open air on Sunday and ordered by the police to leave, stubbornly insisted on their right to assemble in front of public buildings, as long as church people had the right to congregate inside.[68]

In the conflict with the Sabbatarians, Germans, Irish, French, and other immigrant groups stoutly defended their right to observe the Sabbath in the European manner. For them, Sunday was a time for dances, parades, theatricals, picnics, visits to beer gardens, and the outings of singing, sharpshooting, bowling, card and athletic clubs. Restaurants and bakeries were open; bands played in the Milwaukee beer gardens; and stout German burghers assembled "Over the Rhine" in Cincinnati on Sunday, to smoke their pipes, drink beer, and sing. In Chicago, where the Germans had congregated on the North side of the river, shops were open on Sunday, and groups of Germans could be seen "smoking, jabbering and drinking Lauger (sic) beer to their heart's content."[69] The German House of Chicago was built in 1856 largely to circumvent Sunday closing laws.[70] In Cleveland, neighbors complained that Germans came to University Heights each week-end, to "over-indulge" in lager, listen to a noisy band, and disturb the quiet of Sunday.[71] Schurz wrote to his wife in 1855 about the gayety of Watertown's beer gardens, and the target shooting and dancing on Sundays, and observed that "Even the American is reconciling himself little by little to this German mode of celebrating Sunday . . ."[72] Heinzen denounced the "emptiness and purposelessness" of the German middle class who found their greatest enjoyment in the bourgeois pleasures of the beer hall and believed *Gemüthlichkeit* was unthinkable without the amber fluid, but even he stoutly maintained that Sunday was a day for recreation.

Germans were as intolerant in the contest between Continentalism and Puritanism as their American critics, and the Forty-eighters, in particular, made most derogatory references to American "barbarians and Methodists." German bands blared as picnickers paraded past the churches where services were in progress, and the din of the beer halls continued far into Sunday night. When July Fourth fell on a Sunday, and Americans suggested postponing the celebration until the following day, it became a matter of principle for German radicals to insist that the day be observed with appropriate fanfare on the Sabbath. As late as 1869, monster Fourth of July celebrations were sponsored by the Germans of Pittsburgh, Indianapolis, Quincy, Cleveland, Akron, and elsewhere, on Sunday. Seven thousand marched with eight bands through the streets of Pittsburgh. In Cleveland, despite objections from the YMCA, Germans marched to the Public Square, to sing American and German songs, listen to the reading of the Declaration of Independence, and an address by August Willich.[73] In New York, in demonstrations against the Sunday laws, such leading Forty-eighters as Oswald Ottendörfer, Joseph Fickler, Dulon, and Sixtus L. Kapff played a prominent rôle, and as late as 1871, the *Wächter am Erie* debated with the Cleveland *Plain Dealer, Leader,* and *Herald* about the iniquity of Sunday closing laws.

What Germans meant when they defended their "personal liberty" to drink beer was clear, and there can be no doubt about the unanimity of the German element on this issue. Opposition to "temperance legislation" cut across all party and class lines, and was an important issue in local and national campaigns for several decades. Forty-eighters helped make the freedom of man and "the freedom of lager" synonymous terms in the minds of many Americans. In 1855, Weitling, who ordinarily set his mind on higher goals, blasted in his *Die Republik der Arbeiter* against "Protestant Jesuitism," and temperance and Sunday laws, under the title, "The Republic in Peril." He regarded American interference with personal liberty and individual habits as worse than the restrictions he had known in the despotic German states. He spoke of the tyranny of majorities over minorities in a democracy, and although he urged Germans to reduce their consumption of beer, he was enraged by what he termed the attempt "to rob us of our social and civil liberties,"[74] and believed that to admit any restrictions on personal liberty only invited further regulations. In a similar vein, Esselen wrote, "the temperance question is not a question of beer, but of personal liberty,"[75] and the Milwaukee *Banner* and *Volksfreund* disposed of "the temperance swindle" as "an outflow of Puritan bigotry."[76] Champions of the working class made the additional point that taverns and workers' halls where beer was served were the only clubs where the underprivileged could develop a well-rounded "German social life."

The opposition to "the temperance swindle" was not confined, however, to mere debate about the meaning of personal liberty. In Milwaukee a mob, composed largely of Germans, damaged the home of Wisconsin's sponsor of the temperance law, and Germans appeared at the polls on election day with ox-horns filled with beer, which they refilled from beer wagons in the street.[77] Milwaukee papers reported 3,936 glasses of beer had been consumed in one beer hall during a sixteen-hour day, and the *Westbote* observed sarcastically, "No wonder Milwaukee allows itself to be called the German Athens."[78] Cincinnati, in 1854, had eight hundred cafés and saloons, 450 parlors for card-playing, thirty pool rooms and thirty bowling alleys, and in 1860, over two thousand places where liquor was sold. Although the liquor consumption of the Queen City was by no means confined to Germans, the latter were always associated, in the minds of many Americans, with the brewery and saloon business of the city.[79]

Weitling estimated that New York had one thousand beer cellars in the 1850's, and that the annual consumption of beer by the Germans of the city amounted to a million dollars.[80] In St. Louis, the Gambrinus Society sponsored a parade for the devotees of lager beer on May Day, 1858, in which hundreds of Germans marched behind floats furnished by the breweries.[81] In Davenport, Germans and Irish rioted against a sheriff who confiscated several barrels of beer, and marched behind an American flag to the office of the justice of the peace to protest such interference with personal liberty. In 1855, in Chicago, there were serious "Lager Beer Riots," when the cost of liquor licenses was raised to $300. The tyranny of the city administration was likened to the crisis over the Stamp Act during the American Revolution, and a hundred Germans from the North Side, joined by many Irish, marched to the court house, where a mob gathered, shots were fired, and one person was killed, and when the police lost control of the situation the National Guard had to be summoned to quell the disturbance.[82] In New York a mass meeting of Germans was called to protest against temperance legislation, and the *New Yorker Staatszeitung* battled for "unrestricted personal liberty" as vigorously as any radical paper, and reported, without comment or criticism, an attack on a German Methodist minister of Watertown, Wisconsin, who had dared to preach against liquor in that strongly German community.[83]

Such incidents affected the reputation of the entire German group. Americans were shocked by tactless assaults of radical extremists not only on churches and religion, but on an American tradition of Sabbath observance which dated from the founding of the Republic.[84] Forty-eighters who urged the Germans to stress issues more important than Sunday outings and beer received little support, and when Hassaurek recommended that the Free Men's Society of Cincinnati abolish its bar, he almost provoked an insurrection.[85] Rösler von Oels criticized his fellow Germans for unnecessarily irritating their American neighbors by their exhibitions of personal liberty on Sunday.[86] The Whig *Zuschauer am Potomac* demanded respect for religion, as "one of mankind's highest treasures," labeled its foes as bad citizens, and pleaded for a better understanding between Germans and Americans. Heinzen attacked German bock-beer festivals, and maintained that lager beer had made his countrymen stupid, quarrelsome, and reactionary, and destroyed their capacity for cultural and political activity; yet he fought every attempt to regulate personal habits by law. Esselen became disgusted with the "German phalanx, whose flag is a beer-glass, whose symbol is a beer barrel, and whose leaders are saloonkeepers and brewers,"[87] and a writer in the *Atlantische Studien* remarked cynically that "where there are three Germans, one starts a saloon so that the other two may have a place to quarrel."[88]

The controversies over rationalism and religion, personal liberty and blue laws, Continentalism and Puritanism, helped fashion a German-American stereotype in the minds of many Americans of the 1850's, and seriously affected their relations with the foreign-born for years after the Civil War.

FOOTNOTES

CHAPTER 10

1. The *Westbote*, Jan. 27, 1854, deplored all religious discussions in the German press, which tended to divide instead of unify the German element.

2. See also, *Wächter am Erie*, Dec. 15, 1853.

3. *Atlantis* (Cleveland, Jan. 1855) II (N.S.) p. 33.

4. *Humanist*, April 25, 1852, quoted in Sister M. Hedwigis Overmoehle: *The Anti-Clerical Activities of the Forty-eighters in Wisconsin, 1848-1860—A Study in German-American Liberalism* (Ph.D. dissertation, St. Louis University, 1941) pp. 194-95.

5. Karl Heinzen: *What Is Humanity?* (Indianapolis, 1877) p. 30. For a more complete discussion of Heinzen's position, see Wittke: *Heinzen*, especially pp. 148-70.

6. *Atlantische Studien* (Göttingen, 1853) I, 38-39, II, 116-41.

7. *Der Pionier*, Jan. 29, 1859.

8. May 10, 1875.

9. *Atlantis,* Oct. 1855, N.S., III, 305-9; see also *New Yorker Staatszeitung,* Nov. 15, 1853.

10. C. F. Huch: "Die freireligiöse Bewegung unter den Deutsch-amerikanern" in *Mitteilungen des Deutschen Pionier Vereins von Philadelphia* (1909) XI, 1-35.

11. Eugene H. Roseboom: *The Civil War Era, 1850-1873* (Columbus, 1944) pp. 213-14.

12. *Wächter am Erie,* Oct. 6, 1852.

13. *Wisconsin* (American Guide Series, New York, 1941) pp. 492-93; Still: *Milwaukee,* p. 123; and J. J. Schlicher: "Eduard Schroeter, the Humanist," in *Wisconsin Magazine of History,* Dec. 1944, XXVIII, 169-76.

14. Quoted in Rudolf Glanz: *Jews in Relation to the Cultural Milieu of the Germans in America up to the Eighteen Eighties* (New York, 1947) p. 31.

15. *Westbote,* June 16, 1854.

16. *New Yorker Staatszeitung,* Sept. 19, Oct. 5, 19, 26, 31, Nov. 23, 26, Dec. 2, 15, 1853; Sept. 8, 1854; *Belletristisches Journal,* Feb. 10, 1854; *Die Republik der Arbeiter,* Dec. 3, 1853; *Wächter am Erie,* Dec. 15, 1853.

17. See *Wächter am Erie,* Dec. 8, 1852; Philipp Wagner: *Ein Achtundvierziger* (Brooklyn, 1882) pp. 227-28; and J. Hanno Deiler: *Zur Geschichte der Deutschen Kirchengemeinden im Staate Louisiana* (New Orleans, 1894) pp. 84 and 93.

18. *Wächter am Erie,* Sept. 7, 1853.

19. Overmoehle, *op. cit.,* p. 261.

20. Amand Gögg: *Ueberseeische Reisen* (Zurich, 1888) p. 149.

21. See Carl E. Schneider: *The German Church on the American Frontier* (St. Louis, 1939) p. 199.

22. *Wächter am Erie,* Oct. 15, 1853; Still: *Milwaukee,* p. 125; and the *Humanist,* Oct. 16, 1853, quoted in Overmoehle: *op. cit.,* appendix, p. 303; and *Turnzeitung,* April 15, 1854, in *Jahrbücher der deutsch-amerikanischen Turnerei,* edited by Heinrich Metzner (New York, 1892) I, 241-49.

23. Heinrich Kloss: *Um die Einigung des Deutsch-amerikanertums* (Berlin, 1937) pp. 223-24.

24. *Jahrbücher der deutsch-amerikanischen Turnerei,* I, 241-49.

25. Wittke: *Heinzen,* pp. 224-26.

26. *Westbote,* Sept. 16, 1858.

27. *Atlantische Studien,* III, p. 231.

28. Charles E. Snyder: "Unitarianism in Iowa," in *The Palimpsest* (Iowa City) XXX, Nov. 1949, No. 11, pp. 358-59.

29. See Hildegard Binder Johnson, "Adjustment to the United States," in Zucker: *Forty-eighters,* p. 57.

30. See Hense-Jensen and Bruncken: *Wisconsin's Deutsch-Amerikaner,* I, p. 162; *New Yorker Staatszeitung,* Feb. 1, 1853; Koss: *Milwaukee,* pp. 389-407; and *Wächter am Erie,* Oct. 20, 1852.

31. *Wächter am Erie,* Feb. 2, 1853, Jan. 29, 1874; *New Yorker Staatszeitung,* Jan. 14, 1851.

32. Quoted in Overmoehle, *op. cit.,* p. 182.

33. *Ibid.,* pp. 78-80.

34. *New Yorker Staatszeitung,* April 9, 1852; Schneider: *op. cit.,* pp. 195-96; *Wächter am Erie,* June 16, 1860.

35. *Wächter am Erie,* June 29, 1853.

36. See Overmoehle: *op. cit.,* pp. 176-77; *Atlantische Studien,* II, 159-60.

37. *North American Review* (1856) LXXXII, 266.

38. See *Wächter am Erie,* Sept. 5, 1867.

39. *New Yorker Staatszeitung,* March 2, 1855.

40. Stierlin: *Kentucky,* p. 155.

41. Quoted in Donald G. Tewksbury: *The Founding of American Colleges and Universities before the Civil War* (New York, 1932) pp. 74-75.

42. Börnstein: *Memoiren*, II, 106-8.

43. See Emil Klauprecht: *Deutsche Chronik in der Geschichte des Ohio-Thales* (Cincinnati, 1864) pp. 186-87. Hereafter cited as Klauprecht: *Deutsche Chronik*.

44. Roseboom: *op. cit.*, p. 289.

45. Stierlin: *Kentucky*, pp. 155-57.

46. *Wächter am Erie*, Dec. 29, 1853.

47. Dec. 28, 1853; also Jan. 1, 2, 1854.

48. *Westbote*, Dec. 30, 1853.

49. Philipp Schaff: *America* (New York, 1855) pp. 274-75.

50. Still: *Milwaukee*, p. 126.

51. *New Yorker Staatszeitung*, March 23, 1850; July 6, 1850.

52. *Ibid.*, Oct. 28, 1852.

53. *Ibid.*, April 6, 1850.

54. Quoted in Emmet H. Rothan: *The German Catholic Immigrant in the United States, 1830-1860* (Washington, 1946) p. 115.

55. Frederick P. Kenkel: "Subjected to an Acid Test," quoted in Rothan, *op. cit.*, pp. 119-20.

56. Quoted in John A. Hawgood: *The Tragedy of German-America* (New York, 1940) p. 230.

57. Rothan, *op. cit.*, and George P. S. Timpe: *Katolisches Deutschtum in den Vereinigten Staaten von Amerika* (Freiburg, 1937).

58. Stierlin: *Kentucky*, p. 142.

59. Hense-Jensen and Bruncken. *Wisconsin's Deutsch-Amerikaner*, I, 161-63.

60. Overmoehle, *op. cit.*, pp. 289, 290; also 137.

61. Michael Chevalier: *Society, Manners and Politics in the United States* (1839) p. 284.

62. *Lebende Bilder aus Amerika* (1858) in Oscar Handlin: *This Was America* (Cambridge, 1949) pp. 262-63.

63. See J. H. A. Lacher: *The German Element in Wisconsin* (Milwaukee, 1925) p. 41.

64. See *New Yorker Staatszeitung*, Feb. 15, 1854; also *Wächter am Erie*, July 20, 1853.

65. *New Yorker Staatszeitung*, June 29, 1850.

66. *Ibid.*, Oct. 5, 1853.

67. Börnstein: *op. cit.*, II, 168-80.

68. *Wächter am Erie*, June 1, 1853.

69. Observations of Edward L. Peckham, in 1857, quoted in Bessie L. Pierce: *As Others See Chicago, Impressions of Visitors, 1673-1933* (Chicago, 1933) p. 168.

70. Max Stern and Fred Kressmann: *Chicago's Deutsche Männer* (Chicago, 1885) pp. 39-41.

71. Cleveland *Leader*, July 28, 1857; see also, Philipp Schaff: *America* (New York, 1855) p. 41.

72. *Intimate Letters*, p. 147.

73. *Wächter am Erie*, July 1, 6, 1869.

74. *Die Republik der Arbeiter*, May 19, 1855.

75. *Atlantis*, April 1855, II (N.S.) pp. 304-6.

76. Quoted in Dorothy M. Johnson: "Attitude of the Germans in Minnesota toward the Republican Party," U. of Minnesota M.A. thesis (March, 1945) p. 68.

77. *Ibid.*, p. 69.

78. *Westbote*, May 1, 1857.

79. Roseboom: *Civil War Era*, p. 226; Rudolf Glanz: *op. cit.*, p. 44.

80. *Die Republik der Arbeiter*, April 22, 1854.

81. *Westbote*, May 13, 1858.

82. Bessie L. Pierce: *A History of Chicago* (New York, 1940) I, 435-38; also Max Stern and Fred Kressmann: *Chicago's Deutsche Männer* (Chicago, 1885) pp. 23-25.

83. *New Yorker Staatszeitung,* Nov. 24, 1853.

84. At an outing of Knownothings in Newport, Kentucky, in 1855, a glee club sang the following "German song,"

> "Fill 'em up, fill 'em up, fill 'em up here,
> Swei Glass Lager und trei Glass Beer.
> Up mit der Vine und down mit der Beer,
> Don't care nix for Temperance here."

Westbote, Aug. 3, 1855.

85. *Westbote,* Sept. 29, 1854.

86. Koss: *Milwaukee,* p. 359.

87. *Atlantis,* April 1855, N.S., II, 304-6; and Sept. 1855, II, 163.

88. II, 107.

Chapter 11 · *THE TURNER*

THE CONTRIBUTIONS of the German Turner *(Turnvereine)* to American political and cultural history are among the most important results of the German immigration of the nineteenth century. While the Turner movement was not unknown in the United States before 1848, and distinguished Germans introduced physical education to the curriculum of several schools in the earlier decades of the century, the history of the Turner organizations in America really begins with the Forty-eighters.

Friedrich Ludwig Jahn, or "Turnvater Jahn" as he was affectionately known in Turner circles, established his first *Turnplatz* on the Hasenheide in Berlin in 1811, during the dark days of Prussia's humiliation, when most of western Europe was under the heel of Napoleon. In that black hour for all Germans a few dauntless spirits refused to give up hope for a free and united Germany, and the Turner organization was founded. It grew into an effective vehicle of German patriotism and nationalism. Father Jahn was convinced that there could be no rebirth of Germany unless its people became healthy and strong through a carefully planned program of physical training. But in addition to physical culture, he wanted an organization to foster sound patriotic ideals. The old plea of Juvenal, for *mens sana in corpore sano* became the motto of the Turner, and their goal the development of a sound, well-coördinated body, a mind sensitive to liberty and moved by the love of country, and an intellect disciplined for the political struggle to make the Germans united and free. Ardent patriotism and devotion to liberty were fundamental principles of the *Turnvereine* from the day of their inception. During the age of Metternich the Turner had been driven underground, their leaders harassed by the police, and Jahn himself sentenced to five years in jail. Their athletic exercises were declared illegal and their societies ordered to dismantle their apparatus. Although some early members, including the founder, lost their enthusiasm for radical reform in their more advanced years, the spirit of the movement remained thoroughly liberal. Along with the *Burschenschaften* of the university students, the *Turnvereine* were one of the most influential groups in the Revolution of 1848. Turner in large numbers flocked to the black-red-gold banner of the Revolution, fought under Sigel and Hecker in Baden, on the barricades in Dresden and in the streets of Frankfurt and, when the revolution collapsed, paid a heavy price for their rebellion against the reigning princes.[1]

As early as 1824, Jahn's system of physical training had been introduced to the United States by prominent German immigrants. Karl Beck and Karl Follen who arrived in that year found teaching positions in the famous Round Hill boys' school of Northampton, Massachusetts, established by George Bancroft, the historian. Representatives of the best of German cultural life, they were readily accepted in the intellectual circles of Boston. Beck organized a gymnasium on the Turner model, taught classes according to Jahn's system of physical education, and translated his manual, *Deutsche Turnkunst,* into English. Follen taught physical education at Harvard. Francis Lieber, another of Jahn's disciples and a veteran of the war against Napoleon, opened a gymnasium and swimming school in Boston, which attracted considerable attention.

These early ventures were exceptional, however, and the Turner movement made little progress in the United States until the Forty-eighters came. Many refugees were eager to transplant the *Turnverein* to America and, as intellectuals and inveterate reformers, emphasized the liberal traditions of the Turner movement quite as much as physical fitness. The *Turnvereine,* like the *Freie Gemeinde* and *Freimännervereine,* to which many Turner belonged, became centers of German radicalism in the abolitionist movement of the 1850's, and in the Civil War hundreds of their members served in the Union Army. From 1848 to the Civil War, the Turner movement owed its organization, progress, and success in the United States primarily to the Forty-eighters, who saw in the *Turnvereine* another means for the advancement of their political and social ideas.

The first *Turngemeinde* in the United States was organized in Cincinnati in October 1848. According to the accepted account in Turner annals, three Turner from Ludwigsburg arrived in that city on October 11 and found lodging with a tavern keeper who was a friend of Friedrich Hecker. When the latter came to Cincinnati, and official welcoming ceremonies were over, he visited his friend Kienzel in his place of business on Plum Street and the Miami Canal, and stopped in the little hotel which had but recently been renamed the Hecker Haus. The two friends discussed the possibility of establishing a local *Turnverein,* and drew up a constitution and a set of by-laws. When fourteen Cincinnati Germans responded to their call, they erected a fence around an empty lot and began their physical exercises. On New Year's Day 1850, they dedicated their own hall, a primitive board structure, forty feet by eighty feet, and probably the first *Turner Halle* in the United States. The society supported a male chorus and a small library, and began publishing a monthly in 1851. Since that time three generations have carried on the work of the founding fathers, and the society is still active.[2]

The Philadelphia *Turngemeinde* developed from a meeting of young German immigrants in a boarding house and saloon on North Fourth Street in 1849. Some months later it held a ball in the Odd Fellows Hall to raise funds for the purchase of apparatus. By March of the next year the society had fifty-six active members who exercised twice a week in an old Quaker Meeting House which had been converted into a Turner hall. Eighteen months later, after a record of notable progress, the society suffered the secession of the Socialists among its membership, who founded their own *Sozialer Turnverein* and initiated a long court battle with the parent group for control of the property.[3]

The *Sozial-demokratische Turnverein* of Baltimore also dates from the year 1849. In its first twelve months it enrolled 278 members and became the strongest of the seventeen Turner societies then existing in the United States. It defended its liberal principles with great courage in a state where slavery was legal and the nativists powerful, printed a *Turnzeitung* and, in 1860, became the national headquarters for the *Turnerbund.*[4]

The first *Turngemeinde* of New York was founded November 28, 1848, a month after the Cincinnati society was organized, at a meeting held in Becker's Hotel in Hoboken. The members assembled for their exercises in Richter's brewery. By the end of the first year, a minority were dissatisfied with the organization's lack of political activity, and withdrew to found the *Socialistischer Turnverein*. Sigismund Kaufmann was its first speaker, Franz Sigel its first fencing instructor, and from the outset the new group advocated a more revolutionary, socialistic program. Gustav

Struve was active in the early days of the society, and August Schärtner, who had fought in Baden in 1848, and Aaron Frank of Karlsruhe, a young Heidelberg student who had been revolutionary commissar of Bruchsal,[5] were among the leaders of the seceding organization. Brooklyn's Turner society was formed in 1850. Efforts to federate the local societies in the Eastern cities into a national organization were handicapped by the division of opinion between those who gave priority to physical exercise and ignored politics, and more radical members who championed a program of thoroughgoing socialist reforms.

The Turner movement also spread rapidly in the West. Eduard Schultz, a political refugee from Baden, organized the first short-lived *Turnverein* in Milwaukee in 1850. In 1853, August Willich founded the *Social Turnverein,* whose membership at the outset was limited to Forty-eighters. It was the predecessor of the present-day Milwaukee *Turnverein.*[6] In Sheboygan the Turner society, organized in 1854, erected its wooden horses and performed its gymnastic exercises in the public square until it could acquire a hall. Similar groups were established in Madison, Fond du Lac, LaCrosse, and other Wisconsin towns.

The *Sozialistischer Turnverein* of Davenport was founded in August 1852, largely by veterans of the war with Denmark over Schleswig-Holstein. By 1854 it had its own hall where members drilled regularly in uniforms of white duck, gray hats, and red neck-bands.[7] Among the pioneer Turner of Peoria, Illinois, were Ernst Violand and Karl Emil Gillig, a young mechanic who had fought as a lad of nineteen in the German Revolution.[8] The first *Turnverein* of St. Louis was organized in May 1850, and took the name *Bestrebung* (Endeavor). In 1855 the members laid the cornerstone for their first building, and by 1861 the membership had risen to five hundred, of whom a large percentage enlisted in the 17th Missouri Regiment, known in the Civil War as the "Western Turners' Regiment."[9] The library of the St. Louis society had over two thousand volumes in 1883.[10] In Chicago, the Turner first assembled in an empty lot on Randolph and Market streets in 1852, but were able to dedicate their first hall, a frame structure, a year later. In 1857 the *Social Democratic Turnverein* was established, and by 1896 Chicago had twenty-four societies.[11] By 1856 there were *Turnvereine* in twenty-six states and the District of Columbia.[12] German Turner battled for freedom in "bleeding Kansas" in 1857, and in 1859 a Pacific *Turnerbund* was organized in

Sacramento, to unite local groups on the California coast, but after but one *Turnfest* the organization died out during the Civil War.

In the Southern states the Turner encountered special difficulties because of their antislavery views. In Louisville, native Americans disapproved of the Sunday celebrations of the "white jackets," and during the Know-nothing period the Turner Hall burned down under mysterious circumstances. Half the members of the Louisville group joined the Union Army in 1861.[13] In New Orleans, the Turner organized in 1851, and proudly flew the black-red-gold colors over their hall. Five years later the society helped dedicate a monument to Andrew Jackson, and joined in a May Festival with their fellow Turners of Mobile, Alabama.[14] As the Civil War drew nearer, serious disagreements developed between Northern and Southern Turner. The Charleston, South Carolina, society, accused of being "bootblacks for the aristocracy who whip Negroes," was expelled from the *Turnerbund,* and as late as 1870 a bitter controversy developed with the New Orleans *Turngemeinde* over admitting Louisiana's mulatto lieutenant-governor as a guest in the Turner Hall.[15]

The ideals of the Turner were high, and at their best included much more than the development of a sound body. In an address to the Turner on July 4, 1858, Friedrich Röpenach referred to the Declaration of Independence and the Constitution of the United States as "a golden franchise for Paradise for the persecuted and vanquished who had fought for liberty in Europe,"[16] and it was the avowed objective of the Turner to strive in America for the "ideal republic" denied them in their fatherland.[17] The lead article in the first issue of the *Turnerzeitung,* published in Philadelphia in 1853 for circulation among the total membership, and written by Wilhelm Rapp, defined the objectives of the *Turnerbund* broadly enough to include all "political, social and religious reform." Rapp envisaged the Turner Halls as meeting places for the friends of progress and the foes of all special privilege, ecclesiastical despotism, and political corruption.

The membership of the Turner organization included revolutionary communists, atheists, pantheists, ardent nationalists, sober, middle-of-the-road reformers, and cosmopolites who championed the universal brotherhood of man regardless of race, creed, class, or nationality. Turner insisted that their ideals were those of the ancient Greeks, who envisaged the complete harmony between mind and body as man's highest achievement.[18] According to Turner principles, morality must be built upon love for one's neighbor, not the dicta of priest or church. The Turner were regularly reminded by their leaders of their obligation to subordinate individual advantage to the well-being of the majority and to work for the improvement of their adopted fatherland. "America," Rapp wrote on one occasion, "is the rejuvenated and reborn Europe. Anglo-Saxon initiative and love of liberty, Irish strength, and German love of art and depth of soul are united here" in a common enterprise. He urged his fellow Germans to become integrated with other Americans as rapidly as possible and learn the ways of American democracy. In theory, the Turner endeavored to educate men physically, ethically, intellectually, and culturally. Their goal was a more "refined humanity," and their leaders regarded their organization as a vital educational force for progress in culture and freedom and good citizenship. Considerable sums were spent on gymnasia and gymnastic apparatus, and much energy was expended in calisthenics, acrobatic tumbling, and performances on the parallel bars, which men already in middle life still thought essential to the maintenance of physical fitness. But much money also went into libraries, singing societies, debating clubs, lectures, and dramatic performances. The Turner supported free public schools, and wanted physical education included in the curriculum, and religious instruction excluded. At their national conventions prizes were offered for original contributions in prose and poetry, and for the best declamations and debates, as well as for outstanding athletic performance.

Several Turner societies made special provisions for the aid of political refugees. Hecker hoped to make the Turner more active politically, and in 1860 the societies in Baltimore, New York, and elsewhere, gave benefit exhibitions for a Garibaldi fund. On such occasions prominent refugees usually revealed new plans to send the veterans of 1848 back to Europe, to fight for Italian liberty, and then for the freedom of the German fatherland.[19] To men like Willich, the main purpose of the *Turnverein* was to "carry the red flag of socialism."[20]

The history of the early Turner movement in the United States is replete with the names of pioneers who dedicated their lives to its ideals and to the new country where they had chosen to live out their lives. Many regarded Sigismund Kaufmann as the most important pioneer in the history of the American Turner movement. Born in Hesse-Darmstadt and trained for a business career, he had taken part in the Revolution of

1848 at the age of twenty-two. He arrived in the United States practically penniless, entered a law office to read law, and in 1852 was admitted to the bar. He was one of the founders of the New York *Turnverein,* and for many years its "speaker," and he edited its first paper. Kaufmann became a conspicuous figure at Turner conventions, as a kind of Nestor of the movement. An ardent Republican, he was a Lincoln elector in 1860, and a supporter of Greeley in the Liberal Republican revolt of 1872. Kaufmann took an active part in the work of the German Society of New York, and in 1877-79 served as its president.

Eduard Müller, a native of Mainz and an enthusiastic Turner as a young art student in Munich, organized the first *Turnverein* in his native city. In the 1830's, he was banished for seven years because of his liberalism, but returned to Mainz to teach physical education and edit a Turner paper. When he was again in trouble because of the Revolution of 1848, he left for the United States, and settled in New York. He became a member of its *Turnverein,* and in 1852 published a manual on physical education. His enthusiasm for his profession was so extraordinary that he became an eccentric figure. His daily costume was a white linen coat and trousers, which he wore, presumably, in emulation of Father Jahn; in the severest weather he refused to wear a vest, muffler or overcoat, and his long gray locks hung down uncut over his shoulders.[21]

Wilhelm Rothacker, another refugee of 1848, edited the *Turnzeitung* in Davenport.[22] Constantin Conrad, who fled to the United States in 1849, was the leader of the Cincinnati *Turnverein* for eight years. Thereupon he organized a school and a physical training club for girls in Pittsburgh, and lived to become one of the oldest teachers of physical education in the United States. Karl Heinrich Schnauffer, editor of the Baltimore *Wecker,* and Johann Straubenmüller, for many years a distinguished member of the New York school system, were widely known for their Turner lyrics. Both were political refugees of 1848.[23] Heinrich Lohmann, a cigar maker in Bremen who fought with the Turner in the Saxon revolution, was among the founders of the Baltimore *Socialistische Turnverein,* and directed a school for gymnastics for many years. The refugees Eduard Schulz and Fritz Anneke were active in the early Turner school of Milwaukee.[24] Wilhelm Rapp, a student of theology at Tübingen who was tried and acquitted after the Revolution, worked as a journalist on a number of German-American papers, edited the *Turnzeitung* from 1855 to

1856, and was president of the American *Turnerbund* for one term. Franz Sigel, remembered primarily for his military career in Europe and America, was extremely popular with the Turner and spoke at many of their conventions.

With their stress on principle and remaking the world along more radical lines, the Turner combined an irrepressible love for pageantry, parades, and public celebrations, and a special weakness for a kind of student romanticism which many never quite outgrew. The climax of their public demonstrations were the annual *Turnfeste,* attended by delegates from local societies in a given area, and later from the United States as a whole. Such gymnastic spectacles became more and more pretentious and lavish, and no *Turnfest* was complete without a torchlight procession, brilliant displays of fireworks, noisy shooting, and the hilarious singing of student and Turner songs. Bugle calls and the ruffle of drums usually heralded the most spectacular exhibitions of acrobatics and physical strength, and Turner societies paraded on the slightest provocation for patriotic holidays, picnics, and in funeral processions for deceased members, when they turned out with black mourning bands on the sleeves of their uniforms, and marched with muffled drums to the cemetery.

Apparently the first *Turnfest* in the United States was held on September 29 and 30, 1851, in Philadelphia, with the local society acting as host to six or seven hundred visitors from New York, Boston, Baltimore, Newark, and Reading. Kinkel and Struve were honored guests. The delegates were welcomed with shouts of "Gut Heil," the Turner greeting, and many participants, because they were veterans of 1848, addressed each other with the familiar "Du." In white jackets and red ties, to the accompaniment of blaring horns, the Turner marched in military formation to Lemon Hill on the Schuylkill, with a "giant Saladin" carrying a blood-red banner at the head of the parade. While the band played "Hail Columbia" and "The Star Spangled Banner," a Turner from Baltimore climbed a seventy-foot pole to unfurl the United States flag. The speech-making concluded with an address by Kinkel, and the competition for prizes continued throughout the day. In the evening the Turner returned to the city, to spend the night in convivial singing and drinking, and the following day the delegates paraded to Independence Hall to be greeted by the Mayor. Thereupon they proceeded by boat to Red Bank, the

Fourieristic phalanx in New Jersey, in which many radical Turner were interested. The day ended with a ball in the Chinese Museum, interspersed with singing and the building of human pyramids by the strongest and most skillful delegates. The business sessions continued throughout the week. Americans were astonished by such prolonged celebrations, and especially interested in German women athletes who appeared in bloomers.[25]

The Turner of New York inaugurated their local festival in August 1851 with a parade in which they carried a flag inscribed "Liberty, Welfare and Education." Struve later made an address on the same theme.[26] The Boston *Turnverein,* in coöperation with a German singing society, held its outing the same year in the woods of Jamaica Plain, and heard Anton Füster and Eduard Schröter reaffirm their faith in a new German revolution.[27] When the Turner met in New York two years later, their torchlight parade, from the Battery down Broadway to the Turner Hall, was greeted with a shower of stones by the rowdies and loafers for which the city was notorious in pre-Civil War days. On Sunday the Turner marched in a funeral procession to bury a member who had died unexpectedly. On Monday a thousand athletes in costume, three to four hundred members of singing societies, and several other organizations, including two hundred "apprentice Turner" between the ages of seven and fifteen, marched behind four bands, in a parade a half-mile long, to the exhibition grounds. After an address by the president of the New York society, the feats of strength and skill began, and continued according to schedule, despite the late summer heat. Women and children cheered the performers, and helped consume quantities of lager beer. The next day the Turner listened to more speeches at the City Hall, and in the evening crowded the Bowery Theatre for a production of Weber's *Preciosa* by their own members. At the conclusion of the performance the best athletes presented tableaux, and the convention ended with another round of festivities on the New Jersey side, and a ball on the following evening.[28]

These descriptions suffice to characterize the *Turnfeste* in the decade before the Civil War, and their character did not change greatly in later years. Sigel was marshal of the Philadelphia parade in 1854, and the main speaker in New York two years later.[29] In 1859 Friedrich Münch won the essay contest of the Turner, and received a set of Heine and an encyclopedia for his contribution on "The importance of the natural sciences for the education and preservation of the German element in the United States." Similar prizes were offered regularly for the best poetry and musical compositions. In 1859 the Turner staged a sham battle.[30]

The Civil War almost destroyed the Turner movement. Many members went off to fight in the Union Army and did not return. Societies were so decimated that they had to suspend their meetings, and it was not until after the close of the war that the *Turnvereine* could be reorganized. The excellent war record of the Turner helped dispel the earlier hostility of nativists toward this peculiar German institution, and members pointed with pride to their military service as proof of their whole-hearted devotion to the American Republic. In the decades following the Civil War, both physical education and the teaching of German were introduced in the public school curricula of many cities, and as a result, separate schools of physical training maintained by Turner societies declined steadily.

The report of the American *Turnerbund* for October 1865 revealed that the organization then had 5,995 members, organized in ten districts and eighty-two societies. Of the total membership, however, only 2,655 could be classified as "active," convincing evidence that the war and advancing years had diminished both the ability and the enthusiasm for vigorous physical exercise. Four hundred and seventy-five members belonged to singing auxiliaries and 147 to sharpshooting groups.[31] By 1876, total membership had climbed to some fourteen thousand in 185 clubs; the library of the North American *Turnerbund* numbered nearly thirty thousand volumes, and the property of the organization was appraised at $1,854,222, but $739,588 was encumbered by mortgages and other debts.[32] The total membership was divided into 4,572 active gymnasts, 454 fencers, 1,103 singers, 301 sharpshooters, and 7,026 boys and 916 girls who were in training to become full-fledged Turner. In 1948, when the *Turnerbund* celebrated its centenary, it had 25,376 members in ninety-eight societies, and property valued at $4,744,161.[33]

After 1871 the *Turnerbund,* without abandoning its earlier hostility to ecclesiasticism, Puritanism, and religious instruction in the schools, concentrated its attention for a time on political and economic reform. It issued statements advocating greater rights for women, labor reforms, the eight-hour day, factory and child labor laws, and the need for a new political party which would unite all progressives. In addition, the *Turnerbund* adopted resolutions favoring the teaching of German and physical education in the schools, progressive income and inheritance taxes, the Australian ballot, the direct election of the President and senators, public ownership of public utilities, and other reforms which suggest the platform of third parties after the Civil War. There was little to distinguish the Turner during this post-bellum period from other progressive and radical groups except their specific demand that German traditions be preserved for their children and grandchildren, and that the German language be taught in the schools.

As time went on and older leaders died, the *Turnvereine* experienced a marked decline of interest in their original objectives and lost their militant radicalism. They became social organizations, whose halls and recreational facilities provided entertainment and pleasant meeting places for a so-called "passive" membership which was not greatly interested in the original program of the society, knew little or nothing of the society's history, and joined largely to belong to another social club. Even in earlier years, critics like Heinzen poked fun at the "pseudomilitary games," the "student drinking" and the "giant swings" of the Turner organizations, and bemoaned the fact that "the phalanx of liberty" had become mere "philistines in uniform." Hecker, addressing the Turner of St. Louis, deplored the transformation of the movement into a "gymnastic circus" and mere muscle-building. He pleaded for a return to the original objectives which had made the *Turnverein* "the carrier, developer and apostle of the free spirit," and urged its members to take part in public affairs and to champion reforms instead of acting like "tin soldiers" who are returned to their boxes when the Turn Hall is closed for the night.[34] Weitling charged that the Turner movement had abandoned its socialistic principles for mere recreation, and wasted time and money which might better be devoted to the cause of labor.

With the passing years, the Turner seemed to become more deeply absorbed in artificial efforts to preserve the conviviality of student life and to revel in a romantic interest in jackets, ribbons, and uniforms. Many *Turnvereine* suffered from factional controversy over the extent to which they should continue to be a part of the radical movement, and the majority seemed to favor a more congenial and comfortable bourgeois program of physical recreation and social entertainment. Although some stubbornly persisted with their program of social action, others were satisfied with exhibitions of athletic skill and physical stamina, and believed their obligation to liberalism and reform was fully discharged if they continued to oppose prohibition and Sunday closing laws.

In more recent times, local societies built expensive and attractive social halls in which the gymnasium was the least important part of the structure. Such buildings were costly and could be supported only by entertainments open to the general public, and from the receipts from the bar or the kitchen, and frequently the ground floor housed a commodious barroom and dining room. Accounts in the German press indicate that there was much drinking,[35] and occasionally breweries bought stock in the Turner halls, or made liberal contributions toward their building funds, thus acquiring a not always wholesome voice in the society's affairs. On the other hand, it must be added that to this day the New York *Turnverein,* in whose physical activities the women members now exceed the men, and whose membership is open to other nationality groups, still supports a school attended by four hundred children, maintains a library and reading room, dramatic, singing, and chess clubs, monthly lectures and debates, and publishes a magazine, known as *Bahn Frei.* The club placed several of its members on the Olympic teams for the United States in 1924, 1932, 1936, and 1948, and has trained many instructors of physical education for the public schools. Its German school, chartered by the New York Board of Regents in 1911, gives instruction to about seven hundred youngsters from eight to eighteen years of age for two-hour periods each week, and on Saturday. As early as 1857 it was a full-fledged elementary school, with ten teachers and a principal, and Heinrich Metzner, a patriarch of the Turner movement, was a member of its staff for more than half a century. The school reached its peak enrollment of 1,283 in 1884, had to be closed temporarily as a result of the hysteria against all things German during World War I, and in 1943 again found it expedient to drop its German classes until after the close of World War II.[36]

The history of such societies in New York and several other larger cities is exceptional, however. For the most part, as the older generation died or lost control, interest in intellectual activities, lectures, debates, and dramatic performances declined sharply, though amateur dramatics survived for a somewhat longer period. The *Turnvereine* became primarily social organizations, although they never abandoned their interest in physical education entirely, and in later years made their halls recreation centers for the whole community. But the original purpose and spirit of the Forty-eighters has been largely forgotten. A few stalwarts, sometimes of surprisingly advanced years, and occasional recruits from various nationality groups, still work out on parallel bars or go through the calisthenic drills described in the German manuals or demonstrate their skill on the bowling alley, but the majority have become "passive," pay their dues, and use the club house primarily to get good German food and beer and to meet with friends for congenial evenings of billiards, bowling, or cards.

FOOTNOTES

CHAPTER 11

1. "Zehn Jahre aus der Geschichte der Turnerei in Deutschland," in *Jahrbücher der Deutsch-Amerikanischen Turnerei*, edit. by Heinrich Metzner (N. Y., 1892) I, 49-65.

2. See *Der Deutsche Pionier*, VII (No. 5) July 1875, pp. 178-87; *Cincinnati*—(American Guide Series) (Cincinnati, 1943) pp. 218-19. For the list of early members and organizations, see *Jahrbücher der Deutsch-Amerikanischen Turnerei*, I, *passim*, and especially pp. 142-44.

3. "Die ersten Jahre der Philadelphia Turngemeinde," in *Mitteilungen des Deutschen Pionier Vereins von Philadelphia*, XXIV (1912) 29-36.

4. Augustus J. Prahl: "History of the German Gymnastic Movement in Baltimore," in *26th Report Society for the History of the Germans in Maryland* (1945) pp. 16-29.

5. *Jahrbücher der Deutsch-Amerikanischen Turnerei*, I, pp. 24-31. See also, Alfred F. Kierschner: "New York Turn-Verein 100th Anniversary," in *The American-German Review* (Aug. 1950) XVI, No. 6, pp. 7-13.

6. Still: *Milwaukee*, p. 124.

7. Richter: *Geschichte der Stadt Davenport*, pp. 512-25.

8. *Jahrbücher der Deutsch-Amerikanischen Turnerei*, II, 187-88.

9. Scharf: *Saint Louis*, p. 1771.

10. *Ibid.*, p. 901.

11. A. J. Townsend: *The Germans of Chicago*, p. 127.

12. See *Jahrbücher der Deutsch-Amerikanischen Turnerei*, III, 48, 54-56, 237-40; and *Belletristisches Journal*, Nov. 14, 1856.

13. Stierlin: *Kentucky*, Part IV, pp. 26-30.

14. *Belletristisches Journal*, Feb. 29, May 23, 1856.

15. *Wächter am Erie*, March 19, 1870.

16. Baltimore *Wecker*, July 10, 1858.

17. C. F. Huch: "Der Sozialistische Turnerbund," in *Mitteilungen des Deutschen Pionier Vereins von Philadelphia*, XXVI (1912) 1-15.

18. *Jahrbücher der Deutsch-Amerikanischen Turnerei*, I, 202-6.

19. *New Yorker Staatszeitung*, Aug. 30, Oct. 11, 1860; *Belletristisches Journal*, Sept. 14, 1860.

20. See also John H. Strasser: *Chronologie der Stadt New Ulm* for an account of the founding of this Turner colony in Minnesota, promoted by the Colonization Association of the Socialist *Turnerbund*. To this day the town retains many of the characteristics of the old radical spirit of the German Forty-eighters.

21. *Jahrbücher der Deutsch-Amerikanischen Turnerei*, I, 35-37.

22. Joseph Eiboeck: *Die Deutschen von Iowa und deren Errungenschaften* (Des Moines, 1900).

23. See A. E. Zucker: "Carl Heinrich Schnauffer" in *24th Report of the Society for the History of the Germans in Maryland* (1939) pp. 2-8; and *Jahrbücher der Deutsch-Amerikanischen Turnerei*, I, 129-37. See also, M. D. Learned: "The German-American Turner Lyric" in *Reports of the Society for the History of the Germans in Maryland*, VIII-XIV, 123.

24. Hense-Jensen and Bruncken: *Wisconsin's Deutsch-Amerikaner*, I, 156-58.

25. C. F. Huch: "Das erste allgemeine Turnfest in den Vereinigten Staaten von Nord Amerika"—in *Mitteilungen des Deutschen Pionier Vereins von Philadelphia* XXIII (1911) 20-23; and *Jahrbücher der Deutsch-Amerikanischen Turnerei* I, 67-81.

26. *New York Tribune*, Aug. 19, 1851.

27. *Jahrbücher der Deutsch-Amerikanischen Turnerei*, II, 88-90; also Henry Metzner: *A Brief History of the American Turnerbund* (Pittsburgh, 1924).

28. *Atlantische Studien*, IV, 67-70; see also *Die Republik der Arbeiter*, Sept. 10, 1853.

29. *Belletristisches Journal*, May 16, 1856.

30. *New Yorker Staatszeitung*, Aug. 25, 1859. For other celebrations, see *Wächter am Erie*, Aug. 13, 1869, and Ernst Below: *Bilder aus dem Westen* (1894) in Oscar Handlin: *This Was America* (Cambridge, 1949) p. 385.

31. *Wächter am Erie*, Jan. 27, 1866.

32. *Ibid.*, June 1, 1876.

33. See also, for other statistics, Karl Knortz: *Das Deutschtum der Vereinigten Staaten* (Hamburg, 1898) p. 61.

34. *Friedrich Hecker und sein Antheil an der Geschichte Deutschlands und Amerikas* (Cincinnati, 1881) pp. 62-71.

35. See *New Yorker Staatszeitung*, Feb. 20, 22, 1856; and *Wächter am Erie*, June 23, 1873.

36. See Alfred F. Kierschner: "New York Turn-Verein 100th Anniversary," in *The American-German Review* (Aug. 1950) XVI, No. 6, pp. 7-13; and Theodore Huebner: "The German School of the New York Turn-Verein," *Ibid.*, pp. 14-15.

Chapter 12 · POLITICAL RADICALISM

To the doctrinaire radical, the United States of the 1850's was a land of strange contrasts. Its Constitution, obviously the result of many compromises, represented a complicated and delicately poised system of checks and balances which defeated the direct, primary democracy for which theoreticians among the radical Forty-eighters contended. The Bill of Rights was unique, yet the same Constitution protected slavery. On the one hand the American government was a unitary state built on "we, the people"; on the other, it reserved many important powers to the states. The American system seemed to be a strange mixture of democracy and aristocracy, and a curious blend of a republican form of government with an executive whose powers exceeded those of many monarchs.

Refugees found their Anglo-American neighbors a strange bundle of contradictions also. In the field of industry, inventiveness, production, and material progress, they were extraordinarily bold and successful innovators. In the field of religion, education, and politics they seemed extremely conservative. Adolf Douai, one of the ablest German refugees, referred to the American's slavish and superstitious respect for tradition and authority, and pointed, for an example, to the mental gymnastics of American jurists in making the common law of England fit the American pattern instead of insisting on specific legislation to cope with new conditions in a new world. Douai deplored the transformation of the Democratic party from the liberalism of Jefferson and Jackson to the conservatism of the 1850's and the domination of the party by a Southern slavocracy and the mob politics of the larger cities. To the educated European the American political game appeared to be largely a matter of shirt-sleeve politicians and tobacco-chewing bosses, operating with gangs of rowdies and plug-uglies on election day.[1] German radicals believed that the political and social structure needed to be overhauled in accordance with the logic of

161

their theories, and that it was the duty of newcomers to act as censors of American life, "to deal with the sickly aspects" of politics "with the critique of sound reason, sharp logic and an incorruptible love of truth."[2]

The feature of the American Constitution which Forty-eighters cherished most was the Bill of Rights. Its freedoms outweighed all the defects of the Constitution. Free speech and a free press made it possible for every minority to advocate reform, and in the United States the appeal was to the ballot, whereas in Europe it had been all too often to bullets. Moreover, in the United States there were no occupational barriers or artificial class distinctions to inhibit individuals with talent and thrift. With the exception of the South, land was fairly evenly distributed and business and the trades were open without limit to those of ability and initiative. In sharp contrast with the police states of Europe, political and social experiments of every kind could be carried on without rocking the foundations of the state or provoking a revolution.

Conservative Americans, including Germans of the older immigration, regarded many Forty-eighters as leftists, "fanatics of equality," "haunted by the ideas of Rousseau," "the slaves of their democratic theories," and not only reformers but utterly impractical dreamers. Undaunted by such criticisms, with an assurance akin to conceit and a faith in minorities to move mountains by the force of an idea, the extremists plunged headlong into the battle for political reform. Some of their demands were utopian, and their methods revealed a lack of understanding of American conditions, yet the reformers were honest and sincere and ready to sacrifice for their convictions. These men grew to love the land that gave them asylum, though their attacks on its shortcomings were sometimes extremely unfair. Many were victims of their own orthodox, inflexible, doctrinaire attitude, and their lack of tact destroyed the effectiveness of their propaganda and provoked sharp counterattacks. Yet these radicals were part of that leaven of liberalism which has been at work in the American body politic from the beginning and helped make the United States, not a fixed pattern of government, but a process forever finished.

Proposals for constitutional reform came from several sources. As early as 1851, a small party of Germans in Richmond, Virginia, pledged themselves to work for the abolition of the Senate and the Presidency. A German radical club of Cleveland which included prominent Forty-eighters endorsed a similar program. When "the German world reformers" met in Cincinnati in the summer of 1853 to advocate a primary democracy for the United States, the Columbus *Westbote* and the Cincinnati *Volksfreund* ridiculed Hassaurek, Rothacker, and others by comparing their debates and recriminations with scenes in the Polish Parliament or during the last days of the parliamentary assembly at Frankfurt.[3] The Cincinnati *Turnverein* rejected their platform as extreme and impracticable, and on the ground that it would give support to the charges of nativists that German radicals were an unassimilable element in the American population.[4] The *Baltimore Wecker* and the Chicago *Deutsch-Amerikaner*, both edited by political refugees of 1848, were equally critical of the Cincinnati platform,[5] and leading American journals, such as the *National Intelligencer*, denounced "a new untried Utopian system of government," spawned in "the brains of certain longhaired, wild-looking gentlemen in spectacles" who wanted to supplant the republic of Washington and Jefferson with the theories of Kinkel and Cabet. The editor contrasted German radicalism with "Irish conservatism, an impregnable breakwater against the assaults of an ignorant and conceited Red Republicanism."[6] The *United States Magazine*, in July 1850, charged European reformers with "extravagant notions of freedom" and with "instilling . . . principles at war with society."

The most widely known German radical platform was the so-called "Louisville Platform" of 1854, the result of Karl Heinzen's brief and tempestuous sojourn as an editor in the Kentucky river town. In March 1854, he invited the support of the radical Germans of the city for a "new reform party." The deliberations of Heinzen, Bernhard Domschke, and other political refugees resulted in a declaration of principles known henceforth in German-American circles as the "Louisville Platform," and widely publicized by radical German editors in an appeal "To All True Republicans in the Union." The platform was a subject for acrimonious debate for several decades, and divided the German element into two definite groups. To Heinzen, the controversial statement of principles merely recapitulated the demands for "liberty, prosperity and education for all" which he had proclaimed earlier in Europe, and which, though theoretically a part of the Declaration of Independence and the United States Constitution, had never been fully realized in this country.

The Louisville Platform, in forthright language, denounced all racial and class privileges and specifically attacked slavery, all schemes for its extension, and the fugitive slave law of 1850. It called for independence in politics, instead of the blind partisanship of existing political organizations, and denounced the sinister influence of clericalism in American public life. In addition, it advocated free land for actual settlers, and equal political and social rights for Negroes and women. Women's rights and equal suffrage were issues on which Heinzen stood almost alone among his German countrymen. German papers occasionally referred to the feminist lectures of Mathilde Franziska Anneke, the most distinguished of the women Forty-eighters, but with the exception of Heinzen's *Pionier* and the St. Louis *Neue Zeit,* the German press was practically unanimous in condemning the campaign to secure equal rights for the sexes. Outstanding Forty-eighters, such as Dr. Reinhold Solger, Christian Esselen, and Friedrich Hecker, not only opposed the movement but argued that if women were given the vote, cultural progress would be retarded by a hundred years.[7] The Louisville Platform further demanded easier and quicker methods to acquire American citizenship; a new government office for colonization and immigration; internal improvements by the federal government, including the building of a Pacific railroad; penal, judicial, and educational reforms; a miscellany of social legislation; and an end to American neutrality and isolation.

Perhaps the platform's demands for the abolition of the presidency and the Senate were the most provocative. Heinzen by this time had come to regard federalism as an obstacle to direct popular government, and advocated a single, unified legal and governmental system, and the union of executive and legislative functions in one body, under a parliamentary system of ministerial responsibility. In accordance with his philosophy of government, the exact opposite of the prevailing system of checks and balances and separation of powers, the Louisville Platform advocated the immediate abolition of the presidential office. Heinzen regarded "the king in dresscoat" as a dangerous compromise with monarchy. Instead of the two-house legislature, the Louisville radicals favored a unicameral Congress elected directly by the people and subject to recall at any time, and as a substitute for a single executive they proposed an administrative group patterned on the Swiss executive council, subject to congressional control, and carefully watched by a congressional committee whenever Congress was not in session.[8]

The Germans who drafted this declaration of principles at Louisville hoped to organize their countrymen, on a nation-wide basis, into a "Union of free Germans," and they distributed their platform and an accompanying manifesto in German and English to the press and to men in public life. More than a score of German newspapers in the West reprinted the platform, and in the East it was carried by the *Anzeiger des Nordens,* Anneke's *Newarker Zeitung,* the *Long Island Zeitung,* and the Philadelphia *Freie Presse,* a paper strongly sympathetic to labor. The Louisville Platform was formally endorsed by organizations of "free Germans" in Boston, Cincinnati, Indianapolis, and San Antonio, and Heinzen championed its principles for the rest of his life. They became the credo of the small and unique League of Radicals which Heinzen organized in later years. His attacks against the office of chief executive never mellowed, and in 1868 Heinzen's *Pionier* circulated petitions to abolish the presidency. A number of Turner endorsed his proposal, and Schurz and Sumner presented his petitions to the Senate, as did Butler to the House of Representatives. In the elections of 1868 and 1872 Heinzen's followers dropped special ballots into the ballot boxes bearing the words "No President at All," and "the abolition of the monarchical office."[9]

Such extreme proposals created alarm in American circles and were among the reasons for the nativist agitation against German "radicals and infidels," and the Knownothing riots in Louisville in 1855. Actually Germans who advocated such radical measures constituted a very small minority of the total German immigration. The *New Yorker Staatszeitung* repudiated the Heinzen radicals, and the editor of the Columbus *Westbote* made short shrift of every movement that originated with the man whom it once characterized as this "Field Marshal of all incurable world reformers."[10] The *Texas State Gazette,* reporting a convention of German radicals in San Antonio, denounced their propaganda "to undermine and uproot our institutions and laws, religion and its ministers. . . ."[11]

Such radical programs inevitably raised the question of the desirability of founding a "new German party" to influence American politics directly. In the early 1850's, German language papers in Philadelphia and New York, and the *Baltimore Wecker* and the St. Louis *Anzeiger des Westens,* gave the proposal some support.[12] Many Forty-eighters weighed the chances for a new party only to abandon the suggestion as impracticable, and German papers with substantial circulation lists maintained that such political maneuvers would endanger instead of enhance the influence of the German-American group. The *Cincinnati Volksblatt* soberly reminded newcomers that they were the beneficiaries of the free institutions of a free country and were now "enrolled in the practical school of experience in republican living."[13]

More alarming to the general public than these proposals, the best of which were later enacted into law and the worst discarded, was the infiltration of socialist and communist ideas from Europe. Socialism and communism were used as interchangeable terms and have never been too accurately defined. Both were regarded as foreign importations, spawned and nurtured on foreign soil, and the exact opposite of the political and economic theories on which the American Republic was based. Until the end of the nineteenth century American socialism had a decidedly foreign flavor; its program and procedures were imported from abroad, and received their greatest support from recently arrived immigrants, especially German craftsmen.

As early as the spring of 1849, Magnus Gross, later a member of the staff of the *New Yorker Staatszeitung,* lectured on socialism in Louisville.[14] A German workers' society, founded in Detroit in 1850, championed socialist reforms. In Milwaukee, German émigrés of 1848 planted the seeds of socialism among the Turner and workers' movement in the 1850's. Members of the Milwaukee *Arbeiter und Lese Verein* listened regularly to addresses by prominent Forty-eighters, such as Anneke, Schröter, and Franz Schmidt, a former member of the Frankfurt Parliament.[15] Weitling's *Die Republik der Arbeiter,* though published in New York City, had readers in Wisconsin, and papers like the Milwaukee *Volksfreund* and the *Wisconsin Banner* were sympathetic to his program. Louisville had its quota of German communists before the Civil War who looked upon Weitling and Willich as their prophets. The Cincinnati *Arbeiterbund* maintained a hall and a coöperative grocery, and although weakened by internal controversies, the German workers and socialists remained powerful in that city until 1860 and from time to time supported a local labor party.[16] The radical wing of German immigrant labor read scores of little labor papers from New York to New Orleans.

In 1853, the *Sozialer Turnverein* of New York gave a ball and concert for the relief of the "proletarians" in the communist trial of Cologne, and the proceedings of that famous "red" trial were reported in detail in German-American papers of editorial viewpoints as varying as the *New*

Yorker Criminal Zeitung und Belletristisches Journal, Weitling's *Die Republik der Arbeiter* and the *Neu England Zeitung.* The *Turnzeitung* carried essays on "capital and labor" and similar topics, and reflected a strongly socialistic editorial policy.[17] Wilhelm Rosenthal's *Wilde Rosen,* a Sunday weekly, in 1850 championed atheism, socialism, and the class struggle; and the *Beobachter am Ohio,* a radical Louisville sheet, attacked all private property, and urged that capitalists and priests be hanged together, according to the "philosophy of the guillotine and the gallows."[18] When the first American edition of the *Communist Manifesto* appeared in English in *Woodhull and Claflin's Weekly,* it was referred to as "German Communism-Manifesto of the German Communist Party."

Heinzen's program of social reform would classify him with modern socialists, but he was not a communist. He had no desire to destroy individual property rights, but wished to guarantee and safeguard them for all, and he fought violent personal battles with communist leaders. He respected Weitling as an honest and sincere utopian, but he hated Marx, and referred to the latter's dialectics as the antics of an "ape," hopping from one Hegelian thesis and antithesis to another, and denounced his program as nothing short of a "communist factory and barracks state," a jailhouse for individual liberties.[19]

Hermann Kriege's program also was socialistic, and like Heinzen he fell into disfavor with the Pontifex Maximus of the new communist movement, and was viciously attacked in Marx's *Neue Rheinische Zeitung.*[20] Dr. Edmund Ignatz Koch, who fled to the United States in 1850, distributed copies of Blanqui's writings and asked Marx for copies of the *Communist Manifesto* for circulation in New York.[21] Abraham Jacobi, August Willich, and August Becker, accused in the Cologne "red trial" of membership in secret radical organizations, were part of the Forty-eighter immigration.[22] Friedrich Kapp was known in 1848 as a "proletarian" and a "communist."[23] Gustav Struve, an extreme republican and once an intimate of Heinzen, may be classified as a socialist, as his early American papers, the New York *Der Deutsche Zuschauer* and his *Soziale Republik,* clearly indicate. The latter became the official organ of a German workingmen's league under strong Forty-eighter influence, which the German Communist Club of New York tried in vain to control.[24]

August Willich, officer in the Prussian Army until he resigned in 1846 because his liberal views clashed with those of his superiors, learned the carpenter trade, and as a manual laborer found his way into the communist ranks. He studied the communist theories prevalent in Europe before the Revolution, and was greatly influenced by the Communist League of Cologne. In 1848, after fighting with Hecker in Baden, and in 1849, with Blenker and Schimmelpfennig in the Palatinate, Willich fled to Switzerland and England, and in 1853, we find him working as a carpenter in the Brooklyn Navy Yard. He edited the *Deutsche Republikaner,* a radical labor paper in Cincinnati dedicated to the class struggle, from 1858 to 1861, and then went off to war as an officer of the Union Army. Though known to his contemporaries as "the reddest of the red," he too disagreed sharply with Marx and was repeatedly attacked by the Marx-Engels group.[25] Adolf Douai, another of the radicals of 1848, published a series of articles in English on Marx's *Das Kapital* in the *Socialist,* and as late as 1878, though now engaged in the peaceful task of teaching a kindergarten in New Jersey, he testified before a congressional committee on the causes of the panic of 1873. As a spokesman for the Socialist Labor Party, he explained the crash in terms of "planless production," resulting in "overproduction" and "underconsumption."[26]

Kellner, Meyer, Sorge, and Weydemeyer were Forty-eighters more intimately associated with Marx and more favorably disposed toward his leadership, and all carved their niche in the history of American radicalism. Gottfried Theodore Kellner was a Ph.D. from Göttingen who published the radical *Hornisse* in Kassel, during the Revolution. After his press was destroyed, he fled to Belgium and then to New York, where he edited the first number of *Die Reform,* a strictly Marxist paper which had a brief existence. In 1856, he became editor of the Philadelphia *Demokrat.* Although his radicalism diminished with prosperity and advancing years, he remained an active supporter of labor and the socialist movement in the United States. Hermann Meyer, a German Jew and radical pamphleteer, arrived in New York in 1852 and, like Kellner, fell under the influence of Joseph Weydemeyer, worked for the cause in Milwaukee and St. Louis, and helped organize German sections of the First International.[27]

Friedrich A. Sorge, another early German Marxist, was the son of a Saxon preacher whose home was a kind of way station for political refugees in the underground between Poland, Belgium, and France. After fighting in the German Revolution, Sorge escaped to Switzerland, where he supported himself by giving music lessons, for he felt as much at home with Beethoven and Wagner as with Marx and Engels. In Geneva he became identified with the workers' movement, and made important contacts with such radicals as Moses Hess, Johann Philipp Becker, Marx, and Engels. Sorge came to the United States in 1852. In 1857 he became a member of the German *Kommunisten Klub,* founded in New York by freethinking communists. Friedrich Kamm, another Forty-eighter, was its chairman, and Fritz Jacobi, a veteran of 1848 who lost his life in the Civil War, was vice-president. The little group worked hard to exploit the panic of 1857 as an argument for Marxism. For a time Sorge coöperated with republicans such as Heinzen and Douai to overthrow the German tyrants, but as he grew older his interest turned almost exclusively to the communist movement. One of the first independent labor parties was formed in New York from the union of the *Kommunisten Klub* and a German *Arbeiterverein.* Thoroughly honest and incorruptible, Sorge rose to prominence as a Marxist leader in the United States, became general secretary of the First International when that body established its headquarters in New York, and represented the United States at the Congress of the International at The Hague. When he died in 1906, at nearly eighty, he left his library, rich in materials on the early labor movement and socialism, to the New York Public Library.[28]

Joseph Weydemeyer was the favorite of Marx and Engels, and continues to be revered by American communists as one of their pioneers. The son of a Prussian official, he prepared for a military career at the military academy in Berlin. As a young man he was attracted to the radical theories of Anneke and Willich and was greatly influenced by the *Rheinische Zeitung* of Cologne. Presently Weydemeyer abandoned the army for journalism. He worked on the *Triersche Zeitung,* and in 1845 helped edit the *Westphaelische Dampfboot,* a socialist monthly to which both Marx and Engels contributed. In the crucial year of the Revolution, Weydemeyer was associated with the *Neue Deutsche Zeitung,* but unlike many radicals, remained behind in 1849 to keep the communist movement alive in Germany and to raise money for the refugees in London. By the end of 1850 he escaped to Switzerland, after his paper had been banned by the authorities, and in November 1851, with a wife and two children, he landed in New York, with a letter of introduction from Marx to Charles A. Dana. At the time, Marx was a contributor to Greeley's

Tribune, and German-language papers already were taking some notice of his writing.[29]

With the blessing of Karl Marx, Weydemeyer launched his weekly *Die Revolution,* in New York, dedicated to the exposition of Marxian materialism and the class struggle. For this little New York paper which survived but two issues, Marx wrote his famous *18th Brumaire of Louis Napoleon,* and Engels and Freiligrath were other contributors. When the paper folded, Weydemeyer complained bitterly that the workers were being exploited in America by Kossuth and Kinkel, and "most of them are asinine enough to contribute a dollar for this hostile propaganda rather than a penny for the expression of their own interests."[30] Both Engels and Marx had warned their disciple as early as 1851 that "the available Germans who are worth anything become easily Americanized," and he had pointed out that the economic opportunities which the United States had to offer made men "consider bourgeois conditions as a *beau idéal.*"[31] America had no "real proletariat," in the European sense, at whom the propaganda of communism could be directed.

Although his first paper failed, Weydemeyer continued to act as "literary agent for Marx and Engels," and tried to place their articles with the *New York Tribune* and radical German-language papers such as the *Turnzeitung* of New York and the *Neu England Zeitung* of Boston. Weydemeyer fought with Heinzen and other critics of Marx, attacked the "romantic" plans and "political immaturity" of revolutionary exiles such as Kinkel, Fickler, Gögg, Willich, and others, and expounded the gospel of a dictatorship of the proletariat. In June 1852, with four other hopeful spirits and the blessing of the Marxists in London, Weydemeyer organized the Proletarian League of New York, a group which his recent biographer calls "the first nucleus of the newly forming Marxist movement in the United States."[32] Weydemeyer was active in the German labor movement of the 1850's, particularly during an epidemic of strikes in New York in 1853, and in March of that year, with Dr. Kellner, launched *Die Reform,* only to see it expire again on April 26, 1854. After this second failure in radical journalism, Weydemeyer made his living by free-lance writing and lecturing on English Chartism. Finally forced to move for financial reasons to Milwaukee, he found employment as a notary and a surveyor. Here and in Chicago he worked with workers' clubs and *Turnvereine,* sold Marx's publications, and wrote for the *Illinois Staatszeitung.* Returning to New York, he helped survey Central Park, and continued his propaganda in the trade unions and the Communist Club, established in 1857. An ardent supporter of Lincoln, he served as an officer and engineer in the Union Army and was discharged a colonel in 1865. Thereafter, he wrote for the *Neue Zeit* in St. Louis, and was county surveyor. He died in the cholera epidemic of 1866, at the age of forty-eight.

In contrast with the so-called "scientific socialism" of Weydemeyer and the Marxists, the America of the Forty-eighters also had its exponents of utopia. In Cleveland, Joseph Leopold Stiger sold the monthly *Der Kommunist* (1852) for ten cents a copy, and opened a "Political Literary Institute" on Superior Street, where periodicals and other printed matter were available for an admission charge of a cent a day, or 12½ cents a month.[33] Fritz Anneke in the Milwaukee *Volksfreund* described the communist utopia as "the last and highest form of social life on earth . . . the realization of entire and perfect liberty . . . the annihilation of any type of compulsion, theoretical and practical . . . the realization of heaven."[34] Sebastian Seiler, a co-worker of Weitling in France and Switzerland, and a veteran of the revolutions in Baden and Westphalia, expounded unsound theories about labor and money in his papers in New Orleans.[35] Douai, early in his career, maintained that the maximum of liberty was possible only under communism,[36] and Franz Arnold, a revolutionist from the working class, advocated coöperatives and Weitling's brand of communism in the United States after 1849, but later ceased all political agitation and settled down to business and real estate in Chicago.[37] Louisville, in 1850, had a political refugee from Baden, known only as Dr. Krauth and nicknamed "Robespierre." The "Doctor" equated communism with primitive Christianity, and predicted both state and church would wither away.[38] Such men belong among the visionaries and stargazers of the middle nineteenth century, when America was literally fermenting with reform.

The most interesting of the communists among the Forty-eighters was Wilhelm Weitling, the self-educated tailor from Magdeburg. His theories derived largely from Babeuf, Buonarratti, Cabet, Considérant, Fourier, Saint-Simon, Proudhon, and others whom he had met or with whose publications he had become familiar while living in Paris, where he combined tailoring with radical propaganda. As a member of "the League of the Just," one of the many secret societies of the French capital, he prepared his first major treatise, *Die Menschheit wie sie ist und wie sie sein sollte* (Mankind as it is and as it should be), in which he attempted to integrate the rising labor movement with the new doctrine of communism. In contrast with Marx, Weitling's communism was a mixture of rationalism, French utopianism, and certain moral and religious principles derived from primitive Christianity, for although Weitling emphasized his agnosticism and anticlericalism, there was a deeply mystical element in all he wrote. His particular brand of communism stemmed, moreover, from actual experiences as a craftsman and journeyman, and behind the radical theories which he had absorbed in the French secret societies there was an emotional drive which made him a unique personality.

Weitling had left France to plant the seeds of communistic doctrine in the cantons of Switzerland, where he promoted workers' organizations, established coöperative dining halls, published a radical journal, and founded secret communist cells which operated under innocuous names. In 1842 he published his *Garantieen der Harmonie und Freiheit* (Guarantees of Harmony and Freedom) the magnum opus which most completely describes his "system," and *Das Evangelium des armen Sünders* (The Gospel of the Poor Sinner) which tried to prove that the teachings of Jesus, if rightly understood, were identical with communism. The author's portrayal of the Nazarene as a revolutionary leader of the underprivileged led to his conviction for blasphemy and disturbing the peace, and a term in the Zurich jail. Upon his release he was pushed across the border into Germany and eventually made his way to London, where he was hailed as a martyr by the German Communist Club. In 1846 Weitling broke with Marx over the correct interpretation of the communist gospel and proper propaganda techniques, and was read out of the party by his younger and less well-known rival.[39]

Weitling was in the United States when the news of the Revolution reached this country, and hurried back to Germany, but his rôle in the *annus mirabilis* of 1848 was not significant, and his stubborn insistence on complete social revolution, instead of piecemeal reform, found few supporters. Returning to the United States, he tried once more to put his theories into practice.

The philosophical tailor worked hard in America for social security, coöperatives, and old-age pensions. He called the first German labor congress in the United States, and the delegates, meeting in Philadelphia, drafted an interesting platform. For five years Weitling edited and published *Die Republik der Arbeiter* in New York, traveled widely to organize chapters of his *Arbeiterbund,* and promoted labor halls in many cities. In the end, his movement failed because of his disastrous decision to invest its funds in a communist colony in Iowa.[40]

Weitling's *Arbeiterbund* had local affiliates from New York to Milwaukee, and from Detroit to New Orleans. Its founder had devoted disciples in Louisville, in far-off New Braunfels, Texas, and in tiny frontier settlements such as Mayville, Wisconsin. His German Labor Congress of 1850 spoke for some 4,400 workers from *Arbeitervereine* throughout the eastern half of the United States, and gave first place to Weitling's views about currency, coöperatives, and banks where labor could be exchanged for labor.

The avowed purpose of the *Arbeiterbund,* which at its peak probably had five thousand contributing members, was to usher in Weitling's "republic of the workers." Its more practical objectives included sick benefits, old-age pensions, and other forms of social insurance and mutual assistance. For several years German workers sent their dues to the central office in New York. Workers' halls in many cities provided meeting places for social and cultural activities, mutual insurance societies, coöperative dining halls, and little building and loan associations. The larger societies supported singing and theatrical organizations, public lectures and debates, and reading and social rooms. Here workers found diversion and the means for intellectual development, as well as good food and drink, at reasonable prices. Weitling claimed to be the first German leader in the United States to expose the "lodge humbug" of his countrymen, and to denounce the expenditure of the worker's hard-earned dollars for such "silly purposes." Though he enjoyed convivial social gatherings, his primary purpose was to organize labor for social revolution and shake off the prevailing system of wage slavery which was depressing workingmen into a hopeless proletariat. Although the *Arbeiterbund* fell apart in 1855, some local units survived as centers of social and cultural life.

After the Civil War, the German workers' movement played an important rôle in the formation of the first Socialist parties in America—parties so dependent for their support on immigrants that for years German was one of the languages of procedure in their conventions. The seeds sown by Weitling, Weydemeyer, and others continued to bear fruit in many places. Ludwig Bogen, a political refugee of the Frankfurt Parliament, founded the *New Ulm Post* in 1864, and ardently supported the Knights of Labor.[41] Johannes Peyer, an M.D. from St. Gallen, Switzerland, who participated in the student revolt in Vienna in 1848, combined the practice of medicine in Cincinnati with editing the *Arbeiter Abendzeitung.*[42] *Die Freie Presse,* a workers' organ in Philadelphia, counted heavily for support on radical Forty-eighters,[43] and the *Arbeiterhalle* in that city, built originally by an association advocating Weitling's currency reforms, continued as headquarters for a mutual insurance society for workingmen. At the end of the century, its singing society merged with the Philadelphia *Harmonie.*

Spokesmen for the older and more conservative German immigration, such as the Columbus, Ohio, *Westbote* and the *Staatszeitung* of New York, predicted correctly that the new radicalism would not take root in America. The Cleveland *Germania* and the *Westbote* referred repeatedly to the madness, arrogance, and intolerance of men like Weitling, who wanted to teach the American people "true republicanism" and represented their opponents as Philistines, "slaves of capital" and "servants of the moneyed aristocracy." The *Westbote* maintained that the American republic could not be understood from within "the four walls of a New York hotel by a bottle of wine," ridiculed propagandists who could not agree on a definition of socialism and communism, and as "patent reformers" "sat on their nests like clucking hens to hatch a new platform every month."[44] The *New Yorker Staatszeitung* referred to "heroes of revolution" and "European beer politicians" who picked American pocketbooks for their plans of world reform, and warned its readers against intellectual "rowdies and loafers" whom the European Revolution had dumped upon the United States.[45]

The prophets of communism discovered to their sorrow that their German brethren in the United States were far more interested in social evenings, lodges, and beer halls than in coöperatives, a new currency, and utopian colonies in the Middle West. The America of the 1850's, with cheap land and relatively good wages, was not a favorable atmosphere in which to nourish radical plans for a new social and economic system. The absence of caste restrictions and the general acceptance of a philosophy of free enterprise and equality of opportunity bred rugged individualists, not disciples for utopias. Weitling, for example, got a hearing and a following soon after his arrival in the United States, for his European reputation and prestige had preceded him, but his theories, like those of other European reformers, did not strike root, and died as other alien radical systems imported from the outside have done. They could not thrive in the American climate where men who were willing to work and save had an equal chance to rise in the economic and social scale.

The indictment of communistic theories from the pen of Christian Esselen in the *Atlantis* of April 1855 has special importance. "Communism is a contradiction in itself," wrote this radical Forty-eighter. "It speaks of brotherly love, but it is rank egoism. It proclaims liberty, but reduces to slavery. It promises the right of freedom, but subjects to a dogmatic system. Communism is a form of religion. . . . It claims to abolish private property, but in reality dissolves personality. It promises equality, yet sets up a veritable caste system. It promises the well-being of all, yet leads to a state of poverty." In the same vein Karl Heinzen, regarded by European and American communists as a mere bourgeois democrat, observed that communists wished "to make people happy without making them free," and talked too much about "interests" and too little about "principle."

FOOTNOTES

CHAPTER 12

1. Adolf Douai: *Land und Leute in der Union* (Berlin, 1864) pp. 59-116.
2. Philipp Wagner: *Ein Achtundvierziger* (Brooklyn, 1882) pp. 236-38.
3. *Westbote,* Aug. 19, 1853.
4. *Ibid.,* April 28, 1854.
5. *Ibid.,* June 9, 1854.
6. *National Intelligencer,* Dec. 10, 1851.
7. See *Atlantis,* Jan. 1855, II (N.S.) pp. 75-76; *New Yorker Staatszeitung,* Dec. 21, 1855. For reports of Madam Anneke's lectures, see *Ibid.,* Sept. 3, 1852; Jan. 13, 1853; *Belletristisches Journal,* Sept. 3, 1852; *Wächter am Erie,* Aug. 14, 1852.
8. For more detailed discussion of Heinzen's views, and the Louisville Platform, see Wittke: *Heinzen,* pp. 94-95; and Chapters IX and X.
9. See also on these reforms, *Wächter am Erie,* Feb. 26, 1868; and a lecture by Hecker in Cleveland, *Ibid.,* Dec. 15, 1871.
10. Oct. 21, 1851.
11. *Texas State Gazette,* June 22, 1854, quoted in *Americana Germanica,* VII, New Series (1909) p. 176; see also, pp. 208-12; 218-25.
12. See *New Yorker Staatszeitung,* Aug. 18, 1850; Aug. 26, 28, 1851; July 13, 1852.
13. *Cincinnati Volksblatt,* May 14, 1850, quoted in *Westbote,* Dec. 13, 1850.

14. Stierlin: *Kentucky*, p. 111.

15. Koss: *Milwaukee*, p. 337.

16. See *Cincinnati Volksblatt*, Feb. 25, 1851.

17. *Belletristisches Journal*, Aug. 31, 1860.

18. See Stierlin: *Kentucky*, p. 124; also *Westbote*, Nov. 22, 1850; and Joseph Dorfman: *The Economic Mind in American Civilization, 1865-1918* (New York, 1949) III, 42-46.

19. See Wittke: *Heinzen*, Ch. X—"Social Reform Without Communism."

20. See *New Yorker Staatszeitung*, Dec. 2, 1848.

21. Karl Obermann: *Joseph Weydemeyer, Pioneer of American Socialism* (New York, 1947) pp. 35-36.

22. See also, W. F. Kamman: *Socialism in German-American Literature* (Philadelphia, 1917) *passim*.

23. Edith Lenel: *Friedrich Kapp*, pp. 48-49.

24. Hermann Schlüter: *Die Internationale in Amerika* (Chicago, 1918).

25. See *New Yorker Staatszeitung*, Dec. 27, 1853; also *Der Deutsche Pionier*, IX, No. 10 (Jan. 1878) pp. 439-45, 488-95; X, No. 2 (May, 1878) pp. 68-71; No. 3 (June, 1878) pp. 114-17; No. 4 (July, 1878) pp. 144-47.

26. Dorfman: *op. cit.*, III, 42-46.

27. Obermann: *op. cit.*, p. 147.

28. On Sorge, see Hermann Schlüter: *Die Internationale in Amerika*, pp. 87-88; *Deutsch-Amerikanische Geschichtsblätter*, VIII (Oct., 1908) No. 4, p. 148; and Sorge's "Erinnerungen eines Achtundvierzigers," in *Die Neue Zeit* (Stuttgart, 1899) 17. Jahrgang, Vol. II, edit. by Karl Kautsky, pp. 150-60; 189-92; 252-56; 284-88; 317-20; 381-84; 414-16; 445-48.

29. See *New Yorker Staatszeitung*, Nov. 24, 1849; June 8, 1850; Sept. 4, 1852.

30. Quoted in Obermann: *op. cit.*, p. 40.

31. *Ibid.*, p. 28; see also, *Die Neue Zeit* (Stuttgart, 1907) Vol. XXV, p. 58; and for a later, but similar, comment by Engels, Gustav Mayer: *Friedrich Engels* (New York, 1936) p. 276.

32. Obermann: *op. cit.*, p. 55.

33. *Westbote*, Jan. 8, 1852.

34. *Volksfreund*, Jan. 7, 1851, quoted in Overmoehle: *op. cit.*, p. 228.

35. *Belletristisches Journal*, Sept. 28, 1860.

36. See *Die Zukunft* (Berlin, 1878) I, 65-74, 447-55.

37. *Der Deutsche Pionier*, XV (No. 9) Dec. 1883, p. 382-83.

38. Stierlin: *Kentucky*, pp. 120-21.

39. See Carl Wittke—"Marx and Weitling," in *Essays in Political Theory*, presented to George H. Sabine and edited by Milton R. Konvitz and Arthur E. Murphy (Ithaca, 1948) pp. 179-93.

40. See Carl Wittke: *The Utopian Communist, A Biography of Wilhelm Weitling, Nineteenth Century Reformer* (Baton Rouge, 1950). See also C. F. Huch: "Die Anfänge der Arbeiterbewegung unter den Deutsch-Amerikanern," in *Mitteilungen des Deutschen Pionier-Vereins von Philadelphia*, X (Oct. 1910) No. 4, pp. 244-55.

41. *Der Deutsche Pionier*, No. 4 (1886) pp. 347-48.

42. *Ibid.*, XI, No. 2 (May, 1879) p. 55.

43. *Mitteilungen des Deutschen Pionier-Vereins von Philadelphia*, V (1907) pp. 21-25.

44. *Westbote*, April 14 ,1851; also Oct. 25, Nov. 22, 29, 1850.

45. See *New Yorker Staatszeitung*, Sept. 21, Oct. 24, 1850; March 5, 1851; June 12, 24, 30, Aug. 8, 1851. See also, Rudolf Cronau: *Drei Jahrzehnte Deutschen Lebens in Amerika* (Berlin, 1909) pp. 305 and 464, for comments on Heinzen and Sorge.

Chapter 13 · NATIVISM

FROM THE beginning of our history as a separate nation on this Continent, it was a popular American theory that the doors to the United States stood open to the dissatisfied, the persecuted, and the ambitious from all parts of the western world. Immigration helped Americans to expand the vision of their democracy into a haven of refuge where men and women of every national origin could pool their brains and brawn in the building of a land of peace and prosperity. Yet there has never been a generation since colonial days when the politics of the United States have been entirely free of nativism. In every period of American history there have been those who viewed with alarm an unrestricted immigration from alien lands, and feared lest the newcomers prove unassimilable and a menace to American institutions, and on several occasions the nativism of a well-organized and vocal minority has produced political upheavals of considerable consequence. In the 1830's local nativist parties arose on the eastern seaboard, and there were bitter controversies over the use of public funds for Catholic parochial schools. In Charlestown, Massachusetts, an Ursuline Convent was burned down in 1834, and the antagonism between Protestants and Catholics reached alarming proportions because of acts of vandalism which continued into the 1840's.

In the 1850's, America experienced its greatest period of nativism and religious bigotry. In a decade when old political parties were disintegrating, confused voters were looking for new issues and new alignments to divert attention from the increasingly acrimonious debate over slavery. The 1850's also became a decade of extraordinarily heavy immigration from Ireland and the German states, and the immigrant vote, under the control of local political bosses, assumed new and alarming proportions in American politics. Americans had not yet mastered or completely accepted all the implications of the peaceful use of the ballot box. The melting pot seemed to be boiling over as new elements from Europe were dumped into it year after year. Conservative property-holders resented higher taxes for the support of indigent or unhealthy immigrants, and concluded that the newcomers not only were polluting American elections but endangering property rights as well. At the same time, labor feared the effect of immigration on the standard of living.

To these causes of nativism must be added the deep-seated fear of American Protestants that the institutions of the Republic were being threatened by the growing power of the Church of Rome. The Catholic Church grew rapidly before the Civil War, primarily because of the influx of Irish and, to a lesser degree, German Catholics. Because the Knownothingism of the 1850's was so largely anti-Catholic, the Irish bore the brunt of its attack, and the movement was fed by the rantings of anti-popery preachers, the lurid revelations of ex-priests, and a pornographic literature reeking with the alleged immorality of monasteries and convents.

The Knownothing Order, a secret political party whose clandestine methods appealed to a nation of joiners and struck fear into the hearts of old-line politicians who did not know how to cope with such a mysterious phenomenon, became so strong that competent observers seriously considered the possibility of a Knownothing president in 1856. In 1855, governors and legislatures of Knownothing persuasion were elected in seven states, and Horace Greeley, a strong opponent of the movement, guessed that from seventy-five to a hundred members of Congress were openly or secretly connected with the Order. By 1857 it was practically dead. It died of a number of causes, but primarily because it abandoned secrecy and split along sectional lines over the slavery controversy.[1]

Although the Irish were the particular *bête noire* of the Knownothings, Germans received their full share of abuse and denunciation, and there were violent physical encounters between Germans and nativists in several cities. The specific charges against the German group were not the same in all parts of the country, but they stemmed from the attitude of Germans, and especially radical Forty-eighters, toward religion, Americanization, the Puritan Sabbath, temperance legislation, and radicalism in politics and economics.

The superior attitude of German intellectuals toward American culture and institutions was partly responsible for the unfavorable reaction of many Americans toward the German immigrants. In the words of Julius Fröbel, they did too much talking and boasting about "German" industry, "German" philosophy, "German" art, "German" toleration, "German" women, the "German" temperament and the "German" spirit, a spirit that "seemed to stand constantly before a mirror, observing itself," and indulging in a self-adulation that could be attributed either to "vanity or hypochondria."[2] Instead of recognizing the flexibility of American life and becoming attuned to this "Paradise of the poor man" where there was complete freedom and a minimum of government, too many German intellectuals talked only of becoming "the yeast of the fermenting process of the modern age; the oxygen in the process of combustion of national and religious prejudices." Gustav Körner specifically attributed the strong revival of native Americanism "to the arrogance, imperious and domineering conduct of the refugees."[3]

The attitude of certain German leaders toward Americanization was a cause of grave concern to Americans who were disturbed by the slow amalgamation of immigrant groups. The German immigration after 1848 included some unusually obstinate and difficult material to assimilate. A Forty-eighter like Friedrich Kapp advocated complete Americanization in language and customs, for he believed all efforts to develop a German cultural area in the United States would fail. He therefore urged educated Germans to affiliate as closely as possible with Americans of similar intellect and training, and cease consorting with German-American farmers and workingmen. But Kapp was severely criticized by fellow immigrants when he asserted that "America will become the fatherland of those born here," and that the grandchildren of immigrants will completely forget the language of their forbears. Kapp himself in heart and spirit remained a German, and regarded Europe as his spiritual and cultural home. Julius Fröbel advised his countrymen to strive for cultural integration based on the English language,[4] and in the *Atlantis* in 1858, Christian Esselen advocated a "crossing of the best in all nations." "There is no American people," he added, "it is fashioned from those who came from all corners of the earth. The only unity exists in the principle of civil, religious, and political liberty."

Karl Heinzen wrestled with the problem of Americanization for years, and did not complete his naturalization until 1860. He found it difficult to compromise between the cultural patterns of Europe and America. He could understand how one could remain a German in the United States, or become completely Americanized, but he refused to approve the hyphenated "German-American" who, he believed, represented surrender to a hybrid status inferior to both the German and the American. He quarreled with Carl Schurz and thought the latter had been too quick to win acceptance as an American politician and too eager to "serve" the American people instead of influencing them intellectually and culturally as a German. "The Germans feel that he has become an American; no American feels that he has remained a German."

As late as 1866, Heinzen wrote that one might hate Germany and leave it, as he and other Forty-eighters had done, but one could never deny one's nationality, because it was deeply rooted in a man's blood, his education, and the history and traditions of his people. In one of his best public lectures, delivered in the Turner Hall in Boston, Heinzen defined Americanism in terms of the Declaration of Independence, and denounced the Americanization program of the Knownothings as a betrayal of the immigrant's cultural heritage. He pleaded for variety in American life; for harmony between diverse cultures and national strains rather than complete uniformity, and for a common devotion to the rights of man. "We cannot be natural Americans," he concluded; "we will not ape Americanism, and we dare not be inferior to Americans. Therefore let us be Germans without Teutonism, and Americans without Americanism; merely American citizens with a German nature, who will find their Americanization in the unhampered development of true humanism, in the atmosphere of freedom guaranteed by the Declaration of Independence."[5]

Carl Schurz, who made the adjustment to America more completely than most Forty-eighters, resolved quite early that he would see the United States in the most favorable light possible and, because he had decided to make his home here, would not become discouraged. Yet in 1853 he wrote, "I am no less attached to Germany in America than I was in Europe."[6] Twenty years later, in a speech to a *Sängerbund* in Washington, he denounced the nativist attitude but also criticized his German listeners for isolating themselves from their American neighbors. He recognized Anglo-Saxon hegemony in language and tradition; he urged Germans to amalgamate with other Americans and "to give up separate, special interests in politics," and he compared the United States to "a great river into which many streams flow."[7] Yet Schurz, whom Charles A. Dana described as the "red-bearded Teuton" with "the eloquence of Demosthenes and the fire of Kossuth," was frequently abused during his public career as a "Mephistopheles in whiskers" and a "Dutch viper" who sucked the red blood of the American Republic.[8]

Professor Hawgood has suggested that it was one of the "tragedies of German-America" that the German element in the United States received its ablest and most aggressive leadership at a time when the country was in the midst of a revival of militant native Americanism. The Forty-eighters found themselves on the offensive and on the defensive for several decades. The result was an organized resistance on the part of the German element to the normal processes of Americanization. The cultural isolation which resulted persisted for several decades. Moreover, fed by the flattery of American politicians eager for votes which might be delivered *en bloc,* the Germans developed a sense of political importance far beyond their actual strength. The Knownothing crusade of the 1850's enforced an artificial unity upon the German group, awakened the German element from their lethargy, and helped close the chasm which had divided the older and the newer immigration. The more radical Forty-eighters were culturally conscious and politically hyper-conscious, and the Knownothings furnished them with an issue which enlisted their talents of leadership and thus helped build little German cultural islands in the great sea of Americanism.[9]

De Tocqueville once said that "religion in America . . . must be regarded as the first of their political institutions." In seeking an explanation for the nativist attitude toward the German immigration of the middle nineteenth century it must be emphasized again that the agnosticism, materialism, and atheism of the radicals, and their tactless attitude toward venerable American institutions, was a most important factor. Knownothings denounced their Tom Paine celebrations as un-American "manifestations of German infidelity."[10] The *Buffalo Commercial Advertiser,* a nativist organ, grudgingly acknowledged the ability and culture of the Forty-eighters, but found the "religious element . . . lacking in them." Nativists stressed their "infidel doctrines," their "anti-Christian" point of view, their profanation of the Sabbath, their "new, strange and bewildering theories of the destiny of man and of human society" which denied "all imperfection in the nature of man," and their assaults upon the faith of "our revolutionary ancestors."[11] The refugees were described as "disciples of Heine" by Americans who apparently believed that the German poet contended "that there can be no true freedom until Christianity shall be abolished."[12] Many nativists regarded German lodges and societies as actively anti-Christian organizations which "bring from the deep bottom of a sinful heart to the surface, Rationalism and Atheism."[13] A Knownothing paper in Boston likened the German immigration to a "festering boil" whose poison was distributed throughout the country, and added, "Their Catholicism and their atheism produce a pest, wherever they go."[14] In short, here was the fulfillment of the biblical prophecy of Ezekiel—"I will bring strangers upon thee, the terrible of the nations, and they shall draw their swords against the beauty of thy wisdom, and they shall defile thy brightness."

A small group of the most radical German freethinkers discovered some merit in the Knownothing Order, provided only its attacks could be confined to Irish Roman Catholics. They had a low opinion of the Catholic Irish, whom they described as consumers of potatoes, promiscuous begetters of children, "splay-footed bog-trotters," and willing tools of priests and corrupt politicians. The American Protestant German Association of Buffalo, virtually a German Knownothing lodge, endorsed Millard Fillmore, the candidate of the nativists, for the presidency in 1856.[15] Esselen referred to the Irish as "the praetorian guard of brutal terrorism," and described their unsavory record in American elections. Though he deplored the methods of the nativists, he justified their campaign for "Americanism" as opposed to Catholicism, and pleaded for a return to the basic principles of 1776.[16] The *New Yorker Staatszeitung*, satisfied that the rage of the nativists was directed primarily against the Irish, advised its readers to maintain a neutral position in the conflict between Puritanism and Jesuitism.[17] As late as 1876, the Cleveland *Wächter am Erie* denounced "German Knownothingism toward the Irish," and labeled both the American and the German brand of nativism as "bigoted and unjustified."[18] Under the circumstances, Irish found it impossible to coöperate with Germans, though both suffered from the malicious misrepresentations of the nativists. Instead, the Catholic clergy continued to denounce radical German "infidels," "foreign anarchists," and "universal republicans" from Central Europe, and the *Boston Pilot*, organ of the hierarchy in Massachusetts, strongly advocated stricter immigration laws to make it more difficult for radicals and infidels to gain admittance to the United States.

Political and economic considerations also figured in the nativist reaction against Germans and other recent newcomers from Europe. The *Ohio Republican,* a Knownothing sheet, stressed the effect of immigration upon American wages, and charged that Germans were driving "white people" out of the labor market, and, with their "garlic sausage, sauerkraut and beer," forcing Americans to accept a lower standard of living.[19] The argument that Europeans were robbing native Americans of bread and jobs was supported by lurid accounts of the dumping of paupers and criminals in the United States. Such charges were applied to agricultural areas as well. "Foreigners are working the farms," wrote a leading nativist in 1856. "The teeming earth, which has till now sent forth its abundance from beneath the hand of the hardy American farmer, struggles on in a succession of short crops, under the cheap system of European tillage. . . . The foreign squatter has staked out the best portions of the public domain."[20]

Many conservative, patriotic Americans believed republican institutions were in actual peril from the radicalism imported in immigrant ships. An Alabama Congressman, waving over his head a copy of a German Socialist paper published in Richmond, Virginia as he spoke in the House of Representatives, shouted that these Europeans "are incapable of appreciating and enjoying our liberties."[21] Samuel C. Busey, a nativist writer, viewed with alarm the "disaffected and turbulent persons of the earth" and "all the exiled patriots" who found asylum in America.[22] John Bell, speaking in the Senate in 1852, portrayed a "European democracy," based "upon abstractions" which scorns "our American, home-bred ideas of liberty."[23] Another nativist writer regarded German reformers and radicals as an undesirable "class of citizens," who brought from Europe "the pestilent products of the worn-out soil of the Old World," and "a host of extravagant notions of freedom, and . . . crude, undigested theories, which are actually irreconcilable with obedience to laws of our own making." The writer referred specifically to immigrants who "come with their heads full of a division of property," and "socialists [who] are silently making an impression on the people of our great cities, where all the seepings of the country are gathered into one great mass of ignorance and corruption."[24] "Bred to hatred of their own home government," commented another excited critic, "they have acquired an almost instinctive hostility to all governments."[25] Americans actually believed "red republicans" might achieve power and wealth in the United States by riding "on the blood-red waves of Revolution."[26] Such fears for the future of the American system led to the demand for a longer residence requirement for naturalization. To support their plea for more stringent regulations, nativists had only to call attention to the notorious happenings at the polls where the bosses of local machines herded foreign-born voting cattle, Irish and German alike, to the ballot boxes.

Another irritant to older Americans was the insistent clamor of political refugees for a new foreign policy and the demand that the United States abandon its traditional isolation and intervene actively to make the world safe for republicanism. "Revolutionary societies" of refugees demanded "the radical liberalization of the European Continent." To excited nativists, the reception of Kossuth, who "came with the arrogance of a conqueror, though an exile," and of Dr. Kinkel, "the celebrated German socialist professor," was convincing proof of the sinister plans of political refugees to sponsor "seditious movements, aimed alike at our system of neutrality and our form of government."[27] When Irish and Germans organized militia companies to practice the manual of arms, many Americans were convinced that the United States would be drawn into the European maelstrom of revolution, and accused Kossuth and Kinkel of advocating nothing short of "a renunciation of our national policy and the violation of our sacred neutrality."[28] American nationalism resented the German national spirit of the political refuges of 1848. "The foreigner," commented the *Cleveland Leader*, "who sets foot on our shores, resolved to be one of us, should burn his ship and be an American,"[29] stop jeopardizing the peace of his adopted fatherland by his anti-isolationist propaganda, and cease using the United States as a sounding board for his radical theories. Appeals to the "passions, prejudices and animosities of the foreigner," calculated to refresh "the recollections of his youth" were considered dangerous to the peace and security of the United States.[30]

Thus the nativist agitation, as far as the Germans of the 1850's were concerned, reveals a mixture of religious, social, political, economic, cultural, and nationalist motivation. In so far as it was based on legitimate criticisms of the behavior of certain immigrants, it had a rational justification. In part, it was the product of sheer bigotry and intolerance, and reflected the conflict between two distinct social and cultural patterns, European Continentalism and American Puritanism, or "barbarians" and "Methodists," to use the words of German Forty-eighters. Although the controversy also involved the right to drink beer and have a good time on Sunday, its roots were much deeper than mere differences of opinion over Sabbatarianism. Moreover, the Germans suspected the Whigs of a secret alliance with the nativists, and nothing that party could do, either by employing an "erstwhile German revolutionary hero" as a campaign speaker, or by the outright purchase or subsidy of German papers like the Cleveland *Germania* or the *Iowa Staatszeitung,* could dispel that impression.[31]

The Knownothing platforms of the 1850's demanded the exclusion of paupers and criminals, the repeal of state laws allowing foreigners to vote before they had completed their naturalization, a residence requirement of twenty-one years for citizenship, and the repeal of Congressional land grants to unnaturalized foreigners. The platforms invariably included denunciations of the "aggressive policy and corrupting tendencies" of the Catholic Church, favored the exclusion from public office of all save Americans by "birth, education and training," and advocated the reading of the Protestant Bible in the public schools.

Nativism found expression in other channels than secret societies, political action, and the drafting of political platforms, although these were by far the most important areas of Knownothing activity. In Cincinnati, Boston, and other cities, militia companies composed of foreign-born were disbanded.[32] The legislature of New York refused to charter a German *Turnverein* lest it become a "front" for radicalism and turn out to be an anarchist society in disguise.[33] The *Sachem,* a nativist paper of New York, specifically attacked the Germans and believed the foreign-born should be demoted to an inferior "caste" of Americans, somewhere between the Negro and the native Yankee.[34] The *Cleveland Express* objected to German singing societies because they "aid in the perpetuation of foreign clannishness" and consist primarily of "so-called 'German Liberals,' the Socialists, the anti-religious, property-dividing, law-hating emigrants from Germany."[35] A letter-writer to the *New York Tribune* deplored that Castle Garden and the Battery, the most beautiful spots from which to view New York, had been surrendered to "thousands of unwashed immigrants," whose "wandering hordes" blocked Broadway as they made their way from the Castle into the city.[36]

Such charges, however absurd, were nevertheless relatively harmless when compared with the rioting and brawling between nativists and foreign-born in many cities. In the recorded cases of mob violence, the Turner seem to have been involved more often than any other group. Their agnosticism and radicalism made them special targets for conservative, church-going native Americans, and when they organized military companies in self-defense to police their outdoor celebrations, American nativists became alarmed by this "armed minority" within the state.

Rioting between Turner and "rowdies" and "short boys" of New York began as early as 1850. On several occasions the crisis was precipitated by gangs of loafers who drank beer and ate sausages at Turner picnics and refused to pay for what they had consumed.[37] In May 1851, on Pentecost Sunday, a number of German workingmen, including the followers of Weitling, set out from New York for a picnic in Hoboken, at which Franz Arnold and Gustav Struve were the main speakers. The latter had hardly finished his plea for renewed support of republicanism in Europe when a battle royal broke out between the picnickers and New York rowdies, resulting in one death and a number of wounded. From fifty to seventy Germans were arrested and taken into court. The *New Yorker Staatszeitung* maintained that the trouble did not arise from racial antagonisms and would have occurred if only native Americans had been present, and a few extremists blamed the Jesuits for the unfortunate encounter. Nevertheless the New York Germans promptly assembled at the Shakespeare Hotel, appointed a committee, including Ottendörfer, Metternich, and Lievre, to raise a defense fund to insure a just trial, and to sponsor a concert for the benefit of the "wounded."[38] Despite wild charges by nativists that the real purpose of the outing had been to proclaim the "social republic" in America, the prosecution, after many delays, finally dropped the case.[39]

In 1852, rioting between nativists and voters in the German ward of St. Louis resulted in several casualties, and a mob hurled rocks through the windows of the *Anzeiger des Westens,* edited by a Forty-eighter.[40] In 1853, four German militia companies were molested by rowdies in New Orleans while engaged in military drill, and their refreshment stand, always the most important feature of such martial occasions, was destroyed. Several were wounded in rioting in which the militia gave a poor account of itself.[41] In 1854, Philadelphia was the scene of disturbances during a *Turnfest,* and the police broke up a serenade by German singers on the ground that they were disturbing the peace.[42] In New Orleans, nativists were suspected of setting fire to the German theatre.[43]

Such demonstrations were minor when compared with the riots in Cincinnati, Columbus, and Louisville in 1855, cities in which radical Forty-eighters were numerous and active. Cincinnati virtually was in a state of civil war for three days in April, when Knownothings seized control of the voting places, besieged the Germans "over the Rhine," and Turner threw up barricades and mobilized their sharpshooters to protect the German section of the city.[44] In Columbus the members of the *Männerchor,* a singing society founded in 1848, were attacked in June 1855 while returning from a *Sängerfest* in Cleveland. A mob seized the German flags with which the singers planned to parade to their hall, and more serious consequences were avoided only because the Turner met the singers at the depot, and conducted them to their headquarters.[45] A few weeks later a Fourth of July celebration did not end so happily, and the day became known in the German-American annals of Columbus as the "Bloody Fourth." On their way home from the day's outing, Turner, singers, and the German militia company were greeted with a shower of rocks, shots were fired from the ranks of the Turner, and three persons were wounded and one killed. The police raided the German section on the South Side of the city, searched the homes of peaceful citizens without warrants, and made a number of arrests, while a mob, including Negroes, shouted "kill the damned Dutch," and "hang the damned Hessians." Contributions poured in from many cities to defray the legal expenses of a trial, and the national Turner organization appropriated $3,000 for attorney fees. After much excited discussion in the German-language press throughout the United States, the accused were released for want of evidence, but the Germans attempted no further public celebrations in Columbus until 1859.[46] In the German community of Louisville, the home of the famous radical "Louisville Platform," the year 1855 was known as the "Knownothing Year." In August 1855, rioting between Germans and nativists broke out during a local election. Houses, taverns, and groceries of German and Irish citizens were raided, looted, and in some cases destroyed, and there were numerous casualties. Many immigrants left the city with all their belongings, even though the state legislature took steps to indemnify the sufferers, and papers like the *New Yorker Staatszeitung* and the *Buffalo Demokrat* appealed for funds for the relief of Irish and German victims of the outrage.[47]

In 1855 the battles between nativists and foreign-born reached their climax, but less bloody outbreaks occurred in other places for several years longer. Baltimore, notorious in the 1850's for its rowdies, "plug uglies," and inefficient police force, was the scene of a Knownothing riot late in 1855, and in 1858 witnessed a clash between police and Turner who had assembled in the hall of the Social Democratic *Turnverein*.[48] A German was murdered in New Orleans on election day in 1855,[49] and the following year the Turner of Covington, Kentucky, were attacked while dedicating their new flag. The trouble began when Germans refused to give unlimited refreshments to a group of youngsters, and ended with a mob throwing rocks into a Turner parade and marching menacingly around the Turner Hall. The mayor of Covington called upon all Germans to surrender their firearms, and 106 Turner were arrested and released on bail of $1,000 each.[50] In 1859 new outbursts occurred during a German picnic in Louisville and a Fourth of July celebration in Cincinnati.[51]

Mob violence of such proportions did not escape the attention of the authorities in Germany. In their propaganda to prove that America was not a utopia of freedom and tolerance, the governments of Prussia and Saxony stressed the Knownothing riots, and in the latter state, placards were posted in the streets reporting the number of Germans killed in the United States. Accounts of an election-day riot in Cincinnati and of street battles in Louisville appeared in the *Augsburger Allgemeine Zeitung* and other German papers.[52]

The attacks of nativists on "citizens by choice" instead of birth left wounds which did not heal for many years. The files of the German-language press bulge with accounts of the controversy between nativists and foreigners from 1854 to the end of the decade, and only the Civil War crowded the nativist issue into the background. "If one hair is hurt on the head of an abolitionist in Kansas," commented the *Neue Zeit* of New York in 1855, "the 'humane' press of the free states teems with lead articles, but when Germans and Irishmen are murdered by the dozens, one hears not a single word of criticism." The German press urged its readers to unite into a solid phalanx and vote as a unit against the enemies of the foreign-born. Whoever refused to join in the combat against the "common foe" should be shunned as a "traitor to his people, his political friends and his fatherland in the New World."[53] The *Illinois Staatszeitung* stressed the unjust dismissals of "foreigners" from public offices, and the leading New York paper rallied German democrats "to strangle the hydra which was choking their lives."[54] If an occasional German editor had the temerity to point out that not all "Anglo-Americans" were nativists, that nativism existed in every nation, and that the majority repudiated its ugly gospel, he was spurned as a political turncoat and a traitor to his people. More moderate Germans tried to demonstrate the enormous economic value of the immigrant to the United States or attempted to focus attention upon the patriotic rôle of the German element in earlier days by proposing a monument to General von Steuben of Revolutionary fame, but most German leaders, and especially the Forty-eighters, felt that the issue must be fought out in the arena of politics. The German reaction to Knownothingism became an important issue in the political realignment of 1850 to 1860 which witnessed the disruption of the Democratic and the formation of the new Republican party.

FOOTNOTES

CHAPTER 13

1. For further details, see Carl Wittke: *We Who Built America, The Saga of the Immigrant* (New York, 1939) Ch. XIX, "Closing the Gates"; and Ray A. Billington: *The Protestant Crusade, 1800-1860* (New York, 1938).

2. Julius Fröbel: *Die deutsche Auswanderung und ihre culturhistorische Bedeutung* (Leipzig, 1858) p. 78; also 46 and 87.

3. *Atlantis*, II (May, 1855) pp. 392-93, quoted in Overmoehle, p. 253. Koerner: *Memoirs*, I, 549.

4. Fröbel: *op. cit.*, p. 35.

5. For a more complete statement of Heinzen's views, see Wittke: *Heinzen*, Ch. XII, "The Problems of Americanization."

6. Quoted in Claude M. Fuess: *Carl Schurz, Reformer* (New York, 1932) p. 41.

7. *Wächter am Erie*, March 22, 1872.

8. Fuess: *op. cit.*, p. 172. See also Chester V. Easum: *The Americanization of Carl Schurz* (Chicago, 1929).

9. See John A. Hawgood: *The Tragedy of German-America* (New York, 1940) *passim*.

10. *Atlantis* (Jan. 1855) II (N.S.) p. 78

11. See John P. Sanderson: *Republican Landmarks* (Philadelphia, 1856) pp. 219, 226.

12. *Ibid.*, p. 219.
13. *Ibid.*, p. 226.
14. See *Westbote*, July 28, 1854; also *New Yorker Staatszeitung*, April 1, 1854.
15. *Westbote*, March 21, 1856.
16. *Atlantis* (Feb. 1855) II (N.S.) pp. 81-85.
17. *New Yorker Staatszeitung*, Dec. 15, 1853; June 7, 1854.
18. *Wächter am Erie*, Sept. 23, 1876.
19. *Westbote*, June 22, 1855.
20. Thomas R. Whitney: *A Defence of the American Policy* (New York, 1856) pp. 309-10.
21. *New Yorker Staatszeitung*, Jan. 18, 1855.
22. Samuel C. Busey: *Immigration: Its Evils and Consequences* (New York, 1856) p. 13.
23. Sanderson: *op. cit.*, p. 227.
24. *Ibid.*, pp. 219-22; 325.
25. Whitney: *op. cit.*, p. 179.
26. *Ibid.*, p. 171 and 176.
27. Whitney: *op. cit.*, pp. 172 and 177.
28. *Ibid.*, p. 191-97; also Busey, *op. cit.*, pp. 29-30.
29. *Cleveland Leader*, Jan. 31, 1855.
30. Busey: *op. cit.*, p. 61.
31. See *Westbote*, Sept. 24; Oct. 15, 22, 1852; also *New Yorker Staatszeitung*, April 20, 1855.
32. *New Yorker Staatszeitung*, July 17, 1855.
33. Billington: *op. cit.*, p. 330.
34. *Die Republik der Arbeiter*, July 17, 1852.
35. *Cleveland Express*, May 30, 1855.
36. *New York Tribune*, May 30, 1855.
37. *Deutsch-Amerikanische Geschichtsblätter*, X (Oct. 1910) No. 4, pp. 228-33.
38. *New Yorker Staatszeitung*, May 28 and May 30, 1851.
39. *Ibid.*, June 6, 17, 1851; *New York Tribune*, for all of May 1851; *Die Republik der Arbeiter*, May 31, 1851. See also, *New Yorker Staatszeitung*, June 4, 1852.
40. Börnstein: *Memoiren*, II, pp. 152-57; Scharf: *St. Louis*, p. 1838.
41. *Wächter am Erie*, May 4, 1853.
42. Egenter: *Amerika ohne Schminke* (Zurich, 1857) pp. 381-82.
43. *New Yorker Staatszeitung*, May 2, 1855.
44. *Jahrbücher der Deutsch-Amerikanischen Turnerei*, II, pp. 5-16; *Westbote*, April 6, 1855; *New Yorker Staatszeitung*, April 6, June 29, 1855.
45. *Westbote*, June 8, 1855.
46. *Westbote*, July 6, 13, 27, 1855; *Jahrbücher der Deutsch-Amerikanischen Turnerei*, II, pp. 90-93; also 110-20; and *New Yorker Staatszeitung*, July 12, 1855.
47. See Stierlin: *Kentucky*, pp. 164-74; *Westbote*, Aug. 10, 17, 25, 1855; *New Yorker Staatszeitung*, Aug. 8, 1855; and also Klauprecht, *Deutsche Chronik*, pp. 187-96.
48. *New Yorker Staatszeitung*, June 4, 1858.
49. *Westbote*, Oct. 26, Nov. 9, 30, 1855.
50. *Westbote*, May 16, 1856; *New Yorker Staatszeitung*, May 16, 1856.
51. *Westbote*, July 7, 1859.
52. See *New Yorker Staatszeitung*, May 10, Oct. 10, 1855; and Marcus L. Hansen: *The Atlantic Migration* (Cambridge, 1940) p. 304.
53. *New Yorker Staatszeitung*, April 27, 1855.
54. *Ibid.*, Oct. 26, 1853.

Chapter 14 · THE SLAVERY ISSUE

GUSTAV KÖRNER recorded in his diary in 1834, "Negro slavery is the only rope by which the devil holds the American people." Schurz referred to the South's peculiar institution as the "one shrill discord" in the American democracy. Friedrich Kapp, in more philosophical terms, concluded that in the United States Anglo-Saxons and Germans were destined, after a separation of fifteen hundred years, to reunite in the common struggle to extend the frontiers of human liberty.

It was self-evident that radical reformers among the refugees of the 1850's would not compromise with human slavery, which they regarded as the blackest stain on the banners of the new land which claimed their political allegiance. They rebuked their countrymen of the earlier immigrations for their indifference concerning the abolitionist crusade and their blind loyalty to a party which once had espoused the political philosophy of Jefferson and Jackson, and now was controlled by Southern politicians and Northern doughfaces. Such accusations aggravated the undignified quarrels between "Grays" and "Greens," but also helped clarify political thinking and eventually change the political affiliation of a large number of German-Americans. The radical leadership of the Forty-eighters penetrated the innate conservatism of the older immigration and led a sufficiently large number of Germans into the new Republican party to have an important and even decisive influence in several strategic states.

The average immigrant, whatever his national origin, could not be expected to become excited over states' rights, or follow the details of the constitutional theories with which that issue was debated for decades in American political campaigns. Even the most intellectual Forty-eighters dismissed such discussions as of relatively little consequence. They had no difficulty, however, in understanding that a nation could not long remain half free and half slave. They appraised the situation in terms of their revolutionary idealism, and concluded that the United States was involved in a sectional controversy over basic human rights in which one part of the nation defended the exact antithesis of democracy and equality. The fact that Southern leaders, regardless of politics, were unfriendly to further immigration from Europe, and that the majority of the newcomers shunned the South, provided another reason for the German refugee's interest in a new Republican party. Many Germans wanted farms and free homesteads and could not accept with equanimity a policy which would open still unoccupied territories to slavery. Thus a powerful economic interest reinforced the humanitarian motive to abolish slavery, or at least to confine it to existing limits.

The slavery controversy drew many political refugees of 1848 into a new field of political activity. As the hope of the exiles for a new revolution in Germany faded, their idealism and talents for agitation and reform found an outlet in the rapidly mounting controversy over slavery. Their earlier interest in societies of freethinkers to battle the ecclesiastics, and in utopian schemes for a new social order, was drained off into the more practical political battle for a wholly free America. Here was a new "cause" which reached the climax just in time to save many a refugee from intellectual decay and moral frustration. It provided an opportunity to combine with fellow-Americans of other origins on a practical political issue, and in the course of the controversy German refugees became more pragmatic and more American. They discovered that the times demanded a combination of their passion for reform with practical, useful service to their adopted country. Their experiences hastened their Americanization, and helped counteract the separatism and ethnic petrifaction which had resulted from the nativist attacks of the 1850's.

It would be difficult to find in the entire German group even a small minority who were ready to defend the institution of human slavery as such, although there were Germans in Charleston, New Orleans, Texas, and other parts of the South who shared the pro-Southern view of their neighbors about states' rights and related questions. Among German church groups, the Moravians and the relatively small organization of German Methodists openly disapproved of slavery. German Catholics took no stand on the issue, and the Lutheran synods were sharply divided. The Lutheran Synod of Wisconsin, for example, was antislavery, but the Missouri Synod, always obedient to established authority, found biblical justification for the South's peculiar institution. Its journal, designed especially for the clergy, quoted Scripture to prove that slaveholding was not a sin. *Der Lutheraner,* official mouthpiece of the Missourians, argued that sometimes slavery is visited upon men by God as punishment for their sins, and C. F. W. Walther, the most influential of the "Old Lutherans," was careful not to condemn the institution as such though he urged his followers to fight against its worst abuses. The descendants of the Pennsylvania Germans seemed indifferent until aroused in the late 1850's by leaders like Carl Schurz. Isaac Mayer Wise, leader of the American Jewish reform movement in which German Jews played a decisive rôle, openly attacked the abolitionists, as late as 1861, as "fanatics" and "demagogues," warned against the union of German atheism and American Puritanism which he believed responsible for the fanaticism of the abolitionists, and denounced "red republicans and habitual revolutionaries, who feed on excitement and delight in civil wars."[1]

It was left largely, though not wholly, to the leaders of the "Greens" to awaken their fellow Germans to active opposition to the continuance and extension of the slave system. Fenner von Fenneberg spent nearly ten years in the United States after his escape from Germany. His book of *Transatlantische Studien,* published in Stuttgart on the eve of the Civil War, reflected his strong antislavery stand.[2] Friedrich Kapp, in a lecture on Texas published in the *New York Tribune,* urged his countrymen to go to the Southwest to help make West Texas a free state, and Douai's *San Antonio Zeitung* strongly supported his plea. At the time there were approximately eleven thousand German colonists in West Texas, and although the majority were opposed to slavery, they found it expedient not to precipitate a crisis over the issue. The attitude of the political refugees of 1848, however, was altogether different, and Douai was their courageous spokesman. In the spring of 1854, 120 of their group met in convention in San Antonio and Douai published their free-soil platform in his *San Antonio Zeitung.* A storm of indignation, including threats of lynching, followed this forthright avowal of antislavery principles, and Douai had to continue his editorial battles single-handed, without the support of his stockholders. Frederick Law Olmsted, eager to preserve West Texas as free soil, solicited financial support for Douai's paper from Henry Ward Beecher and others, persuaded Theodore Parker and other friends to subscribe and secured new type for the publisher in New York, on liberal credit terms. Probably due to Olmsted's interest in the matter, the *New York Times* carried an editorial on the need for free-soil immigrants for Texas, and published a review of Kapp's *Die Sklavenfrage in den Vereinigten Staaten* (New York, 1854). Despite such encouragement from outside, the movement to win West Texas for freedom failed. Southerners threatened the Germans with mob violence, merchants stopped advertising in the *San Antonio Zeitung,* and in May 1856 its owner sold out to the opposition and moved to New York.[3]

The extent to which Germans were slave owners in Texas and elsewhere in the South has been a matter of controversy. The largest slave owner among the Texas Germans was the Society for the Protection of German Immigrants, which in 1846 stocked its farm with twenty-five Negroes.[4] In 1854 the main speaker at a German celebration in Houston on Independence Day deplored the radicalism of the "newcomers," and urged his hearers to avoid the sectional controversy.[5] *Der freie Verein* of Sisterdale, Texas, organized by radicals in 1853, incurred the violent opposition of conservative Germans when its statement of principles included a plea for the abolition of slavery,[6] and in New Orleans the editor of the *Deutsche Zeitung,* a "rabid abolitionist" refugee, was forced to leave the city to escape mob violence.[7] The *Louisiana,* another German paper issued in New Orleans in the spring of 1855, was antislavery also,[8] and in the same year the St. Louis *Anzeiger des Westens* "went over to the abolitionists."[9] In 1860, however, neither Lincoln nor Douglas got a single vote in New Braunfels, stronghold of German liberalism and culture in Texas.[10]

The leading journals of the freethinkers, such as the *Deutsche Republikaner* of Cincinnati, the Milwaukee *Corsär,* the Pittsburgh *Courier,* the *Baltimore Wecker,* and Heinzen's *Pionier* were avowed abolitionist papers and irreconcilable enemies of the Democratic party from the outset. Editors of older, conservative German papers described such publishers as "sentimental Negrophiles." Christian Esselen charged Louis Agassiz with distorting the scientific theories of race to give comfort to the slaveholders, and his *Atlantis* kept up a relentless attack on the South's peculiar institution. Gustav Struve opposed the project to colonize the freed Negroes in Liberia, because he believed its primary purpose was to defeat the program of the abolitionists, and advocated a separate German party to combat slavery.[11]

The *Turnvereine* in the 1850's were especially responsive to humanitarian appeals, and many local societies took a positive stand against slavery or its expansion. In 1855 the national convention of *Turnvereine*, meeting in Buffalo, drafted an antislavery platform. As a result, local groups from Houston, Texas, Charleston, South Carolina, Savannah and Augusta, Georgia, and Mobile, Alabama, seceded immediately, to be joined by the *Turnverein* of New Orleans two years later. Turner groups in Baltimore, St. Louis, Covington, Newport and Louisville, Kentucky, and Wheeling remained loyal to the national society, however, and as late as 1860 the *Turnzeitung,* although issued in Baltimore, called upon its readers to vote for Lincoln. The following spring, when a company of Baltimore Turner marched off to join the Union Army, the office of the *Baltimore Wecker,* where the *Turnzeitung* was published, was stormed by Southern sympathizers and states' rights men, who smashed the windows and destroyed machinery in the printing plant.[12] Undaunted by mob violence, the *Wecker*, proud creation of a Forty-eighter, continued to advocate emancipation and the preservation of the Union, and defended Lincoln's policy in almost every detail. George Dietz, an enthusiastic Turner who wrote many lyrics in praise of freedom, resigned his position on the editorial staff of the *New Yorker Staatszeitung* in 1854 when that paper refused to condemn the Kansas-Nebraska Act.[13]

Caspar Butz published a biting satire in 1855 on the occasion of the celebration of the Fourth of July, in which he excoriated the noisy, annual demonstrations of artificial patriotism on the anniversary of the Declaration of Independence; depicted the miseries and sufferings of the slaves, and urged his German countrymen not to participate henceforth in such celebrations until all Negroes were free.[14] Heinzen's attacks on slavery began in 1851, and he never compromised in his crusade for the equal rights of colored men. He rejected all theories about racial inferiorities, and belabored the churches for their hypocrisy in luring black men into the fold of the "religion of love" and then refusing to take a stand against the slave system and the slave traffic. Heinzen regarded emancipation as an international issue. He was bitterly disappointed because so many German-Americans were apathetic toward this great moral question. "Opposition to the politics of slavery in America," he wrote, "is a battle against reaction in Europe. This republic cannot and will not be able to do anything for European freedom until it has shaken the yoke of slavery from its own."[15]

The incident which reopened the sectional controversy after its "final settlement" by the Compromise of 1850 was the Kansas-Nebraska Act sponsored by Stephen A. Douglas four years later. That law produced a chain reaction of events which led directly to the Civil War, although such an outcome was farthest from Douglas' intentions, for he introduced the controversial measure for a variety of reasons, one of which may well have been a desire to find a formula which would postpone the sectional conflict until the forces of Nature would provide a permanent solution. To radical Forty-eighters like Heinzen, however, Stephen A. Douglas was henceforth a "Douglas Iscariot," and his "popular sovereignty" doctrine but another name for treason to the Republic and the whole human race. The controversy over slavery became so violent that old party lines were shattered and a new political party was born. The majority of German Forty-eighters seized upon the issue to arouse German-Americans who were not abolitionists against a Democratic party which had produced "bleeding Kansas," defeated legislation for free homesteads, and become a protagonist of slavery.

The Kansas-Nebraska Act affected the German-language press as few other issues have done. Forty-eighter editors called for a new "radical German party," and Germans assembled in mass meetings in Chicago, Buffalo, Boston, Cincinnati, Louisville, and far-off Galveston, to oppose the repeal of the Missouri Compromise and the opening of a large part of the public domain to slavery. In Chicago, the protest was led by George Schneider, the Forty-eighter who edited the *Illinois Staatszeitung;* and George Hillgärtner, erstwhile Heidelberg lawyer and revolutionist, branded Douglas as an "ambitious and dangerous demagogue" and a "blemish upon the honor of the State of Illinois." The Senator's likeness was displayed in the Chicago Market House, under the caption "the Benedict Arnold of 1854," and after a parade down Michigan Avenue, the crowd burned the "Little Giant" in effigy. A petition, protesting the repeal of the Missouri Compromise, was sent to Gustav Körner, lieutenant-governor of Illinois.[16]

In New York, when the *Staatszeitung* defended Douglas, a crowd, wearing green paper hats and led by Lindenmüller, a refugee from

Berlin, marched to the newspaper office to protest. A mass meeting of
New York Germans developed into a noisy affair in which all semblance
of parliamentary procedure was ignored, and the assembly had to be
hastily adjourned when it turned into a battle royal between older and
newer immigrants. Forty-eighters, led by the speaker of one of the German free congregations, played a conspicuous rôle in these turbulent
proceedings. Several weeks later another anti-Nebraska meeting was
held under more peaceful conditions. Prominent Forty-eighters, such as
Dietz, Sigismund Kaufmann, Försch, Gottlieb Kellner, and others denounced the *New Yorker Staatszeitung*[17] for its conservative attitude.
In Cleveland a German mass meeting, called on a few hours' notice,
attracted a crowd of seven hundred who listened intently to an address
by Hassaurek of the Cincinnati *Hochwächter*. Three delegates, including
Jakob Müller, were sent to a state-wide meeting in Columbus, where
German radicals wrote a platform denouncing both existing major political parties and favoring a new organization. Although the conservative
Cincinnati Enquirer severely criticized the German extremists, the *Cleveland Leader* defended them as true lovers of freedom, heaped special
praise upon Friedrich Hecker, and philosophized that the "place of birth
does not determine who is an American."[18]

A large section of the German-language press branded Douglas as
"the tool of the czar of Russia." When the Columbus *Westbote,* which
agreed that Nebraska should remain closed to slavery but continued to
defend Douglas, protested against recent violent demonstrations by radical
Germans, its editor received fifteen cancellations by return mail from
the Germans in Sandusky.[19] Even papers like the *New Yorker Criminal
Zeitung, und Belletristisches Journal,* whose major interest was literary
and cultural, felt it expedient to clarify their position on the Kansas-
Nebraska question.[20] The Cincinnati *Hochwächter,* the Milwaukee *Corsär*
and Heinzen's *Pionier* urged the Germans to leave the Democratic party
at once. The *Deutsche Republikaner* and the *Volksblatt* of Cincinnati
discussed the possibility of organizing a German free state settlement in
Kansas.[21] The *Virginnische Staatszeitung* reported that Germans had
voted against the Democrats in a recent state election.[22] "We firmly
believe," observed the Cleveland *Forest City Democrat,* "that the Germans are to be the executioners and exterminators of American slavery.
If that element of our citizenship withdraws their support from the

party that upholds slavery, it will go by the board before the close of this century."[23]

Out of the turmoil over "bleeding Kansas," and the subsequent events for which the Kansas-Nebraska Act was the primary cause, the new Republican party was born, and in the shifting political affiliations of the period from 1854 to 1860 the votes of the foreign-born proved to be of great importance. Within the German group, there was a prolonged struggle between "Grays" and "Greens," and German Catholics and Lutherans distrusted the leadership of radicals whom they regarded as heretics and "sacrilegious despoilers of churches." When Hassaurek lectured in Quincy, Illinois, on "Slavery and Jesuitism," he was hooted down by a mob, and his meeting ended in a bloody brawl.[24]

So much has been written of the rapid and easy transition of the German group from old-line Democrats in 1852 to eager Republicans in 1856 and 1860, that it must be emphasized that influential voices continued to be raised among the Germans in defense of Douglas and the Kansas-Nebraska bill. The *New Yorker Staatszeitung*, financially the most successful of the German press, consistently maintained that the slavery question must be settled within the framework of the United States Constitution, by the individual states and territories. It recognized slaves as property, guaranteed by the fundamental law of the land. The *Staatszeitung* reminded immigrants that they were as free to settle in slave territory as in free, and pointed to thousands of Germans living happily in the South. The paper demanded that aliens settling in the territories be given the franchise on the same terms as American citizens, and forecast that the unreasonable agitation of "green" Forty-eighters would result in a resurgence of nativism against all the foreign-born. When a national day of prayer was suggested to prevent passage of Douglas' bill, the *Staatszeitung* sarcastically called attention to the new unholy and unnatural alliance between beer drinkers and fasters; freethinkers and religious bigots; "champions of endless progress" and the Knownothings.[25]

In Ohio, four German papers, the *Demokratische Tageblatt* of Cincinnati, *Der Deutsche* of Holmes County, *Der Deutsche in Ohio,* and the Columbus *Westbote* remained faithful to Douglas and the Democrats. The *Westbote* circulated widely in the Middle West. After reading an article in the *Indiana Volksblatt*, deploring such "childish demonstrations" as the burning of Douglas in effigy in Chicago, the editor of the *Westbote* reminded the Germans that the Senator from Illinois had never failed to defend immigrants against nativists, and berated "phantasy politicians" who "know as much about American conditions as a caffir knows about Hegel's philosophy."[26] In a long editorial on July 7, 1854, the *Westbote* contrasted the principles of 1776 with those of the revolutionists of 1848 and the self-styled "reformers" of 1854, and Louis Fieser, the editor, suggested that the founding fathers "did not try to build a temple for fairies in a world of fairy-tales" or "A Republic for angels." He compared the practical men of 1787 with the "quacks" and "political miracle men" of 1848 who were leading simple-minded Germans into dangerous political waters and advocating a strongly centralized government which would endanger states' rights and individual liberty.[27] In the campaign of 1860, the *Westbote* still supported Douglas, as a "true Democrat," though it denounced the Lecompton Constitution and other blunders in applying popular sovereignty to Kansas. German Democrats of the old school contended that a defection from the party of Jefferson and Jackson would only strengthen the Whigs and their Knownothing allies, and that the triumph of nativism would harm Germans far more than Douglas' popular sovereignty. In their opinion, the record of the Democratic party was above criticism on such questions as Sunday and temperance legislation, bank monopolies, and the treatment of the foreign-born.

The *New Yorker Staatszeitung* reprinted letters from Germans in the South warning against the dangers of civil war, and pointing out that even Southerners who disapproved of slavery would fight to defend states' rights and the guarantees of the Constitution.[28] Germans were advised to use their political influence to neutralize the power of the slaveholders but not to disrupt the Union,[29] and the New Orleans *Deutsche Zeitung,* under a new editor, warned against the unfair propaganda of the abolitionists.[30] Dr. Abraham Jacobi argued that slavery eventually would break down from its own economic inefficiency.[31] The *New Yorker Staatszeitung* asked its readers to resist the "impractical and short-sighted theorists" of the newer immigration and their "progressive press," and called for the preservation of the Union at all costs.

The controversy between "Grays" and "Greens" over the slavery question continued until the first shots of the Civil War were fired at Fort

Sumter. In states like Wisconsin, the older German church groups remained staunch Democrats and were profoundly distrustful of freethinkers and radicals. The worst anti-draft riots in that state occurred in the German settlements near Port Washington, where the majority of the population were German Catholics and Democrats.[32] The Milwaukee *Volksfreund* in 1854 described the Republican party as a "Holy Alliance of . . . abolitionists, Whigs, Know-Nothings, Sunday and Cold Water Fanatics," and the Republicans to insure a hearing for their cause, subsidized a paper in Milwaukee, edited by Bernhard Domschke, to counteract the influence of the city's three German Democratic papers. Although Lincoln carried Wisconsin in 1860, Douglas received 58% of the vote of Milwaukee. Four years later, the German wards still manifested little enthusiasm for "the Great Emancipator."[33] In Columbus, Ohio, the *Westbote,* organ of Democrats and "Grays," opposed all organizations tainted with abolitionism, although the editor himself favored gradual emancipation. He supported Douglas for president, opposed suffrage for Ohio Negroes, and stressed the preservation of the Union as the paramount issue. The largest German wards in Columbus continued to roll up Democratic majorities in 1856, 1858, and 1860.[34] Cleveland had a German "Douglas-Johnson Club" in 1860, and the *Germania* supported the Illinois Democrat for president.[35]

Francis Lieber described Forty-eighters as "rabid democrats—novices, and therefore fanatics in politics."[36] The *New Yorker Staatszeitung* maintained that only full-fledged citizens should edit newspapers in the United States, ridiculed Heinzen and his group as European beer politicians and ex-revolutionaries living on American pocketbooks, and viciously attacked "socialistic and communistic" newcomers who were confusing the rank and file of the Germans in America.[37] A correspondent from San Francisco reported that peace had been restored in the German community of California only after the departure of Julius Fröbel and the suspension of his radical newspaper, and that the Germans now were back in the Democratic fold.[38] Similar reports came from Iowa, where a number of Germans reacted violently against the radical antislavery propaganda of Esselen's *Atlantis.*[39] The Indianapolis *Volksblatt* never left the Democratic fold, and the Louisville *Anzeiger* and the Buffalo *Demokrat* returned to their earlier affiliation after a brief flirtation with the radical anti-Nebraska group.[40]

Such items indicate that the struggle for the votes of the Germans was more protracted and complicated than generally has been recognized. The German element remained divided throughout the 1850's, and the battle between "Grays" and "Greens" did not end immediately with Lincoln's call for volunteers. The desertion of Germans from the old-line Democracy was neither sudden nor unanimous, and there were dissenters even among the Forty-eighters, although as a group the latter bore the brunt of the political battle for the German vote.

FOOTNOTES

CHAPTER 14

1. Bertram W. Korn: "Isaac Mayer Wise on the Civil War," in Hebrew Union College *Annual*, XX, 642.

2. Ferdinand Daniel Fenner von Fenneberg: *Transatlantische Studien* (Stuttgart, 1861).

3. See Laura Wood Roper: "Frederick Law Olmsted and the Western Texas Free-Soil Movement," in *American Historical Review* (Oct. 1950) LVI, No. 1, pp. 58-64; and *New Yorker Staatszeitung*, Jan. 24, Feb. 27, 1855; and *Belletristisches Journal*, Oct. 9, 1857.

4. Biesele: *Germans in Texas*, p. 196.

5. *New Yorker Staatszeitung*, May 1, 1856.

6. *Ibid.*, May 1, 1856.

7. *Ibid.*, Feb. 22, 1855 and Dec. 5, 1860.

8. *Belletristisches Journal*, May 11, 1855.

9. *New Yorker Staatszeitung*, April 18, 1855.

10. Biesele: *Germans in Texas*, p. 204.

11. *New Yorker Staatszeitung*, Aug. 2, 1851.

12. See Augustus J. Prahl: "History of the German Gymnastic Movement of Baltimore," in *26th Report—Society for the History of the Germans in Maryland* (Baltimore 1945) pp. 16-19; and also *New Yorker Staatszeitung*, Oct. 24, Dec. 26, 1855, for the secession of the Charleston group; and *Ibid.*, March 6, 1856, and *Belletristisches Journal*, Aug. 10, 1860.

13. *New Yorker Staatszeitung*, Feb. 17, 1854.

14. B. A. Uhlendorf: "German-American Poetry" in *Deutsch-Amerikanische Geschichtsblätter*, XXII-XXIII, pp. 165-66.

15. For further details, see Wittke: *Heinzen*, Ch. VIII.

16. Pierce: *History of Chicago*, II, 207.

17. *New Yorker Staatszeitung*, Feb. 24, March 10, 17, 1854.

18. *Cleveland Leader*, June 20, 1854; see also, Cleveland *Forest City Democrat*, March 10, 1854.

19. *Westbote*, March 17, 24, 1854.

20. *Belletristisches Journal*, March 10, 1854; for further evidence of the indignation of the German liberals see extracts from the Chicago *Daily Democrat, Free West, Illinois Journal*, and *Belleville Advocate*, in Albert J. Beveridge: *Abraham Lincoln* (Boston, 1928) II, 228, footnote.

21. *Belletristisches Journal*, June 22, 1855.

22. Cited in *New Yorker Staatszeitung*, June 16, 1855.

23. March 7, 1854.

24. *Westbote*, Dec. 7, 1855.

25. See *New Yorker Staatszeitung*, Jan. 25, Feb. 22, March 17, 28, May 19, Dec. 28, 1854.
26. *Westbote*, March 31, June 30, 1854.
27. July 7, 1854.
28. June 15, Nov. 17, 1855.
29. *Belletristisches Journal*, April 10, 1857.
30. *New Yorker Staatszeitung*, July 20, 1855.
31. *Ibid.*, Feb. 27, 1855.
32. *Wisconsin* (American Guide Series) New York, 1941, p. 43.
33. Still: *Milwaukee*, pp. 152-3; 161.
34. *Westbote*, Dec. 15, 22, 1859; Aug. 8, 1856; July 22, Oct. 21, 1858; December 1, 1859; Nov. 8, 1860; April 18, 1861.
35. *Cleveland Plain Dealer*, July 10, 1860; *Cleveland Leader*, July 13, 1860.
36. Freidel: *Lieber*, p. 233.
37. *New Yorker Staatszeitung*, April 6, 1854.
38. *Ibid.*, Nov. 3, 1855.
39. *Ibid.*, March 7, 1855.
40. *Ibid.*, April 10, Aug. 1, 1855.

Chapter 15 · *THE BATTLE FOR THE GERMAN VOTE*

WHILE THE Kansas-Nebraska bill was still being debated in Congress, Salmon P. Chase predicted, "It will light up a fire in the country which may, perhaps, consume those who kindle it." No other act of Congress in American history produced such an immediate political reaction. By undoing the "finality" of the compromise settlement of 1850, and annulling a sectional agreement which had endured for thirty years, Senator Douglas and President Pierce, as Greeley pointed out, made more abolitionists in three months than the crusaders for equal rights for Negroes had been able to make in fifty years. The decade of the 1850's witnessed a veritable revolution in the political parties of the United States. The Whig party went to pieces completely with the reopening of the sectional controversy, figured significantly for the last time in the campaign of 1852, and was virtually dead by 1856. The composition of the Democratic party changed radically during the decade. But the most important result of the Kansas-Nebraska Act was the birth of the Republican party, composed originally of northern Whigs, Anti-Nebraska Democrats, the remnants of the Free Soilers, and the more extreme abolitionists.

On February 28, 1854, a group which had assembled at Ripon, Wisconsin, called for the formation of a new party, and that place has been recognized ever since as the birthplace of the Republicans. In July of the same year, mass meetings at Jackson, Michigan, launched the new organization on a state-wide basis. Before the close of the year, the political revolt over the Kansas issue had spread through the western states and into the older East, and the fall elections of 1854 revealed the new movement as a lusty infant, destined to grow stronger with each succeeding campaign. By 1855, political giants and realistic politicians like William H. Seward were ready to bid for the leadership of the new party, and a year later it staged its first campaign on a national scale.

Our major interest in these momentous political changes is the rôle played by the Germans. Signs of the political importance of this bloc of foreign-born voters were evident before 1854. By 1850, Germans were being chosen for local offices in increasing numbers. The Cincinnati City Council, for example, included ten Germans in 1852, and the power of the Cincinnati Germans was further recognized by the appointment of the able jurist Stallo to the common pleas bench. In the presidential campaign of 1852, speakers for both major parties no longer referred to "Dutchmen," but to "most thrifty colonizers" who came from a "nation of thinkers." Both parties distributed profitable printing contracts among the German-language press. The Whigs tried especially hard to develop a favorable German press, and their candidate, General Winfield Scott, made flattering comments about Irish and German immigrants whose bravery he had tested on the battlefields of the Mexican War. As the number of immigrants to the United States mounted in the 1850's, special appeals to the foreign-born vote became more frequent.

The campaign for the German vote produced bitter controversy in the German-language press. Democrats were quick to discover the vulnerability of the new party because of the presence of so many Knownothings in its ranks, and organized *Sag Nichts* branches in 1855 to keep the Germans from joining "sore head Knownothings and Freethinking Germans" in the opposition camp.[1] The Democratic *Westbote* ridiculed "German Confusionists" who advocated a fusion of Germans, nativists, Yankee bigots, and temperance fanatics,[2] and the *New Yorker Staatszeitung* insisted that no self-respecting German could ally himself with rabid abolitionists. The paper carried on a violent newspaper war with such radical journals as the *Hochwächter* and the *Deutsche Republikaner* of Cincinnati, the St. Louis *Anzeiger des Westens,* the *Turnzeitung,* Esselen's *Atlantis,* Heinzen's *Pionier,* and others which it accused of favoring the "political suicide" of fusion.[3] The Minnesota *Staatszeitung,* as late as the summer of 1858, denounced "the miserable hypocrisy of the white northern abolitionists who, with freedom on their lips . . . will put into the bargain of Negro emancipation the cold-water humbug and the puritanic Sunday laws,"[4] and The Catholic *Seebote* of Milwaukee disposed of the Republicans as "temperance men, abolitionists, haters of foreigners, sacrilegious despoilers of Churches, Catholic killers . . . a blood-thirsty tiger ever panting for your gore."[5] The close connection between the Knownothing, temperance, and free-soil groups in the new party could not be denied. In Ohio, for example, the Cleveland *Wächter am Erie,* and two Cincinnati papers edited by Forty-eighters, urged their readers to vote for Chase for governor in 1855, but rejected the rest of the Republican ticket because of the open alliance of free soilers with nativists in the state party organization. In Indiana, John M. Wilson, who became an elector for Lincoln in 1860, was reported to have referred publicly in 1855 to "the lop-eared, big-mouthed, thick-headed Dutchman . . . the foam of beer still in his horse-tail mustache, and stinking . . . of garlic and onions . . ."[6]

In 1856, Republicans made their first bid for control of the national government. A year before the actual campaign began, Democratic German-language papers noted a serious defection among the Germans of the Middle and Far West. The Michigan *Volksblatt* and the *Indianapolis Freie Presse* had switched to the Republicans, and of fifteen German papers published in Ohio in 1855, only five were loyal to the Democrats. The *Wächter am Erie,* the *Hochwächter,* the Toledo *Staatszeitung,* and the *Sandusky Intelligenzblatt* supported Chase and the free-soil, fusion ticket in Ohio in 1855. In New York City, the *Demokrat* and the *Abendzeitung* went over to the Republicans in the fall of 1855, leaving the *Staatszeitung* to carry on the fight for the Democrats. The Albany *Freie Blätter* and the *Buffalo Telegraph* also were in the Republican camp. When the Chicago *National Demokrat* deserted its old allegiance, the Peoria *Illinois Banner* charged that it had betrayed its principles for fat printing contracts. Apparently the "newer journals" and their "exciting articles" from the pens of the refugees of 1848, were causing great confusion among the German voters.

In 1856, the Republicans, on the anniversary of Bunker Hill, nominated John C. Frémont, glamorous pathfinder from California, for president, and W. L. Dayton of New Jersey for vice-president. The Democrats, avoiding both Pierce and Douglas because of their close connection with the Kansas question, chose James Buchanan of Pennsylvania, an old Jacksonian who had been out of the country during most of the recent controversies, for president, and John C. Breckenridge of Kentucky as his running mate. The Republican platform flayed the Pierce administration for its handling of the Kansas issue and denied that the Constitution permitted the legalization of slavery in the territories. The Democrats defended popular sovereignty and the Kansas-Nebraska Act, and condemned the "political crusade" of the Knownothings as a violation of the free spirit of America.

German-language newspapers of whatever political persuasion seemed confident that "the adopted citizens" would decide the election. A battery of Forty-eighters promptly entered the contest on behalf of the Republicans. Friedrich Hecker spoke in Pittsburgh, New York, Rochester, Philadelphia, Buffalo, and other German centers, and was selected in Illinois as a presidential elector-at-large. In Buffalo, though frequently interrupted by hecklers, he stressed the argument that failure of German-American refugees to support Frémont would be tantamount to "a betrayal of their flag and their past."[7] Gustav Struve, who had refused to become naturalized because "the battle against European despots [was] his major objective" in life, appealed to his "comrades of 1848 and 1849" to battle for liberty in America "in the spirit of the martyrs of the German Revolution."[8] Julius Fröbel presided at a Republican meeting in the New York Academy of Music which Struve addressed. Brentano issued his appeal to vote Republican from his farm in Michigan in the form of an open letter to the *Kalamazoo Telegraph*.[9]

Dr. Hermann Kiefer, a veteran of the battles of Ubstadt and Philipsburg in Baden, now practicing medicine in Detroit, became chairman of the German Republican Executive Committee of Michigan.[10] Hassaurek stumped for the Republicans in Wisconsin, Indiana, Illinois, and other states, and Esselen supported Frémont with vigorous editorials. Although Heinzen predicted Frémont's election, he refused to become a member of a party committee, partly because of his chronic independence and partly because he was not yet naturalized. Bernhard Domschke denounced the Milwaukee Democrats for defending "religious tyranny and physical slavery."[11] George Schneider promoted Frémont clubs among the Chicago Germans, and to counteract the influence of his *Illinois Staatszeitung,* the Douglas forces launched the rival Chicago *Demokrat.*[12] Emil Praetorius and Heinrich Börnstein spoke for the Republicans in St. Louis, and Caspar Butz contributed his various talents to the Republican cause. Schurz, an eager Republican from the outset, wrote late in 1856, "My brief activity brought me such widespread influence that I shall probably not keep out of official life very long."[13]

In the East, Adolf Douai campaigned among the Germans of Massachusetts and Connecticut. In his address in the Tabernacle in New York he made it clear that he preferred freeing the Negro to saving the Union.[14] Dr. Reinhold Solger was as influential in building the Republican party among the Germans in the East as Schurz was in the West. The leaders of the New York German Republican group included Friedrich Kapp; his law partner, Franz Zitz, a veteran of the Frankfurt Parliament; Wilhelm Loewe aus Calbe, another former member of the Frankfurt group; Eduard Kapff, Eduard Pelz, and Försch, all Forty-eighters; and Joseph Goldmark, the ex-revolutionist from Vienna. Dr. Gabriel Riesser, a former member of the Frankfurt Parliament who was visiting in the United States, took part in the campaign for Frémont,[15] though an alien. Dr. Adolph Wiesner, another Forty-eighter, was a leader of the Republicans in Baltimore.[16] The *Turnzeitung,* rabidly for Frémont, represented the Republican standard bearer as the candidate of "labor and the settler." In New Jersey, Fritz Anneke, though disturbed by the Knownothing connections of the party, supported Frémont. Of the older German leaders, the most active campaigners for the Republicans in 1856 were Friedrich Münch, the sage of Missouri; Samuel Ludvigh and Gustav Körner of Illinois, and Judge Stallo and Stephan Molitor of Cincinnati.

The Democratic press was aware of the disturbing influence of the Forty-eighters in German-American politics. The Cleveland *Plain Dealer* fumed about "hair-lipped" German revolutionists who wanted to reduce America to "an agrarian level," and warned against "Red Republicans" who were worse than "Black Republicans"—"a lawless, reckless set of impostors" who "left their country for their country's good" to come here "to get up riots and carry on revolutions."[17] The *New Yorker Staatszeitung,* though less insulting, agreed that the revolutionists had "learned nothing and forgotten nothing," and were "impetuous, arrogant, intolerant, loud in boasting and feeble in performance."[18]

The Republican leadership utilized every device to woo the German vote. Frémont announced that he favored letting foreigners vote after only three years' residence in the United States. The party subsidized German newspapers or made it financially worthwhile to convert papers like the *Minnesota Deutsche Zeitung* from a Democratic into a Republican organ. The San Francisco *Star of Empire* regularly published several pages of German. A German printing establishment and a new Republican paper, known as the *Union und Washington Correspondent,* were established in the nation's capital, edited by Karl Burgthal, a refugee of rather doubtful past from Vienna, and appeared half in German and half in English.[19] Germans paraded in Republican rallies with transparencies lettered with German campaign slogans, and frequently a whole section in Frémont parades was reserved for Germans.[20] Campaign songs were written in German, among them several compositions by Friedrich Schünemann-Pott, leader of the freethinkers,[21] and a bureau was organized by German Republicans to help immigrants with their naturalization papers.[22] The national convention of the Republican party in 1856 was addressed by Schneider of the *Illinois Staatszeitung* and several other prominent German editors. Philadelphia Germans meeting in the *Arbeiterhalle* formally endorsed Frémont, organized Frémont clubs, and published German campaign songs, and the "German Republican Central Club" included such refugees as Franz Arnold, Nikolaus Schmitt, and Adolf Douai. In September and October, Hecker, Julius Fröbel, Douai, and Münch addressed large gatherings of German Republicans in Philadelphia halls decorated with pictures of von Steuben, DeKalb, Muhlenberg, Gallatin, Christopher Saur, Conrad Weiser, and Kosziusko. On such occasions the Turner marched into the hall with banners streaming, bands blaring, and torches blazing; German singing societies sang appropriate airs, and the meeting usually closed with everybody singing, in German, the "Free Soil Marseillaise." In spite of such demonstrations, however, Buchanan carried Philadelphia and Pennsylvania in 1856.[23]

The Democrats had no other strategy save to label the Republicans an unholy alliance of bigots, nativists, Yankee Puritans, and drys. The *Westbote* suggested that "our German-Republican trumpeters of liberty be sent for ten days to Oberlin where the water cure would cure them of their insanity."[24] The *New Yorker Staatszeitung* solicited letters from Forty-eighters like R. Weil von Gernsbach to prove that not all refugees had gone mad. Von Gernsbach, who described himself as "also a political refugee from Baden, albeit an unknown soldier of freedom," insisted that "Red Republicans" like Hecker, Struve, and Brentano could not speak for the rank and file of the emigration of 1848.[25] A communication from Theodor Mögling, who had fought with Hecker and was American consul in Zurich, argued that Buchanan had befriended the victims of 1848, had given a banquet for political refugees in London in 1854, and therefore deserved the votes of the Germans in America.[26] Hassaurek was accused of selling his convictions for Republican gold, and Struve and Brentano, still unnaturalized, were told not to instruct German Americans how to vote.[27] A few Forty-eighters, such as Joseph Fickler and Oswald Ottendörfer, campaigned for the Democrats in 1856. Fickler tried to discredit Hecker and Struve by emphasizing their blunders in 1848 and 1849, and maintained that unity and democracy were at stake in the United States in 1856 as they had been in the German Revolution eight years earlier.[28]

In many ways the campaign of 1856 was as exciting as the famous Log Cabin and Cider campaign of 1840, though now a genuine moral issue was involved. The Democrats enjoyed their last triumph for a long time to come when Buchanan received 174 electoral votes to Frémont's 114. Although the latter's strength was concentrated in eleven northern states, the result of the election proved that the Republicans had become a major party. Schurz concluded that the results showed that Americans responded more quickly to a new idea than did German or Irish immigrants, but he took great satisfaction from the fact that Frémont had received twenty-five thousand German votes in Wisconsin.[29] The *Westbote* pointed out that in Ohio the rural German vote had remained Democratic, but could not deny the success of "the radical mustaches" in cities like Cincinnati and Cleveland.[30] Republican papers like the *New Yorker Abendzeitung* and the *Illinois Staatszeitung* were disappointed by "the low intellectual level" and the "lack of education" of the Germans in Indiana and Pennsylvania. The *New Yorker Staatszeitung,* greatly pleased with the outcome, proceeded to read the Forty-eighters out of the German group, and rejoiced that Germans "could not be ruled by Brentano and Co."[31]

Actually, 1856 was but the prelude to 1860, and German radicals continued their propaganda, arranged lectures on slavery in Chicago and elsewhere immediately following Frémont's defeat, and proposed a permanent federation of German Republicans, freethinkers, and other German societies. August Thieme, of the Cleveland *Wächter am Erie,* noting that half the Germans had voted for Frémont in 1856, promised Forty-eighters would do much better in 1860! In the interval between 1856 and 1860, the Democrats continued to hope that Germans would find their new political bedfellows increasingly uncongenial. The party capitalized on John Brown's raid at Harper's Ferry in 1859, to argue that all "Black Republicans" were fanatics who would lead the country into disunion and destruction. Heinzen, on the other hand, hailed Brown as a hero, and proposed a "John Brown Association" to prepare Americans for the appeal to arms. In Cincinnati, several hundred Germans heard August Willich pay tribute to the new martyr of the abolitionists, and in Davenport, Iowa, the *Demokrat* appeared in heavy black borders, and leading Germans draped their business houses in mourning on the day when Brown was executed.[32] Not all Forty-eighters, however, approved the violent methods of Brown and his associates, and some feared their political effect. But according to the *Missouri Republican,* it was the "Red Republicans" of 1848—"all Robespierres, Dantons and St. Justs . . . red down into their very kidneys,"[33] who were primarily responsible for such violent measures.

Unfortunately for Republican strategy, several incidents occurred after 1856 which proved quite disconcerting to the German constituency. Gustav Struve, who had supported Frémont in 1856, suddenly urged his countrymen to refrain from voting, because he believed Republicans wanted to make naturalization more difficult. The *New Yorker Criminal Zeitung und Belletristisches Journal* advocated an independent German ticket.[34] More disturbing was the defeat of Carl Schurz for lieutenant-governor of Wisconsin. With his usual self-confidence, he had predicted that he would "advance at a single step from the position of alderman in Watertown to that of lieutenant-governor of Wisconsin."[35] His nomination had attracted nation-wide attention in the German-language press, and when the leading Forty-eighter went down to defeat, although the rest of the Republican state ticket was successful, the effect upon the Germans was startling. Schurz himself believed he was the victim of an election fraud, but the Democrats contended he had been betrayed by the nativists in his own party. Fortunately for the Republicans, Schurz quickly recovered his equanimity. In February 1858 he wrote to his old friend Kinkel, "I am more popular with the Americans than the Germans, for among the latter are those who envy me . . . I was a phenomenon to the Americans."[36] His remarkable bilingualism brought him many invitations from Republican state organizations to speak in both East and West, and the Republican party gladly supported his speaking tours. The party also financed additional German-language papers, though many did not survive the campaign by more than a few months.[37] The St. Louis *Anzeiger des Westens* complained of the niggardly attitude of the party with reference to patronage, and pointed out that in St. Louis the reward for fifty-three thousand votes had been a job for one German as turnkey in the local jail.

Such disappointments were trivial, however, compared with the storm of indignation that swept the German element when the Massachusetts legislature, still under the influence of the Knownothings, proposed, and finally passed, the "two year amendment," depriving naturalized citizens of the right to vote or hold office until two years after the completion of their citizenship. Many Republican legislators had supported this discrimination against the foreign-born. The Germans deeply resented such a challenge to their dignity as adopted citizens of the United States. Heinzen demanded the defeat of the "Republican Know-Nothings" in 1860, and protests against the Massachusetts amendment poured in from all over the Union. The Boston Germans met in the Turner Hall, led by Heinzen, Louis Prang, and Adolf Douai, who urged their listeners to support only that party which "does not measure civil rights by place of birth, or human rights by color of skin." Cincinnati Germans appealed to Hecker, Kapp, Schurz, Douai, and others to prepare a manifesto setting forth the principles of German Republicans, and there was a widely discussed proposal for a national convention of German-Americans.[38] The *Buffalo Telegraph,* the *Toledo Express,* the *Sandusky Intelligenzblatt,* the St. Louis *Westliche Post,* the *New Yorker Abendzeitung,* and the *Turnzeitung,* among other German papers, denounced the Massachusetts amendment and called for retaliation. Obviously the Republican party was faced with an embarrassing problem. To win and hold the German vote, it had to give positive proof that it deserved the immigrant's support, which meant repudiating Massachusetts nativists and former Knownothings.

Fortunately for the Republican leadership, the sober second thought of some of the most prominent Forty-eighters convinced the Germans that neither a secession from the party nor a national convention to launch a new party would be wise. Hecker, Willich, and Schurz, among others, took a moderate position, and influential German papers in the Middle West refused to follow the lead of the "hot-heads." American dailies, like the *Springfield Republican,* agreed that the Massachusetts amendment was a stupid blunder. "When you get a German between slavery on one side and Know-Nothingism on the other," commented the editor, "you get a stubborn fellow in a very tight place, and he is quite as apt to let slavery slide for this time in order to make his vote tell against the Know-Nothings."[39] Salmon P. Chase denounced the "two year amendment" in a letter to the Sandusky Germans in 1859,[40] and state Republican conventions in the West, where the German vote was important, adopted resolutions censuring the Massachusetts legislature. That body, however, stubbornly refused to change its course, and finally passed the amendment.

Extremists like Heinzen shouted for revenge, and the Republican national organization rushed Schurz to Massachusetts and other states, to quell the spreading revolt among the German element. After dining with Longfellow, Schurz delivered one of his great speeches at Faneuil Hall in Boston, on "True Americanism." It was reprinted not only in the German-language press, but also in influential Republican papers, such as the New York Tribune. In the course of his remarks, Schurz laid the major responsibility for the "two year amendment" at the door of Governor Banks, although the latter actually had tried to get the waiting period reduced to ninety days.[41] Schurz urged the Germans to await developments and refrain from organizing a separate party. Later in the year he campaigned in Minnesota and Wisconsin and other parts of the strategic Middle West, where huge crowds greeted "that tremendous Dutchman" with parades, serenades, and the booming of cannon. In Minnesota alone he traveled six hundred miles by horse and buggy and by boat, to deliver thirty-one speeches before audiences composed largely of Germans, and in St. Paul he spoke for an hour and a half in German and for another hour in English.

"The phlegmatic brethren in the West," wrote the editor of the New Yorker Criminal Zeitung und Belletristisches Journal on March 21, 1860, "must demand a formal repudiation of nativism by the Republican convention in Chicago, or the party will be defeated." Prominent Forty-eighters echoed the demand, and Heinzen advocated reducing the residence requirement for citizenship from five years to three years. Fully aware of the crisis in their party, leaders like Chase, Seward, and Lincoln proclaimed their opposition to all discriminations against "adopted citizens," and beginning with Ohio, Republican state conventions repudiated the Massachusetts amendment. Republican managers of the national convention of 1860 saw to it that plenty of beer was on hand to convince Germans that the party was not dominated by narrow-minded Puritan Yankees.

Forty-two German-born delegates were among those who assembled in Chicago in 1860 in the convention which nominated Lincoln. The number included Hermann Raster, able journalist; Hassaurek and Jakob Müller from Ohio; Louis Dembitz of Kentucky; Caspar Butz of Illinois, and Douai and Kapp from the East; Friedrich Hecker and George Schneider, and Carl Friedrich Haussner, a less well-known radical refugee from Prussia. Schurz was chairman of the Wisconsin delegation and a member of the committee on resolutions. German delegates came armed with instructions from German Republican Clubs and committees, to insist upon a straightforward statement of the absolute equality of native and foreign-born Americans. The party was forced to choose between "Eastern nativists and the German vote of the West."[42]

The German delegates held a pre-convention meeting at the German House in Chicago, and it was here that "the Dutch plank," finally adopted by the Republicans, originated. Among the most influential members of this pre-convention gathering, in addition to such prominent Forty-eighters as Kapp, Douai, and Solger, were Professor Johannes Gambs, a former teacher of gymnastics who left Hesse after the Revolution; Elias Peissner, a lawyer, under suspicion in 1848, and now a teacher of German at Union College; Heinrich Vortriede, a refugee from Westphalia who edited the *Buffalo Telegraph;* Dr. Adolph Wiesner, the Maryland Turner and Frankfurt leftist; Karl Dänzer, a political refugee who had studied law at Heidelberg and now edited the *Anzeiger des Westens* in St. Louis; Schünemann-Pott, the freethinker; August Becker, an Ohio editor; Jakob Müller of Cleveland; Dr. Hermann Kiefer of Detroit; Bernhard Domschke and Dr. Johannes Georg Günther, brother-in-law of Robert Blum, from Wisconsin; Karl Röser, imprisoned in 1848 and now the publisher of the Wisconsin *Demokrat;* Dr. Wilhelm Hoffbauer of Iowa, a physician who belonged to the Left in the Frankfurt Parliament; and Carl Rotteck, a refugee lawyer who was a farmer and journalist in Muscatine. Adolf Douai and Caspar Butz acted as secretaries, and the deliberations of the convention were dominated completely by the liberal spirit of 1848. The delegates demanded a free Kansas, free homesteads, and repudiation of the Massachusetts nativists, and announced their readiness to support

Seward, Chase, Lincoln, or Wade for the presidency. Their resolutions were circulated among all the delegates of the Republican National Convention, and after listening to speeches by Hassaurek and Schurz, in which the latter boasted that three hundred thousand German votes hung in the balance, that body unanimously incorporated the "Dutch plank" in its platform. It put the party on record as opposed "to any change by which the rights of citizenship heretofore accorded to immigrants from foreign lands shall be abridged or impaired," and promised "full and sufficient protection to all classes of citizens, whether native or naturalized, both at home and abroad."

A Forty-eighter writing for the Cleveland *Wächter am Erie* reported that the convention of 1860 "reminded him of the Frankfurt Parliament." "Never before [had he] been so much aware of how precious liberty is."[43] The *Westbote* sourly referred to the "Dutch plank" as a mere "plaster for this Massachusetts wound,"[44] and Horace Greeley reminded the Germans that although the Republican party welcomed "friendly counsel," it would not brook "dictation." "He who votes in our election as an Irishman or German," he added, "has no moral right to vote at all."[45]

Seward of New York was the favorite candidate of the Germans. His forthright stand, during a long career, against all forms of nativism, and his high intellectual qualifications had endeared him to the German element, and he had the support of influential papers like the *Illinois Staatszeitung* and the *Baltimore Wecker*. The *Wächter am Erie* believed that many Germans favored the nomination of Ben Wade, and that all Germans were opposed to Bates and Banks.[46] Lincoln, always a shrewd politician, had not overlooked the German vote. For a time he struggled with a German grammar in an effort to learn the language. He bought the German *Illinois Staatszeitung* of Springfield, Illinois, for $400 and had Dr. Theodore Canisius edit it to advance his political ambitions. In 1858, when invited by Chicago Germans to make a Fourth of July address, Lincoln flatteringly referred to his fellow citizens of German origin as genuine lovers of liberty, "not selfishly, but upon *principle,—*not for special classes of men, but for all men."[47] German workingmen regarded him as the "champion of free labor and free homesteads,"[48] and the *Baltimore Turnzeitung* endorsed the Illinois candidate in the early spring of 1860. However, when the "rail splitter" was finally nominated, the majority of the Germans accepted the result without much enthusiasm, for they would have preferred Seward or Frémont. "Lincoln is not loved by the people as Frémont is," wrote one of the New York German editors. "It would have been fortunate if the convention had selected a different candidate."[49]

The fortunes of the Democrats in 1860 need not concern us here, nor the split in the party between the Douglas and Davis factions in the convention, which proved especially embarrassing to Oswald Ottendörfer, publisher of the *New Yorker Staatszeitung* and a friend of Douglas. The Douglas group published a German campaign biography of their candidate, employed German campaign speakers, subsidized papers, and organized "German Republican Guards" as an antidote to the "Wide Awakes" of the Republican party, but to little avail. Their pamphlets ridiculed the German lager-beer legion, under the command of Schurz, and the "Dutch plank," and German Democratic papers denounced Lincoln as a "dictator" and his party as "Black Republicans" steeped in "Asiatic despotism." The *Cleveland Plain Dealer* viciously attacked Schurz as "a red republican, save for his heart, which is black," and referred to Forty-eighters in general as "infidels," "communists," "cowardly, avaricious Dutchmen," "conscienceless atheists . . . traitors, hired slanderers."[50] One prominent Forty-eighter, Joseph Fickler, campaigned for the Constitutional Union party in 1860.

The Republican appeal for German votes was spearheaded by a galaxy of stump speakers recruited largely from among the Forty-eighters, and reinforced by such spokesmen for the older immigration as Körner, Münch, and Francis Lieber. Reinhold Solger was especially active in the East; Carl Schurz, whom Lincoln called "foremost among the Republican orators of the nation," was the most influential German Republican in the West. As a member of the National Committee, he had charge of its foreign department, employed German, Scandinavian, and Dutch speakers, and circulated a proposed Republican homestead bill in several foreign languages. "Vote yourself a farm" proved to be a powerful slogan among the foreign-born.

Hassaurek spoke to a German meeting in Cleveland for two and a half hours. August Thieme, editor of the *Wächter am Erie,* stumped for Lincoln in Ohio. Hecker spoke in New York and Philadelphia, although Schurz had superseded him as "the idol of the Republicans." In Philadelphia "German Invincibles" paraded with bands and torches to celebrations to ratify the Chicago platform, and "Fillmore Rangers and German Republicans" marched together to welcome Schurz to the city.[51] When Seward and Charles Francis Adams campaigned in far-off Minnesota, Seward visited the St. Paul *Turnverein* and Adams found it politic to call on a German brewer and taste of his beer, for "as he is inclining to Republicanism, we felt afraid to decline his civility."[52]

Surpassing all others, Schurz performed herculean labors for the Lincoln ticket. His speeches were a sensation among Americans as well as Germans, for he spoke with equal eloquence in English and German. Wherever he went, torchlight processions of American "Wide Awakes" and German Turner escorted him from station or hotel to the hall in which he was to speak. He was serenaded by German singing societies and bands; rockets and Roman candles were shot off in his honor, and ladies and children presented him with huge bouquets.[53] During the campaign of 1860, he traveled twenty-one thousand miles, and received $1,800 for expenses from the Republican organization. In July, Schurz wrote from Peoria, Illinois, to his wife, "The Germans are coming over in masses. The jubilation is almost oppressive."[54] At Belleville, Hecker appeared with him on the same platform. In St. Louis, Schurz spoke German on one day and English the next. At Terre Haute, he interrupted his campaign to bowl for an hour with German friends, and wrote his wife that he was "quite as good at it as he used to be."[55] At Fort Wayne, an Irishman tossed a cabbage head through the window of the hall in which Schurz was speaking.[56] The *Chicago Press* reported "a tremendous stampede of German voters in Southern Indiana, and the Wabash counties of Illinois, to the Republican ranks."[57]

In the East, Schurz made major addresses in New York and Philadelphia, and spoke frequently in old Pennsylvania German centers, such as Reading, Lancaster, and Carlisle. "The old Pennsylvania Dutch, who only half understood me," he told his wife, "run after me like children. The Democrats are beside themselves, and wherever I have spoken, they telegraph like mad in all directions for German speakers to neutralize my efforts."[58] Francis Lieber admitted that Schurz's attack on Douglas at Cooper Institute was "the most effective speech . . . he had ever heard in America."[59] "After twelve years," wrote a correspondent from Portsmouth, Ohio, "the Revolution of 1848-49 is bearing fruit in America."[60] Even the *New Yorker Staatszeitung* grudgingly conceded Schurz's success, though Democrats continued to attack him as a hireling of the Republicans, a professional politician and an office-seeker. Copies of his major speeches were widely circulated.

The result of the campaign of 1860 is well known, but the controversy over the part which Germans played in the outcome rages on among historical scholars. Samplings of the vote in solidly German centers like New Ulm, Minnesota, and Hermann, Missouri, outstanding centers of German liberalism and rationalism, reveal that in the former the vote for Lincoln exceeded that for Douglas by five to one, and in the latter it was solidly Republican. In Cincinnati the German wards made the city Republican in 1860. In the German Fifth Ward, for example, a Democratic majority of 3,074 in 1855 became a Republican majority of 1,739 in 1860.[61] In Philadelphia a Democratic majority of 3,000 in the October balloting became a 5,000 majority for the Republicans by November. In Newark, New Jersey, the German wards showed heavy Republican gains.[62] Milwaukee remained Democratic, but Wisconsin went Republican. Several scholars have concluded that the foreign-born vote in the Northwest was decisive for Lincoln, and that a change of one vote in twenty would have given these states to Douglas. In seven Northwestern states, with 283,000 foreign-born voters, Lincoln's majority over Douglas was slightly under 150,000.[63] The discussion over the decisiveness of the German and foreign-born vote in the election of Lincoln continues, but all agree that it was important, that Forty-eighters produced a political revolt among large numbers of their countrymen, and that the new Republican administration had an obligation to the German leadership in the distribution of political spoils.

Scores of Germans hung around the federal capital in 1861, looking for the loaves and fishes for the faithful, and bitter and petty disputes broke out over the spoils of office. Schurz and Hassaurek were looking for diplomatic posts. The editor of the Cincinnati *Volksblatt* wanted a consulate. George Schneider of the *Illinois Staatszeitung* became consul in Denmark, and later, collector of internal revenue in Chicago. Hermann Tzschirner, well-known Saxon revolutionary, got a job in the New York Customs House. Hermann Raster received a political appointment, and August Thieme, the Cleveland editor, became a pension agent. Dr. Solger, after some delay, became assistant registrar in the United States Treasury in Washington.[64]

Seward was reported to have announced that no citizen of foreign birth should receive a mission to Europe. The story created a sensation among German Republicans who wanted to be sent abroad. Schurz made it clear early in 1861 that he was an active office-seeker, and at Lincoln's inauguration he occupied a prominent place on the platform. The new President was puzzled as to how he could satisfy the desires of his German friend, and the whole German group regarded Schurz's fate as a test case of the administration's attitude. Schurz wanted to become minister to Sardinia. Much to Seward's dismay he began to recruit a regiment of German cavalry. Finally he was appointed minister to the Court of Madrid. He was convinced that the Catholic Archbishop of New York and the Bishop of Albany had intervened with Seward and Weed to block his appointment to Sardinia, and explained to his wife that the hierarchy did not "want a free-thinking German sent to Italy at a time when the temporal power of the Papacy may be the chief issue of political controversy."[65]

FOOTNOTES

CHAPTER 15

1. Roseboom: *The Civil War Era*, pp. 301, 309.
2. *Westbote*, Oct. 6, 1854, quoting the *Indiana Freie Presse*.
3. *New Yorker Staatszeitung*, Jan. 24, April 25, July 20, 25, 1855.
4. Quoted in Dorothy Johnson: "Attitude of the Germans in Minnesota Toward the Republican Party," M.A. Thesis, U. of Minnesota, p. 63.
5. Quoted in Ernst Bruncken: "Political Activities of Wisconsin Germans after 1854," *Proceedings of the State Historical Society of Wisconsin* (Madison, 1901) p. 201, and Overmoehle, *op. cit.*, p. 181.
6. *Westbote*, Aug. 23, 1860. The identical statement was attributed to Schuyler Colfax in the campaign of 1864.
7. See *Westbote*, Oct. 10, 1856; *New Yorker Staatszeitung*, July 29, 1856.
8. *New Yorker Staatszeitung*, July 26, 1856.
9. *Ibid.*, July 25, 1856. The *New Yorker Staatszeitung* characterized Struve and Brentano as "ruins of the Revolution."
10. *Liberty Writings of Dr. Hermann Kiefer*, edited by Warren Washburn Florer (New York, 1917) p. 51. Hereafter cited as *Liberty Writings*.
11. Overmoehle, *op. cit.*, p. 179.
12. Pierce: *History of Chicago*, II, pp. 218-19.
13. Schurz to Henry Meyer, Nov. 20, 1856, in *Intimate Letters*, p. 174.
14. *New Yorker Staatszeitung*, July 25, Aug. 30, 1856.
15. *New Yorker Staatszeitung*, Sept. 17, 1856; *Belletristisches Journal*, Nov. 7, 1856.
16. Cunz: *The Maryland Germans*, p. 272.
17. July 22, Oct. 12, 1856.
18. Oct. 30, 1856.
19. See *New Yorker Staatszeitung*, Jan. 12, Feb. 27, Oct. 28, 1856.
20. Albert J. Beveridge: *Abraham Lincoln*, II, 427.

21. See *Mitteilungen des Deutschen Pionier Vereins von Philadelphia*, II (1906) 27-29.
22. *Belletristisches Journal*, Oct. 3, 1856.
23. See C. F. Huch: "Anschluss der Deutschen Philadelphias an die Republikanische Partei im Jahre 1856" in *Mitteilungen des Deutschen Pionier Vereins von Philadelphia*, XI (1911) pp. 1-32; *New Yorker Staatszeitung*, Oct. 25, 1856.
24. Sept. 19, 1856.
25. *New Yorker Staatszeitung*, Aug. 7, 1856. See similar letters from Samuel Stern, a Jewish refugee, *Ibid.*, Oct. 28, 1856; and Friedrich Wiechel, who wrote to repudiate Julius Fröbel; *Ibid.*, Oct. 17, 1856.
26. Oct. 31, 1856.
27. *New Yorker Staatszeitung*, Nov. 13, 1856; also Sept. 11, 1856.
28. See *Ibid.*, Oct. 9, 17, 30, 1856; *Westbote*, Oct. 17, 1856.
29. Schurz to Henry Meyer, Nov. 20, 1856, in *Intimate Letters*, p. 174.
30. Oct. 24, 1856.
31. Nov. 25, 1856.
32. See *Westbote*, Dec. 8, 1859; and F. I. Herriott: "The Conference in the Deutsches Haus, Chicago, May 14-15, 1860," in *Transactions of the Illinois State Historical Society*, (1928) p. 108.
33. Quoted in *Wächter am Erie*, June 8, 1861.
34. See *Westbote*, Sept. 2, 23, 1858; *Belletristisches Journal*, Oct. 22, 1858; *New Yorker Staatszeitung*, Dec. 18, 1858.
35. Schurz to Henry Meyer, Sept. 20, 1857, in *Intimate Letters*, pp. 178-79.
36. Schurz to Kinkel, Feb. 15, 1858, *Ibid.*, p. 184.
37. The *Leuchtthurm* of New Philadelphia, Ohio, was one of these. It was financed by a Republican running for Congress, who employed a "green German" to edit his election sheet. See *Westbote*, April 29, Oct. 1, 1858. Other papers which received subsidies from the party included the *New Yorker Abendzeitung*, the *Toledo Express*, and the *Iowa Staatszeitung*. See *Westbote*, Sept. 4, 1857; Dec. 9, 1858.
38. *New Yorker Staatszeitung*, Aug. 17, 1859; and *Belletristisches Journal*, April 1, 1859.
39. Quoted in Herriott: *loc. cit.*, p. 151.
40. Roseboom: *op. cit.*, pp. 351-52.
41. See Fred H. Harrington: *Fighting Politician, Major General N. P. Banks* (Philadelphia, 1948) p. 45.
42. See *Wächter am Erie*, March 14, 17, 1860; *Belletristisches Journal*, March 16, 1860.
43. May 23, 1860.
44. May 31, 1860.
45. Herriott: *loc. cit.*, p. 149.
46. May 5, 1860.
47. See James G. Randall: *Lincoln, the President* (New York, 1945) I, 166 ff.
48. David C. Mearns: *The Lincoln Papers* (New York, 1948) II, 452.
49. See *Belletristisches Journal*, May 25, 1860; also July 27, 1860.
50. See *Wächter am Erie*, Oct. 3, 1860.
51. See David C. Mearns: *The Lincoln Papers* (New York, 1948) I, 251; and C. F. Huch: "Beteilung der deutschen Republikaner Philadelphias an der Presidentenwahl im Jahre 1860," in *Mitteilungen des Deutschen Pionier Vereins von Philadelphia*, XXI (1911) 33-48.
52. Theodore C. Blegen: *Grass Roots History* (Minneapolis, 1947) p. 225.
53. See *Cleveland Leader*, July 10, 1860, and Claude M. Fuess: *Carl Schurz, Reformer* (New York, 1932).
54. *Intimate Letters*, p. 214.
55. *Ibid.*, p. 218-19.
56. *Westbote*, Sept. 13, 1860; *New Yorker Staatszeitung*, Sept. 8, 1860.
57. Quoted in *Cleveland Leader*, June 11, 1860.

58. *Intimate Letters*, p. 224.
59. Freidel: *Lieber*, p. 300.
60. M. A. Becker to Schurz, Oct. 14, 1860.
61. *Wächter am Erie*, Nov. 17, 1860.
62. *Ibid.*, Nov. 12, 1860.
63. On this issue, see W. E. Dodd: "The Fight for the Northwest, 1860" in *American Historical Review*, XVI, 774-88; Arthur C. Cole: *The Era of the Civil War* (Springfield, Illinois 1919); Donnal V. Smith: "Influence of the Foreign-Born of the Northwest in the Election of 1860," in *Mississippi Valley Historical Review*, XIX (Sept. 1932) pp. 192-204; and Andreas Dorpalen: "The German Element and the Issues of the Civil War," *Ibid.*, XXIX (June 1942) pp. 55-76; and Joseph Schafer: "Who Elected Lincoln," in *American Historical Review*, XLVII (Oct. 1941) pp. 51-63.
64. See David C. Mearns: *The Lincoln Papers* (New York, 1948) II, 496-97; (letter of Körner to Lincoln, March 28, 1861); and Rhoda E. White to Lincoln, Dec. 15, 1860, *Ibid.*, pp. 341-43; and *Wächter am Erie*, Oct. 19, 1861; March 18, 1863; June 7, 1865; and *Westbote*, March 21, 28, 1861.
65. Schurz to his wife, March 15, 1861. For this item, I am indebted to Dr. Arthur R. Hogue, who has a number of unpublished Schurz letters.

Chapter 16 · *IN DEFENSE*
OF THE UNION

Iɴ ᴛʜᴇ conflict between liberty and slavery, civilization and barbarism, loyalty and treason, the Germans will play, not a subordinate, but a leading rôle. The spirit of 1848 is abroad again." Thus wrote the editor of the *New Yorker Criminal Zeitung und Belletristisches Journal,* himself a political refugee of the Revolution, on April 26, 1861. Forty-eighters who thirteen years earlier had fought for liberty in the German fatherland, rallied in 1861 to battle for the principles of freedom, popular sovereignty, and national unity which inspired their efforts in 1848 and 1849. Arnold Ruge wrote from London to remind his friends that the war between the states was more important for Europe than the Revolution of 1776. "It is a cleansing of the air of the Republic and the rehabilitation of its significance for the world."[1]

The record of the foreign-born in the war to preserve the Union was a convincing manifestation of national unity and a complete refutation of the nativists who had questioned the loyalty of America's "adopted citizens" in the decade of the 1850's. To be sure, many recent arrivals had no family ties to keep them at home, and there was a preponderance of males of military age among the German immigration. Furthermore, bounties for volunteering proved as attractive to immigrants as to native-born Americans. Throughout the war, recruiting officers met immigrants on their arrival in New York, and some were solicited for military service while still at home. Many Irish Americans opposed the emancipation of the Negro because they feared his competition in the labor market; some resisted the draft, and others enlisted with the hope of eventually striking a blow at England. The draft law caused serious trouble among the Germans of Milwaukee; there were anti-draft riots in Ozaukee County,

Wisconsin, and Forty-eighters had difficulty in arousing German farmers of the state to an interest in the war and an understanding of its signifi- cance.[2] Discipline in some military units composed primarily of foreign- born was not always of the best, but hardly worse than in other units of the laxly administered Union Army. Yet the fact remains that the foreign- born played an honorable, and in many cases distinguished, part in the Civil War, and served the country of their adoption with as much valor and devotion as the native-born.

The statistics of the actuary of the United States Sanitary Commission fix the number of persons born in Germany who volunteered for the Civil War at 176,817. Some estimates place the number of native Germans in the Union Army at 216,000. Neither figure is accurate, and does not in- clude those of German stock and language who came from Austria, Switzerland, and other areas where German was spoken. It is clear, how- ever, that the enlistment of Germans exceeded the proportion normally expected from this group.[3]

The number of Germans who saw service under the Confederate flag is difficult to ascertain. In 1860, the total German population of what became the Confederate States of America was approximately seventy thousand, of whom more than one-fifth lived in New Orleans. German companies and units of other nationality groups were recruited in Louisi- ana, Georgia, South Carolina, Virginia, and Texas. The Turner of New Orleans fought for the South under the command of a former reporter for the *New Orleans Deutsche Zeitung,* and the *Turnverein* of Houston was one of the best drilled companies in the South.[4] A careful scholar has concluded that it is practically impossible to draw a clear line of division between Germans who entered Texas before 1848 and those who came after that date, as far as their attitude toward slavery was concerned. Undoubtedly the overwhelming majority of Germans in the South would have preferred to remain neutral in the war, but vigilance committees and conscription made such a position untenable. Germans with Union sympathies were persecuted in Virginia and Texas, and some Texas Germans fled into the desert, or into Mexico, or across the Union lines, and several were lynched while in prison. On several occasions during the war, German soldiers on both sides of the line were heard singing the same familiar German folksongs.[5] The only well-known Forty-eighter who favored the South was Dr. Adelbert J. Volck of Baltimore, who harbored Confederate soldiers in his home, smuggled medical supplies into the Southern lines, and eventually was locked up in Fort McHenry on orders of General Butler.[6]

In Missouri, the struggle for control of the state in 1861 was especially critical, and it is generally conceded that the Germans of St. Louis played a decisive part in the outcome. The federal arsenal in this strategic border state was guarded at the outbreak of the war by only a handful of United States soldiers, and Southern sympathizers were eager to seize the supplies stored there. Three German Turner companies, from the German section of St. Louis, many of whose members had learned to shoot in 1848, offered their services to Captain Nathaniel Lyon and agreed to hold the arsenal against attacks by pro-Southern "Minute Men." Frank Blair secured the necessary authorization from Washington for the enlistment of the Turner companies, and the city's brewers hauled in fresh supplies of beer daily for the German volunteers who held the arsenal and filled the air with their German songs.

Four volunteer regiments were recruited in two days to hold Missouri in the Union. One was commanded by Franz Sigel, another by Heinrich Börnstein, and a third, consisting of a band of "bearded" Germans known as the "black hunters" (schwarze Jäger), was commanded by Nikolaus Schütter. Blair commanded the fourth. The German volunteers defied the pro-Southern Governor Jackson, surrounded Camp Jackson where the state militia and Southern sympathizers were quartered, forced their surrender, occupied the capitol at Jefferson City, and attempted to cut off the escape of the Confederates into Arkansas. St. Louis was in an uproar early in 1861, and Southern sympathizers were stunned to see "these shuffling, heavy, stupid-looking men" recruited among the German population and jeered the "Hessians" as they plodded through the heart of the city. Street fighting between "Dutch" and "rebels" continued in St. Louis for several days.[7] One need not accept the extreme claims of German-American historians to agree that the Germans played an important rôle in the early months of the battle for Missouri. The state might eventually have been won and held for the Union in any case, but the prompt intervention of German volunteers and Turner companies helped decide the issue between Unionists and Secessionists.

This chapter is not concerned with the military events of the Civil War, or with a detailed account of the experiences of all German units in the

Union Army. Any attempt to describe the fortunes of the most important German immigrants of the 1850's on all the battlefields of 1861 to 1865 is out of the question. It may be true that Germans who immigrated before 1848 furnished a larger percentage of Civil War soldiers than the Forty-eighters, but the record of the latter group, in view of its relatively small numbers, was remarkable. Many Forty-eighters had had experience in the artillery and engineering corps, or in making military maps, and the talents of such specialists were much in demand.

When President Lincoln issued his first call for volunteers the response was immediate and enthusiastic. It has been estimated that six thousand Germans enlisted in New York, and four thousand in Pennsylvania. In the course of the war, Ohio furnished eleven German infantry regiments, three batteries, and one cavalry regiment.[8] In Cleveland, a German singing society was immediately converted into a military company, and of the nine thousand men who came from Cuyahoga County, more than twenty-five percent were Germans. Companies of fifty or more were formed in Piqua, St. Mary's, and smaller towns in Ohio.[9] Judge Stallo administered the oath in German to the first regiment of his countrymen recruited in Cincinnati. The 7th, 8th, 9th, 37th, 58th, and 107th Ohio Volunteers contained many German companies whose· officers used German as the language of command. The 107th Ohio, organized in 1862, consisted of German companies from Cleveland, Sandusky, Akron, and Stark County.[10] A suggestion to unite all Ohio German regiments in a single brigade under Willich or Schimmelpfennig was often made but never carried out.

Six months after Fort Sumter, there were six thousand Germans from Illinois in the Army. The 32nd Indiana regiment contained many Germans, and Wisconsin furnished Irish, German, and Scandinavian regiments. In New York, Friedrich Kapp proposed a regiment of *Sensenmänner* (Germans equipped with scythes) because he had learned of their effectiveness against cavalry during the Polish Rebellion.[11] Heinrich Fach, a Forty-eighter, became lieutenant-colonel of the volunteer artillery organized in Germania Hall in New York City. Its colonel was an expert chess player, and another of its officers was Max Conheim, the playwright. The "Garibaldi Sharp Shooters Corp" consisted of three Hungarian, one Italian, one French, one Spanish, and four German companies, and was commanded by Colonel Utassy, had an Italian next in command, and a

German captain who was the leading tenor of the Teutonia singing society and had fought in Schleswig-Holstein in 1848. The 8th Volunteers, known as New York's Steuben regiment and commanded by Colonel Ludwig Blenker, another veteran of 1848, marched off under escort of hundreds of Germans, led by their singing societies, and behind a flag with the inscription "Ubi libertas ibi patria," presented by the ladies' auxiliary. The 5th and 11th New York regiments were composed largely of members of the *Liederkranz* and the Teutonia *Männerchor,* whose musical directors laid down their batons to become army buglers.[12]

Many German names appear on the muster roll of regiments organized in St. Louis and Missouri. The histrionic Heinrich Börnstein became colonel of the 2nd Missouri and, though only fifty-six years old, resigned after three months' service, with a farewell address which would have done credit to Napoleon after a hundred battles.[13] By 1862, Missouri had produced four German generals, among them the well-known Sigel and Osterhaus. The 24th Illinois Infantry was known as the "Hecker Regiment."[14] The 9th Wisconsin published its own little paper in the field, known as *Der deutsche Krieger.* Reinhold Solger claimed that seventy-five thousand Germans were under arms before the end of 1862, and that one-third were in German regiments under German officers.[15]

"The spirit of 1848" was especially manifest among the Turner societies. Of the total membership of ten thousand in 1861, between five and six thousand entered the Union army, and it has been estimated that, in addition, some two thousand former members enlisted in the Turner regiments. In Philadelphia, eighty-six of a total membership of 260 enlisted at once, and the society offered membership in the *Turnverein* to all recruits who joined its military unit. Within a week the number reached four hundred. After drilling in their own gymnasium and dance hall, the company departed for New York to become part of Blenker's regiment. In Chicago, 105 Turner had enlisted by April 17, 1861, and marched off as the "Turner Union Cadets." In Cincinnati, two hundred Turner joined the army immediately after the fall of Fort Sumter, and in three days Colonel Robert McCook enrolled 1,500 men for the 9th Ohio Volunteer Regiment. Wearing a plug hat, he drilled his men in their gym suits, and his outfit became known in Ohio as the "Turner regiment."[16]

The Baltimore Turner enlisted *en bloc* in April 1861. Composed largely of German artisans and workers, they responded eagerly to the appeals of their leading Forty-eighters, whereas the members of the Germania Club, composed of Baltimore's more prosperous élite, had so little sympathy with the radicals of 1848 that their social hall was closed during the war by order of General Butler as a hotbed of secessionist sentiment.[17] The New York *Turnerschützenregiment* recruited 265 from New York City, 95 from Williamsburg, 65 from Newark, 45 from Bloomingdale, 50 from Brooklyn, 35 from Poughkeepsie, 22 from Albany, 75 from Buffalo, 12 from Syracuse, 15 from Jersey City, and others from smaller places, and invited Franz Sigel, an active Turner, to become their commander.[18] Their enthusiasm for conviviality and amateur theatricals undimmed by barracks routine, the New York Turner regiment in the summer of 1861 celebrated the birthday of Father Jahn at Camp Hamilton by putting up lanterns and floral decorations, singing Turner lyrics, and listening to speeches and declamations.[19] Three months later, a Turner regiment stationed at Newport News celebrated the anniversary of Schiller's birth with several acts from *Die Raüber* and *Wallenstein's Lager*.

Through various activities and organizations, the Germans contributed to the comfort of their soldiers at the front. A Milwaukee bock-beer *fest* netted a hundred dollars for the volunteers' fund.[20] German societies gave dances, fairs, and bazaars to raise money for those at the front or for the relief of their families. The DeKalb Regiment, the last of six German outfits recruited in New York in 1861, marched off with two beautiful flags made by the ladies' organizations. In Cleveland, Toledo, and other cities, women's auxiliaries *(Frauen Hülfe-Vereine)* knit socks and made underwear and bandages which were dispatched at regular intervals to the men in the field.

Friedrich Hecker laid down his plow on his Illinois farm to raise a regiment for the Union Army, and in June 1861 the "Hecker boys" entrained from Chicago. With that flowery oratory for which he was noted, the Colonel accepted the regimental flag and promised that, though his hair had turned gray and his beard snow white, he would fight as vigorously for liberty in 1861 as in 1848. Seven months later Hecker resigned his commission, exasperated by red tape and graft, the inability to get proper supplies and equipment, the lack of military discipline, pillaging, camp-following women, and the stupidity of some of his superiors. Later Hecker reëntered the service, and was severely injured at Chancellorsville.[21]

Adolf Engelmann, one of Hecker's greatest admirers, and a veteran of the Mexican War who had returned to Germany to fight in the Revolution of 1849, became an officer in the Union Army. Karl Eberhard Salomon of Saxony, who fled to the United States after 1849, became colonel of the 5th Missouri Volunteers and later of the 9th Wisconsin, and fought bravely in the early battles to hold Missouri for the Union. Friedrich Salomon, another Forty-eighter, was a captain in his brother's regiment, and rose to be a major general. Alexander Schimmelpfennig, trained in a Prussian military school and a veteran of Kossuth's Hungarian Revolution, was a colonel in the Army of the Potomac, fought in the Second Battle of Bull Run and at Gettysburg, and was severely wounded at Chancellorsville. Max Weber, Sigel's comrade in 1849, and a graduate of the Polytechnic Institute and the military school in Stuttgart, commanded a German Turner Regiment from New York, and fell, severely wounded, at Antietam. Peter Joseph Osterhaus, a veteran of the Prussian Army, though not directly involved in the Revolution, left Germany in 1849, settled first as a merchant in Illinois, and in 1851 moved to St. Louis where he entered the Union Army, ten years later, as a private. He was mustered out a major general, took part in no less than thirty-four engagements, including Vicksburg and Sherman's march from Atlanta to the sea, and was regarded by many competent military experts as the best of the German officers.[22]

The ardent Republican, Gustav Struve, enlisted as a private in 1861, became a captain in Blenker's regiment, and resigned when he disapproved of his superior's policies. Bernhard Domschke closed his desk as editor of a Milwaukee paper to become a lieutenant in a "Sigel Regiment," spent nearly two years in Libby Prison, and after his exchange in March 1865, published a book describing his prison experiences.[23] Captain Ernst F. Hoffmann, who had commanded a battery at the battle of Waghäusel, and had fled with Sigel into Switzerland, was a typical soldier of fortune who had fought not only in Baden, but in Schleswig-Holstein, for the British in the Crimean War, and as a staff officer with Garibaldi. At the outbreak of the Civil War he was manager of the Turner Hall in Cincinnati and owned a saloon called "The Tavern of the German Republic," where freethinkers were accustomed to meet. He volunteered for military service at once, and commanded a battery of Cincinnatians under Sigel in the early campaigns in Missouri and Arkansas.[24] Germain Metternich, an artillery officer in the Revolution, became lieutenant colonel of the 46th New York, and was killed in Georgia while trying to quiet a group of drunken soldiers.[25]

Karl A. Knoderer, who had resigned public office in Baden to join the revolutionists, fell in the Civil War as a colonel of the 167th Pennsylvania. Captain Hermann Ignatz Dettweiler, a veteran of Waghäusel, was severely wounded.[26] John Albert Neustätter, who fled with Schurz after the capitulation of Rastatt, was an artillery officer in the Union Army.[27] Franz Grimm, a radical journalist from Braunschweig, fell at Shiloh, as a captain in the 43rd Illinois.[28] Bernhard Maria Wiedinger, journalist and teacher, from Constance, and a former revolutionary, was elected captain of a company in the original Hecker Regiment, but had to resign his commission because of poor eyesight.[29] Julius Stahel, a veteran of the Kossuth uprising, fought at Bull Run, in McClellan's Peninsular Campaign, and with Burnside and Hooker, and rose to the rank of major general. Friedrich Knefler, a German Jew who also had fought with Kossuth, became a brigadier general in the Civil War.

August Willich, a former Prussian officer and a comrade of Hecker in 1848, is generally regarded as one of the ablest soldiers among the Forty-eighters. A strict disciplinarian and a bold fighter, he took part in a number of engagements of the Civil War, was severely wounded, and left the army with the rank of brigadier general. After the war, his friends elected the disabled veteran auditor of Hamilton County, Ohio, and expected him to live on the fees of his office. Unfortunately he left too much to his deputies, looked upon his post as a pure sinecure, and was sued for illegal collection of fees. Though ably defended by Stallo, he left office under a cloud. He died in 1878 on a farm at St. Mary's, Ohio.[30]

Fritz Anneke, a dashing young artillery officer of 1848-49, was in Switzerland when the Civil War broke out, and was urged to return to the United States where experienced men were badly needed. The American Consul in Zurich refused to provide traveling expenses, however, and Anneke's passage finally was paid by a loan from the old Revolutionary Fund collected by Kinkel in the United States a decade earlier. Although employed to drill artillery companies, Anneke had great difficulty getting a commission until the governor of Illinois finally made him a colonel. Anneke's military career was marked with much controversy and friction with his superiors. In March 1862 he was relieved of command of a battery, but two months later was back in service under Halleck. The following summer, again because of differences with his superiors, he was court-martialed, although the charge that he had deserted was without foundation and arose from a mistake in the transmission of orders.[31]

The list of Forty-eighters who held commissions of various ranks during the Civil War could be greatly extended to include: Albert Arndt, who fell at Antietam; Franz Backhoff, a major under Sigel in Missouri, who had refused to fire upon the people at Rastatt, and served two years in jail; Colonel Gottfried Becker, former editor of the *Turnzeitung;* Hans Boebel, a freethinker and Turner who lost a leg at Gettysburg; Andrew Brickel, a major in the Army of the Potomac; Colonel Adolf Dengler, a "Latin Farmer" from Belleville, who had defended Freiburg in the Revolution and fell at Vicksburg; Heinrich Dietrich, a captain at Gettysburg; Christian Essig, Sigel's adjutant in Baden; Ernst F. M. Fähtz, an Austrian who had fought in Hungary, Baden, and Schleswig-Holstein, and became lieutenant colonel of a Maryland regiment; Carl Gottfried Freudenberg, who participated in the Revolution in Mannheim as a lad of fifteen, and was colonel of the 52nd New York; Joseph Gerhardt of Bonn, who commanded a battalion in 1848 and organized the Turner of Washington, D. C., for the Civil War; Emil Haas, a regimental surgeon; Wilhelm Hexamer, an engineer who commanded a battery at Antietam; Heinrich Huhn, a Turner and actor who was adjutant of an Ohio regiment; Wilhelm Peter Heine, an artist from Dresden who had been with Admiral Perry in the Far East, and served in the engineer's corps of the Union Army; Wilhelm Jacobs, wounded at Chancellorsville; Konrad Krez, a lawyer and poet who became a brigadier general; Fritz Leser, adjutant of a Turner regiment from Missouri; Franz Mahler, wounded at Gettysburg; Friedrich Poschner, colonel of an Ohio regiment; Heinrich Ramming, a journalist who became colonel of a Missouri regiment; Adam Senges, a colonel of the 15th New York artillery in the Army of the Potomac; Albert Sigel, a prisoner of 1849, who fought alongside his better-known brother Franz as colonel of a Missouri regiment; and other Forty-eighters, such as Adam Schumacher of the Ninth Ohio; Hermann Ulffers, an army engineer; Colonel Adolf von Hartung, of the 74th Pennsylvania Regiment; Rudolf von Rosa of the 46th New York; and Heinrich von Treba, who succeeded Willich as commander of the 32nd Indians.[32]

In view of the religious unorthodoxy of many Forty-eighters, it is interesting to note that several Germans served as chaplains in German regiments. The 3rd Ohio, obliged to choose a chaplain, selected Adolf Gerwig, a freethinking Forty-eighter who had studied theology at Heidelberg and taught school in America, where he became a great admirer of Theodore Parker. Gerwig announced that "he would not be a preacher who howls and prays, but a friend, comforter, teacher, and hospital helper," who would regale his men with instructive lectures instead of sermons. Early in 1862, he was found dead in his quarters with his pistol beside him.[33] August Becker, another ex-theologian who escaped into Switzerland in 1848, and in 1854 became editor of the *Baltimore Wecker,* served three years as chaplain of the Steuben regiment of New York. Wilhelm Stengel, a former law student at Tübingen and a journalist in Cincinnati, was chaplain of the 9th Ohio Turner Regiment, but resigned to become a captain. Edmund Märklin, who fought with Sigel in 1848 and was too old for active service in the Civil War, became an army nurse for the 34th Wisconsin Volunteer Infantry.[34]

The Union Army was no model of efficiency or military discipline, and it required years to develop a well-officered and well-integrated fighting force. Volunteers were regarded with suspicion by West Point officers. On the whole the record of the German outfits was entirely creditable. Many died on the battlefield, or returned maimed or with health shattered by long months in prison camps. On the other hand, there were cases of insubordination, drunkenness, profiteering, and laxity in discipline among the German units and their officers also. Whether such offenses by the foreign-born received more attention in the press than similar violations of orders by native Americans remains an unsettled question. Unfortunately, controversies over the competence and valor of the Germans became extremely acrimonious in several cases, in which outstanding Forty-eighters were the chief targets for criticism.

German militia companies had enlisted to "save Washington," fully expecting something of a lark and a short war. As military routine became more difficult and monotonous, men complained about their duties, resented taking orders and became insubordinate. Financial irregularities, arising largely from the licensing of sutlers for the armies, gave rise to shocking tales of speculation and graft in which a few German officers were involved. Sometimes the cause of trouble was nothing more serious than too much lager beer, apparently an essential item for German outfits, though drinking to excess was a rather general vice in the army, beer and whiskey were easy to get, and brawling frequently followed from over-indulgence.

The Germans, like everybody else, wanted commissions, gold braid, and the prestige of military titles, and the Civil War had its quota of political generals and unprincipled adventurers. Money and influence helped men get commissions for which they were not qualified, and Lincoln was hounded for appointments. Heinzen pointed out that before the war every German adventurer and vagabond had become an editor—now he aspired to become a general! Heinzen's editorials flayed the politicians and incompetents among the Forty-eighters who suddenly strutted about in officers' uniforms. With savage delight, he called atten-tion to their former occupations—one had been a stationer, another a politician, still another a tavern keeper, and others suddenly had blossomed forth with titles of nobility. Heinzen intensely disliked the uncritical flattery which the German press heaped upon German soldiers and officers. He deplored the pressure upon Lincoln for commissions, and ridiculed the sentimental demonstrations with which German volunteers were sent off to the front.[35] "The first theatre of war for most of the German colonels was the beer house," Heinzen wrote in 1861. Otto von Corvin, a member of Blenker's staff, agreed with many of these criticisms of the German officer class. This veteran of the Revolution of 1848 reported the Civil War for European readers as the American correspondent for the *Augs-burger Allgemeine Zeitung,* and acquired his American citizenship by enlisting in the Union Army.[36] Like Heinzen, he discovered vagabonds and "bums" among the German refugees, and ex-German officers who had left the fatherland because of financial troubles or for mere adventure and regarded the United States as the "overseas orphanage for cracked-up German officers."

At a time when military experience of any kind was at a premium, it was relatively easy for an ex-private in a European army to become a lieutenant in America, and for lieutenants to become generals. "Foreign military humbuggers" who claimed to have fought in twenty-five battles in Europe called for volunteers and hoped to become colonels of their newly created regiments. Obviously, when officers were elected by their own men there could be little discipline. Administration was so lax and inefficient that a colonel was often credited with a regiment when in fact he had raised only a company or two. Nevertheless he drew rations for an entire regiment, and occasionally borrowed "companies" from other outfits to pad his totals on inspection day. "The mania to become a colonel" led to the hunting down of recruits, at one to five dollars a head, and the offer of good food and booty. A New York German paper described a recruiting office with a bugler and drummer outside, and a whiskey bottle, cheese and sandwiches on the table inside.[37] There were cases in which Union Defense Committees and other patriotic organizations spent as much as ten thousand dollars to recruit a single regiment, and new regiments continued to be raised when existing units should have been consolidated into organizations of respectable size and effectiveness.

When the German "Cameron Rifles" marched to the New York City Hall to receive their battle flag, a deputy sheriff arrested their colonel for failure to collect a debt of $85 owed by his quartermaster.[38] The Republican *Baltimore Wecker* complained in 1861 of the misconduct and poor discipline of German troops under German officers ordered to protect the city. They were described as a howling and shouting mob who brandished weapons of murder in drunken sprees and menaced peaceful citizens. Mutinies occurred occasionally among German troops, as well as resignations, courtmartials, or dishonorable discharges of officers in the quartermaster's department who were accused of cheating the government and their comrades in handling military supplies.[39]

Such incidents were relatively few and were limited to no particular group in the army. To a large extent, they resulted from ineffective administration by the War Department. Yet they provided the ammunition for new attacks upon foreign-born soldiers by Americans still under the spell of nativism, and precipitated feuds between native and adopted citizens that threatened the unity of the war effort. Many Americans regarded the Germans as aggressors in these controversies, and it is true that in some cases the latter demanded special consideration for their group. Four months after the outbreak of war, the German press complained that German officers had not been properly recognized, and that the War Department was influenced by a recurrence of nativism. German radicals assembled in New York to insist on Willich's promotion from colonel to brigadier, and advocated sending a committee to the President to demand ten German brigadier generals.[40]

When Frémont was removed from his command in Missouri by the President because of his ill-advised attack on slave property, many German papers, such as the *Westliche Post,* the *Illinois Staatszeitung* and the *Anzeiger des Westens,* edited by Forty-eighters, became sharply critical of the President's policies. A German Republican Convention in New York State criticized Lincoln in formal resolutions.[41] In Chicago, Rapp and Butz, among others, addressed a mass meeting whose sole purpose was to laud Frémont and protest the President's "halfway measures," and similar meetings were held in Iowa, Wisconsin, and Ohio. Enthusiastic supporters of Frémont collected dimes to buy the General a sword. In St. Louis, the Germans paraded in his honor and heard an address by Emil Praetorius. Such incidents reveal the growing friction between the moderates in the Lincoln administration and the more radical Forty-eighters, but they were overshadowed by more important charges against three German generals—Blenker, Schurz, and Sigel, all well-known refugees of 1848.[42]

Ludwig Blenker had been a wine merchant in Worms, a petty officer in the Greek Revolution, and commander of Ludwigshafen in the German Revolution of 1848. Thereafter he fled to Switzerland and the United States, where he lived for a time on a farm and operated a small business in New York. In 1861 he became colonel of the 8th New York regiment, and in due time commander of a brigade. At Bull Run, his four German regiments fought well and received high praise for their valor. Blenker undoubtedly was vain and loved pomp and circumstance. When McClellan became general of the Army of the Potomac, Blenker led a torchlight procession to his headquarters. He loved the blare of bands and gaudy uniforms, yet officers of merit testified to his ability to organize, feed, and discipline a brigade of volunteers, and no one questioned his personal courage.

Unfortunately a number of German adventurers flocked to his standard, and petitioned for commissions and other preferments, and presently papers like the *New York Demokrat* were pointing to the "orgies of foreign princes, counts and barons on Blenker's staff." Matters reached a climax when a Prussian prince joined the brigade. For uncompromising republicans like Heinzen and Struve, this was the last straw. The latter promptly resigned his captaincy, issued a brochure protesting Prince Salm-Salm's appointment to a colonelcy, and announced that as a republican he could not serve under a Prussian prince. Heinzen unlimbered his biggest journalistic guns in the *Pionier,* and resolved to drive Blenker out of the army.

Ugly charges of financial irregularities circulated about the luckless General, and although Struve wrote to the *Illinois Staatszeitung* to defend Blenker against the accusation that he collected a hundred dollars each month from sutlers whom he had licensed, the charges continued to spread, and created the impression that the German brigade was rapidly getting out of hand. Newspaper stories recounted that Blenker's troops robbed the surrounding country of food and livestock, and did private pillaging of personal possessions which could have no military value. The German-language press and the *New York Tribune* aired the charges. The *New Yorker Criminal Zeitung und Belletristisches Journal* defended Blenker, and several German editors hinted that Schurz was plotting to supersede Blenker as a field commander.[43]

Heinzen's *Pionier* surpassed all other papers in the violence of its attack on Blenker. Heinzen challenged the military competence of a "swindler and jail bird" who shared the profits of others, who exploited his men, and employed a lawyer to delve into the General's record abroad. Charges were forwarded to the War Department which alleged thieving and embezzlement in Europe and grave financial irregularities in this country. Heinzen apparently made little effort to sift truth from scandal-mongering, and treated all information that reached him as of equal validity. When Blenker's appointment as a general reached the Senate for confirmation, at least three senators spoke against it, and charged him with illegal financial transactions, selling sutlers' licenses to the highest bidder, and making his outfit "a nursery of European princes and barons, essentially anti-republican in their sentiments."

Schimmelpfennig, a fellow officer, characterized Blenker as a "bum," and behind the scenes there was intense rivalry between the friends of Blenker, Schurz, and Sigel. Nevertheless Blenker was confirmed as a brigadier general. But his career was at an end. Without issuing an explanation or defense, he left the army, and died on a farm in New York in November 1863. The *New Yorker Abendzeitung* believed he died "of a broken heart, hounded to death by a band of professional slanderers and political fanatics," and victimized by adventurers and bogus nobility on his military staff. He died poor, and there is no proof that he profited personally from the transactions of sutlers who sold beer, champagne, and other products to his men. McClellan continued to speak highly of Blenker's ability as an officer.[44] Several members of his quartermaster's department, however, were convicted of financial irregularities.

Carl Schurz, far better known than Blenker, quickly tired of his diplomatic post in Madrid and yearned for the more exciting life of an army officer. Though his limited experiences in 1848-49 provided no sound basis for his claims, he was convinced that he had special talents for a military career, and what he had not learned in the field he would learn from books on military history and tactics. Before the end of 1861, Schurz was writing from Spain to complain that at a time when the war was in a most critical stage, and "the cause which is at stake is the cause of my life," he was "condemned to elegant leisure." In 1862 he was back in the United States, ready to be photographed in the uniform of a brigadier general—big leather boots, blue uniform with conspicuous buttons and epaulettes, gloves and riding whip, or in a cossack outfit of fur cap, cape, boots and spurs. German papers of diverse political opinion, such as the *Westbote* and the *Illinois Staatszeitung* seriously questioned Schurz's competence in military matters and doubted the wisdom of his appointment.[45] The *Westbote* described the "German Demosthenes" as "an inflated, ambitious demagogue," "an orator, a man of education, and an office-seeker of amazing tenacity and impudence," and a "political general" far inferior to Blenker.[46] Adolph Steinwehr, writing to Sigel on January 26, 1863, asked the latter's help in securing another command, for "it is a great humiliation for me to be obliged to serve under Schurz."

In a letter to Caspar Butz, Schurz argued that the army was "in the hands of the pro-slavery element," that "it was necessary to inject an anti-slavery element," and give a new direction to policy in Washington, and pointed out that he accepted a minor military appointment at considerable sacrifice.[47] Shortly before, Schurz had written to Sumner from Stafford Court House to ask why he did not have a higher rank, and had referred to "the influence" which he wanted to develop in the army and to his relations with his "large constituency." He was particularly anxious to silence "the jeers of the German pro-slavery papers over the German Republican leader," and urged the Senator from Massachusetts to see the President and get him a major general's commission. In still another letter to Sumner, in 1863, he referred again to his "influence with a large class of citizens." Schurz frequently wrote to the President in a highly critical vein, and turned out to be one of Lincoln's troublesome generals in this respect. Schurz had many fine qualities of mind and character, but a sense of humor and modesty about himself was not among them. His sincerity and devotion to the cause are unquestioned. He tried hard, by studying military tactics, to learn the business of being a general, and he achieved the commission of a major general, but his military competence remains a subject of controversy.

Schurz's division, consisting of many German troops, figured in the disaster of the 11th Army Corps at Chancellorsville, where Stonewall Jackson's fast-flying columns fell upon both flanks of the corps and drove it to rout. Schurz and Schimmelpfennig insisted that they had urged General Howard to make reconnaisance and redraw the whole front, and that their troops fought against great odds as well as could be expected. They pointed out that seven thousand in the corps were Americans and only five thousand Germans. Hooker blamed his defeat squarely upon the flight of the 11th Corps; Schurz held Hooker and Howard responsible for the disaster. In response to a specific request from Schurz, General O. O. Howard issued a statement to counteract the "false and malicious attacks" of the press on the "disgraceful flight" of the "flying Dutchmen." The New York Times, however, referred to Schurz and his men as "Dutch cowards"; the Chicago Times, as late as 1870, spoke of the "Dutch Panique" of the "lager beer devotees" at Chancellorsville, and the Louisville Journal characterized the German army as a "rabble of liberty shouters."

The German-language press immediately closed ranks to refute such attacks by "stinking nativists," and for once Heinzen's Pionier and Ottendörfer's New Yorker Staatszeitung were in agreement, although the latter still doubted Schurz's competence and suspected his dealings with Blenker, Sigel, and Halleck. Kapp called a meeting at Cooper Institute in New York to demand justice for German soldiers and to express resentment over their treatment as mere "auxiliary troops," and intimated that "the American people do not deserve what the Germans are doing for their cause."[48] In Cleveland, Chicago, and St. Louis, Germans demonstrated against Halleck, urged a German National Committee to obtain justice for the foreign-born, and called for more vigorous opposition to Copperheads and a more efficient administration in Washington.[49]

The controversy raged for months. Meantime the 11th Army Corps was being liquidated, the German units were not refilled, and the men were assigned to other regiments, leaving both Schurz and Steinwehr without commands. The German press blamed Hooker. Early in 1865, Schurz was attached to the staff of General Hancock and charged with recruiting another army corps, but by that time the war was practically over, and he resigned his commision on May 6.

Although Schurz was the best-known Forty-eighter, Franz Sigel probably had the greatest knowledge of military tactics and the most practical experience in 1848-49. A native of Baden, Sigel was educated at the gymnasium in Bruchsal and the military academy of Karlsruhe. In 1847, his liberal views led to his resignation from the army and he turned to the study of law at Heidelberg. In the Revolution of 1848 he had four thousand men under his command. After the failure of the first uprising he fled to Switzerland, but returned in 1849 to command at Heppenheim and Küferthal. He served as general adjutant to Mieroslawski, the Polish commander-in-chief, and after the latter's retirement assumed supreme command, and for a short time acted as minister of war as well. Military historians agree that his operations at Waghäusel, Sinsheim, Durlach, and Steinmauern, and his final masterly retreat with a defeated army into Switzerland, were highly successful tactical maneuvers by a bold and able leader.

When the Civil War broke out, Sigel was teaching school in St. Louis, and had seriously considered going to Italy to fight for Italian unification.[50] He immediately organized a regiment of volunteers and played a major rôle in the fight to hold Missouri in the Union. He fought well at Pea Ridge, Arkansas, and in several other engagements in the same campaign, and was a master strategist in commanding several retreats.

While Frémont was in charge in Missouri, Sigel was in high favor, a fact which did not help his relations with Halleck when the latter superseded Frémont. Sigel was convinced that the new commander, a West Pointer, had the regular army officer's contempt for volunteers, regardless of their ability. When Halleck ordered some of Sigel's troops elsewhere, the German protested the depletion of his forces, resented such interference with his command, and chose to regard Halleck's orders as deliberate insults to his dignity. Halleck, on the other hand, disapproved of the free and easy manner of the German troops toward their officers, and complained of their lack of discipline. Sigel brashly offered his superior a new plan of campaign, and the friction between the two men reached a climax when a letter from Sigel to his father-in-law, referring to Halleck as a "slick lawyer," was stupidly given by Dr. Dulon to the *New Yorker Volkszeitung* for publication. The letter, which appeared in both English and German language papers,[51] made Sigel's "affair" "the affair of the Germans at large." Meanwhile the irascible Forty-eighter had resigned, and met with Governor Körner in St. Louis to enlist the latter's good offices with the authorities in Washington. What Sigel wanted was an independent command, and he believed he deserved it. In further disagreements with Halleck and Curtis about the Battle of Pea Ridge, he charged the former with duplicity and failure to perform his duty. Sigel "absolutely demands a Major-General's commission, on pain of a German rebellion," observed the *Philadelphia Gazette* on February 4, 1862, and the *New York Post* commented sharply on his "clamors for recognition of his great merits," and his practice of praising himself "by accusing his superior officers."

Sigel's resignation touched off the usual German demonstrations and resolutions.[52] Kapp and the Germans of New York demanded a congressional investigation. The Wisconsin legislature took similar action. The Cleveland *Wächter am Erie* contrasted Halleck the nativist with Frémont, "the friend of the Germans," and the *Illinois Staatszeitung* demanded pressure upon the President to make Sigel a major general, with his own command. In Chicago a movement was started to buy Sigel a homestead. Actually only $260 was collected and, at the General's suggestion, turned over to the German Hospital in Philadelphia. Funds also were collected to buy Sigel a sword. The impressive weapon was ready by November 1862, at a cost of $2,000, and consisted of 70 ounces of silver in the blade, with the General's initials set in diamonds, the handle decorated with the figure of a knight fighting a dragon, and the blade engraved with "Defender of Liberty." Prominent Forty-eighters, like Rapp, Brentano, Butz, and Dr. Ernst Schmidt, comprised a Sigel Committee of Chicago which not only worked for the better recognition of the merits of their hero but contemplated sending Sigel to lead a new revolution in Germany, à la Garibaldi's dramatic entry into Italy. Sigel portraits were sold in the offices of German newspapers; the women of St. Louis gave him a silver cup; and when the General went to Washington to see the Secretary of War he was greeted by, and addressed, huge crowds en route.

Several congressmen from Illinois and Indiana, as well as Colonel Blair and Senator Trumbull, called on the President early in 1862, and were assured that Sigel would get a division and a major general's commission at the earliest possible opportunity. In the early summer of 1862, Sigel became a major general—but the controversies over Carthage, Pea Ridge, and with his superiors followed him into his new post. The German element eagerly awaited developments. When it appeared that the new major general had only two small brigades instead of an independent larger unit, and that he was third in command in Virginia, under Pope and Banks, the latter a general with an unsavory record for nativism, the German press found additional reasons for concern. Rumors of a second resignation were bandied about in the press, and Germans signed petitions asking Lincoln to give their favorite a corps, "subordinate to the President only" and recruited by the magic of Sigel's name. Sigel festivals were held in several cities and poems were written in his honor.

It is pointless to follow Sigel's controversies and campaigns in all their details. He fought in the Second Battle of Bull Run and filed charges against his superior, General McDowell, as a result of that encounter. After Rappahannock he was the bitter enemy of Pope and Hooker, and when the latter became commander-in-chief in the Eastern theatre the press reported once more that Sigel had resigned. He demanded a court of inquiry when Pope referred unfavorably to his part in the Virginia campaign, and in direct appeals to the President requested better equipment and assignment to another command.

Many Germans honestly believed that if Sigel had been supreme commander the war would have ended in a much shorter time. The General became a symbol of their participation in the war, and they were extremely sensitive about the treatment of their favorite. Would he continue in the army? Would he succeed Howard as head of the 11th Corps? Had Chase interceded for him with Stanton and Lincoln? Kapp and others went to Washington to persuade the President to let Sigel raise one hundred thousand volunteers, and the press continued to highlight the conflict between Germans and "nativists" over what would be proper recognition for the German element.

In the summer of 1863, when Sigel's staff was dissolved and the General went to Bethlehem, Pennsylvania, on leave, a delegation from St. Louis waited on the President to ascertain why Sigel was not in the field.[53] The agitation of the Germans finally reached a point where Kapp, Sigismund Kaufmann, and Weil von Gernsbach joined several others in an open letter to the *New York Demokrat* requesting that the Germans desist from further demonstrations. "Sigel can handle his enemies," the appeal concluded—"God protect him from his friends." But Sigel continued to correspond about his troubles with Schuyler Colfax, Speaker of the House, and Congressman Robert Schenck of Ohio. In a letter to Colfax, he wrote with reference to Halleck, "I would rather die in the coal region than to apply to him in any form or manner."[54]

In March 1864, Sigel was put in charge of the Department of West Virginia. On May 15, he was defeated by Breckinridge in a small but bloody engagement at New Market. Grant was sharply critical of Sigel's tactics; Sigel blamed his physical condition for the results of the battle. Superseded by General Hunter, Sigel took charge of a division of reserves at Harper's Ferry, to guard the Baltimore and Ohio Railroad. In July he was relieved of this command also, after he had retreated before Early's raid on Washington. Deeply hurt by what he described as "a severe censure," he demanded an investigation of his whole military career since 1861, and in a letter to Secretary Stanton referred to "the national prejudices and even persecution" which he had to endure. He was given leave of absence, and finally resigned his commission on May 4, 1865.

Sigel's loyalty to the Union cause was never challenged, whatever tactical errors he may have made in the field or in his public relations. In 1863, when the controversy over his status in the army was at fever heat, Sigel stumped the country to urge the defeat of the Copperheads. He had no traffic with German radicals who met in Cleveland to find some one to supersede Lincoln in 1864. He fought with Brough to defeat Vallandigham for the governorship of Ohio, and referred to the possible victory of the peace-at-any-price Democrats as "a national calamity" and "an immortal shame to this Republic."[55] He made addresses in critical states like New York, Pennsylvania, and Ohio, and spoke in both English and German. In nearly every speech he equated the cause of the North with the cause of liberty and humanity for which Forty-eighters had fought in Europe, and he told a Utica audience that he came "to fight a little with the enemy in the rear, because I cannot just now fight the enemy in front." Germans turned out in great numbers to hear him and greeted their hero with serenades, parades, and the recitation of the popular poem, "I Fights Mit Sigel." There can be no doubt that Sigel's influence was important in the critical campaigns of 1863.[56]

After the war, Sigel was editor of the *Baltimore Wecker,* worked for railroad, shipping, and insurance companies, German Republican committees, various social organizations, and the Turner. He was nominated for secretary of state of New York in 1869 and held several minor posts under Grant and Harrison. An ardent civil service reformer, he fought the Tweed Ring in New York, and when high in the seventies founded the *New York Monthly,* whose German correspondents and contributors were largely Socialists, for the exile of 1848 never abandoned his interest in radical reform. When Sigel died in 1902, Schurz delivered his funeral oration.

The violent controversies over the war records of Blenker, Schurz, Sigel, and others were soon forgotten. The sacrifices of the Germans in the Civil War gave them a real sense of belonging to their adopted fatherland and helped dispel the last vestiges of nativist hostility. Germans in the post-war period were appointed and elected to public office, and as veterans could claim the gratitude and the political support of their fellow citizens. The Civil War permanently closed the breach between "Grays" and "Greens" and brought to an end the storm-and-stress period of the Forty-eighters. Many learned their final lesson in Americanization on the battlefield. The most violent phase of their radicalism was passed, and the gap between Forty-eighters and other Americans nearly closed. The defects of American democracy no longer seemed so serious in the light of their sacrifices for the preservation of the Union. Although German-Americans continued to stress their cultural and social organizations and activities, they never again exercised the political influence they had in American affairs from 1854 to 1865.

FOOTNOTES

CHAPTER 16

1. Ruge to *Anzeiger des Westens,* quoted in *Wächter am Erie,* July 10, 1861.

2. See Joseph Schafer: "Four Wisconsin Counties," in *Wisconsin Domesday Book, General Studies* (Madison, 1927) pp. 158-68.

3. See Wilhelm Kaufmann: *Die Deutschen im Amerikanischen Bürgerkrieg* (Munich, 1911); A. B. Faust: *The German Element in the United States* (New York, 1909) Vol. II;

and Fred A. Shannon: *The Organization and Administration of the Union Army 1861-1865* (Cleveland, 1928) 2 vols.

4. *Wächter am Erie*, May 11, 1861.

5. See Ella Lonn: *Foreigners in the Confederacy* (Chapel Hill, 1940) especially pp. 121, 124, 424, 437; see also E. Merton Coulter: *The Confederate States of America, 1861-1865* (Baton Rouge, 1950) pp. 47-48; 443-444.

6. See Cunz: *The Maryland Germans*, pp. 313-14.

7. See, for these incidents, Francis Grierson: *The Valley of the Shadows* (New York 1948) pp. 225-26, 232; Scharf: *St. Louis*, pp. 483-536; Börnstein, *Memoiren*, II, 247-329; and Daniel Hertle: *Die Deutschen in Nordamerika und der Freiheitskampf in Missouri* (Chicago 1865), pp. 44-113.

8. *Wächter und Anzeiger*, Aug. 9, 1902, p. 121.

9. *Westbote*, May 2, 1861.

10. *Wächter am Erie*, Aug. 27, 1862.

11. *Belletristisches Journal*, Aug. 2, 1861.

12. *Ibid.*, May 3, 17, 31, April 26, 1861.

13. See also Scharf: *St. Louis*, pp. 453-82; and Virgil C. Blum: "The Political and Military Activities of the German Element in St. Louis, 1859-1861," in *Missouri Historical Review*, XLII, No. 2, pp. 103-29.

14. Max Stern and Fred Kressmann: *Chicago's Deutsche Männer* (Chicago, 1885) pp. 52-57.

15. *Westbote*, April 10, 1862; *Wächter am Erie*, Nov. 19, 1862.

16. See *Cincinnati* (American Guide Series) (Cincinnati, 1943) pp. 218-19; Carl Wittke: "The Ninth Ohio Volunteers" in *The Ohio Archaeological and Historical Quarterly* (April 1926), Vol. XXXV, pp. 1-18; Bessie L. Pierce: *History of Chicago*, II, 256; and *Jahrbücher der Deutsch-Amerikanischen Turnerei*, I, 62-71, 81-82, 97-100; III, 141-44, 170; and *Chicago und Sein Deutschtum* (Cleveland, 1901-2).

17. Cunz: *The Maryland Germans*, pp. 274-75, 311.

18. *Belletristisches Journal*, May 3, 1861.

19. *Ibid.*, Aug. 23, 1861.

20. Still: *Milwaukee*, p. 158.

21. *Westbote*, June 27, 1861; Jan. 30, 1862. Caspar Butz dedicated three poems to the Hecker regiment. See Caspar Butz: *Gedichte eines Deutsch-Amerikaners* (Chicago, 1879) pp. 69-73.

22. See Emil Mannhardt: "General Peter Joseph Osterhaus" in *Deutsch-Amerikanische Geschichtsblätter*, IV (July 1904) pp. 54-62.

23. *Twenty Months as a Prisoner of War* (Milwaukee, 1865). See also *Wächter am Erie*, June 22, 1864; March 22, 1865.

24. See *Wächter am Erie*, March 26, 1862 and *Pittsburger Volksblatt*, March 25, 1862.

25. *Westbote*, Sept. 5, 1861; May 29, 1862.

26. *Der Deutsche Pionier*, X (No. 7) Oct. 1878, p. 272.

27. *Ibid.*, XI, No. 10 (Jan. 1880) p. 385.

28. *Mitteilungen des Deutschen Pionier Vereins von Philadelphia* XXII (1911) pp. 25-28.

29. *Chicago und Sein Deutschtum* (Cleveland, 1901-1902) pp. 152-53.

30. See *Wächter am Erie*, May 27, 1869 for the Hamilton County episode.

31. See *Belletristisches Journal*, Aug. 16, 1861; *Westbote*, March 6, 1862; *Wächter am Erie*, March 19, May 24, 1862; Aug. 22, 1863; and Stierlin: *Kentucky*, pp. 200-1.

32. See Ella Lonn: "The Forty-eighters in the Civil War," in Zucker: *Forty-eighters*, pp. 182-220.

33. *Wächter am Erie*, Oct. 12, 1861; Feb. 8, 1862.

34. See Hense-Jensen and Bruncken: *Wisconsin's Deutsch-Amerikaner*, I, 186-87; also 203-9; and Uhlendorf: "German-American Poetry," in *Deutsch-Amerikanische Geschichtsblätter*, XXII-XXIII, 200-2.

35. See Wittke: *Heinzen*, pp. 179-84.

36. *Der Deutsche Pionier*, XVII, No. 3 (1886) pp. 283-84.

37. *Belletristisches Journal*, Aug. 16, 23, 1861.

38. *Ibid.*, Aug. 30, 1861.

39. See *Westbote*, Aug. 8, 1861; June 11, 19, 1862; and the cases of Captain Jacob Löwenthal and Schumann, in *Ibid.*, July 10, 1862.

40. *Westbote*, May 15, 1862.

41. *Wächter am Erie*, Sept. 18, 1861.

42. See *Wächter am Erie*, Nov. 8, 1862; also Nov. 10, 1861; and *Westbote*, Sept. 26, Nov. 21, 1861.

43. *Wächter am Erie*, June 28, 1862.

44. For further details, see Wittke: *Heinzen*, pp. 180-84.

45. *Westbote*, April 3, 1862; *Illinois Staatszeitung*, April 24, 1862.

46. *Westbote*, July 3, 10, 1862.

47. See *Wächter am Erie*, April 12, 1862.

48. See *Wächter am Erie*, Sept. 3, 1870; May 16, 30, 1863; Nov. 21, 1863; and Kapp: *Aus und über Amerika*, II, pp. 279-87.

49. *Wächter am Erie*, June 24, 27, 1863.

50. See *Belletristisches Journal*, July 19, 1861; Jacob Picard: "General Franz Sigel" in New York *Sonntagsblatt Staats-Zeitung und Herold*, Nov. 20, 27, 1949; and Wilhelm Blos: *General Franz Sigel's Denkwürdigkeiten aus den Jahren 1848-49* (Constatt, n.d.).

51. Wilhelm Kaufmann: "Sigel und Halleck," in *Deutsch-Amerikanische Geschichtsblätter*, X (Oct., 1910) No. 4, pp. 210-16.

52. See *Westbote*, Jan. 23, 1862; *Wächter am Erie*, Jan. 8, 15, 22, Feb. 12, April 9, May 28, June 4, Nov. 12, 1862.

53. *Philadelphia Freie Presse*, June 18, 1863.

54. Sigel to Colfax, Feb. 11, 1864.

There is a quantity of Sigel material, letters, army reports, and scrap books, from 1861-1865, in the Western Reserve Historical Society Library, stressing not only the military but the political phases of the Sigel controversy, and it is on this material that this account is primarily based.

55. Sigel to L. D. Campbell.

56. See *Philadelphia Evening Bulletin*, Oct. 1, 1863; Wheeling *Daily Intelligencer*, Oct. 15, 1863; *Pittsburgh Gazette*, Oct. 9, 1863; *Cleveland Leader*, Oct. 13, 1863.

Chapter 17 · *THE POLITICS OF THE POST-WAR YEARS*

IN THE decades following the Civil War, German-Americans, with the exception of a few issues, were divided on public questions like most other Americans. The influence of the fighting Forty-eighters gradually declined as they grew older and they and their constituents became Americanized. Several issues proved of particular import to German voters, however, and prominent Forty-eighters, now no longer regarded as refugees, continued to be influential in matters of public policy. Schurz, Sigel, and others lived into the dawn of the twentieth century, but the majority of their fellow refugees ceased to be politically active long before.

A substantial number of radical Germans lost faith in Lincoln before the close of the war, and became disgusted with what they considered his ultra-conservative policies toward emancipation and Southern slaveholders. Ardent and uncompromising champions of complete equality for the Negro, like Heinzen, accused the President of prolonging the war unnecessarily by policies of conciliation and moderation. Such radicals demanded immediate emancipation, the confiscation of rebel property, complete racial equality, and the use of colored troops. It is well to remember that not only radical Germans, like Heinzen, Butz, Schurz, and others criticized the administration in Washington for being too soft, but influential American editors, such as Joseph Medill and Murat Halstead, and political leaders like Thaddeus Stevens, Sumner, Chandler, and Wade shared their irritation with Lincoln. When emancipation finally came, Forty-eighters like Heinzen and Butz believed it did not go far enough,[1] and August Thieme, of the *Wächter am Erie,* agreed with Wendell Phillips that the war was in vain if it did not result in

244

the complete reconstruction of Southern society and a revolution in the Southern economy.

The French invasion of Mexico, at a time when the Union was fighting for its life, aroused the entire German press, and many editorials condemned the President for indecisiveness and tardiness in dealing with so flagrant a violation of the Monroe Doctrine. The release of the Confederate agents, Mason and Slidell, in the "Trent affair," was regarded as a national humiliation and a capitulation to British arrogance. The *Wächter am Erie* concluded that the Government was fighting an unreal war, marked by "halfway measures" and "missed opportunities."[2] Heinzen found fault with Lincoln's Gettysburg Address, and rewrote it in terms of revenge for the martyr, John Brown. In 1863 his *Pionier* carried caustic editorials against appeasement and a negotiated peace. Radicals of the Heinzen, Butz, and Sigel variety wanted the South reduced to a conquered territory, the rebels severely punished, their property confiscated, and a new order created based on unconditional surrender and the enfranchisement of the Negro.[3] The *Wächter am Erie* editorialized on the bearing of the fighting on the cause of "humanity and liberty" throughout the world,[4] and when the war finally ended, German refugees in London, including Freiligrath, Karl Blind, and Kinkel, sent a formal message congratulating the North on its victory.[5]

As early as 1863, dissatisfaction with the halfway measures of the Lincoln administration led to demands for a new political party. Heinzen's *Pionier* was not the only German paper to suggest in 1864 that Frémont be nominated to replace Lincoln. Leading German papers in the North, edited by other Forty-eighters, favored a convention of radicals, and clubs were organized in many cities to press the radical demands. The result was a call for a national convention of dissatisfied German-Americans. In October 1863, a "preliminary" convention met in Cleveland to make plans for the following year. The attendance was small; influential Forty-eighters like Brentano, Schurz, Solger, and Sigel refused to take part, and Heinzen's disciples, who were in the majority, clashed repeatedly with a minority led by Kapp. The delegates approved a platform calling for unconditional surrender, complete abolition, drastic reconstruction of the South, vigorous enforcement of the Monroe Doctrine, and American support for European revolutions, for the Heinzen faction insisted that the "North American Republic cannot be safe and enjoy liberty as long as the rest of the world is in chains." The Cleveland *Wächter am Erie* and the Boston *Pionier* were designated as the official organs of the new radical organization.

Although the Cleveland convention of 1863 was repudiated by the majority of the German-language press and the Forty-eighter group, the Heinzen minority continued to agitate for Frémont, champion of Negro rights, for the Republican nomination for the following year. The Frémont boom may have originated in Missouri, where the General continued to be popular, and it received support from many non-German groups, but Germans were especially active in organizing Frémont Clubs in New England and the middle western states, and a number of their papers endorsed the movement.

Caspar Butz of Chicago characterized Lincoln as "the weakest and worst man that ever filled the Presidential chair," and with Pruessing, Dr. Ernst Schmidt, and representatives of German workingmen, signed the call for a Frémont convention. A "German Political Club" in Cleveland, whose presiding officer was the Forty-eighter Jakob Müller, demanded punitive measures against the South, including the confiscation of Southern estates and their redistribution as homesteads for veterans, and in St. Louis and Cincinnati, radical Germans took similar action.[6] Twenty-seven German delegates from ten states met in Cleveland in 1864 in advance of the larger group of radical Republicans who had come to nominate Frémont for president. Heinzen dominated the German delegation, and Frémont's adjutants collaborated closely with his group. Their platform was similar to the principles approved the preceding autumn, except that the Germans advocated a new party and rejected all compromise proposals from Lincoln Republicans.

About four hundred delegates attended the convention proper, although a thousand were expected. They assembled on May 31, 1864, in Elmer's Hall in Cleveland, and continued their deliberations in Chapin's Hall. Heinzen and five other Germans were members of the platform committee of fourteen. Kapp, Emil Praetorius, and other prominent Forty-eighters from New York and Missouri were conspicuous for their absence. The platform of the "Radical Democracy" demanded the extinction of slavery by constitutional amendment, the popular election of presidents and for one term only, the enforcement of the Monroe Doctrine, and the confiscation and redistribution of rebel property. Frémont was chosen to head the ticket, and Heinzen, Butz, and several other Forty-eighters became members of the national executive committee.[7]

The response of the Germans was anything but unanimous, even in radical circles. Demonstrations in St. Louis, New York, and Cincinnati to ratify the nomination proved disappointing. The *Wächter am Erie* compared Frémont's attitude toward the Lincoln administration with that of the Copperheads, and deplored the effort to split the Republican strength in a decisive campaign. The *New Yorker Abendzeitung* and the *Illinois Staatszeitung* ridiculed the proposal for a separate German organization, and the *Toledo Express* first accepted Frémont, and then in July, with other papers, switched to Lincoln. Two German papers launched in Fremont, Ohio, to support "the Pathfinder" died an early death. Radical German clubs in Hoboken and New York flirted with the Frémont movement for a short time but finally endorsed Lincoln, and George Hillgärtner started a new paper in St. Louis for the specific purpose of supporting the President for a second term.[8]

The Republican administration press pictured the Frémont Convention as a strange collection of adventurers, fanatics, visionaries, and Ishmaelites. The *Cleveland Herald* spoke of "impetuous hair-brained Germans," and Thurlow Weed characterized the radical uprising as a "slimy intrigue." Undaunted by such attacks, Heinzen went with Wendell Phillips to call on Frémont in Nahant, Massachusetts, to map the strategy of the campaign, and apparently left completely satisfied, for the *Pionier* continued to refer in extravagant terms to Frémont's many virtues. Thaddeus Stevens and Elihu Washburn of Illinois were sufficiently impressed by the activities of the dissenters to urge Schurz to give up his military duties and stump the country for Lincoln's reëlection, and Schurz directed the party's foreign-language bureau in 1864 as he had done so successfully four years earlier.

On September 22, when Frémont withdrew from the race, Heinzen commented dolefully, "The party founded at Cleveland is now an army that has been dismissed, without a flag . . . and yielded without a battle." He was charitable enough, however, to attribute Frémont's withdrawal to the latter's fear of a Democratic victory. The *Pionier* and the St. Louis *Westliche Post* were bitterly disappointed, but other papers, like the *Pittsburger Volksblatt,* seemed both relieved and pleased. German Frémont clubs changed almost overnight into Lincoln clubs; Schurz went into action as the leading Republican stump speaker among the Germans; the majority of the German radical press finally supported Lincoln for reëlection, and although some Germans may have stayed away from the polls, the majority probably voted for the President, if for no other reason than to avert the disaster of a Democratic victory.[9]

Lincoln's second inaugural address again disappointed the Heinzen radicals among the Forty-eighters. A few weeks later the bullets of the fanatical Booth ended the career of the War President, the polemics ceased with his death, the Lincoln legend began to grow and the stature of his critics to shrink to size. Radical Republicans, regardless of national origin, hoped that Lincoln's mild policies would be reversed, and expected Johnson to reconstruct the South in a way that would make treason forever odious. August Thieme, of the Cleveland *Wächter am Erie,* hailed the new President as a distinguished son of the common people who knew "the traitors of the South" so well that he would not let his heart run away with his head in meting out just retribution.[10]

It was not long before the Tennessee tailor, originally welcomed as the superior of the Illinois rail-splitter, reversed his policy to follow in the footsteps of his predecessor, thereby precipitating a struggle with the Radical Republicans in Congress for control of the party and the country. By August 1865, Heinzen's *Pionier* was demanding the impeachment of the President. Johnson was accused of personal prejudice, keeping the Negro "in his place" and surrendering defenseless freedmen to their former masters—in short, he had turned into "a traitor to the North and to his party." Germans in Philadelphia and Chicago refused appointments to public office from the President.[11] In 1866, Sigel stumped the Northern states for the Radicals; Körner and the *Belleviller Zeitung* approved when Congress overrode Johnson's vetoes; the *Turner,* in convention at St. Louis, accused the President of frittering away the fruits of victory; and papers like the *New Yorker Abendzeitung* and the *Wächter am Erie* charged Johnson with giving aid and comfort to Copperheads, "having the Constitution on the brain," and "restoring" the Southern "Junker class" to power. Meanwhile, Democrats, eager to recapture the German vote, resorted to their old strategy and stressed the temperance fanaticism of prominent Republican leaders, on the not entirely groundless assumption that the German vote "floated on beer." In the summer of 1867, sizeable meetings of Germans in several cities protested the invasion of their personal liberty by temperance crusaders, and in Chicago, Schmidt, Raster, and other prominent Forty-eighters led the demonstrations.

Schurz continued to be the most successful speaker for the Republicans among the German voters. His "lectures" dealt with reconstruction, the financial policies of the government, the status of the Negro, and the temperance question, and wherever he went he was greeted by his German compatriots with tremendous demonstrations. Hassaurek addressed the German Republicans of Cleveland for two hours on "the party of Union, freedom and human rights" and urged them to remain true to their "mission" in America. The *Wächter am Erie,* the *Illinois Staatszeitung,* and the *Baltimore Wecker* advocated Johnson's removal from office. Sigel, Kapp, Weber, Karl Goepp, and the visiting historian Hermann von Holst addressed the "Republican German Campaign Club" in Cooper Institute in New York on the same anti-administration theme, and Sigel proposed a German party under the leadership of the radical *Turnvereine.* Most German leaders, however, rejected such plans to isolate the Germans politically, and urged them to work within the existing parties.[12]

Schurz was temporary chairman of the Republican convention which nominated Grant in 1868. The campaign, as far as the distinguished Forty-eighter was concerned, was a repetition of many speeches, serenades, torchlight processions, Turner demonstrations and boxes of Rhine wine and cigars from admiring friends. There was no indication that Schurz and his German confreres would break with "the Hero of Appomattox" four years later. Most Forty-eighters were as much under the spell of his magic name as other Americans who remembered only that Lincoln had found a general to bring the war to a victorious close. Heinzen, however, opposed Grant from the outset.

Meanwhile Schurz achieved the distinction of election to the United States Senate from Missouri. "My good friends," he observed, "consider my election the beginning of a new era in Germanism in America. . . . Only Heinzen scolds away lustily in the old manner." On January 16, 1869, Schurz wrote his wife, with pardonable pride—"How I should like to take my old mother and my father to the gallery of the Senate and let them look upon their son in the highest position which a foreign-born person can reach in this country, and which no German before has attained."[13] The new Senator learned rather quickly that he would not only be showered with congratulations but hounded by German office-seekers as well. His term witnessed confusion and violence in the South under radical reconstruction, and unprecedented inefficiency and corruption in the Federal Government in Washington.

The Liberal Republican revolt to prevent Grant's reëlection in 1872 started in Missouri, and had the endorsement of such prominent representatives of the older German group as Körner and Friedrich Münch, and of Hecker and Schurz for the Forty-eighters. Early in 1872 the *Cincinnati Courier,* a German Republican paper, called for a Liberal Republican national convention. The Democratic Columbus *Westbote* published Hecker's invitation to his followers to unite with all anti-Grant Republicans and Democrats in a convention to cleanse the "Augean stables," and Hecker made a vigorous address along the same lines to the Germans in the Turner Hall of Chicago.[14] Cincinnati sent Hassaurek and other liberal Germans as delegates to the proposed convention, and a Liberal Republican meeting in Columbus, attended largely by Germans, listened to addresses by Dr. Philip Blesch and Christian Heddäus, a German minister of high repute among his countrymen, in which the speakers urged a revolt against "Grantism." The Cleveland delegation of eighteen members included August Thieme and August Willich. The *Westbote* reported that the Germans of New Orleans were coming to the national convention a hundred strong and with their own band.[15] Only an extreme minority, many of whom were followers of Heinzen, refused to join the revolt against the regular Republicans. Heinzen himself hoped for Grant's reëlection so that the presidential office might fall into such utter disrepute that it would be abolished.[16] Sigel, on the other hand, appeared on the same platform with the President in New York and campaigned for Grant's reëlection, and Hermann Raster, Grant's collector of internal revenue for Chicago, bitterly assailed Schurz for treason to the party.

The campaign of 1872 promised to reunite the German Republicans with the Democrats, and to heal the party breach of the 1850's over slavery and secession. Most Germans were weary of radical reconstruction and eager to end corruption in the government by civil service reform. Many favored lowering the war tariffs. Schurz and Hecker championed civil service and made the issue popular among their German followers by highlighting the scandals of the Grant era and reminding their listeners of the efficient bureaucracies which they had known in the father-land. In the fall of 1871, Schurz lectured on civil service reform in Cleveland and Cincinnati to large crowds for an admission charge of fifty and seventy-five cents, and Hecker advocated the establishment of "vigilance committees" in every city to scrutinize the administration of local, state, and federal government.[17] Liberal papers like the *Wächter am Erie* opposed Grant primarily because of his support of the spoils system. When Caspar Butz lost his job as commissioner of the state penitentiary in Joliet, Illinois, because of a change in party, and others became convinced that "No Dutch need apply" at the White House for appointments while Grant was President, civil service reform received new support from the complaint that Germans never had received proper recognition in the distribution of public offices.[18]

One other incident, an aftermath of the Franco-German War, had some importance in explaining German opposition to Grant in 1872, for it convinced many Germans, including Forty-eighters, that the administration was pro-French and prejudiced against the "new Germany" of Bismarck and its Hohenzollern Kaiser. Senator Schurz charged Grant's Secretary of War with violating American neutrality legislation by selling surplus government war materials, arms, and ammunition in 1870 and 1871 to agents of the French. The transaction apparently had been carried on by a devious route through contacts between Belknap, in Grant's cabinet, Remington and Sons, and a neighbor of the Remington family. A committee appointed to sift the charges found them to be substantially correct, but concluded that no law, either domestic or international, had been violated.[19]

Schurz and Sumner, who supported him, stirred up a tremendous furor among German-Americans by their charges against Grant's Secretary of War. The venerable Gustav Körner wrote in 1872 that "as a German" he could not vote for a President who had permitted the sale of Springfield rifles and American bullets to the French, and therefore had "perhaps 100,000 brave Germans on his conscience."[20] The *Wächter am Erie* referred to "the blood money that came from the sale of arms to France," and the three German papers of Cleveland forgot their political differences and argued that "the Germans have a special score to settle" with the President.[21] Daniel Hertle, a refugee who came to the United States in 1850 and happened to be in the Palatinate in the fall of 1872, described in a letter to the press the bitter reaction of the Germans of the fatherland toward the munitions deal.[22] In Nashville, Tennessee, Germans pledged support to Greeley in 1872 primarily because of his friendly attitude toward Germany during the war with France.[23] To such tactics the Grant press replied by attacking Schurz and his kind as "mad cossacks" who were "traitors to America," and put the interest of the country of their origin above that of the land which gave them refuge in their time of trouble.[24] Thomas Nast, himself a native German, and a leading cartoonist for *Harper's Weekly,* caricatured Schurz's part in the whole episode under the caption of "Carl's Boomerang," and admonished him that "little children should not investigate French firearms." Heinzen, almost alone among the Forty-eighters, defended the legality of the sale of surplus arms to France.

The call for a Liberal Republican convention in Cincinnati, which originated in Missouri where Schurz's influence was at its zenith, was endorsed by tariff reformers like J. D. Cox of Ohio and many other anti-Grant groups. The convention turned into a most heterogeneous gathering, and not idealists but practical politicians controlled its deliberations. The tariff question was the greatest stumbling block to agreement, and a preconvention caucus struggled over a formula which would reconcile sincere tariff reformers with ardent protectionists like Horace Greeley, the support of whose *New York Tribune* seemed essential to success. The same political jockeying occurred in choosing a candidate to head the ticket. Although a majority favored Charles Francis Adams, he was not named on the first ballot, largely because of a mistaken sense of loyalty to "favorite sons." Adams himself was en route to Europe as an arbitrator at Geneva in the *Alabama* case. When the smoke of battle finally cleared away, the delegates found to their dismay that Horace Greeley had been nominated. His candidacy proved hard to swallow, not only for Democrats, who had no choice but to forget their pride and nominate him in their convention also, but for many Republicans as well. Probably no one was more dumfounded and disappointed than Schurz, whose influence over the convention had been almost completely neutralized when the delegates maneuvered him into the position of chairman.[25]

An examination of important samples of the German-language press reveals that the Germans as a whole, and the reformers in particular, wanted Adams to lead the fight against Grant in 1872. The *Wächter am*

Erie, the *Cincinnati Volksblatt,* the *New Yorker Criminal Zeitung und Belletristisches Journal,* and even the Columbus *Westbote* had urged Adams' nomination. Dr. Karl Dänzer, editor of the *Anzeiger des Westens,* and J. Rittig, a Forty-eighter from Prague who published the *Louisville Anzeiger,* worked for Adams as members of the Cincinnati Convention. Schurz favored the Massachusetts statesman from the beginning. In pre-convention discussions of available candidates, the German press admitted Greeley's sterling character and pioneering intellect, but found him unsuitable because he was bone dry, rode too many hobbies, was an extremist on the tariff, and had no capacity for administration. Governor Jacob D. Cox, a man of fine character and great ability, was opposed by the same group because "there is still too much of Oberlin clinging in his coat-tails."[26]

Greeley's nomination was a bitter pill for Germans to swallow, and many either remained with Grant or stayed away from the polls on election day. German voters admitted that the Liberal Republican standard bearer had always dealt fairly with the foreign-born and had valiantly supported equal rights for Catholics, Protestants, and Jews, but unfortunately he also had been a lifelong supporter of the temperance crusade! Papers like the *Wächter am Erie* and the *Pittsburger Volksblatt* pointed out that temperance was not an issue in the campaign, and the Cleveland *Anzeiger,* a Democratic paper, favored Greeley because of his liberal views on religion. Friedrich Münch, seventy-three years old and probably the senior member of the Cincinnati Convention, conceded that the practical politicians had outmaneuvered the idealists, but he decided to accept the "bargain" and vote for Greeley.[27] Hecker, because of his profound dislike of Grant, had to "choke down the Cincinnati ticket," although his first reaction was to advise the Germans to stay away from the polls. His brother-in-law, Dr. Heinrich Tiedemann, another veteran of 1848, supported Greeley with less hesitation, and Hassaurek took the stump for the fusion candidate late in the campaign. In Wisconsin, Schurz, Konrad Krez of Sheboygan, and Emil Rothe of Watertown, the last a life-long Democrat, worked hard for the Liberal Republican ticket, and other Forty-eighters came out of retirement to take an active part in the reform movement.[28]

Among the leaders of the German-language press, the St. Louis *West-liche Post,* the Cleveland *Wächter am Erie,* the *Deutsche Zeitung* and the *Demokrat* of Davenport, the Peoria *Deutsche Zeitung*, the *Belleviller Zeitung*, the *Milwaukee Herold* and the *Seebote*, the Chicago *Freie Presse*, the Detroit *Abendpost*, the Buffalo *Volksfreund*, the Columbus *Westbote*, the *Louisville Anzeiger*, the Council Bluffs *Post*, and the LaCrosse *Nordstern* finally, and with considerable reluctance, endorsed Greeley's candidacy. The German press of Wisconsin, with two exceptions, supported Greeley, and of the eleven German papers in Iowa, only two favored Grant. Some of the largest German papers, like the *New Yorker Staatszeitung*, the *Philadelphia Demokrat,* and the St. Louis *Anzeiger des Westens,* continued to deplore the Liberal Republican blunder in nominating Greeley, and refused to give him their support. The *New Yorker Staatszeitung* would endorse neither Grant nor Greeley, but the New York *Demokrat, Abendzeitung,* and *Criminal Zeitung* finally supported the General for a second term. In July the Cleveland *Anzeiger,* originally for Greeley, was bought by the "Grant party," and distributed at half the price of its competitor, the *Wächter am Erie.* The *Cincinnati Courier,* the *Baltimore Wecker,* and the *Illinois Staatszeitung,* edited by Wilhelm Rapp, also finally recommended Grant to their readers.

Such a summary of German editorial opinion indicates great confusion among the German voters. Newspapers edited by Forty-eighter reformers and refugees took opposite positions in the campaign in 1872. If the active "Grant Men" among them did not exceed a dozen, they nevertheless included such leaders as Sigel, Hermann Raster, and Jakob Müller, Republican lieutenant-governor of Ohio. In an address to his German neighbors in the German Theatre of Cleveland, Müller labored hard to explain his position. He admitted that reforms were sorely needed, but contended that a union with the Democrats was not the way to get them. He referred to the temperance issue and the Puritan background of many Republicans, but argued that the "Romanism" of the Democrats was worse. He blamed Congress, not the President, for the spoils system, and assured his hearers that whereas the sale of arms to France was a bad mistake, Grant and his party sympathized with Germany during the Franco-German War. At no point in his long address did Müller attack Greeley on a single issue.[29] Francis Lieber, widely known as a political scientist and publicist, supported Grant, and the party publicized his endorsement as an antidote for Schurz's support of Greeley and compared "the stable and unswerving" Lieber with the "fickle and treacherous" leader of the Forty-eighters.[30]

In February 1872, Schurz had written to his brother-in-law, Adolf Meyer, in Germany, "I cannot become President it is true; however, between us I can say it, that to make the next President will be my task, and furthermore, I can do it."[31] He went to work in the campaign of 1872 as if he were determined to prove his prediction. He knew what difficulties he would encounter among the Germans and he had serious doubts about the wisdom of Greeley's nomination, yet Schurz became one of the leading stump speakers in 1872, as he had been in the critical campaign that elected Lincoln a dozen years earlier. Again, large crowds listened to him with great respect. In September he made six speeches in Ohio, four of them in German, to help his followers resolve their doubts in favor of Greeley and reform. Old-line Democratic papers, like the Columbus *Westbote*, once his bitter foe, blessed him for his courageous exposure of Republican corruption, and everywhere he was greeted with serenades, parades, and ovations.

The supporters of Grant were genuinely disturbed by Schurz's campaigning and tried hard to undermine his influence with the German voters. Accounts suddenly appeared in several German-language papers accusing Schurz of a land swindle in the 1850's, when he sold lots in "Schurz's Addition to the City of Watertown," Wisconsin. Like others in the period when the West was booming, the enterprising young German had tried his hand at speculation and high finance by placing a heavy mortgage on the Addition and selling it off in individual parcels. Several buyers, the Republicans charged, lost their initial payments because Schurz had not extinguished the debt on his holdings. Schurz's friends replied that he had pointed out to all buyers that the land he was selling off in lots was still encumbered by a mortgage; that buyers had received warranty deeds only, and that when the plot was finally sold at auction for the mortgage, Schurz was too poor to redeem it.[32]

The Grant press also represented the traitor from the Republican ranks as "a professional foreigner," and an "agent of Bismarck" and Prussia. Nast drew Schurz sitting at the piano playing "My Heart is on the Rhine," with Uncle Sam looking over his shoulder and saying, "Look here, stranger, there is no law in this country to compel you to stay."[33] The *Cleveland Leader* charged that Schurz collected two hundred dollars for every speech, and repeated the story of the alleged Watertown swindle. Another paper claimed that while he was minister in Spain, Schurz had overdrawn his salary by four hundred dollars. The *New York Herald* maintained that Schurz supported Greeley on orders from Bismarck and after the campaign would be raised to the German peerage and given the Iron Cross.[34] Such stupid misrepresentations rallied the German press to Schurz's defense, and papers like the *Illinois Staatszeitung,* which had disagreed with the Senator on the munitions question, were as vigorous in refuting the charges as the press which had been friendly to Schurz from the beginning.

Greeley's decisive defeat in 1872 ended the Liberal Republican revolt and opened the door to four more years of Grant, whose second administration proved worse than the first. A detailed analysis of the causes for Greeley's defeat is unnecessary, for the contrast between the glamorous hero of Appomattox and the eccentric New York printer was too great to be overcome. German leaders could not claim a decisive rôle in the outcome. Many Germans apparently did not vote at all in 1872, finding it impossible to support either candidate with conviction. In Ohio, Hassaurek and Willich and several liberal German papers tried throughout 1873 to keep the Liberal Republican revolt alive, but without success.

The influence of the Forty-eighters declined rapidly after 1872, and their activities as a group becomes more difficult to trace, although German voters could still be aroused on special issues for another decade. One was the perennial temperance question, which always provoked heated reactions, regardless of party affiliations. Hecker and the editors of the Cleveland and St. Louis German dailies viewed the temperance agitation of the 1870's as a recurrence of the nativism of pre-Civil War years, and believed it originated in a deep-seated hatred for the foreign-born. Sunday closing ordinances, enacted in many cities during the 1870's, precipitated sharp political controversies. Cleveland, for example, attempted to enforce Sunday closing in 1873. A German saloonkeeper promptly put up a table before his place of business and loaded it down with Bibles, a pitcher of ice water and several glasses of milk and lemonade, and at Lied's Garden, where a concert had been scheduled, the proprietor pulled the American flag to half-mast and draped it in mourning, to express his contempt for the fanatics who controlled the city government.[35] When a "People's Party" defeated the "Law and Order ticket" of Chicago by eleven thousand votes in 1873, congratulations poured in from near-by cities, and the *Illinois Staatszeitung* jubilantly credited the victory to the Germans.[36] In 1874, while "fashionable church ladies" of Cleveland were invading the saloons for prayer meetings, Hecker lectured in the same city on "The Present-day Conflict between Fanaticism and Civic and Economic Liberty," an address which he repeated in Erie, Buffalo, and other cities. In Indiana, the German press sponsored a convention in Terre Haute to combat the "temperance disease" which was ravaging the state. German Republican papers were alarmed to find a steady stream of German voters returning to the Democratic fold because of the temperance question, and it is significant that the Republican platforms adopted in 1875 in Ohio, Wisconsin, and Iowa made no reference to the controversial issue.[37]

The question of sound money versus an inflated currency of greenbacks or silver was of more public significance, and figured in political campaigns from the close of the Civil War to the present century. On this issue, German voters responded as champions of sound currency whenever they really understood what was at stake. Papers like the *Wächter am Erie,* for example, sympathized in the 1870's with the Granger movement and the Anti-Monopoly party but repudiated their unsound proposals on money. Though otherwise extremely critical of Grant, the editor gave him unstinted praise in 1874 for his courageous veto of the inflation bill passed by Congress on the heels of the panic of 1873. Hecker campaigned in several states for sound money. In Ohio, the campaign for governor between Rutherford B. Hayes and "Old Bill" Allen in 1875 was fought largely over the currency question. Allen, despite his Jacksonian hard-money antecedents, had revived the "rag money" issue, and made a surprisingly strong race. Near the close of the campaign, the Republican organization rushed Schurz into Ohio to mobilize the German vote. Returning from a flattering reception in Germany, Schurz made nine speeches, beginning with a notable exposition of the economics of the money question in the Turner Hall of Cincinnati. The *Volksblatt* and the *Freie Presse* of Cincinnati and the Cleveland *Wächter am Erie* supported Schurz's plea for Hayes and sound money, and when the latter emerged victorious, by a precariously small majority, Charles Francis Adams wrote from Massachusetts to congratulate Schurz on his decisive contribution to the cause of good government and sound money.[38] A survey of leading German papers, including the *New Yorker Staatszeitung,* the *Detroit Post,* and papers in Pittsburgh, Milwaukee, and Chicago indicates that German editors were practically unanimous in their support of a sound currency in the 1870's. True to his lifelong convictions, Schurz was still fighting for sound monetary standards in 1896, when Bryan and McKinley engaged in their famous "Battle of the Standards." Schurz made a notable address in 1896 on sound money before the American Honest Money League and the *Deutsch-Amerikanische Gutgeld Liga*, of which he and Ottendörfer were honorary presidents, and the Republican National Committee distributed copies of his important speeches on this issue throughout the country.

By 1876, a sharp division occurred among Forty-eighters still active in politics. The choice in the presidential campaign of that year had to be made between Samuel J. Tilden, a Democrat with a good record for reform, including prosecution of the notorious "Tweed Ring" of New York City, and Hayes, a sound-money man of undoubted integrity, but tainted with temperance ideas. Furthermore, the German press charged the Republican candidate with voting as a member of the Centennial Commission to close the Philadelphia Fair on Sundays, and of accepting the support of the "American Alliance," regarded as a successor to the Knownothings. Hayes's friends replied that the charges were false, and found it politic to point out that whenever Hayes was in Cincinnati he stopped regularly each morning for his "eye-opener" at John Roth's beer garden.[39]

Sigel campaigned for Tilden in 1876, and Ottendörfer supported him in the *New Yorker Staatszeitung*. Hans Balatka, the Milwaukee Forty-eighter, Jakob Müller of Cleveland, Hassaurek, Schurz's brother-in-law, Edmund Jüssen, Dr. Hoffbauer of Dubuque, Iowa, and other Forty-eighters endorsed Tilden. Gustav Körner did likewise. The *Philadelphia Demokrat* and the Cleveland *Wächter am Erie* supported the Democratic candidate. Friedrich Münch reported that the Germans in the West were weary of the promises and scandals of the Republican administration and were turning in large numbers to Tilden, although the *Cincinnati Volksfreund* insisted that only a minority in that city were deserting the Republican banners.

To the chagrin of many Germans who had followed him in 1872, Schurz returned to the regular Republican party in 1876. He had played an important part in a conference of "Independents" in New York in the spring of the year, and received the almost unanimous endorsement of the German press for his persistence in advocating reform. His pledge to support Hayes in 1876 startled many of his friends, who reminded him of his earlier statements that the Grand Old Party could never be reformed from within, and pointed out that support of the Republican candidate made a farce of his earlier association with the Independents.[40] In an open letter to Oswald Ottendörfer of the *New Yorker Staatszeitung* Schurz tried to justify his decision, on the ground that the real issues in 1876 were sound money and civil service reform, and on both Hayes's position was unassailable. His critics were not satisfied, however, and hinted that his real motive was to get back into the good graces of the regular Republican organization and share in the spoils of office. The *Wächter am Erie* lamented the apostasy of "Old Karl," and the *Dayton Volkszeitung* noted the degeneration of a real statesman into a "paid stump speaker."[41]

Schurz confined his campaign speeches to a discussion of civil service reform and sound money. Since Ohio, as usual, was a critical state, the Republican National Committee sent Brentano, Hecker, and Schurz to address the Germans in Cleveland and other cities. Praetorius and Butz spoke for Hayes in the Middle West, and organizations like the Baltimore and Cincinnati *Turnvereine* endorsed the Republican candidate. The Turner movement as a whole, however, was as badly divided as the German-language press between Hayes and Tilden. All the "great men" among the Germans apparently felt called upon to issue manifestos to enlighten their fellow countrymen on the campaign. The outcome was one of the most confusing in the annals of American politics, and the disputed election of 1876 had to be settled by a special electoral commission which labored until the very eve of inauguration day to reach a conclusion. The basis of their decision which awarded the victory to Hayes has long been a matter of controversy among historians. It was a tribute to the American democracy and the devotion of the common people to the American tradition of law and order that the decision of 1877 was accepted without resort to violence. Mass meetings in various parts of the nation protested against the "Hayes-Tilden scandal," and thousands of voters were convinced that Tilden had been robbed of the presidency by a shabby political trick.

Germans played their part in these popular demonstrations, and some reminded Hecker and Schurz that they had taken up rifle and bayonet to vindicate the popular will in 1848. Neither of the famous Forty-eighters replied to such irresponsible suggestions; the storm died down, and Schurz became Secretary of the Interior in the cabinet of the new President. Here he made a distinguished record as an administrator, and made his own department a "demonstration station" for civil service reform. Regular Republicans, like Blaine, denounced the German-American maverick for introducing "Prussian methods" into the American democracy. As president of the National Civil Service League, Schurz continued to demonstrate his devotion to reform.

For some years longer, the "tremendous Dutchman" continued to play a rôle as one of the nation's leading independents. In 1884 he was back in the Democratic fold and spoke for Cleveland at a huge German-American meeting in the Academy of Music in New York. Ottendörfer presided, and the greatest Republican and the greatest Democrat among the Forty-eighters stood on common ground. Schurz inflicted his gratuitous advice on Cleveland as he had done on Lincoln, but although he disagreed frequently with the first Democratic President since the Civil War, he continued to give him his support. In 1896 Schurz opposed Bryan because of the latter's financial heresies, but in 1900 he emerged from semi-retirement and along with Emil Praetorius and several others of the old Forty-eighter group argued against the "new imperialism" of the Spanish-American War which had drawn the United States into the whirling eddy of world politics. The German press, as a whole, opposed imperialism, and in the campaign to keep America true to her old traditions Schurz was joined by such distinguished citizens as Mark Twain, Finley Peter Dunne, Charles W. Eliot, William James, Henry van Dyke, Jane Addams, and Samuel Gompers.

FOOTNOTES

CHAPTER 17

1. See a poem by Butz, in Caspar Butz: *Gedichte eines Deutsch-Amerikaners* (Chicago, 1879) pp. 74-75.
2. January 1, 1862.
3. See Wittke: *Heinzen*, pp. 184-89.
4. Dec. 31, 1864.
5. *Wächter am Erie*, May 24, 1865.
6. *Wächter am Erie*, Feb. 13, 1864; March 16, 1864.
7. *Wächter am Erie*, June 1, 1864.
8. *Wächter am Erie*, March 19, June 25, Sept. 28, Oct. 1, 1864.
9. See Wittke: *Heinzen*, pp. 189-95; and *Wächter am Erie*, Sept. 28, 1864.

10. April 19, 1865.
11. See *Wächter am Erie*, Sept. 1, 1866, citing the *Illinois Staatszeitung* and the *Philadelphia Freie Presse*.
12. See *Wächter am Erie*, Sept. 19, 1867; also Aug. 22, 1867; also June 1, 1869.
13. *Intimate Letters*, p. 467; also p. 468.
14. *Westbote*, April 6, 17, 1872; also March 6, 9, 1872.
15. *Westbote*, April 27, 1872; also March 9, April 6, 17, 20, 1872; and *Wächter am Erie*, April 5, 16, 25, 1872.
16. For Heinzen's views on "No President at All," see Wittke: *Heinzen*, pp. 204-9.
17. *Wächter am Erie*, May 23, Oct. 18, 1871.
18. *Wächter am Erie*, May 1, 16, 1873.
19. See W. B. Hesseltine:`*Ulysses S. Grant, Politician* (New York, 1935) pp. 265-6.
20. *Wächter am Erie*, Oct. 4, 1872.
21. *Wächter am Erie*, March 19, Oct. 4, 1872; also *Westbote*, Aug. 3, 1872.
22. *Wächter am Erie*, Oct. 19, 1872.
23. *Westbote*, May 28, 1872.
24. *Ibid.*, March 6, 1872.
25. See Hesseltine: *op. cit.*, pp. 271-90.
26. See *Wächter am Erie*, April 29, 1872; *Westbote*, May 8, 1872. To radical Forty-eighters, Oberlin was the epitome of a pious hypocrisy. On February 4, 1861, Schurz wrote to his wife from Hillsdale, Michigan, "I spent Sunday in Oberlin with a pious doctor's family, who would not cook a noon meal on the Sabbath. Imagine my situation. No meat for breakfast, dinner or supper. I am prepared to be pious, but I have no desire to travel on an empty stomach. . . ." *Carl Schurz MSS.*, Wisconsin State Historical Society Library. I am indebted to Dr. Robert G. Gunderson for this item.
27. *Wächter am Erie*, May 6, 8, 10; June 1, 12; Aug. 20, 1872.
28. Hense-Jensen and Bruncken: *Wisconsin's Deutsch-Amerikaner*, I, 238-40.
29. *Wächter am Erie*, Aug. 16, 1872.
30. Freidel: *Lieber*, p. 412.
31. Letter of Feb. 3, 1872, made available to me by Dr. Arthur Hogue.
32. See *Watertown Weltbürger* and Cincinnati *Volksfreund*, quoted in *Wächter am Erie*, Sept. 11, 18, 1872.
33. Fuess: *Schurz*, p. 182.
34. See *Wächter am Erie*, Sept. 9, 1872; *Westbote*, Aug. 7, 1872; *Cleveland Leader*, Sept. 11, 1872.
35. *Wächter am Erie*, July 28, 1873.
36. *Ibid.*, Nov. 8, 1873.
37. See *Wächter am Erie*, March 18, 20, 23, 1874; July 9, 1875.
38. F. W. Clounts: "The Political Campaign of 1875 in Ohio," in *The Ohio Archaeological and Historical Quarterly* (January 1922) XXXI, 38-95.
39. See Philip D. Jordan: *Ohio Comes of Age, 1873-1900* (Columbus, 1943) p. 263; see also *Wächter am Erie*, Sept. 2, 11, 1876.
40. *Wächter am Erie*, July 8, 1876.
41. *Ibid.*, July 14, 28, Aug. 25, Sept. 4, 1876.

Chapter 18 · THE JOURNALISTS

IN PRECEDING chapters, the names of Forty-eighters who turned to journalism in the United States appear frequently, for it was primarily through the printed page and the lecture platform that the leaders of the German immigration tried to make their contribution to the American scene. The editor's desk has always been an effective sounding board for reform. Many German newspapermen had valuable experience in their profession in the fatherland; others, especially intellectuals who were university trained, took up journalism as a source of revenue during their first difficult months in the United States and remained in the profession the rest of their lives.

The first great expansion in the German-language press resulted from the migration of the political refugees of 1848 and 1849. Men of talent and militant idealism, they raised the level of German-American journalism and made their liberal traditions an active force in American politics. The number of German newspapers in the United States nearly doubled from 1848 to 1852, and in the next three years German papers of many varieties were established. Radical, freethinkers' weeklies and monthlies, dedicated to "enlightenment and social progress," were especially numerous.

In 1840 the total number of German papers in the United States was approximately forty, and by 1848 it had grown to seventy. Among the older papers, the *Alte und Neue Welt* of Philadelphia and the *New Yorker Staatszeitung* had a substantial circulation before 1848, but German farmers and artisans generally were too poor or too little interested to subscribe for newspapers and journals, and their quality was not impressive. In 1843 the *Cincinnati Volksblatt* was the only German daily in the United States, and even the *New Yorker Staatszeitung* was issued only three times a week. Before 1848 it has been estimated that not more than three new German papers appeared annually; in 1849 eleven were established; in 1850, twelve; and in 1851, twenty-four. In the state of Wisconsin, a German population of approximately 150,000 in 1853 supported twelve papers, and in the preceding three years eleven new papers had appeared in the state. With the exception of the Catholic *Seebote,* all were radical, independent sheets.

The half-dozen years after 1848 witnessed a remarkable expansion of the German-language press, although some of the new ventures proved short-lived.[1] In 1851 the *New Yorker Staatszeitung* had a circulation of 4,800, and Heinzen's New York *Schnellpost,* 1,150. Five years later the *Staatszeitung* had a daily circulation of 15,300; two other dailies in New York had a combined circulation of 5,700, and four German weeklies reported 16,200 readers. Before the close of the decade, Pittsburgh had five German dailies, a total exceeded only by St. Louis. Most German papers at the beginning of the 1850's were Democratic; by the end of the decade many had transferred their political allegiances to the Republican party, and a number of new Republican papers published in the German language had been founded. German-language papers invariably increased in number just before an important political campaign and decreased immediately after the election.[2]

More important than statistics of uncertain accuracy is the influence which reformers and refugees exercised on the contents and tone of the German press. The period from 1850 to 1870 has been characterized as the golden age of the German-language press in the United States. Certainly the level of journalism at this time was far superior to that of the preceding years. After 1870, when the influence of the Forty-eighters began to wane, the press went into another decline, greatly accentuated by the forces of Americanization which noticeably reduced the number of readers. The veteran *New Yorker Staatszeitung* conceded that the level of German-American journalism rose sharply after 1848 because of the activity of highly educated refugees and the higher caliber of the German immigration as a whole. After Kapp returned to Germany he spoke disparagingly of the 1850's, and commented that "any half-baked student or cracked-up candidate in theology, or printer's journeyman, or failure of any kind . . . was good enough to become the editor of a German newspaper" in America,[3] but the improvement in both style and content of the German-language press could not be denied.

With some notable exceptions, much of the editing of German papers was done before 1850 with paste-pot and scissors. The publisher copied and translated from English papers printed in the neighborhood or received by mail. The style was corrupted by colloquialisms and grammatical errors, the use of English words, and still worse "German-Americanisms," and papers were filled with cheap novels and serials, and news and "filler" geared to the lowest level of readers. Many papers were supported by politicians and contained few editorials save the violent political exchanges which marked every election year. Many German books were on the same level. The German classics were little known and seldom owned; the best sellers were cook, prayer, veterinary, and farm books, and publishers complained that Germans would buy neither books nor newspapers, but read the copies available in the taverns.[4]

The intellectuals of the new immigration shuddered at the bad grammar and spineless editorials of the German press, and resolved to introduce higher standards. The papers which they founded were more independent, better written, and gave greater importance to editorials. The era of personal journalism in the American press had its counterpart in the German language field during these years, and scores of Forty-eighters published papers which were as much their personal organs as the *Tribune* was the mouthpiece of Horace Greeley. The views of the editor controlled and determined the character of the paper. Newcomers regarded their older competitors with scorn, ridiculed their timidity and the dullness of their columns, and exposed their atrocious German. In some cases they converted stodgy old papers into fighting journals for progress and reform; more often they launched new journals of opinion and made incredible sacrifices to maintain them. To the older group, these younger enthusiasts were "German riders of moonbeams"; "cosmopolites" whose diatribes jeopardized the status of the German element in the United States; a "student democracy" of impractical star-gazers; "knights of new ideas" who pulled "sun, moon and stars down from the sky" in their eagerness to establish their "paper democracy." Before the end of the 1850's so scholarly a person as Friedrich Münch maintained that the German-language press had become too erudite for the average German-American to understand.[5]

The ardor of the new editors was so unrestrained that it sometimes led to a kind of fishwife journalism. Personal abuse and disgraceful feuds characterized German-American journalism, and editors of radical sheets seem to have been the most frequent offenders. The unusual violence of editorial controversy occasionally resulted in threats to horsewhip the offenders, and in several cases ended in actual physical encounters. The intolerance of some reformers, and their utter impatience with American customs knew no bounds, and in their determination to call every spade a spade, and in their contempt for anemic double-talk, editors stooped to indefensible personal slander and abuse. Vile expletives were the spice of their arguments, and slander, overstatement, and deliberate falsehoods were part of the equipment of their editorial arsenals.

In San Francisco two rival German editors beat each other in the streets before taking their quarrel to the courts. One of the litigants was Ferdinand von Löhr, a student of medicine at Giessen and a veteran of Blenker's forces in the Revolution, who was practicing medicine and editing the *California Demokrat* in San Francisco.[6] In Cincinnati, Hassaurek and one of his competitors were hauled into court because they threatened to extinguish each other in a duel.[7] Heinzen lost a libel suit against the *New Yorker Staatszeitung* in 1852; in Louisville he was involved in a horsewhipping incident, and the *New Yorker Staatszeitung* in nearly every issue in 1851 published a column of "Heinzeniana," in which the editor replied in the crudest manner to the latest attacks of this belligerent journalist.[8] Conditions finally became so intolerable that Hassaurek's *Hochwächter,* itself one of the worst offenders, joined with the Columbus *Westbote,* the *Philadelphia Freie Presse,* and other more moderate journals to urge an armistice among the embattled editors, and proposed a convention to elevate the tone of the German-language press.[9]

The scandalous and scurrilous attacks of impatient, irritable, and tactless world reformers on benighted colleagues and venerable American institutions must not obscure the fact, however, that the Forty-eighter group contained a remarkably large proportion of able, independent and honest journalists. Refugee editors were widely scattered throughout the country, and even those of only average ability made a significant contribution to the standards of German-American journalism. Editors of successful metropolitan papers achieved local and national prominence and shared in the rewards of public office, unmistakable evidence that they had "arrived" politically. Others were known only to their local constituency.

Nikolaus Schmitt, whom August Thieme, editor of the Cleveland German paper, had met when both sat in the Frankfurt Parliament, was the son of a lawyer, and studied jurisprudence at the universities of Würzburg, Heidelberg, and Munich. Denied a place in the public service of Bavaria because of his radicalism, Schmitt edited the *Boten für Stadt und Land* in his native city of Kaiserslautern from 1832 to 1849, and exercised considerable influence in the Palatinate as a spokesman of the political opposition. In the Frankfurt assembly Schmitt affiliated with the left, opposed a union of Austria and the German states, fought hereditary monarchy, advocated abolishing capital punishment and the nobility, and demanded guarantees of academic freedom in the universities. After the collapse of the Revolution and a period of exile in Switzerland, Schmitt came to America in 1850. With Joseph Reichard, another Forty-eighter, he published the daily *Volksvertreter* in Philadelphia for six months, and then founded his better-known monthly, the *Gradaus*. He wrote scholarly articles on Pennsylvania history and a biography of Steuben, and died in Philadelphia in 1860 at the age of fifty-four.[10]

August Thieme, the *Wächter am Erie's* most distinguished editor, was born in Leipzig, the son of poor parents. He achieved the doctor's degree in the university of his native city. After a brief career as a teacher, he became an advocate of radical reform, wrote for the newspapers, published his *Hirschberger Wochenblatt,* and made political speeches, especially on Sundays. In 1848 he was probably the youngest member of the Frankfurt Parliament and sat with the extreme left. Thieme continued to participate in the activities of the rump parliament in Stuttgart and was an organizer for the people's militia. He came to the United States late in 1849, settling first in Buffalo as a teacher and journalist. In 1852 he was called to Cleveland to edit the *Wächter am Erie,* whose first number appeared on August 9, 1852, and he remained the guiding spirit of this notably influential German paper until his death twenty-seven years later. At the time when the *Wächter* was established, Cleveland had an unusually active group of German Forty-eighters who wanted a paper committed to the principles of the "Greens." Heinrich Rochotte, a captain in 1848 who brought his company flag with him to America, Jakob Müller, and several others launched the new enterprise by selling eighty shares of stock at five dollars a share. Out of a total German population of 1,500, four hundred Clevelanders subscribed for the new weekly, which was printed on the presses of the *Cleveland Plain Dealer*, and sold at five cents a copy. From the outset the *Wächter* was antislavery, and its radical editorial policies led older Germans to regard it as a communist paper. During the Frémont campaign in 1856, the *Wächter* became a daily. After 1879 it was a Democratic paper, though still under the control of Jakob Müller, one of its original founders. It survives after nearly a century, as the Cleveland *Wächter und Anzeiger,* but its character has completely changed and no longer reveals either the intellectual caliber or the courageous reforming zeal of its first distinguished editor.

Bernhard Domschke was one of the many Forty-eighters who eventually settled in Milwaukee. Born near Dresden, he had prepared for the ministry, but joined the freethinkers instead in founding "free congregations." Domschke was a talented music critic and an enthusiast for the theatre as well. In May 1849 he took part in the revolution in Dresden. In July 1851 he landed in New York, where he tried to make a living as a teacher in Brooklyn, and organized a "free congregation." The following year he was called to Boston to act as speaker of a group of freethinkers founded by Eduard Schröter, and became assistant editor of the *Neu England Zeitung,* a paper sufficiently radical to win the approval of Karl Heinzen. Domschke became Heinzen's assistant in Louisville, on the *Herold des Westens,* and helped draft the "Louisville Platform." In 1854 Domschke made antislavery speeches in Milwaukee, and the Republican party subsidized his *Der Corsär,* which he managed to keep alive as a party sheet for fourteen months by living in the most frugal manner and sleeping in an unheated room on a bed of newspaper exchanges. After the demise of the *Cörsar,* Domschke published the *Milwaukee Journal* and later the weekly *Atlas,* but he complained bitterly that the citizens of the "German Athens" failed to support his various enterprises. In 1861 he resigned from the *Milwaukee Herold* to join the army. After the war he was active as a journalist until his death in 1869.[11]

Gottlieb Theodor Kellner of Kassel wrote his Ph.D. dissertation on the physiocrats, and prepared himself to teach political science. In 1848, with his cousin Heinrich Heyse, he founded a Social-Democratic club in his home town; published *Die Hornisse,* with a circulation of nine thousand; made speeches for reform throughout Hesse; and was elected to the Hessian Diet. His paper was suppressed, and in 1851 its editor was arrested. After six months in jail, Kellner was liberated in a dramatic jail break and escaped to the United States, where he tried to make a living by lecturing and newspaper work. In 1856 Kellner moved to Philadelphia, where he achieved distinction as editor of the *Philadelphia Demokrat,* a patron of the theatre and the arts, and a Turner and promoter of many German social and cultural interests.[12]

Baltimore's most brilliant Forty-eighter was Carl Heinrich Schnauffer, founder of the *Baltimore Wecker,* a typical radical, antislavery, and anti-clerical paper. Born in Stuttgart, Schnauffer was being trained for a business career in Mannheim when he fell under the spell of Hecker and Struve, and became a regular contributor to the liberal *Mannheimer Abendzeitung* in 1846. He fought with Hecker and Willich in 1848, fled across the Swiss border, was deported to France, and finally came to Baltimore, via England, in 1851. In his three short years among the Maryland Germans before his death in 1854, he not only edited a paper, but did distinguished writing as a poet and pamphleteer. His *Totenkränze,* a collection of poems, were a memorial to the martyrs of 1848 and 1849. He published a drama entitled *Cromwell and the English Revolution,* and a short play, *Christ und Jude,* written in the spirit of Lessing's *Nathan der Weise.*[13]

August Becker, like Schnauffer, belonged to the German *literati.* A native of Hesse-Darmstadt, the son of a preacher, and a student at the University of Giessen, Becker was such an enthusiastic *Burschenschaftler* that his student radicalism resulted in a six-year jail sentence in the 1830's. Released after serving four years of his term, Becker went to Alsace and Basle. In Switzerland he helped organize the workers in Weitling's co-operatives and communist clubs. Sensing that another revolution was imminent, Becker returned to Hesse, edited *Der jüngste Tag,* made revolutionary speeches, and in 1848 was elected to the Hessian legislature. When he arrived in Baltimore in 1852, he tried various jobs, including writing for the *Wecker* and acting as agent and manager for a prominent German actress. In later years his career as a journalist took him to the Cincinnati *Hochwächter,* the *Cincinnati Republikaner,* and the *New York Demokrat.* During the Civil War, as chaplain of a New York regiment, he wrote an account of his experiences in the Peninsular Campaign for the St. Louis *Westliche Blätter.* He held a political job in the dead letter office in Washington for a short time, but returned to the more exciting life of a newspaper editor, and worked in turn on the *Baltimore*

Wecker, the *Cincinnati Volksblatt,* and the *Cincinnati Courier.* A warm friend of Hecker, he spent part of his last summer on the latter's farm in Illinois, and died in the spring of 1871.[14]

Theodor Gülich, a veteran of the Revolution in Baden, was the first editor of the *Davenport Demokrat,* a weekly established with a capital of forty dollars contributed by Iowa Democrats. His associate was Rudolph Reichmann, another Forty-eighter who settled in Iowa. Gülich was one of the founders of a free German school in Davenport, and a member of its city council. In 1861 he moved to Burlington and published the *Iowa Tribune.*[15] Ludwig Bogen, a member of the Frankfurt Parliament, edited the *Post* in New Ulm, Minnesota, in 1864. Albert Wolff, pardoned on condition that he leave Germany, was on the staff of the *Minnesota Staatszeitung* for nearly four decades. Karl Röser, a lawyer who had been a rebel both in 1830 and 1848, founded the *Milwaukee Demokrat* in 1853.

Dr. Wilhelm Vette, a Forty-eighter, edited the *Michigan Demokrat* and the *Milwaukee Banner und Volksfreund.* Fenner von Fenneberg, provisional commander-in-chief of the militia in the Palatinate in 1849, was on the editorial staff of the *New Yorker Abendzeitung* and the *Cincinnati Republikaner,* and was frequently accused of shifting his editorial viewpoint to conform to the wishes of his latest political patron.[16] Sebastian Seiler, a colleague of Weitling in propagandizing Switzerland for a communist utopia, published an independent German weekly in New Orleans. Julius Fröbel published a German paper in San Francisco shortly after the gold rush. C. F. Bauer, another Forty-eighter, once edited the *Milwaukee Herold,* and Georg Philipp Lippe, who had come to the United States in 1849 with Lorenz Brentano, issued the *Schuylkill Demokrat* of Pottsville, Pennsylvania, from 1850 to 1864.[17] Wilhelm Wagner, an ex-minister and a refugee of 1849, edited the *Deutsche Anzeiger* of Freeport, Illinois.[18] Joseph Killian, a lieutenant in the Revolution, in turn owned and edited the Allentown, Pennsylvania, *Westbote,* the Cleveland *Anzeiger* and *Columbia,* the Mansfield, Ohio, *Courier* and the Bucyrus *Deutscher Courier.*[19] Joseph E. Marx, a Forty-eighter, edited the *Toledo Express,* and Karl Resch and Theodor Dietsch, political refugees from Baden and Saxony respectively, worked for the *Louisville Anzeiger* in the early 1850's. L. Stierlin, historian of the Germans in Kentucky, who fled to Belgium late in 1848 to escape the Prussians, edited both the *Beobachter* and the *Anzeiger* in Louisville.[20]

Dr. Karl Lauenstein, active in the student movement of 1848, edited the *Cincinnati Volksfreund* in 1866, and later the *Evansville Demokrat*. Franz Umbscheiden, who fought under Blenker in 1849, and was trained for a legal career, was on the staff of the *New Yorker Staatszeitung* from 1860 to 1864, and later edited the *New Jersey Volksmann*, the *New York Demokrat,* and the *Freie Presse* of Elizabeth, New Jersey.[21] Dr. Gustavus Bloede, a prisoner in Dresden in 1849, and probably better known as the husband of the poetess "Marie Westland," combined his study of medicine in New York with editorial work on the *New York Demokrat*.

A number of German-language papers, though published in a foreign language for a special German constituency, slowly developed into American dailies supported by advertising and emphasizing local news and the usual devices for building circulation in urban areas. Some were distributed to the hinterland by mail or local agents. Such papers more nearly resembled their English competitors, and had no special theories to propagate. They were commercial enterprises, published for profit, and in time became American newspapers published in the German language. Needless to add, they survived longest, and held a clientele even after their readers were able to read and understand American dailies.

The *New Yorker Staatszeitung,* the oldest German language newspaper in the United States today, reached its highest standard of excellence and influence under the able editorship of Oswald Ottendörfer. Ottendörfer was born in Zwittau, Moravia, in 1826, and died in New York in 1900. He studied law and philosophy at Prague and Vienna, and as a youth of twenty-two joined the Vienna student legion and later the Robert Blum battalion. He took part in the revolutions in Vienna, Prague, and Dresden, and in the fighting over Schleswig-Holstein, and on several occasions narrowly escaped being shot as a traitor. In 1850 he landed in New York and found a job in the business office of the *New Yorker Staatszeitung*. After the death of Jacob Uhl, the owner, Ottendörfer helped his widow operate the *Staatszeitung,* and in 1859 the two were married. The young refugee had a definite political philosophy. He championed the rights of minorities and the federal system, and was a foe of centralization in government. Throughout the 1850's the *Staatszeitung,* while not condoning slavery, supported Stephen A. Douglas and the current views of the Democratic party toward the Union, the Constitution, and the South. During the Civil War the *Staatszeitung* was frequently charged with Copperhead sympathies, but the paper continued to grow, and under Ottendörfer's able direction became a significant metropolitan daily, with considerable influence in New York politics. In the post-war years Ottendörfer was a reform Democrat, who fought Tammany Hall and in 1874 ran unsuccessfully for mayor of New York City. Deeply interested in civic affairs and public charities, he gave generously to the establishment of a home for aged men on Long Island and to the Ottendörfer branch of the New York Public Library. A memorial fellowship, perpetuating the name of the *Staatszeitung's* most distinguished editor, is awarded annually to an American student of the German language and literature.

Of the many German papers published through the years in St. Louis, the *Anzeiger des Westens* and the *Westliche Post* have been the most important and the most successful. The former was established in 1835. In 1836 Wilhelm Weber, a law student at Jena who wanted to fight for Polish freedom in 1830, and later was imprisoned in Leipzig for seditious remarks, assumed the editorship. A man of superior ability and wide interests, he became librarian of the Mercantile Library of St. Louis. In his efforts to breathe new life into the *Anzeiger,* he recruited the help of such older German leaders as Engelmann, Münch, and Körner. Though not himself a Forty-eighter, Weber advocated the program of the "Young Germany" movement. His successor as editor of the *Anzeiger* was Heinrich Börnstein, who considered himself a Forty-eighter, and was one of the most colorful figures in the history of German-American journalism. An actor, theatre manager, medical student, patron of the arts, and veteran of the Austrian army, he had written plays and been a correspondent for several newspapers in Vienna, and as early as 1842 had begun writing from Paris for the German press in New York, and for Wilhelm Eichthal's *Deutsche Schnellpost* in particular. His theatrical career took him to many Italian and German cities, and he was in Paris in 1848 when the Second French Republic was established under Louis Philippe. Before the end of the year, Börnstein landed in New Orleans, made his way up the Mississippi, and settled in St. Louis, where he revealed amazing talents as a promoter. Besides acquiring ownership of the *Anzeiger,* he ran a hotel, a theatre, a brewery, and several saloons. Börnstein gave his paper a strong free-soil complexion and was one of the first to announce his support of the new Republican party. His career as a volunteer officer in the Union

Army was brief. He did not win laurels on the battlefield, but he showed unusual courage as an editor during the war years, and on more than one occasion enraged citizens of St. Louis threatened to destroy his newspaper office and printing plant. Lincoln gave him an appointment as consul to Bremen, and eventually Börnstein returned to his beloved Vienna to prepare two volumes of reminiscences of a career which covered two continents and lost nothing in the telling.

Associated with Börnstein, and editor-in-chief of his St. Louis newspaper, was Charles L. Bernays, who had been educated in law at Munich, Göttingen, and Heidelberg, and had been a confrere of Marx and Heine in Paris. Bernays came to the United States in 1848. He too obtained a colonel's commission during the Civil War and received an appointment from Lincoln as consul in Zurich. The *Anzeiger des Westens* suspended publication before the end of the war, but was revived by Karl Dänzer, another revolutionist of 1848 who had fled to Switzerland to escape a sentence for *lèse-majesté*. In 1852, Dänzer arrived in Cincinnati, and two years later was associate editor of the *Anzeiger des Westens* in St. Louis. In 1857 he founded the *Westliche Post,* but near the close of the Civil War returned to the older St. Louis paper, reorganized the *Anzeiger,* and became both editor and president of the company.[22]

The *Westliche Post* for several decades was the vigorous rival of the *Anzeiger des Westens.* Its real influence begins with 1864 when Emil Praetorius became editor-in-chief. A native of Hesse-Darmstadt, Praetorius had been a student at Heidelberg and Giessen, and had a degree of doctor of law. Because of the Revolution he came to the United States, and in 1853 joined the German colony in St. Louis, where he remained a prominent figure until his death in 1905. After a brief venture in the leather business, Praetorius' keen interest in public affairs led him into journalism and public speaking, for which he had both training and talent. He lectured widely on esthetics, philosophy, and history, was an abolitionist Republican and in 1860 worked enthusiastically for Lincoln's election. In 1862 he championed complete equality for the Negro in the Missouri legislature and founded *Die Neue Zeit,* which merged with the *Westliche Post* in 1864, when he superseded Theodore Olshausen, a refugee from Schleswig-Holstein, as editor-in-chief. In 1867 Carl Schurz joined forces with Praetorius. Before the War the former had worked for the Watertown, Wisconsin, *Anzeiger* and published his own *Deutsche Volks-*

zeitung, subsidized by the Republican party. Schurz considered St. Louis the center of German influence in the Middle West.[28] Under Schurz and Praetorius the *Westliche Post* became a distinguished paper, and for forty years it was an important political and cultural force in the upper Mississippi Valley. Other distinguished Forty-eighters who were on the staff of the *Westliche Post* at various times included Hermann von Lindemann, liberal editor of the *Dresdner Zeitung* in 1848, and George Hillgärtner. Before the close of the latter's career in America he edited the three most successful German language papers in the Middle West: the *Illinois Staatszeitung;* the St. Louis *Anzeiger des Westens;* and the *Westliche Post.*[24]

The life span of the *Illinois Staatszeitung* extends from April 1848 to World War I. Hermann Kriege was one of its first editors, but the paper took on real vitality in 1852 under George Schneider, a native of the Rhenish Palatinate trained in journalism. In 1848 he escaped a jail sentence by leaving for the United States, and in 1851 joined the staff of the *Illinois Staatszeitung* in Chicago, where he had Hillgärtner and Daniel Hertle, a refugee from the Palatinate, among his early associates. Under Schneider's direction the paper blossomed into a daily. When the *Illinois Staatszeitung* led the revolt against Douglas in 1854, the latter valued Schneider's influence so highly that he made a personal call to try to regain the editor's good will. In 1856 and 1860 Schneider was a delegate to the Republican national conventions, and in 1880 a presidential elector for Garfield. He became collector of internal revenue for Chicago, and a bank president.

The *Illinois Staatszeitung* had a succession of able editors. When Schneider became collector of internal revenue he sold out to Lorenz Brentano, and during the latter's editorial regime the paper was the leading Republican organ in the Northwest. Brentano also held several appointive and elective offices, was consul in Dresden under Grant, and served a term in the United States Congress. Hermann Raster, another bright star in the *Staatszeitung's* galaxy of distinguished refugees, was a university man from Anhalt, who had been a parliamentary stenographer during the Revolution of 1848, and led the uprising in Dessau in 1849. He came to the United States in 1851, and after hardships in New York City which would have broken the spirit of a weaker character, Raster secured the editorship of the *Buffalo Demokrat,* and then returned to

New York to work for the *New Yorker Abendzeitung*. In 1867 he came
to the *Illinois Staatszeitung*. He was a power in the Republican party, a
delegate to several of its conventions, and for one year collector of the
port of Chicago. He bitterly opposed trade unions and an eight-hour day,
and was one of the worst "red baiters" at the anarchist trial following the
Haymarket Riot in Chicago. Wilhelm Rapp, another talented journalist
of the *Illinois Staatszeitung,* fought with the Tübingen volunteers and
served a one-year jail sentence before coming to America. He remained
on the editorial staff of the Chicago German daily for thirty-five years,
after short intervals on the *Turnzeitung* in Cincinnati and the *Wecker*
in Baltimore, and in 1891 acquired the ownership of the *Illinois Staatszeitung*. A heavy-set, bearded Teuton, he was something of a mythical
figure in Chicago, where he enjoyed an extraordinary reputation for
courage and great learning. As early as 1853 he translated some of Jefferson's writings into German, and in 1890 he published his own colorful
reminiscences.[25]

The list of able journalists who made the Chicago paper a power among
the Germans of the Middle West may be completed with a reference to
Adolph Wiesner and Caspar Butz. The former, a native of Prague and
a member of the German Parliament in 1848, came to the United States
primarily to write a book on "The Spirit of World Literature," but never
realized his literary ambition and turned to lecturing and journalism.[26]
Caspar Butz, a Westphalian, who edited radical journals in Germany
before emigrating in 1848, had a checkered career in America. He was
in the hardware and building business in Chicago; served a term in the
Illinois Legislature; was clerk of the Superior Court of Chicago and held
several political jobs; published the *Monatshefte,* a radical journal opposed to Lincoln's conservative policies; participated in several independent political movements; wrote respectable poetry, and was on the editorial staff of the *Illinois Staatszeitung* and several other German papers.[27]

The little radical sheets in which refugees undertook to propagate their
theories of political, social, and economic reforms present a sharp contrast
with the larger German dailies of cities like New York, Milwaukee, St.
Louis, Chicago, and Cincinnati. The death rate among the journals of
opinion was unusually high, yet the propagandists continued to struggle
against incredible odds, certain that the world wanted to hear their message. Such men were not interested in the normal functions of a news-

paper. They had pet theories to advocate and a battle of ideas to fight, and they crowded news reports into the background to reserve space for their learned essays. Usually they wrote in a literary style superior to that of the commercial German-language press, and covered an amazing range of interests.

Karl Heinzen is outstanding in this category of radical reformers, and ranks near the top among German-American journalists of the nineteenth century, as far as ability and perseverance are concerned. His American career included editorial work on smaller German papers, such as the New York *Deutsche Schnellpost,* the *New Yorker Deutsche Zeitung,* his own short-lived *Janus,* and the Louisville *Herold des Westens,* and above all the *Pionier,* the special organ of his peculiar brand of radicalism which he edited for more than a score of years. Moving from Louisville to Cincinnati to New York, he finally established the *Pionier* in Boston, and when it merged with the Milwaukee *Freidenker* in 1880 he could look back upon more than a quarter-century of independent and belligerent crusading for principles which he had proclaimed in his youth and never abandoned.

The circulation of the *Pionier* probably never exceeded five thousand, and usually was much smaller. Nevertheless this was the Bible for Heinzen's disciples throughout the United States. Heinzen regarded the *Pionier* as his personal organ of truth and justice, and he and his wife shunned no sacrifice to keep the paper alive. In Cincinnati they lived in cramped quarters which served as residence, editorial office, and printing plant. Mrs. Heinzen helped set the type and mailed each issue. During the panic of 1857, when circulation dropped below six hundred, the editor accepted payments in kind in lieu of cash, although the subscription rate for the weekly was only three dollars a year, and advertising rates twenty-five cents for five lines. In 1858 a constable confiscated the editor's little library. Heinzen probably never earned more than a thousand dollars a year, and constantly bemoaned the fact that he had no money for books, and so little time to read and study. In 1859 Heinzen moved the *Pionier* to Boston, which he regarded as the most civilized city in the United States. When the Germans of Boston complained that his paper contained almost no local news, Heinzen replied with great irritation that he had no intention of printing a conventional newspaper. Five-sixths of his subscribers lived outside Boston.

An examination of the files of the *Pionier* reveals a remarkable collection of editorials, scientific articles, selections from the world's great literature, essays on diet, education, music, and geography, book reviews and bibliographies, digests and extracts from Darwin, Louis Blanc, Humboldt, Chopin, Poe, Dickens, Shelley, and Harriet Beecher Stowe, and other material appropriate to periodicals designed for the intelligentsia. From the selections from great literature to the editor's pungent editorials, all the material had to fit Heinzen's philosophical system. His invective was biting and blasting, and he had an unquenchable thirst for controversy. No other German-American editor made so many enemies unnecessarily, but few papers had the spice of the *Pionier,* and its literary style was equaled by few contemporary publications and excelled by none. William Lloyd Garrison called it "the ablest, most independent, and highest toned of all the German papers in the country."[28]

Die Republik der Arbeiter, the organ of Wilhelm Weitling, survived in New York from January 1850 to July 1855. Started as a monthly and sold for 6¼ cents a copy, it expanded into a weekly, only to decline again into a monthly before suspending publication altogether.[29] Weitling wanted a paper for the working class which would advocate his schemes for banks of exchange, currency reform, coöperatives, communist colonies, social insurance, and welfare programs, and the first issue of *Die Republik* virtually recapitulated the basic theories found in Weitling's major works. The paper was started with total assets of $1.50, and the editor went from house to house among the Germans of New York City ringing doorbells, and in four days secured four hundred subscribers. By the end of the first year the circulation reached four thousand, but a year later the paper was in serious financial difficulties, though editorial expenses were four dollars a week, total operating costs twenty-one dollars a week, and Weitling moved six times in five years to cut expenses. *Die Republik* had a surprising circulation outside New York, for it was the organ for Weitling's Workingmen's League which had members in nearly every state. Advertising, offered at five cents a line, was practically nonexistent. The paper published treatises on economics, contributions from workers, extracts from exchanges of similar viewpoints, histories of communist settlements, articles on foreign policy, and miscellaneous material ranging from drama and poetry, religious parables, science and invention, medicine, agriculture, to labor news.

Many other radical journals were published in the tradition of the *Pionier* and *Die Republik der Arbeiter*. Among the better known were the *Menschenrechte*, of Rothacker and Johann Rittig, in Cincinnati; Fritz Anneke's several enterprises; his wife's *Deutsche Frauenzeitung;* Hassaurek's violently anticlerical *Hochwächter*, Gustav Struve's several papers edited with the help of his faithful Amalia, in which he espoused many panaceas from vegetarianism to revolution; and the *Albany Freie Blätter*, which gave battle to the "superstition and follies of Christianity." But such papers were doomed almost from the outset, for Germans preferred their beer, lodges, singing societies, *Turnvereine*, and saccharine serials and local gossip "which could be consumed without mental effort or too much reflection." Frequently advertising was refused lest it jeopardize the independence of the paper and blunt the editor's zeal for attacking the established order. Heinzen had the stamina to carry on for more than a quarter-century, but most of his fellow radicals would have endorsed Weitling's conclusions, after four years of fruitless effort, when he wrote: "Whoever publishes a paper because of a principle in which he believes had better not reckon, from the outset, on the interest and continued support of the public," and may well wonder "whether it was worth sacrificing the ordinary comforts of the senses, a family, property and profits," for principle.[30]

It is refreshing to find a few refugees who took a less grim view of life and, instead of stressing the defects of human nature and society, wrote about more pleasant themes. Franz Sigel, with his father-in-law, published a *Review* devoted to military science and belles lettres, intended primarily for Turner, singers, and members of militia companies. In Milwaukee, Otto Ruppius, a novelist and ex-revolutionist from Saxony, for a time edited the weekly *Westliche Blätter*, which was devoted to literary themes, and not controversies. A musician and writer, Ruppius was the author of many novels written in German with American settings, and his work may be compared with that of the better-known Charles Sealsfield and Ferdinand Gerstäcker. When Ruppius edited the Sunday edition of Börnstein's *Anzeiger des Westens*, also known as the *Westliche Blätter*, he filled it with selections from modern and historical German novels and other material from the field of belles lettres.[31]

In 1861 Sigel, Kapp, and Hugo Wesendonck joined with Frederick L. Olmsted, O. B. Frothingham, George Opdyke, and others, in promoting a new monthly, the *Interpreter,* intended to educate Americans and Germans to a better understanding of each other. Seven years earlier, Esselen and J. H. Klippart had made a similar effort in Cleveland, with the *American Liberal,* edited by "ripe scholars and men of research and thought." Both ventures died after a few issues.[32] Esselen's *Atlantis,* despite much attention to controversial issues, was essentially a journal of essays on politics, science, philosophy, art, and literature, and belongs in the category of belles lettres. It probably never had more than a thousand readers. The *New Yorker Criminal Zeitung und Belletristisches Journal* was established in 1851 by Rudolf Lexow, a Forty-eighter from Schleswig-Holstein, and in 1852 he was joined by his cousin, Friedrich Lexow, a gifted poet who had published *Das Volk* in Schleswig and had served one year of an eight-year sentence for subversive activities. The *Belletristisches Journal,* as the name implies, was a weekly devoted primarily to poetry, novels, and cultural and literary material, and only incidentally concerned with the news of the day. It managed to survive for sixty years, and in the 1880's its circulation reached 71,500.

FOOTNOTES

CHAPTER 18

1. See Gottfried Menzel: *Die Vereinigten Staaten von Nordamerika mit besonderer Rücksicht auf deutsche Auswanderung dahin* (Berlin, 1853) pp. 231-32; *Belletristisches Journal,* Feb. 25, 1853. For a list of German papers in 1848, see *Mitteilungen des Deutschen Pionier Vereins von Philadelphia,* XVI (1910) pp. 39-40; see also a table for 1856, in *New Yorker Staatszeitung,* Feb. 14, 1856.

2. By 1873 the number of German language papers had grown to 356, including 56 dailies. See *Wächter am Erie,* June 10, 1873; Aug. 8, 1874; and *Westbote,* March 22, 1873.

3. Kapp: *Aus und über Amerika,* I, 317.

4. See *Atlantis* (March 1855) II (N.S.) pp. 232-40; *Atlantische Studien,* III, pp. 73-74; Lenel: *Kapp,* p. 77; Ludwig von Baumbach: *Neue Briefe aus den Vereinigten Staaten von Nord Amerika* (Kassel, 1856) p. 104.

5. See *Westbote,* July 15, 1853; Feb. 17, 1854; Feb. 20, 1859.

6. *Belletristisches Journal,* July 10, 1857.

7. *New Yorker Staatszeitung,* Dec. 6, 1853.

8. See *New Yorker Staatszeitung,* for example, for March 1851. For a case in Louisville, see L. Stierlin: *Kentucky,* pp. 162-63.

9. *Westbote,* Aug. 12, 1853; see also Karl Heinzen: *Editoren Kongress* (Boston, 1872).

10. *Wächter am Erie,* Feb. 22, 1860; see also *Westbote,* April 12, 1850.

11. See J. J. Schlicher: "Bernhard Domschke: A Life of Hardship" in *Wisconsin Magazine of History,* XXIX (March 1946) No. 3, pp. 319-32, 435-56.

12. See *Mitteilungen des Deutschen Pionier Vereins von Philadelphia,* X (1909) pp. 26-31.

13. See Cunz: *The Maryland Germans*, pp. 276-81; *Der Deutsche Pionier*, III (No. 14) June 1871, p. 108; and *New Yorker Staatszeitung*, Sept. 6, 1854.

14. *Wächter am Erie*, April 1, 1871.

15. See Hildegard Binder Johnson: "German Forty-eighters in Davenport," in *Iowa Journal of History and Politics* (January 1916); and Richter: *Geschichte der Stadt Davenport*, pp. 408, 483-89.

16. *Westbote*, Sept. 26, Nov. 14, 1851.

17. *Der Deutsche Pionier*, XIV, No. 6 (Sept. 1882) p. 238.

18. *Wächter am Erie*, Feb. 17, 1875.

19. *Ibid.*, Oct. 8, 1875.

20. Stierlin: *Kentucky*, pp. 131-32, 142, 164.

21. *Wächter am Erie*, Dec. 19, 1874.

22. See *Der Deutsche Pionier*, XII, No. 5 (Aug. 1880) p. 198; also Börnstein: *Memoiren*, I, 322-23, II, 117-18; and Scharf: *St. Louis*, pp. 933-34.

23. See Fuess: *Schurz*, p. 54; and *Intimate Letters*, pp. 373-74, 376.

24. See Caspar Butz: "George Hillgärtner" in *Der Deutsche Pionier*, XIV, No. 12 (March 1883) pp. 468-70.

25. See *Erinnerungen eines Deutsch-Amerikaners* (Chicago, 1890); also "Wilhelm Rapp" in *Deutsch-Amerikanische Geschichtsblätter*, VII, No. 2 (April 1907) pp. 58-61.

26. *Wächter am Erie*, Oct. 3, 1867.

27. See *Der Deutsche Pionier*, XVII, No. 1 (1886) pp. 36-37.

28. For further details, see Wittke: *Heinzen*, Chapter V, entitled "The Struggles of a Radical Journalist."

29. See Wittke: *Weitling*, especially Chapter IX.

30. *Die Republik der Arbeiter*, Sept. 9, 1854.

31. Börnstein: *Memoiren*, II, 221. Of further interest concerning Ruppius and Gerstaecker is Leroy H. Woodson: *American Negro Slavery in the Works of Friedrich Strubberg, Friedrich Gerstaecker and Otto Ruppius* (Washington, 1949).

32. See *Wächter am Erie*, Nov. 10, 1861; and *Cleveland Leader*, Dec. 29, 1854; and H. A. Rattermann: "Christian Esselen: Eine Charakterstudie aus der Vergangenheit," in *Deutsch-Amerikanische Geschichtsblätter* (Chicago, 1912) XII, 405-61.

Chapter 19 · THE GERMAN
SOCIAL PATTERN

WHEREVER GERMANS settled in sufficient numbers to support group activities they introduced the social patterns of the fatherland, for like all immigrant groups, they did not shed lightly the customs of the Old World. Life in a strange land is difficult enough for the first-generation immigrant without asking that he abandon immediately all the ways of his fathers. Shut off by language from a normal cultural exchange, the immigrant seeks spiritual solace in his memories. The result is a cultural isolation, perhaps most keenly felt by the most highly educated, who band together with stubborn persistence to preserve their inherited social patterns.

In urban centers, large and small, Germans nurtured social organizations of many kinds to perpetuate the life they had known at home. These included societies devoted to music, lodges ranging from benevolent, fraternal, and mutual insurance societies to purely social clubs, bowling and card clubs, *Turnvereine* and organizations of sharpshooters, and societies whose basis for membership was the section of Germany from which the immigrant came. For the more intellectual, reading and library associations, and societies for the promotion of the arts and letters, and for German workingmen's associations primarily concerned with raising the economic level of their class, "Workers' Halls" served the same social objectives. Spring and summer months were marked by outdoor picnics and merrymaking. In the winter season Germans concentrated on masquerade balls, theatrical performances, and musical entertainment, or gathered to commemorate a local tradition or a festival peculiar to the part of Germany from which they came. On such occasions German cooks prepared native dishes, many of which ultimately found their way into the cook books of American housewives. In the German sections of larger cities, spacious and attractive beer gardens dispensed beer, food, and enjoyable music, and on Sundays entire families sought recreation and entertainment in the Continental European fashion.

Such a German social and cultural pattern existed in the United States before the Forty-eighters came, although on a smaller and less pretentious scale. But America's *Deutschtum* took on a new life after 1850. Like a stone thrown into still water, the Forty-eighters produced waves in the German-American pool high enough eventually to affect the entire American cultural pattern.

Forty-eighters refused to give up "the intellectual achievements of a thousand years in the old world for the culture of the primeval forest," and protested that they would be more than mere "cultural fertilizer." They resolved to do battle for German art, music, science, and literature in America, and among them were newcomers immodest enough to compare their mission in the United States with "the Revival of Letters in the West" when medieval scholars fled from Constantinople to escape the Turks. In this sense they spoke about creating a "New Germany" across the sea. Men like Schurz, Kapp, and Esselen realized the folly of trying to create separate German states in America, opposed "German particularism," and argued that Germans could best perform their cultural mission by distributing themselves as widely as possible over the United States. Kapp believed that the cultural treasures of German intellectuals would decisively affect the America of the future.[1] Esselen acknowledged the superior practical, inventive genius of the average American, but insisted that what was needed was philosophers and natural scientists, not just inventors of sewing machines and revolvers. On this higher level he thought the newcomers from Europe could make their most important contribution,[2] and build the spiritual bridge over which the European Enlightenment would make its transit to the United States. Many Forty-eighters felt that with a few notable exceptions the Germans who settled in America before 1850 had manifested little interest in the values of the mind and spirit. To work as they pleased, and enjoy their beer and their recreation when they pleased, seemed to constitute the sum of existence for the German artisan and peasant class. Their folk festivals had little intellectual content beyond providing a day's recreation, and their theatres were hardly more than side shows at annual bazaars.[3]

Before the end of 1850 New York had seventy thousand Germans concentrated in a special area of the city, and strong enough to support two theatres. Concerts at the Shakespeare Hotel were largely attended.[4] In Richmond, Virginia, five thousand Germans in a total population of thirty-eight thousand supported a theatre, a number of German societies, two newspapers, and a "People's Garden" for Sunday outings.[5] Louisville, in the decade before the Civil War, had a singing society, a *Turnverein,* a German theatre, a German school, and several organizations of free-thinkers.[6] Heinrich Börnstein was largely responsible for arousing the Germans of St. Louis to support dramatics, dances, lectures, and outdoor festivities.[7] In Texas, in the triangle between Houston, San Antonio, and New Braunfels, Germans founded singing, shooting, athletic, and other social and cultural organizations. Before the end of the century Cleveland had thirty singing societies, four *Turnvereine,* twenty-four organizations with memberships based on the German state or province from which the immigrant came, a German Medical Society, an educational society, a shooting club, and two societies for German "pioneers."[8]

Militia companies were popular with immigrant and native-born groups alike before the Civil War, for they satisfied both the martial and social desires of their members. In New York nearly every nationality group had its own military organizations. The Germans, like the Irish, loved to parade in gaudy uniforms and discharge firearms and cannon during military maneuvers. Cincinnati, St. Louis, New York, Louisville, Chicago, Milwaukee, and other cities supported German militia companies known as "Steuben Fusiliers," "German Huzzars," or "Lafayette" and "Jefferson Guards." The achievements of these amateur soldiers seem to have been greater at the banquet table and the bar than on the drill ground, and eating and drinking on drill day were equally stressed with proficiency in the manual of arms. Yet many companies enlisted *in corpore* during the Civil War and some made notable records in the Union Army.

For Forty-eighters, fresh from military adventures in the German Revolution, such organizations proved especially attractive, and many were elected officers because of their European experiences. At the annual banquets of these military organizations, leading Forty-eighters frequently made the major addresses. In 1856, for example, Sigel, an adjutant in the state militia, spoke with several other refugees at the banquet of the 5th New York Regiment, a wholly German unit, and pleaded for a popular militia in a people's republic.[9] Three years earlier, Sigel's manual of arms for Turner had sold in an edition of two thousand at twenty-five cents a copy. In 1858, at a Steuben Day festival of the Germans of New York, the German militia paraded with other German societies and took part in a tournament of sharpshooters. In Chicago, the German militia turned out regularly on Washington's Birthday, the Fourth of July, and for funerals. There were German militia companies in Mobile, Richmond, and other Southern cities. The number of officers in these organizations was surprisingly large, and as elected officials they were expected to pay for the drinks after every martial exercise. On parade, German companies usually carried two flags, the American national banner and the colors of the German Revolution.

Closely akin to the militia companies were the German sharpshooters (*Schützenvereine*). Their number expanded remarkably after 1848. Their annual *Schützenfest,* where members competed in the shooting galleries for prizes, was a German-American institution imported directly from the fatherland. At the close of the competition, and after much parading, banqueting, and oratory, the champion marksman was crowned king of the sharpshooters with ceremonies like those of Germany. In 1854 the first *Schützenfest,* attended by competitors from several states, was held in Philadelphia, though local competitions had been held in Columbus, Ohio, and Louisville two years earlier. In later years the festivities frequently extended over three days or a week, and clubs prospered to the point of maintaining their own shooting galleries and picnic grounds. In 1868 the *Schützenfest* in New York lasted ten days; sponsors collected $25,000 to cover expenses, and a special newspaper (*Festzeitung*) was published under the editorship of Sigel. Four years later, at the national *Schützenfest* in Highland, Illinois, the sharpshooters fired 78,000 shots in a week at fourteen targets, for prizes of $12,000. Prior to 1870 the colors of the Revolution always flew over the shooting galleries and picnic grounds of the *Schützen,* for their ranks included many refugees of 1848.[10]

The non-Catholic German immigration responded enthusiastically to the American craze for lodges and secret societies. The Sons of Hermann (*Hermannssöhne*) were established in the United States in 1848, the Order of the Harugari in 1850, and in 1851 there were five German for every three American lodges among the Red Men. The Druids and Odd Fellows were popular also, and Kossuth's visit to the United States re-

vived interest in Freemasonry. The first German Masonic lodge on the
Pacific coast, the Hermann Lodge of San Francisco, was established in
1858. The Old Free Order of Chaldea proved less popular and did not
survive. A Gottfried Kinkel Lodge of the Order of the Sons of Liberty
was established in Milwaukee in 1851, along with a Teutonia Lodge of
German Odd Fellows.

Although the lodge movement spread rapidly in the 1850's and thereafter, Forty-eighters were less active in this field, and some vigorously
opposed the mania for secret societies. Esselen thought lodges silly, dis-
ruptive, and undemocratic. Heinzen believed they contributed nothing
to the enlightenment of the human race, and stressed the art of eating and
drinking to the exclusion of cultural matters. He characterized Masonry
as an "insane humbug," in which grown men strutted about blindfolded,
with aprons around their bellies. To Weitling, the "silly antics" of the
"lodge humbug" were particularly distasteful because they diverted attention from his labor movement. To such reformers lodges were the enemies
of progress, robbed their members of time and money that might better
be spent on worthier causes, dulled their intellects by medieval rituals—
in short, they were organizations in which "fools with colored rags and
aprons and stupid faces participate with German humility and docility
in old English nonsense."[11]

German immigrants were surprised and disappointed to find that
Americans had no folk festivals. The Fourth of July was the one exception, but the celebration of Independence Day consisted primarily of
noise-making and shooting, and seemed devoid of all spiritual content.
Thanksgiving Day, the other typically American holiday, displeased
radical German freethinkers because of its religious character. Newly
arrived immigrants therefore resolved to introduce the German "Volks-
fest" as an antidote for the noise, dullness, or pietism of American national
holidays.

Some of the first German May Festivals in New York were sponsored
by Weitling's Workingmen's League. On Pentecost Sunday, 1854, while
faithful Catholics were entering a church across the street for early mass,
Weitling's workingmen were loading picnic wagons for the march to
the Battery and the picnic grounds where, with ample supplies of beer
and food, whole families spent the afternoon and evening in singing, playing games, and dancing to guitar and accordion.[12] New Year's Eve and

Christmas were observed with music, declamations, and dancing. In 1853 the Germans of California held their first May Festival, and spent the day outdoors competing for prizes in athletic exercises, dancing the mazurka, waltz, polka, and schottische, listening to speeches, and singing folk songs.[13] When such celebrations were molested by gangs of rowdies, Germans fought back vigorously in defense of their right to preserve their national customs in America.

Germans complained that Americans did not know how to celebrate Independence Day with proper dignity. In St. Louis, Heinrich Börnstein and his liberal German followers started a Fourth of July parade at six o'clock one Sunday morning in order not to interfere with church services and to avoid a clash with native Americans and Irishmen who threatened to break up their procession. Armed with revolvers, bricks, and knives, and with German militia at the head and rear of the parade, the Germans marched through the heart of the city through lines of angry Americans and Irishmen and reached the picnic grounds without serious trouble. Here they listened to the conventional oratory and a reading of the immortal Declaration, and then spent the rest of the day in dancing, singing, and playing games.[14] In Columbus, Ohio, a similar celebration was ushered in by artillery fire before daybreak, and at high noon, Turner, militia, and German volunteer firefighters marched to the picnic grounds, where they were joined by their families for the festivities of the day.[15]

Steuben Festivals, commemorating the birthday of the German Inspector General of Washington's army during the American Revolution, were popular in the eastern states, and were planned during the 1850's as patriotic counter-demonstrations against nativist attacks on the foreign-born. Forty-eighters frequently provided the oratory for these occasions, and Struve, Försch, Füster, Kapp, Ottendörfer, and Schramm appeared on several programs.[16] German societies, especially Turner and working-men's clubs, observed the anniversary of the death of Robert Blum, and university men gathered for convivial evenings to live again their student days, or for a reunion of their student corps. In 1858, former students of the University of Jena assembled in a brewery on Fourth Street in New York for the three hundredth anniversary of their alma mater. The colors of sixty student corps, busts of Schiller and Goethe, and crossed rapiers decorated the hall, in which hung a banner which read "Semper floreat alma mater, 1558-1858." Among the men of Jena who listened to orations in German and Latin on that occasion were a number of prominent Forty-eighters.[17]

Special reference must be made to the introduction of the German Christmas in the United States, for the German impact upon the holiday season was especially significant during the decade of the 1850's. In many cities, stores and shops, as late as the 1860's, were closed on Christmas day only in the sections settled by Germans,[18] and in Cincinnati, in the German quarter "over the canal," Christmas Eve was a popular time for weddings. Christmas trees were expensive in the 1850's and had to be chopped down in the woods with one's own hands. Twenty-five years later, 220,000 trees from the Catskills and Maine were available in the New York City market at costs of from ten cents to two dollars a tree. Refugees yearned for the "poetry of the Christmas tree" in this "barren land." The editor of the *Wächter am Erie,* who witnessed the transition from the American to the German Christmas in his own lifetime, commented in 1875: "Whoever can recall how little Christmas was celebrated here two decades ago, and can compare it with to-day, will hail with joy the progress of German institutions and customs."[19]

There is a widely known legend that Pastor Heinrich Schwan of Zion's German Lutheran Church of Cleveland used a Christmas tree for the first time in a Christmas church service in 1851, and Clevelanders claim that the custom spread from their city into other parts of the nation. Actually, Gustav Körner referred in his diary as early as 1833 to decorated Christmas trees in Belleville, Illinois, and there are references to Christmas trees in Cincinnati in 1835, and elsewhere in the early 1840's, and the Germans of Wooster, Ohio, had lighted trees in their homes in 1848. More important than the tree which Pastor Schwan decorated with candles, apples, and candy in front of his church in 1851, was the denunciation by Congregational and Presbyterian Clevelanders of the "heathenish custom" and the "plain case of idolatry" by which churches were defiled by impious "foreigners." Nevertheless, German Christmas customs spread rapidly in the United States. Forty-eighters did not introduce the Christmas tree, Christmas music, or German Christmas cakes, but their sentimental insistence upon their preservation helped impress them upon the country.[20] Louis Prang, a refugee of 1848, introduced the commercial Christmas card to the American public. Although such cards were prepared for sale probably as early as the 1840's, it was not until about 1862 that the custom of sending them to friends and relatives became common. Louis Prang promoted the greeting card movement in America in 1856 and produced cards at his lithograph shop in Boston every year after that date.

The renaissance in the German-American theatre begins with 1850, for the German theatre developed into an institution of high standards only after the new immigration became sufficiently influential to make its influence decisive. Before the Forty-eighters came, German theatrical performances were undistinguished and almost exclusively amateur. To guarantee an audience and not lose money it was necessary to follow the play with a dance, beer and other refreshments, and in many cases the price of admission included these after-theatre accessories. German dramatics were performed in an atmosphere that represented a combination of theatre and beer garden. In New York City, before 1850, German theatre directors like Eduard Haman staged their productions in the drill hall of the militia, in taverns, or in an abandoned church. Dramatic performances were free in New York beer halls, and the management depended on the sale of drinks to meet expenses. The period from 1843 to 1849 was particularly barren. Philadelphia had amateur German dramatic productions as early as 1840, but practically all were in connection with dances. In the first amateur theatres in Milwaukee, in 1850, men smoked pipes or cigars and drank beer served by noisy waiters, and the women cracked nuts and ate apples, while most of the audience waited impatiently for the dance which followed the play.[21]

Under such conditions most performances were mediocre, and the selection of plays limited to light comedy and farce. The repertoire seldom was more pretentious than pieces by Theodore Körner, Kotzebue's comedies, and Kleist's *Kätchen von Heilbronn*. On rare occasions a company attempted Grillparzer or Schiller, almost as unknown to the German-American stage before 1850 as Shakespeare, Lessing, or Goethe. Stage settings and scenery were shabby and the hall usually was filled with tobacco smoke. As late as 1856, a Baltimore theatre manager, to attract patronage, offered a gold watch to the man who would bring the most ladies to the New Year's Day performance. First prize went to a local swain who paid the admission for ninety-seven women, and second prize to a man who brought forty-eight.[22] The Forty-eighters revolted against such mediocrity, were offended by the beer-hall manners of the average German theatregoer, and were particularly incensed to have dramatic performances followed by dancing. Above all, they insisted on a better selection of plays and actors of higher caliber.

The flowering time of the Milwaukee stage begins with 1853, with a presentation of Schiller's *Die Räuber,* always popular with liberals and refugees. The revival continued into the 1860's, although the Civil War seriously affected German theatricals. By 1855 Milwaukee had a professional German theatre, and Schurz wrote with pride to his wife that German dramatics were now well launched, on a respectable level, not only in Milwaukee, but in other cities like New York and Philadelphia.[23] In Chicago, German dramatics of high quality originated with plays produced at the German House in 1856. Chicago's new German Theatre was supported by Forty-eighters such as Butz, Schneider, and Francis Hoffmann and, despite many vicissitudes, survived until 1870. Its first Sunday performance was Schiller's *Kabale und Liebe*. The company presented German classics at a time when the Chicago stage was given over to slapstick comedy and vaudeville, "Mose, the Butcher Boy," and "The Fast Young Man,"[24] and Shakespearian performances could be given only when a star happened to be in the city. Chicago had a number of "People's Theatres" *(Volkstheater)*, and the *Turnvereine* sponsored plays of a lighter kind. After the Civil War Chicago supported a German professional company, under the direction of the Milwaukee Theatre, and the organization gave regular theatrical performances in German until 1931.[25]

In New York, the *Deutsches National Theater* gave a benefit performance in 1853 for Christian Nees von Esenbeck, a noted radical of 1848 who had lost his professorship at the University of Breslau.[26] The St. Charles Theatre of New York, besides presenting a standard repertoire, produced several plays by Max Conheim, a Jewish Forty-eighter who wrote for the German-American stage. Most of his plays were undistinguished, but his propaganda play, *Fürsten zum Land hinaus, oder die Schul' ist aus,* was especially interesting because several scenes were laid in the Shakespeare Hotel, rendezvous of refugees, and portrayed the final triumph of republicanism in Germany.[27] The New York *Stadttheater,* first German playhouse to give performances on a regular schedule, opened in September 1854 for daily performances in an auditorium seating twenty-five hundred, but the management quickly learned that a steady diet of Schiller, Goethe, Lessing, and Shakespeare would not balance the budget.[28]

The renaissance in the German theatre in St. Louis was in large measure due to Heinrich Börnstein. He and his wife were accomplished actors, with considerable European experience. In 1853 Börnstein organized the *Philo-dramatische Gesellschaft* of St. Louis, an amateur group which he directed and with whom he and his wife acted and worked as stage managers. Among the several comedies which he wrote for the organization was one entitled *German Immigration and the German Society*. The company survived for three years and was later reorganized as a professional group. A large part of its receipts went to charity. In 1857 and 1858, the Turner of St. Louis gave regular theatrical performances on Sundays, and in addition, the city had several *Volkstheater*, affiliated with beer halls and beer gardens. In 1859 Börnstein managed the St. Louis Opera House, the first successful professional theatre in the city, and donated a profit of $1,200 from the first evening's performance to the local society for aid to German immigrants. In one season Börnstein gave twenty dramatic readings in St. Louis for the benefit of a German ladies' society, and in 1860 offered a prize for the best German play on an American theme. The St. Louis Opera House encountered many difficulties, including trouble with the police over Sunday performances. In 1861, when its director went to war, the theatre was closed. After the Civil War a professional German theatre was organized in St. Louis which survived until World War I.[29]

In Cincinnati the rapid improvement of German productions was directly attributable to Forty-eighters. In 1851 Friedrich Hassaurek and Karl Obermann founded a German Theatre, known as *Das Deutsche Institut*, which survived until 1861. Under competent directors, and with the help of professional actors, the *Institut* gave four performances a week. On one occasion Heinrich Börnstein brought his St. Louis troupe for guest performances to the Cincinnati theatre, and its professional talent included Antonie Grahn, who played *Maria Stuart* for the first time in Cincinnati to a packed house; Johann Rittig, a refugee who played in the German theatres of Cincinnati, Milwaukee, St. Louis, Louisville, and Chicago, but is better known as a journalist; and Alexander Pfeiffer, a German tragedian who emigrated in 1851 after a clash with his manager in Mannheim over his liberal views, and played *Hamlet, Wilhelm Tell, Don Carlos,* and *Faust* in Cincinnati, St. Louis, and Chicago.

On the eve of the Civil War the monopoly enjoyed by German drama in Cincinnati, according to the *Cincinnati Enquirer*, was challenged only by the minstrel shows at several local theatres. The *Enquirer* repeatedly commented on the good attention and the "quiet" which prevailed in the German theatre "over the Rhine," in contrast with the disorder of American playhouses.[30] In the first two months of 1861 the Cincinnati German Theatre gave fifty productions, but suffered a crushing blow from the Civil War; and in the post-war years the *Turnvereine* presented plays, including the German classics, on an amateur basis. After several successful years, the *Stadttheater in der Turnhalle* in 1875 was transformed into a professional city theatre, only to fail financially when its director ran off with the box office receipts.[31] A sudden decision in 1881 to enforce Sunday closing laws struck especially hard at German theatricals, and it was not until 1890 that a *Theaterverein* finally was organized to underwrite a professional company. In 1918 the hysteria of World War I forced the German Theatre Company in Cincinnati to disband.[32]

Detroit's German Theatre Society had the vigorous support of Dr. Hermann Kiefer, the emigré physician who aided every liberal and cultural movement in his adopted city and was especially interested in a good German theatre. In Davenport, Iowa, the first German plays were given by amateurs, in 1855, in the converted lobby of a tavern. Shares were sold at five dollars to support a German Theatre Society, and Heinrich Lischer, owner of the Davenport *Demokrat* and a protégé of Börnstein of St. Louis, became the first director of the society. Its first performance was the ever-popular *Einer muss heiraten*. In 1856 German theatrical productions in Davenport were shifted to Germania Hall. Two years later the company presented Schiller's *Kabale und Liebe,* and in 1859, *Die Räuber*. In 1862 the Davenport Germans organized a stock company to build a theatre with a seating capacity of fourteen hundred.[33] New Braunfels, on the Texas frontier, had a German Theatre Society before the Civil War, and in the following decade little German theatre troupes carrying a movable stage on wagons made the rounds of the smaller German communities of the state.[34]

No other immigrant group contributed as much to the development of chorus singing of high quality as the German immigration of the middle nineteenth century. Wherever Germans settled, singing societies were organized to sing folk melodies and the music of the great composers of the fatherland. In *Gesangvereine* with various names, such as *Liederkranz, Orpheus, Arion, Männerchor, Eintracht,* and *Harmonie,* German artisans, business and professional men met regularly to practice four-part music. They were not expected to have special talent, but once a week, frequently on Sunday, they assembled to rehearse under a paid director. In Philadelphia the German workers' singing society paid their director fifty dollars a year, plus the receipts of an annual benefit concert.[35] The *Akron Liedertafel,* founded in 1855 with thirteen members, paid its first director $8.33 a month.[36]

What organizations of this kind contributed to the raising of the musical level of the American people can be fully appreciated only when one realizes that at the beginning of the last century bands which tried to play a Haydn symphony in New York were pelted with eggs and vegetables as crowds shouted for "Yankee Doodle." Music on the frontier was on an even lower level. Here fiddlers scratched away by ear, with no concept of harmony, but a great eagerness to play faster than their rivals. Only dance and folk tunes seemed to please the untrained American ear, and as late as 1854 the New York Philharmonic could not play the German masters without fear of cat-calls from the audience.

The oldest German singing societies in New York, Philadelphia, Baltimore, Cincinnati, and St. Louis antedate the coming of the refugees of 1848,[37] but the musical life of most German-American communities had its flowering time after 1850. Forty-eighters not only supported but gave intelligent direction to the German desire to preserve the musical traditions of the fatherland in a country where musical tastes were surprisingly low. In 1848 three new German singing societies were founded in New York, and three in Philadelphia. The first convention of German singers in the East *(Sängerfest)* was held in the latter city in 1850, and societies from several cities competed for prizes. Thereafter, *Sängerfeste* were held annually in Baltimore, New York, and Philadelphia, until the Civil War intervened. By 1855 New York State had thirty-seven German singing societies, and two years later Pennsylvania had fifty-nine. The first singing society in Texas was the *Germania,* of New Braunfels, established in March 1850. Adolf Douai directed the San Antonio *Gesangverein,* and took his singers to the first *Sängerfest* in New Braunfels in 1853.[38] Dr. Georg Fein, a Baltimore Forty-eighter, was one of the founders of the *Concordia* society, and in 1851 the Baltimore *Arion* serenaded Kossuth when he visited the city. In 1850 Dr. Tiedemann addressed the *Sängerfest* in Philadelphia on the continuing struggle for a social-democratic republic in Germany,[39] and the guests drank a toast from the goblet of Robert Blum which had been brought to America by Nikolaus Schmitt. Tiedemann, Kapp, Kellner, Schünemann-Pott, and other Forty-eighters spoke frequently at the banquets of *Sängerfeste* in leading eastern cities.[40]

Philipp Reiter, a Forty-eighter, directed the Philadelphia society when it won first prize at the New York *Sängerfest* in 1852. In 1854 the German singers of New York dedicated three new flags, including the black-red-gold banner of the Revolution, and the red flag under which many members had fought in Baden.[41] The delegates to the sixth German *Sängerfest* in New York in 1855 heard addresses by Försch and Metternich, and Struve and Willich were among the refugees present.[42] In Cleveland, Jakob Müller toasted the German singers' organization as "the product of 1848-49." Hans Balatka, who organized the first musical activities of Milwaukee, directed a *Sängerfest* in Chicago in 1857, and the Chicago *Männerchor,* founded in 1852, was a direct creation of the Forty-eighters.[43] From 1848 to 1870 the latter were honored guests at these great musical conclaves; concert and banquet halls invariably were decorated with the colors of the Revolution, and oratory and songs stressed the liberation and unification of Germany.

The first *Sängerfest* in the West was held in Cincinnati in June 1849.[44] In 1852 the Columbus *Männerchor* was host to the German singers of Cincinnati, Wooster, Canton, Dayton, and several other Ohio towns. The Cincinnati singing society, which won first prize on this occasion, had the honor of entering the picnic grounds at the head of the procession through a door opened by children arrayed in spotless white. At the picnic which followed the singing, Turner exhibited their prowess, and German militia discharged their cannon.[45]

The German *Sängerfeste* developed steadily in size, expense, and conviviality, if not in performance. During a picnic in Philadelphia in 1857 in connection with one of these musical tournaments, six hundred barrels of beer were consumed.[46] The following year the singers listened to an address by a famous Forty-eighter and another by Senator Douglas, who spoke in flattering terms about Germany's contributions to America and emphasized the beneficent effect of German sentimentality on the cold, practical nature of the native American.[47] In 1859 the singers, meeting in Cleveland, presented the opera *Allessandro Stradella,* a favorite with German audiences. The society from Detroit carried off first honors; a mass chorus of four hundred voices appeared in concert; and the ceremonies ended with a parade from the Public Square to the picnic grounds in which the singers were "accompanied by the Light Dragoons, Artillery Companies and Turners." The *Cleveland Herald* commented that "Yankeedom" might learn from the "merry, careless, laughter-loving and beer-drinking" Germans.[48] Chicago's musical life took on new vigor with the arrival of Hans Balatka from Milwaukee in 1860. German Jews participated in all these musical activities, and the German-Jewish press gave detailed accounts of the *Sängerfeste*. At the fourth annual meeting of the German singers of Indiana, the editor of the *Israelite* was the principal speaker.[49]

In later years, *Sängerfeste* usually started with a torchlight procession in the evening, and a parade the following morning. As guest conductor in Cleveland, Hans Balatka rehearsed a mass chorus in parts of Mozart's *Magic Flute* for a public concert attended by over five thousand people, and the orchestra played the overtures from *Martha* and *Wilhelm Tell*. After the prizes had been awarded, the night was usually spent under the mellow patronage of Bacchus and King Gambrinus. In 1857 a national *Sängerfest* in Philadelphia represented fifty-nine. societies and nearly fifteen hundred singers. Turner carried colored lanterns through gaily decorated streets to light up historic Independence Square. In front of the headquarters for visiting delegates stood a huge transparency representing Cecilia, the patroness of music, with laurel wreaths for two female figures symbolizing music and poetry. Inside the hall, shields fastened to the walls bore the names of the heroes of song since the fourteenth century, quotations from German and English poets, and the flags of the participating societies. Unfortunately, because the police forgot to enforce local closing ordinances, a "Sacred Concert" scheduled for Sunday evening was sparsely attended. On Monday, however, the singers gave a grand concert in the Academy of Music, beginning with the majestic strains of Luther's "A Mighty Fortress," and ending with Wagner's "Pilgrim's Chorus." After a night of drinking and singing in the taverns, visitors and their hosts proceeded the next day to a picnic ground on Lemon Hill, where Schünemann-Pott spoke about music "as the holy sacrament of true religion" and the bond that unites all mankind. Still not surfeited with social pleasures, the singers staged a grand ball. The next day delegates transacted whatever business demanded attention, and the *Sängerfest* finally closed with a banquet, more toasts, and general hilarity, expenses of $9,000 for the week and a deficit of $2,500 to be assessed upon the local hosts.[50] The reaction of the American press to such festivities was generally favorable, although occasionally a paper injected a sour note by commenting that they contributed "to the perpetuation of foreign clannishness and the consequent suppression of National American sentiment."[51]

Singing societies and *Sängerfeste* had to be largely rebuilt after 1865 because of the effects of the Civil War on their membership, but the task seems to have been accomplished in a remarkably short time. As early as 1867 a *Sängerfest* in Indianapolis, staged in a hall specially built for the occasion, netted a profit of $2,382.[52] In 1868 the North American *Sängerbund* met in Chicago for five days, with a mass chorus of twelve hundred voices.[53] But by the 1870's the *Sängerfeste,* despite receipts from concert and banquet tickets, had become a financial burden for the local hosts, and the metropolitan press, including German-language papers, criticized the heavy drinking which featured such song festivals, and noted a marked deterioration in standards of performance. The New York *Journal of Commerce* quoted Cicero's *Inter pocula silent Musae.* Competent musicians agreed that the orchestra usually was superior to the singers, and several American papers suggested that it would be well for Germans to develop mixed choruses so that women might exercise a wholesome restraint upon their convivial celebrations.[54] When Cleveland was selected as the convention city for 1874, a "Temple" was specially constructed for the occasion with a bar located under the orchestra pit for the sale of drinks. The New York Philharmonic Orchestra of eighty-five pieces and high-priced soloists were engaged for the main concerts. Although the program was excellent, the performance left much to be desired, and the six-day festival ended in friction and recriminations. Visitors complained about the hospitalities and rooming facilities, and compared the quality of Cleveland beer unfavorably with their familiar local brews.[55] Such experiences led to demands to reduce expenses, improve the level of performance, and reduce drinking and carousing. In these criticisms, veteran Forty-eighters heartily joined. Heinzen reiterated that "beer is the only national theme" of German social gatherings in the United States, and the Fremont, Ohio, *Courier* summed up the discussion in the couplet,

> Behüt uns, Herr, vor Krieg und Pest,
> Vor Schützen, Turn' und Sängerfest.[56]

Fortunately the German immigration after 1848 also made its contribution on somewhat higher musical levels. Forty-eighters like Goldmarck, Schurz, and Sigel were good musicians. Hans Balatka, creator of the Milwaukee *Musikverein,* though not a great musician, had a good voice, played well on the cello, and was a tactful and able director. In May 1850 he directed the first concert of the society, supported by an orchestra of twenty pieces. A string quartette, two of whose players were refugees, played Mozart. The next year Balatka directed an orchestra of thirty and a chorus of nearly eighty, and gave a benefit performance for the refugees of 1848. Many native Americans came to hear these blond musicians from "the land of Philosophers," and their generous support made it possible to give monthly concerts. In 1853 Balatka presented the opera *Czar und Zimmermann,* and two years later, *Norma.* In an amazing repertoire which included fourteen operas in seven years, Weber's *Freischütz* and Mozart's *Magic Flute* seem to have been strong favorites. In 1859 Balatka's musical amateurs disintegrated because of a heated controversy over the merits of the music of Richard Wagner, and in 1860 their director moved to Chicago where, nine years later, he became the conductor of the Chicago Philharmonic Society.[57]

The most distinguished orchestral group among the Forty-eighters was the Germania Orchestra of New York, consisting of twenty-three musicians, nearly all refugees. One of the first orchestras to tour the country, it established a record of eight hundred concerts in six years. The orchestra's best-known members were Carl Bergmann and Carl Zerrahn, and both made musical history in the United States. Bergmann was a native of Saxony, an accomplished cellist, and had directed orchestras in Vienna, Breslau, Budapest, Warsaw, and Venice. Implicated in the Revolution of 1848 in Vienna, he arrived in New York in the fall of the next year and joined the Germania Orchestra. In 1850 he became its conductor. Carl Zerrahn had studied music in Hanover and Berlin, left Europe because of the Revolution, and joined the refugee orchestra as a flutist. After the financial failure of the Germania Orchestra, Bergmann directed the Philharmonic Society and the Arion singing society of New York. He was a popular guest conductor at *Sängerfeste,* and at a time when it required courage to play Wagner and Berlioz before American audiences, Bergmann featured both. He was an excellent arranger of scores and a composer of some merit. Zerrahn is remembered as the conductor of the Händel and Haydn Society of Boston, a post which he filled for forty-two years, and for his work as conductor of the Boston Philharmonic from 1855 to 1863, of the concerts of the Harvard Musical Association from 1865 to 1882, and of the Worcester Music Festivals from 1866 to 1897. Zerrahn taught singing, harmony, and composition at the New England Conservatory of Music until 1898. His influence on the development of choral singing in the United States is universally recognized. In 1869 and 1872 he directed mammoth choruses of ten thousand voices at the Boston "Peace Jubilee" and the music teachers' convention—feats which, however, belong in the category of musical stunts rather than serious musicianship.

During the eight years of its existence, the Germania Orchestra traveled extensively on the seaboard and in the hinterland. It was the first orchestra to play Beethoven's Ninth Symphony in Boston. In May 1853 it played in Chicago, with Bergmann conducting, and in June, in Cincinnati and Cleveland. Unfortunately American audiences were more interested in minstrels than Mozart. A report of the concert in the *Wächter am Erie* deplored the small audience, but lauded the program, which included Beethoven, Rossini, and Mendelssohn, and flute solos by Zerrahn; and commended the organization for its uphill efforts "as the high priests of the art" among American audiences.[58] After the concert the orchestra found it desirable to serenade prominent Clevelanders, on a "few of the principal streets." Crude as some of the performances must have been, the *Cleveland Plain Dealer's* music critic was amazed by the precision of the performers, and one may judge his own musical competence from the comment, "There is no such thing as one bow going up while the other goes down." Occasionally the Germania Orchestra persuaded soloists like Jenny Lind and Ole Bull to appear on its programs.

Many Forty-eighters made their first American dollars by giving piano or singing lessons in well-to-do families, and thus introduced European standards of music appreciation. They also introduced the German musical terminology throughout the United States. Some of the refugees were musicians of real talent. Otto Dresel, for example, a native of Giesenheim who came to the United States in 1848, was for fifteen years Boston's foremost resident pianist. Theodore Hagan had received much of his education in Paris, and while still a young man contributed to newspapers in Cologne and Hamburg, published a book on *Civilization and Music,* and directed the Hamburg municipal theatre before the Revolution. Driven out because of his liberal views, he published novels and dramas in England, founded the German *Musikzeitung* of New York, and became one of the ablest music critics of his generation. Otto Ruppius played in Louisville in the spring of 1852 with the pianist Bernard Plagge in a concert for violin and piano advertised in the Louisville papers as a performance by "Prussian refugees." Ruppius organized a Musical Association and an orchestra in Louisville, and gave two concerts a week, and special promenade concerts during the summer months.[59] Later he became "professor of music" in Nashville, where he conducted an amateur orchestra.

Georg Matzka, a child prodigy on the violin from Coburg, graduated from the conservatory in Prague, and was concertmaster of the orchestra of the Duke of Coburg until his radical sentiments in 1848 lost him the ducal favor. After spending several years in European travel, Matzka came to the United States in 1853. His major instruments were violin, viola, and piano; he taught music in New York; composed for orchestra and string quartettes, and was concertmaster of the New York Philharmonic and Theodore Thomas' Orchestra.[60] Wilhelm Mayerhöfer, a native of Prague and a teacher in the Conservatory of Leipzig, was another refugee who settled in New York, to give music lessons and play the organ in several churches.[61] Gustav Stoeckel, who had been politically active in the Palatinate, became a music teacher in New Haven in 1849. After many years as choirmaster at Yale, the university gave him an honorary degree and appointed him to the faculty. Carl Anschütz, after a short stay in London and Amsterdam, conducted Ullmann's Opera Company and the German Opera Company of New York. Karl Barus, who arrived in the United States in 1849, directed an orchestra in Cincinnati after his unsuccessful effort as a "Latin farmer" in Michigan. The musical activities of these and other immigrants of equal talent support the statement of a distinguished American historian of music that much of the credit for the phenomenal development in American musical tastes from "Yankee Doodle" to *Parsifal* in two generations belongs to the European immigration of the middle nineteenth century.

FOOTNOTES

CHAPTER 19

1. See also, Oscar Canstatt: *Die Deutsche Auswanderung* (Berlin, 1901) pp. 215-16; and Philip Wagner: *Ein Achtundvierziger* (Brooklyn, 1882) p. 234.

2. *Atlantis* (Dec. 1855) III (N.S.) pp. 440-41, 468-69.

3. See *New Yorker Staatszeitung*, Jan. 5, 1850; June 16, 22, 1854; *Belletristisches Journal*, Oct. 26, Dec. 14, 1860; and Franz Josef Egenter: *Amerika ohne Schminke; Eine Quellensammlung zur Darstellung des amerikanischen Lebens in der Wirklichkeit* (Zurich, 1857).

4. *New Yorker Staatszeitung*, Nov. 29, 1850.

5. Lonn: *Foreigners in the Confederacy*, p. 3.

6. *Der Deutsche Pionier*, I, 46-50.

7. Börnstein: *Memoiren*, II, 222.

8. *Cleveland und sein Deutschtum*, p. 97.

9. *Belletristisches Journal*, March 21, 1856; see also April 17, 1857; and *Westbote*, Sept. 19, 1856.

10. *Wächter am Erie*, Feb. 13, 1868; *Westbote*, May 22, 1872.

11. *Die Republik der Arbeiter*, June 12, 1852.

12. *Die Republik der Arbeiter*, June 10, 1854.

13. *Westbote*, June 24, 1853.

14. Börnstein: *Memoiren*, II, pp. 120-23.

15. *Westbote*, July 8, 1853.

16. *Belletristisches Journal*, July 24, 1857; July 30, 1858; *New Yorker Staatszeitung*, July 28, 1858; June 30, 1859; June 16, 1860.

17. *Westbote*, Aug. 26, 1858; and *Belletristisches Journal*, July 23, 1858; Dec. 3, 1858.

18. *Westbote*, Dec. 30, 1853; Dec. 19, 1856; Dec. 27, 1860.

19. *Wächter am Erie*, Dec. 27, 1875, also Jan. 5, 1875.

20. See "The Christmas Tree Legend," in *The American German Review* (Dec. 1948) XV, No. 2, p. 8; Hertha Pauli: *The Story of the Christmas Tree* (Boston, 1944) p. 3; Elbert J. Benton: *Cultural Story of an American City, Cleveland, Part III* (Cleveland, 1946) p. 26. Also Western Reserve, *The Historical Society News* (Cleveland) IV, No. 12, Dec. 1949.

21. See Börnstein: *Memoiren* II, 222-23; C. F. Huch: "Das deutsche Theater in Philadelphia vor dem Bürgerkriege," in *Mitteilungen des Deutschen Pionier Vereins von Philadelphia*, VI (1907) pp. 13-31; and Fritz A. H. Leucks: *The Early German Theatre in New York, 1840-1872* (New York, 1928) pp. 18-47.

22. *Westbote*, Jan. 11, 1856.

23. *Intimate Letters*, p. 151.

24. Max Stern and Fred Kressmann: *Chicago's Deutsche Männer* (Chicago, 1885) pp. 37-38.

25. See Esther M. Olson: "The German Theatre in Chicago," in *Deutsch-Amerikanische Geschichtsblätter* (1937) XXXIII, 68-123; A. J. Townsend: *The Germans of Chicago*, p. 125.

26. Leucks: *op. cit.*, p. 62.

27. *New Yorker Staatszeitung*, Dec. 10, 1853.

28. Leucks: *op. cit.*, pp. 75-99.

29. Alfred H. Nolle: "The German Drama on the St. Louis Stage," in *German-American Annals*, XV, 28-65; also Börnstein: *op. cit.*, II, 221-26; 238-46.

30. *Cincinnati Enquirer*, April 21, 1853.

31. *Wächter am Erie*, April 5, 1875.

32. Ralph Wood: "Geschichte des Deutschen Theaters von Cincinnati," in *Deutsch-Amerikanische Geschichtsblätter* (1932) XXXII, 411-522.

33. *Wächter am Erie*, Nov. 15, 1862; also *Das Deutsche Theater* in *Davenport* (Davenport, 1906) pp. 6-7; and Richter: *Geschichte der Stadt Davenport*, pp. 618-51.

34. *Wächter am Erie*, Aug. 28, 1869; Biesele: *Germans in Texas*, p. 221.

35. *Mitteilungen des Deutschen Pionier Vereins von Philadelphia*, XVII (1910) pp. 1-13.

36. *Akron Times-Press*, June 23, 1930; June 4, 1933.

37. For a list, see *Mitteilungen des Deutschen Pionier Vereins von Philadelphia*, I (1906) pp. 1-32.

38. Biesele: *op. cit.*, p. 222.

39. *New Yorker Staatszeitung*, June 18, 1850.

40. C. F. Huch: "Die ersten deutschen Sängerfeste in Amerika," in *Mitteilungen des Deutschen Pionier Vereins von Philadelphia*, XIX (1911) pp. 1-15; also I (1906) pp. 1-32.

41. *New Yorker Staatszeitung*, May 26, 1854.

42. *Ibid.*, June 30, 1855; *Belletristisches Journal*, June 29, 1855.

43. Townsend: *The Germans of Chicago*, p. 121.

44. Klauprecht: *Deutsche Chronik*, p. 182.

45. *Westbote*, June 11, 1852, and *Die Republik der Arbeiter*, June 26, 1852.

46. *Westbote*, July 3, 1857.

47. *New Yorker Staatszeitung*, July 1, 1858.

48. *Cleveland Leader*, June 18, 1859; also *Cleveland Herald*, June 18, 1859.

49. Rudolf Glanz: *op. cit.*, p. 33. When Philo Jacoby, editor of the *Hebrew*, won numerous prizes in Germany as a representative of the San Francisco *Turnverein* and shooting club, the German-American press pointed with pride to his achievements. *Westbote*, Sept. 6, 1873.

50. See C. F. Huch: "Das siebente allgemeine Sängerfest in Philadelphia, 1857" in *Mitteilungen des Deutschen Pionier Vereins von Philadelphia*, XXIV (1912) pp. 16-25.

51. *Cleveland Express*, referred to in *Cleveland Leader*, May 31, 1855.

52. *Wächter am Erie*, Aug. 15, 1867.

53. Pierce: *History of Chicago*, II, 425.

54. *Wächter am Erie*, July 1, 1871.

55. See *Wächter am Erie*, June 17, June 26, 29, 1874; also *Westbote*, April 30, 1873.

56. Quoted in *Westbote*, June 26, 1872.

57. Still: *Milwaukee*, pp. 115-19.

58. *Wächter am Erie*, June 15, 1853.

59. Stierlin: *Kentucky*, pp. 138-40.

60. *Der Deutsche Pionier*, XVI (No. 4, July 1884) pp. 163-64.

61. *Ibid.*, XII, No. 7 (Oct. 1880) pp. 280-81.

Chapter 20 · *LEARNING AND LETTERS*

To the better-educated immigrants among the German Forty-eighters the American educational system seemed sorely in need of improvement. Some were ready to admit that the average education of the masses probably was better in the United States than in Germany, but textbooks were poor and the curriculum one-sided, narrow, and superficial, with too much stress on the utilitarian, and even in the larger cities classes were held in poorly constructed and poorly equipped schoolhouses. It came as a severe shock to Europeans when they learned that teachers in America were paid less than day laborers, and that teaching methods were almost completely unaffected by modern European pedagogical theories, and consisted largely of the mechanical routine of simple questions and answers, after the fashion of a catechism. Physical education was not included in the curriculum of most schools, and it was a rare American pedagogue who had ever heard of Fröbel or Pestalozzi. Many Forty-eighters were qualified for teaching positions, and some had had experience as teachers in German schoolrooms. Many a refugee made his living in the early months after his arrival by teaching in the schools or as a private tutor in American families.

From New York to Iowa the German-language press, aroused from its lethargy by the editorial talent of Forty-eighters, pleaded for better educational facilities for the children of German immigrants, and enthusiastically supported projects to raise funds for German private schools. In New York delegates of Weitling's Workingmen's League joined with Turner, freethinking and other German societies to demand better instruction, especially in the sciences, and many organizations eventually established schools of their own. In Wisconsin "Forty-eighter schools" in-

300

fluenced the curriculum from kindergarten to higher schools resembling the German gymnasium. Teachers introduced new texts, sometimes their own, applied the theories of European pedagogues, and in many areas maintained standards of education superior to those of the neighborhood.[1]

Part of the demand for separate German schools arose from the desire to preserve the German language in the United States and have it taught to the children of immigrants. Not all Forty-eighters believed that German-Americans could be made bilingual, however. Esselen, for example, favored public schools with English as the language of instruction, and argued for tax-supported institutions which would function as agencies of Americanization to unify the various nationality groups. He stressed the need for uniform pedagogical methods, a standard curriculum, a system of secondary education like the French lycée or the German gymnasium, teacher-training schools and a university to prepare teachers for the public schools, but he did not advocate priority for the German language in the course of study.[2]

Dr. Adolf Douai, one of the outstanding refugee pedagogues of 1848, realized that the future of the German nationality group depended upon their ability to preserve the German language. Although he would have preferred maintaining both languages, he was sufficiently realistic to know that children of immigrants prefer English, and that public schools are easier to support than private schools. Hermann Raster opposed legislation which would force all schools to use English as the language of instruction, and Douai pointed to the Pennsylvania Germans as a horrible example of what happened when immigrants gave up their native tongue and consequently lost all "significance in the intellectual progress of America." Weitling, although urging his followers to teach their children German, "the spiritual music of the inner life of a people," admitted that time and conditions in a new country would eventually defeat their hopes to preserve their mother tongue. Few immigrants of either the first or second generation became truly bilingual. To most of the second generation the language of their fathers no longer communicated live cultural values, and became an encumbrance rather than an advantage. German schools established by Forty-eighters after the middle of the last century had a cosmopolitan character and objective that went far beyond a desire to perpetuate a national German culture in the United States.

In New York City, Rösler von Oels, with eleven years' teaching experience in the German gymnasium, founded a German school in 1850 which was continued after his financial failure by Dr. Eduard Feldner and others who shared his liberal views. In a barren schoolroom with meager equipment and furniture, Rösler von Oels provided excellent instruction on the elementary level for a pitifully low tuition fee which parents tried to scale down still further by demanding secret rebates, apparently on the theory that the school was a charitable plan to help "green Forty-eighters" make a living in the United States. Feldner kept the school alive for nearly four years after its founder left New York, and in 1854 opened a German boarding school in Hoboken.[3] In 1855 Dr. Rudolf Dulon acquired the Feldner school. The new director's earlier activities in politics and religion had made him a highly controversial figure in German-American circles, but his severest critics agreed that the school was a model institution, staffed by well-qualified teachers recruited largely among fellow refugees. Dulon's daughter was the principal teacher in the elementary class, and Franz Sigel instructed in the higher grades. Examinations were conducted in public in the Shakespeare Hotel; distinguished refugees, like Struve, addressed the student body on such occasions, and the enrollment reached 250 in two years' time. The school survived to the outbreak of the Civil War. Its elementary classes were more successful than the higher grades, in part because attendance on the upper levels was small and parents frequently put their children to work before they had completed the course of study. In 1866 Dulon became director of a German *Realschule* in Rochester, and shortly before his death in 1870 published a significant volume on *The German School in America*.[4]

The best-known private school in Baltimore was "F. Knapp's German and English Institute," which opened its doors in 1853 with sixty pupils. By 1860 the enrollment reached 650, and included all school-age groups. One hundred and fifty came from American families and the student body included several Jewish children. Friedrich Knapp, the director and founder, was a Württemberger who taught in the schools of Reutlingen in 1840. In 1848 he lost his position because of his republican principles, was hailed into court on a charge of treason which could not be proved, and finally demoted to a school in a remote and tiny village. In 1850 Knapp arrived in the United States and began his American career as a private tutor and bookkeeper in Baltimore for William A. Marburg. Before opening his own school in 1853 he was principal of the German Reformed parochial school. The Knapp Institute was open to children of all faiths and nationalities, and was conducted according to the theories of Pestalozzi. On its staff were several refugees, including Heinrich Lohmann of Bremen, who died in Baltimore in 1889.[5] Henry L. Mencken has described Knapp's School in its declining years in his reminiscences, *Happy Days,* published in New York in 1940. In Mencken's day Knapp "still wore . . . the classical uniform of a German schoolmaster—a longtailed coat of black alpaca, a boiled shirt with somewhat fringy cuffs, and a white lawn necktie," and the old "Suabian," with "closely-clipped mutton-chop whiskers" still opened each session with songs which he conducted with his violin while his daughter played the parlor organ.

In St. Louis in 1860, Franz Sigel was one of a staff of four teachers in the German *Realschule,* and Emma Pösche, wife of the director, conducted a boarding school for girls in affiliation with the main institution.[6] Louisville supported a German-English school in the 1850's,[7] and in 1852 R. Dollmätsch, an eccentric refugee from Baden, who described himself as an "architect, engineer and geometer," opened a school to teach mechanical drawing, and apparently did most of his instructing on Sunday.[8]

In Milwaukee the Forty-eighters were prime movers in launching the Milwaukee *Schulverein* and in founding and supporting Peter Engelmann's famous German-English Academy. Engelmann had studied at the universities of Berlin and Heidelberg, had taught in the gymnasium at Kreuznach, and had edited a revolutionary newspaper in Germany. Before settling in Milwaukee in 1850 he had been an unsuccessful Latin farmer in the East. He opened his school in Milwaukee in July 1851, with forty children. In 1865 it reached a peak enrollment of 450, divided into eleven classes with sixteen teachers. The director's salary at the beginning was twenty-five dollars a month, and the tuition seventy-five cents to a dollar a month. Night classes were added for a fee of $1.50 a month. Engelmann was one of America's ablest pedagogues and a man of unusually broad interests and learning. For a quarter of a century he directed what many Milwaukeeans, regardless of national origin, considered the best school in the city. Its pedagogical methods influenced the Milwaukee public schools, and its curriculum included physical education and manual training, singing and drawing, and emphasized rational methods of pedagogy instead of mere learning by rote. In 1857, with a score of intellectual

Germans, Engelmann organized a Society for Natural Sciences, to collect specimens for a scientific museum, and the Society became known as Engelmann's Museum of History and in 1880 was incorporated as the Wisconsin Natural History Society. Two years later its collections were presented to the city of Milwaukee, and in due time the institution became a municipal museum under Carl Dörflinger, its first director.[9] Although Engelmann's school overshadowed all others, mention must again be made of the girls' school, organized in Milwaukee by the German feminist, Mathilde Anneke.[10]

In general, the influence of Forty-eighters on education was more pronounced in the West than in the East, although everywhere the flowering time for German private schools falls definitely in the Forty-eighter era. The Revolution made well-trained German teachers available for American schools, and the private school movement was supported by *Turnvereine,* organizations of German workingmen and other German groups. Wherever such societies were too weak to support an entire curriculum they frequently sponsored classes for children on Saturday or Sunday and for adults after working hours. Forty-eighters helped awaken the German artisan class for a campaign for better schools for their children, and the workers responded eagerly to their appeals. School festivals, fairs, bazaars, picnics, and other devices to raise money were familiar activities in German-American communities to collect funds for privately supported schools.[11]

Militant freethinkers considered it especially important to establish free schools where children would be uncontaminated by theology or sectarianism. It was a major objective of the rationalists to promote schools as part of their program of enlightenment, and many of their educational projects had the support of the *Turnvereine.* Free schools were organized in New York in the 1850's by such Forty-eighters as Struve and Professor Füster, and when the cornerstone for the Free German School of New York City was laid, and at the dedication exercises of the building somewhat later, prominent Forty-eighters, including Struve, Füster, Dr. Försch, Ottendörfer, Wiesner, and Hugo Wesendonck made addresses. Within a year the enrollment reached one thousand.[12]

Alexander Loos, a former student of theology and a refugee from Prussia, taught in the school of the *Freie Gemeinde* of Jersey City in

1852.[13] Wilhelm Müller, another refugee and author of a volume of *Radical Essays,* was a teacher in the school of the Social Democratic *Turnverein* of Baltimore.[14] Johann Straubenmüller, an outstanding German-American pedagogue from Württemberg, directed the "Free German School" in New York in 1863.[15] The first teacher of a similar school in Davenport, Iowa, was Johann Heinrich True, a radical from Hanover.[16] In 1852 a German-American school was organized in Louisville, and two years later had an enrollment of 245. It provided education completely divorced from religion, and managed to survive despite financial troubles until 1863. The freemen's society of St. Louis, under the dynamic leadership of Börnstein, supported a school which conducted evening classes for adults and a lecture series on scientific and cultural subjects. A similar society in Cleveland opened a school in 1853 with thirty pupils, one teacher, and an assistant instructor in physical education. "Everything papal and reactionary," to use the words of the *Wächter am Erie,* was excluded from the curriculum, and English received equal attention with German.[17] The school developed to include all grades and, in the traditional German manner conducted its examinations in public.[18]

A catalogue of German refugees who taught in private or public schools in America would be surprisingly long. Besides the outstanding pedagogues already mentioned, it would include a former director of the Rhenish *Sängerbund,* who taught in Rochester; Heinrich Grube, a member of the Frankfurt Parliament;[19] E. F. M. Fähtz, an Austrian revolutionist who taught in Maryland and Pennsylvania; Dr. Peter Unger, a Forty-eighter on the staff of Baltimore City College from 1855 to 1857;[20] J. S. Kahrmann, a member of several faculties, including that of the Free German School of Davenport, supported by such Forty-eighters as Hans Reimer Claussen, Heinrich Köhler, and Heinrich Lambach.[21] Karl Söhner, a friend of Hecker, Itzstein, and Brentano, and civil administrator for one of the districts of Baden in 1849, taught languages and music in Indianapolis after 1850, and supplemented his salary by selling musical instruments and sheet music.[22] Alexander Jakob Schem, a Westphalian who studied at Bonn and Tübingen, was professor of languages at Dickinson College, Pennsylvania, contributed to several encyclopedias and the New York *Tribune Almanac,* published an eleven-volume *Deutsch-Amerikanisches Konversations Lexikon* in 1873, and was superintendent of German instruction in the city schools of New York for seven years.

Anton Eickhoff (1827-1901) another refugee from Westphalia, taught at St. Louis University before turning to politics and journalism.[23] Two private German schools were organized in New Braunfels, Texas, in 1852 and 1853. In 1863 Leopold Biesele, a young lieutenant in the revolutionary levies of 1849, became a teacher in Texas at $250 a year, and remained in the school system of the state for twenty years.[24]

Adolf Douai, the versatile Forty-eighter, was outstanding both in journalism and education. He established German-American schools in New Braunfels and Boston, and also taught in New York and Hoboken. His publications in the field of education include a German grammar, a phonetic primer, readers specially designed for schools supported by Turner, a book on the kindergarten, another on physical education, an outline of history, and a philosophical work, *The Idea of God*. Men of such catholic interests and intellectual stature had standards for the teaching profession, introduced new methods, helped enrich the curriculum, broke new ground in the field of adult education, and would have made significant contributions to any age.

Practically every German immigrant indoctrinated in the fatherland with the value of physical exercise advocated the introduction of physical education into the American curriculum, and the *Turnvereine* for years provided the directors of physical education for city schools. Eduard Schultz, who fought in Baden and the Palatinate, probably was the first instructor in physical education *(Turn-unterricht)* in Milwaukee where he conducted his first class in Becker's *Café français*. Later, in collaboration with Fritz Anneke, another devoted Turner, he developed a bath house, swimming pool, school, and riding academy.[25] Heinrich Lohmann, a teacher in Knapp's Institute in Baltimore, taught fencing, swimming, and physical education in several cities, and supplemented his income from school teaching by selling cigars.[26] Gymnasia were established features of schools like Knapp's and Engelmann's. In 1868 the *Turnvereine* opened a seminary in New York to train teachers of physical education. In 1870 the school was moved to Chicago and, after the Chicago fire, to Milwaukee, where under its famous director G. Brosius, it offered a teacher-training program which stressed not only physical and health education and dietetics, but sciences, languages, music, and cultural history as well.[27] The demand for physical education in the American school curriculum was strongly supported in the German-language press.

The *Kindergarten,* as the retention of the name in its German form implies, was another educational innovation of the Germans in the 1850's. The institution is based on the theories of Friedrich Fröbel, who prophesied that only Americans would understand his new techniques and recognize their importance. In the early 1850's the German-American press was discussing the kindergarten as an educational innovation, and a small brochure dealing with the subject was published by Wiebe, Lindemann, and Loos in 1852.[28] The controversy about who taught the first kindergarten in America remains unsettled. The wife of Carl Schurz listened to Fröbel's lectures in Hamburg in 1849, and her sister, Madame Ronge, established a kindergarten in Manchester, England. As a girl of seventeen, the future Mrs. Schurz was connected for a short time with another kindergarten opened by her sister in London. It may be that Mrs. Schurz operated a kindergarten on a small scale for her children and others from the neighborhood in Watertown, Wisconsin, in 1856. The statement repeated in many textbooks on the history of education that she began the Watertown experiment a year earlier may be challenged, however, because Mrs. Schurz spent little, if any, time in Wisconsin in 1855 and was in Europe during most of the year, recuperating from an illness. We know that Mrs. Schurz interested Elizabeth Peabody of Boston in her project in 1859, and that Dr. Henry Barnard heard Madame Ronge lecture in England in 1854, while attending the International Exhibit of Educational Systems, for he recounted his observations two years later in his *American Journal of Education.* Miss Peabody began editing the *Kindergarten Messenger* in 1873, an important contribution to American educational literature which contained many translations from German sources. Miss Peabody lectured widely and was primarily responsible for the demonstration school established at the Philadelphia Centennial Exposition in 1876.

Caroline Louise Frankenberg, who also learned the kindergarten technique under Fröbel in Germany, opened a "play school" in Columbus in 1858, and the kindergarten connected with Douai's Academy in Hoboken was organized in 1861.[29] Wilhelm Riepe, a Westphalian whose European career was ruined by the Revolution, established the first kindergarten in Davenport in connection with a private school in which he made several significant educational experiments.[30] In 1860 a New York paper urged the formation of a national organization to support "this flower of the German spirit." The kindergarten in the first ward of Milwaukee had an enrollment of seventy-two pupils in 1872, and a year later the first publicly supported kindergarten was established in St. Louis.[31]

To perpetuate German influence in American education, it was necessary to establish training schools for teachers to replace the pioneers when they retired. As early as 1837, German leaders in convention in Pittsburgh advocated a teachers' seminary and authorized a committee to raise the necessary funds. Such an institution actually opened its doors in 1841, only to collapse almost immediately. Arnold Ruge wrote from England to urge the founding of a university on the German model, and plans to that end were initiated in several cities including Cincinnati, where German Jews were enthusiastic for the project. In 1858, when a delegation of Chicago Germans went to Leipzig to recruit teachers, the press revived the agitation for a German university in the United States.[32] In 1860 an appeal for a German-American Teachers' Seminary appeared in the German-language press signed by such outstanding Forty-eighters as Schurz, Kapp, Schünemann-Pott, Butz, Douai, Solger, Dulon, Thieme, Domschke, Hecker, Kiefer, and Ludwig Greiner of Newark, New Jersey, as well as representatives of the older immigration such as Körner, Stallo, and Münch.[33] In Detroit, Dr. Hermann Kiefer was primarily responsible for the establishment of a local seminary which survived for a decade after 1861.

Actually, the movement made little progress on a national scale until 1870, when it received new strength from the spirit of national pride awakened among German-Americans by the Franco-Prussian War. In August 1870, 117 German-American teachers, men and women, recruited largely from the declining faculties of the private schools, met in Louisville to organize a German-American Teachers' Federation. The Federation met annually thereafter, and its activities were marked by significant discussions of pedagogical problems and the publication of a journal of high quality. Throughout its existence the group was suspected by the nativists and under fire from the clergy and the advocates of parochial schools because it stressed the complete separation of church and state and opposed Bible reading and hymn singing in the schools. At a meeting in Detroit in 1874, in which Douai and Madame Anneke were prominent, the delegates appealed for support for a German-American

Teachers' Seminary and appointed a committee headed by Douai to push the project to a conclusion.[34] In 1876 many German papers urged that an appropriate gift by German-Americans on the occasion of the Centennial of the birth of their adopted country would be a good teachers' seminary. Forty-eighters like Ottendörfer, Tellkampf, and Wesendonck sponsored the appeal for funds. Wesendonck helped organize a Seminary Society in New York, and in Cleveland a German workers' society collected contributions for the project.

Despite the panic of 1873 and the long depression which followed, and although German was being taught in many public schools, the *Nationale Deutschamerikanische Lehrer Seminar* opened its doors in Milwaukee in 1878, and absorbed Engelmann's German-English Academy as its preparatory department. From 1891 to 1907 the teachers' seminary had an affiliation with the *Turnlehrer Seminar,* which prepared teachers of physical education. Because the seminary was supported primarily by the freethinking element it never gained favor with German Catholics or Lutherans. In later years the Milwaukee Teachers' Seminary received some support from the German-American National Alliance. In 1919 it closed its doors, a casualty of Americanization and the hysteria of World War I, and in 1926 the school organization, with its library and an excellent publication, the *Monatshefte für Deutschen Unterricht,* was amalgamated with the German department of the University of Wisconsin.

The lecture platform was another vehicle to carry the message of Forty-eighters to German audiences. Some believed their lecture fees would support them and their families; others hoped to use the platform to raise funds for various projects. The number who felt qualified to go on the lecture circuit was surprisingly large, and the subjects on which they were prepared to discourse was even larger. Unfortunately their remuneration was pitifully small, and their hopes soon turned to ashes. Few had the drawing power or the ability as public speakers of a Hecker or a Schurz.

In 1855 Julius Fröbel, Solger, and Wislicenus gave a series of lectures in the hall of the New York Mercantile Library. Cincinnati had a series on natural science in the Turner Hall, and in Dubuque, George Hillgärtner opened a series of twelve lectures under the auspices of the *Turnverein.* Lyceums, lecture courses, and public debates were held in such outlying places as Kenosha, Wisconsin, and other towns on the frontier which had attracted political refugees.[35] Dr. Löwe discoursed on Freiherr von Stein, the early Prussian reformer, in New York in 1859; Struve on the House of Habsburg and "Human Progress," and Wiesner on the German Pioneers of Pennsylvania, and the English Revolution. As early as 1850, Anneke and his wife recounted their experiences in the Revolution to American audiences, but when Madame Anneke had the temerity to speak for equal rights for women, Kapp dismissed her arguments as "mere phrases."[36] Dowiat talked to audiences in Pittsburgh and Washington in 1858 on "The Secret History of the Revolution of 1848." Kapp lectured on Baron von Steuben and German immigration, preparatory to publishing notable volumes on both subjects. Dr. Kellner frequently appeared as a speaker in the Shakespeare Hotel in New York, and before his fellow Germans in Philadelphia, and a military organization in New York invited Germain Metternich to talk about instruments of warfare, and Sigel about problems of immigration. Dr. Füster dealt mostly with cultural history. In 1856 the German Reading Club of New York sponsored a series of addresses by Kapp, Dulon, Wiesner, Heinzen, Jacobi, Dr. Schramm, and other prominent refugees.[37]

Rapp and Solger were especially popular with the Turner of Baltimore before the Civil War; Hassaurek and Willich spoke frequently under similar auspices in Cincinnati. Hecker's appeal to German audiences did not diminish with the years, and as late as 1875 when he lectured on subjects from mythology and archaeology to modern feminism, the "old Forty-eighters" turned out to hear him for an admission fee of twenty-five cents.[38] August Willich lectured to the Humboldt Verein of Columbus in 1873 on "The Origin, History and Destiny of Man in the Light of Humboldt's Cosmos," but the local German paper reported that the talk was too philosophical and scientific and the audience disappointingly small.[39] Heinzen spoke on many topics, and although his material makes good reading on the printed page, he was a poor public speaker and usually spoke while seated. His lecture tours were signal failures, and left him, to use his own words, "richer in enemies and poorer in cash."[40] Esselen had much the same experience despite the rich content of his lectures, and agreed with Heinzen that German audiences had to be educated to follow serious discussions and appeals to reason, rather than oratory.

The most successful Forty-eighter in the lecture hall, with the exception of Schurz and Hecker, was Reinhold Solger. This gifted scholar and author was born in Stettin in 1817 and died in the United States shortly after the close of the Civil War. The son of a Prussian bureaucrat, Solger was educated at Greisfwald and Halle, and moved in the circle of Ruge and the Neo-Hegelians. In 1843 he was a tutor in England; in 1847 he met Bakunin, Herwegh, Herzen, and Bernays in Paris. In 1848 he served as interpreter and translator for General Mieroslawski and went with the defeated rebels into Switzerland. In Bern he lectured on English literature, and in Zürich he helped establish a German periodical. In 1852 he met Carlyle, Bulwer, and Dickens in England. In 1853 he arrived in Philadelphia, and after a short stay, moved to Boston, which became his American home. Except for two years during the Civil War spent in the Treasury Department in Washington, Solger made his living by writing and lecturing, especially in the field of history and German philosophy, and in 1861 he ventured into the relatively new field of comparative and constitutional law. His command of English was excellent, and he spoke with idiomatic correctness, power, and elegance. In 1857 and 1859 he was invited to give the Lowell Institute Lectures in Boston.[41]

To men of such intellectual interests, the hundredth anniversaries of Schiller's birth in 1859 and that of Alexander von Humboldt ten years later provided an opportunity to honor two great Germans and impress their American countrymen with the distinguished achievements of German literature and scholarship. Interestingly enough, the hundredth anniversary of Goethe's birth produced no echoes in America, and few in Germany, for that matter. But the anniversary of Friedrich Schiller, author of *Wilhelm Tell,* and a champion of freedom, in contrast with Goethe, "the hireling of princes," aroused real enthusiasm among the Germans of the United States. Along with Freiligrath, Herwegh, and Heine, Schiller was a favorite of the Forty-eighters, and the Schiller anniversary celebrations were largely their work, although the older immigration joined in the festivities. Kapp concluded that with the Schiller celebrations the Germans in America reached "the high point of their development and spiritual significance for the United States," and the "end of an epoch in the history of German immigration."

In New York the festivities began with a dramatic performance of a piece written by Germain Metternich dealing with Schiller's birth, and a symphony concert in Cooper Institute. Speakers at the commemoration exercises included Dr. Löwe, Dr. Karl Schramm, and Dr. A. Wiesner, well-known Forty-eighter intellectuals. William Cullen Bryant represented the American literary world, and the prize for the best original poem went to Dr. Reinhold Solger, the principal speaker at the Boston celebration. A special Schiller number of the New York *Illustrierte Zeitung* sold thirty thousand copies on the day of issue. The building of the *New Yorker Staatszeitung* was illuminated for the occasion, and the *New Yorker Criminal Zeitung und Belletristisches Journal* wrote enthusiastically "ten years ago this would have been impossible. Our nationality group will not perish in America," and suggested that celebrations in honor of Schiller and Robert Blum be made annual affairs.[42]

In St. Louis, plans for a Schiller fest were temporarily delayed because of uncomplimentary references in the columns of the *Westliche Post* to Börnstein's eagerness to be master of ceremonies, but when the day came the newspaper rivalry between *Westliche Post* and *Anzeiger des Westens* was forgotten and the Germans staged a celebration which began with artillery salvos at dawn and ended with fireworks and an entertainment in the hall of the Mercantile Library, at which Ruppius directed the music and Börnstein read an address prepared by Arnold Ruge.[43] In Columbus the festivities continued for several days, and a performance of *Wilhelm Tell* was followed by a banquet with toasts to Schiller, German literature, the fatherland, the ladies, and Alexander von Humboldt, and the reading of a poem by Freiligrath.[44] The Germans of Philadelphia celebrated with a torchlight parade and floats, including one representing Schiller's famous poem, "The Bell." The houses were illuminated and draped with bunting and the halls decorated with busts of the poet. Dr. Kellner made the principal address. Similar festivities marked the occasion in Cincinnati. In Hoboken *Don Carlos* was performed and Dr. Feldner was the principal orator. Brentano made the main address in Chicago, and Butz recited an original poem. Dr. Kiefer spoke in Detroit. In Milwaukee Schurz was the orator of the occasion. In New Orleans several of Schiller's plays were produced in German, and the German societies paraded with three bands. The main float carried a bust of the poet in a Temple of the Muses, with the names of Goethe, Lessing, Irving, and Cooper inscribed on its four sides and a statue symbolizing immortality in the center. The festivities ended with music and oratory in St. Charles Theatre, and a concert and ball in the

Odd Fellows Hall. A bust of Schiller, presented to the city, stood in Fillmore Square until 1864.[45] In Yorktown, Texas, twenty-one Germans managed to produce *The Bride of Messina*,[46] and in little Greenville, Mississippi, the German singing society arranged a Schiller Fest. In Richmond, Virginia, the celebration extended over three days. Special memorial medals were sold and the proceeds used for libraries of German literature; German language papers issued special editions, German restaurants gave free meals to the poor, and German bakers and housewives prepared baked goods, known as "Schiller Torten."

The hundredth anniversary of the birth of Humboldt in 1869 made a strong appeal to liberal-minded German-Americans, but the occasion did not develop into a great German national festival like the Schiller celebrations a decade earlier, although it had the enthusiastic support of the German press. In Cincinnati the Brewers' Association contributed $500 toward the expenses of an appropriate celebration. In Boston the Germans considered raising a scholarship in the natural sciences; in Newark, New Jersey, they discussed the founding of a German hospital, and in St. Louis the establishment of either an observatory or a botanical garden, projects obviously appropriate to the memory of the great scientist. In New York and Pittsburgh there was strong support for a monument to Humboldt. Milwaukee, Chicago, and Detroit proposed the creation of a university on the German model. The Germans of Cleveland promoted a Humboldt Library, and in Detroit Dr. Kiefer urged a Central Planning Committee to mobilize German-Americans for the support of "Cosmos Societies," a museum, and lectures by distinguished German scientists such as Vogt, Büchner, and Moleschott.[47]

The *Humboldt Feier* of Cleveland was a typical German-American folk festival. A concert on the evening of September 13 was followed by a parade the following morning, inaugurated by artillery fire at daybreak. The parade consisted of four divisions, with bands and floats, and the nineteen societies represented included the Hebrew Literary Association, Slovenske Lipa, the Free German School, and the German veterans of the Civil War. The marchers proceeded to the Rink, where an orchestra played, the singing societies performed, and one of Butz's poems was read. In full view of the audience, a bust of Humboldt was decorated with great solemnity, and in English and German speeches the great naturalist was lauded as "the high priest of German science and learning," who "belongs to the world" and whose research "penetrated heaven and earth, broke the bonds of superstition and fixed our eyes on the true destiny of man." Nevertheless the editor of the local German paper found it necessary to comment on the lack of respect and dignity of the audience. The celebration concluded with a banquet and a ball, and toasts in German and English.[48] Heinzen referred to the Humboldt parade in New York as "conceived in beer and buried in beer." He prepared a special lecture on the contributions of the great agnostic to human well-being in which he referred to Humboldt as "the scientific Columbus of the Western Hemisphere," "the great liberator" who never "degraded natural science by making her a handmaiden of theology."[49]

The development of libraries and the book trade is further evidence of the intellectual and cultural renaissance among the American Germans after 1848. In 1845, when Philip Schaff traveled in the United States, he found it difficult to buy German books or to receive German periodicals with any degree of regularity. Both the *New Yorker Staatszeitung* and the *New Yorker Criminal Zeitung und Belletristisches Journal* commented on the great increase in the book trade as early as 1853, and attributed the change to the heavy recent immigration of men "who are transplanting German science and enterprise" to America.[50]

In 1852 Maas and Cursch, German publishers of Philadelphia, announced a German edition of the complete works of Thomas Paine. Friedrich Wilhelm Thomas, a venturesome publisher of the 1850's who specialized in cheap editions, sold editions of Schiller, Goethe, Lessing, Zschokke, Heine, Uhland, and Shakespeare, and a German version of *Uncle Tom's Cabin* by Adolf Strodtmann, and published editions of Heinrich Zschokke and Humboldt in installments every week or two at ten cents a copy, then reissued the series in book form. In 1869 he sold many copies of the jubilee edition of Humboldt's *Kosmos*.[51] John Weik, a New York publisher, published an "American Popular Library of German Classics" beginning with Heine, at the rate of a hundred pages every two weeks at twenty-five cents a copy, and apparently sold enough copies to make the venture pay.[52] By 1855 there were at least four respectable German bookstores in New York, as many in Philadelphia, and two in Cincinnati. Goethe and other authors appeared in installments in the *feuilleton* of German newspapers, and in the halcyon days of literary piracy, when there were no adequate copyright laws, the latest works of European authors were published in cheap American editions shortly after their appearance abroad. Heine's works were issued in Philadelphia in 1854; Luft, Bickler and Company of Milwaukee printed a cheap edition of the complete works of Ludwig Börne in 1858; and Freiligrath's volumes were available in a New York edition two years earlier.

The boom in the publishing business undoubtedly was affected by the sudden increase in the number of interested German readers. Kapp reported finding editions of the German masters in the blockhouses of "Latin farmers," and described an auction of Freiligrath's works in a Forty-eighter settlement in the Northwest, where payments were made with wood, flour, and other products. The auctioneer had been a teacher in the Palatinate before he was accused of radicalism, and among those attending the sale were a *Juris doctor* of Darmstadt, a former justice from Hesse who was a "Latin farmer" in the West, a tailor expelled from Dresden at the time of the Revolution, and a doctor who was a veteran of the Hungarian Army.[53] Esselen insisted that more German classics were sold in the United States than in Germany, and added, "Schiller, Goethe and the other classicists are to be found in thousands of copies in the huts of workers, on the counters of merchants, in the blockhouses of the western farmers." He suggested publishing an inexpensive edition of Feuerbach's *The Nature of Christianity* to be sold with the works of Paine and Humboldt, and because America had few public libraries he recommended that his readers buy the *Brockhaus Conversations Lexikon,* available from a Cincinnati bookdealer at fifteen dollars.[54]

German reading societies *(Lesevereine)* sprang up in many cities with the primary objective of developing subscription libraries. Börnstein promoted a reading room, modeled on the Parisian *cabinet de lecture,* above an apothecary's shop in St. Louis, where maps, lexicons, newspapers and journals were available at five cents a visit. The "German Reading and Educational Society" of St. Paul *(Lese und Bildungsverein),* founded in 1852, subscribed to the leading German-language papers of New York, Boston, St. Louis, and Cincinnati. Before the end of the decade, Brandeis and Hartmann were operating a successful German loan library in New York, and under the prodding of labor reformers like Weitling and others, German workers supported reading rooms and libraries in their workers' halls.

Finally, the amazing literary output of the Forty-eighters themselves must be briefly noted. Gustav Struve, identified with many ventures in journalism and German-American literature, finished his *World History* in 1860, the *magnum opus* of his career and the culmination of thirty years of study and research. The *New Yorker Criminal Zeitung und Belletristisches Journal* once referred to it as "the first flower of German-American literature—an education in freedom."[55] Struve also published a volume on *The Age of Revolution,* beginning with 1789, but his tragedy, *Abelard and Heloise,* written in collaboration with his wife, proved less successful. Kapp's biography of von Steuben was reissued in an English translation with a foreword by George Bancroft. Among other works of this prolific Forty-eighter was a biography of General de Kalb, a history of German immigration, and several volumes on American themes which he published after his return to Germany. Eduard Pelz is best remembered for his literary sketches of emigration and immigrant life, though he wrote on many other subjects. Adolf Douai, among other books, wrote *Fata Morgana,* a novel of no great literary distinction which was awarded first prize in a competition sponsored by the *Anzeiger des Westens.* Solger, in 1862, won a prize offered by the *New Yorker Criminal Zeitung und Belletristisches Journal* with his novel, *Anton in Amerika.* Julius Fröbel wrote a small book on *America, Europe and the Political Perspective of the Present,* and Börnstein sponsored a German translation of Thomas Hart Benton's *Thirty Years' View.*

Many Forty-eighters published memoirs. Dr. Anton Füster's *Memoir of the Revolution of 1848 and 1849* dealt largely with his experiences in Vienna. Heinzen published two volumes of reminiscences, a small collection of poems, several plays of little merit, and a number of volumes of collected essays and lectures. Schurz's speeches and reminiscences have long been important source material for historical scholars. In addition, he wrote an excellent biography of Henry Clay for the *American Statesmen Series* (1886), and in his later years was a frequent contributor to the *New York Evening Post* and *Harpers' Weekly.* Wilhelm Rapp published a collection of essays and addresses in 1890, and Hermann Raster a collection of travel letters the following year. Struve, Douai, and Karl Theodor Griesinger prepared accounts of their American experiences for German publishing houses. Philip Betz, another Forty-eighter, published a small volume of the recollections of Carl Heinrich Schnauffer, dating from the time when both were refugees in France and Switzerland. Hardly less important to the historian than the reminiscences of such giants among the Forty-eighters as Schurz, Sigel, and Heinzen, are volumes like Philip Wagner's *A Forty-eighter,* published in 1882 in Brooklyn, which recount the experiences of average Germans without much formal education. Although the book expresses disillusionment with many phases of American private and public life, its author never failed to appreciate that individual liberty made the United States unique among the nations of the world.

Theodor Olshausen, editor of the *Davenport Demokrat* and the St. Louis *Westliche Post,* published several volumes on the history of the Mississippi Valley and a study of the Mormons. Johann Straubenmüller published in Baltimore in 1858 a poetic version of Pocahontas and the founding of Virginia. Hassaurek, in his later years, wrote in English about his experiences in Ecuador as American consul, under the title *Four Years Among the Spanish-Americans,* published an historical novel, *The Secret of the Andes,* and a volume of German poems. Peter Bernhard Wilhelm Heine, a Saxon revolutionist and Dresden painter who came to the United States in 1851, spent years in the Orient in the American Navy, and published *A Journey Around the World to Japan* and *Japan and Its Inhabitants.* Ruppius turned out German novels on American themes, with titles such as *The Pedlar* and *The Prairie Devil.* In 1885, after nearly a decade of effort, a number of better-known German-American authors founded "A National Association of German-American Writers and Journalists" with headquarters in Milwaukee, and a membership that included such prominent Forty-eighters as Schurz, Sigel, Praetorius, and Krez.

Konrad Krez is generally regarded as the ablest poet among the German-Americans of his generation, although he pursued the muse only as an avocation, practiced law in Wisconsin, served in the Civil War, and filled several elective and appointive offices. In 1875, he published a volume of poems with the title *Aus Wisconsin.* Other Forty-eighters, like Heinzen and Schnauffer, wrote poetry of more than average merit.[56] The muse of Caspar Butz was concerned with the cause of freedom the world over, from American abolitionism to the sufferings of Poland, Italy, and Cuba. Madame Anneke published a number of poems, and Mathilde Sorge, wife of Friedrich Sorge, Marx and Engels' leading disciple among the German-Americans, wrote "The Sleeping Proletariat," a call to the workers to rally round the red flag. Schnauffer's collected poems were published in 1879, many years after his death. Niclas Müller, a rebel from Baden and an itinerant printer and publisher in the United States, wrote poems of considerable merit for the *New Yorker Staatszeitung* and *Der Deutsche Pionier* of Cincinnati. Some found their way into anthologies of German-American authors, and were translated into English by Charles T. Brooks.[57] Finally, there was a steady stream of "Turner poetry" by "Turner poets," such as Rothacker, Schnauffer, and Straubenmüller, whose theme was patriotism, liberty and social revolution,[58] and the contrast between the freedom of America and the despotism of Europe.

When Esselen reviewed Marxhausen's *Deutsch-Amerikanischer Dichterwald,* the first anthology of German poetry produced on this side of the Atlantic, he commented: "Such a collection should treat preferably of American themes—it should include none of the old *Gefühlsduselei* of German romanticism—it should rather attempt to catch the poetic content of American life, of this young vigorous country. There is a poetry of progress, of development, which is more magnificent than the poetry of reminiscence. . . ." Many poems by Forty-eighters caught the spirit of a young, expanding, and free America.. Yet through much of the poetry of the refugees runs a sentimental yearning for the homeland, whose shortcomings became less apparent in the mellow glow of memory. Konrad Krez's "An mein Vaterland" might have been written in any age of ferment, when men and women have been driven from the land of their fathers by the cruelty of tyrants and dictators. Its opening stanza in poignant, moving lines, perhaps best describes the peculiar psychology of the refugee, and therefore deserves quotation.

> Kein Baum gehörte mir von deinen Wäldern,
> Mein war kein Halm auf deinen Roggenfeldern,
> Und schutzlos hast du mich hinausgetrieben,
> Weil ich in meiner Jugend nicht verstand
> Dich weniger und mehr mich selbst zu lieben,
> Und dennoch lieb ich dich, mein Vaterland![59]

FOOTNOTES

CHAPTER 20

1. See *New Yorker Staatszeitung,* Jan. 22, April 19, 1851; *Wächter am Erie,* Jan. 17, 1868; *New York Tribune,* April 6, 1854; and Richter: *Geschichte der Stadt Davenport,* p. 455.

2. *Atlantis,* III—Aug. 1855 (N.S.) pp. 92-97.

3. See *New Yorker Staatszeitung,* June 29, Oct. 19, 1850; Aug. 27, 1853; April 7, 1854.

4. See *Belletristisches Journal*, Feb. 23, July 13, 27, Sept. 28, 1855; July 18, 1856; July 24, 1857; July 20, 1860; *New Yorker Staatszeitung*, Aug. 11, 1859; and *Wächter am Erie*, April 16, 1870.

5. Cunz: *The Maryland Germans*, pp. 230-31; and *Westbote*, May 24, 1860.

6. *Belletristisches Journal*, Jan. 20, 1860.

7. H. Schuricht: *Geschichte der Deutschen Schulbestrebungen in Amerika* (Leipzig, 1884) p. 57.

8. Stierlin: *Kentucky*, p. 140.

9. Still: *Milwaukee*, pp. 121, 382; Koss: *Milwaukee*, pp. 333-35; Hense-Jensen and Bruncken: *Wisconsin's Deutsch-Amerikaner* II, pp. 191-93; *Wächter am Erie*, May 23, 1874; and Frieda Meyer Voigt: *The Engelmann Heritage* (Milwaukee, 1951).

10. For further details, see Dora Edinger: "A Feminist Forty-eighter," in *The American German Review* (June 1942) VIII, No. 5, pp. 18-19, 38.

11. See also, L. Viereck: *Zwei Jahrhunderte Deutschen Unterrichts in den Vereinigten Staaten* (Braunschweig 1903) pp. 53-57.

12. *Belletristisches Journal*, Sept. 16, Dec. 23, 1859; Feb. 17, 1860.

13. *Der Deutsche Pionier*, IX, No. 9 (Dec. 1877) pp. 357-58.

14. Cunz: *The Maryland Germans*, p. 273.

15. *Ibid.*, pp. 272-73; see also *Jahrbücher der Deutsch-Amerikanischen Turnerei*, I, 179-81.

16. Richter: *Geschichte der Stadt Davenport*, pp. 555-56.

17. April 23, 1853; April 7, July 18, 1860.

18. For other data on "free schools," see *New Yorker Staatszeitung*, Sept. 13, 1856; Jan. 22, April 21, Oct. 20, 1859; also May 21, 1855.

19. *Wächter am Erie*, July 19, 1869.

20. Cunz: *The Maryland Germans*, p. 272.

21. See Richter: *Geschichte der Stadt Davenport*, pp. 558-60.

22. *Der Deutsche Pionier*, XV, No. 10 (Jan. 1884) p. 418.

23. See also, Anton Eickhoff: *In der neuen Heimath-Geschichtliche Mitteilungen über die deutschen Einwanderer in allen Theilen der Union*. (New York, 1884.)

24. Biesele: *Germans in Texas*, pp. 165-66, 212.

25. Koss: *Milwaukee*, p. 318.

26. *Jahrbücher der Deutsch-Amerikanischen Turnerei*, I, 96.

27. H. Schuricht: *Geschichte der Deutschen Schulbestrebungen in Amerika* (Leipzig, 1884) pp. 101-5.

28. See *New Yorker Staatszeitung*, Sept. 26, 1851; Sept. 17, 1852; *Belletristisches Journal*, Sept. 24, 1852.

29. See Elizabeth Jenkins: "Froebel's Disciples in America," in *The American-German Review*, III, 15-18. See also, Louise Hall Sharp: *The Peabody Sisters of Salem* (Boston 1950) pp. 289 and 326.

30. Richter: *Geschichte der Stadt Davenport*, pp. 556-58.

31. J. W. Stearns, in his *The History of Education in Wisconsin* (Milwaukee, 1893) p. 75, refers to the Milwaukee kindergarten: "so far as is known (as) the first kindergarten in Wisconsin."

32. See also *New Yorker Staatszeitung*, Oct. 18, 1854 and *Belletristisches Journal*, July 16, 1858.

33. *Wächter am Erie*, July 18, 1860.

34. *Wächter am Erie*, Aug. 3, 1874.

35. *Wisconsin (American Guide Series)* (New York, 1941) p. 199.

36. *Wächter am Erie*, Nov. 6, 1852; Koss: *Milwaukee*, p. 318; Stierlin: *Kentucky*, p. 144.

37. See *Belletristisches Journal*, Jan. 26, 1855; Dec. 12, 1856.

38. See *Wächter am Erie*, Feb. 8, 1875; also *Westbote*, Jan. 11, 1873.

39. *Westbote*, March 1, 1873.

40. See Wittke: *Heinzen*, pp. 138 *et seq.*, and 295-99.

41. See Kapp: *Aus und über Amerika*, I, 356-80; and A. E. Zucker: "Reinhold Solger" in *24th Report of the Society for the History of the Germans in Maryland* (1939) pp. 8-16.

42. November 11, 1859.

43. Scharf: *St. Louis*, p. 1832.

44. *Westbote*, Oct. 27, Nov. 17, 1859.

45. J. Hanno Deiler: *Geschichte der New Orleanser Deutschen Presse* (New Orleans, 1901) pp. 29-30.

46. Kapp: *Aus und über Amerika*, I, p. 329.

47. See *Liberty Writings*, pp. 70-74; *Wächter am Erie*, Aug. 30, 1869; *Belletristisches Journal*, Aug. 26, 1869.

48. *Wächter am Erie*, Sept. 7, 15, 1869.

49. See Heinzen's *The True Character of Humboldt: Oration Delivered at the German Humboldt Festival in Boston* (Indianapolis, 1869).

50. See *New Yorker Staatszeitung*, Sept. 1, 1853; Dec. 20, 1853; *Belletristisches Journal*, March 4, 1853.

51. *Mitteilungen des Deutschen Pionier Vereins von Philadelphia*, V (1907) pp. 24-25.

52. *Westbote*, April 13, 1855.

53. Kapp: *Aus und über Amerika*, I, 327-28.

54. *Atlantis* (Nov. 1855) III (N.S.) pp. 394-99.

55. June 1, 1855.

56. See Gottlieb Betz: *Die deutschamerikanische patriotische Lyrik der Achtundvierziger und ihre historische Grundlage*, in *Americana-Germanica* XXII (Philadelphia, 1916).

57. See Philip A. Shelley: "Niclas Müller, German-American Poet and Patriot," in *Studies in Honor of John Albrecht Walz* (Lancaster, Pa., 1941) pp. 1-20.

58. See B. A. Uhlendorf: "German-American Poetry, A Contribution to Colonial Literature," in *Deutsch-Amerikanische Geschichtsblätter*, XXII-XXIII (1922-23) pp. 109-235. See also, Dieter Cunz: "Carl Heinrich Schnauffers Literarische Versuche" in *Publications of the Modern Language Association of America*, LIX, No. 2 (June 1944) pp. 524-539.

59. Professor Zucker recently has given us the following English translation:

> In all thy forests was no tree mine own;
> No blade of rye in all thy fields was mine;
> Thou cast me out defenseless and alone,
> So young and simple I could not divine
> That I should love thee less, myself the more,
> Still, Fatherland, I love thee as before!

Chapter 21 · *THE REWARDS OF LABOR IN FREE AMERICA*

ARLIER CHAPTERS have stressed the contributions of German Forty-eighters to American politics and culture, and have dealt largely with important political and social movements in which this extraordinary group played a significant part. No less important, although less dramatic, were the contributions of the Forty-eighters to the building of America through their more prosaic efforts to earn a living and support their families in a new land whose opportunities were open to men and women of courage, initiative, perseverance, and thrift. The fact that some of the more prominent refugees found life especially hard, and that there were a number of failures among them, must not obscure the fact that the majority found their American experience satisfying, and achieved a greater measure of material success in the land of their choice than they would have had in the land of their origin. This was particularly true of craftsmen and workers, who were part of the backbone of the American democracy, but it was also true of many professional men.

It is generally agreed that the Germans by 1850 had made little impression on the artistic life of America, with the exception of notable contributions in the field of music. German critics readily admitted that in the appreciation of art, painting, and sculpture, their countrymen lagged behind their American compatriots.[1] Although the number of artists of merit among the Forty-eighters was too insignificant to affect the prevailing artistic tastes of Americans, several deserve brief mention.

One was Theodor Kaufmann, a native of Hanover who had studied painting with Peter von Cornelius of Düsseldorf and Wilhelm von Kaulbach in Munich. He fled to Switzerland and Belgium after the Revolution and arrived in New York in 1850, where his first earnings came

from selling drawings of religious characters and scenes. Paradoxical
though it was, there were Forty-eighters talented with pencil and brush,
who painted altar pieces and frescoes for frontier churches where the
standards were low enough to secure them commissions. Kaufmann
started an art school in New York, and Thomas Nast was one of his
pupils, but he had little financial success either as a painter or as director
of a school, and became the typical itinerant, poverty-stricken portrait
painter and photographer who took commissions wherever he could find
them. He painted a portrait of Julius Fröbel, and after his discharge
from the Civil War did a series of war scenes, including paintings of
Admiral Farragut, General Sherman, and Lincoln's assassination, and
Louis Prang reproduced some of his more popular pieces in his new
color process. In 1871 Kaufmann published an *American Painting Book*
in Boston. The emigré painter died in obscurity and poverty in New
York at the age of eighty-six, and is remembered, if at all, only for eight
etchings which trace the development of the Idea of God (*Die Entstehung
der Gottesidee*), copies of which, with the artist's explanatory text, are
in the Library of Congress.[2]

Henry Ulke, whose activities on the Berlin barricades in 1848 led to
a prison sentence, was an illustrator for *Leslie's* and *Harper's Weekly*.
Like Kaufmann, he also made daguerreotypes and photographs, and
painted portraits on commission. His oil painting of President Grant
was hung in the Red Room of the White House.[3] More significant was
Ulke's interest in the natural sciences, and in the course of his wanderings
as a painter he collected thousands of specimens of beetles which are
preserved in the Carnegie Institute of Pittsburgh.

Philadelphia harbored a group of Forty-eighter artists, sculptors, musicians, and poets who met regularly during the 1850's at a favorite table
(*Kneiptisch*) in one of the local taverns. The group contained its quota
of unlovable characters, known in more stable immigrant circles as
"Revolutzer" and "Stänker." Christian Schussele was one of the more
successful painters and art teachers of the Philadelphia group. A product
of the art academy of Strassburg, he produced a number of historical
paintings, including "Franklin before the Lords in Council" (1856);
"Men of Progress" (1857); "Zeisberger preaching to the Indians," painted
in 1859 for the Moravians of Bethlehem, Pennsylvania; "King Solomon
and the Iron Worker" (1860), and "Washington at Valley Forge" (1862).[4]

Anton Hochstein, who immigrated with his family from Bavaria in 1849 as a young man of twenty, was a painter in oils and water color, but made his living illustrating seed catalogues.[5] Karl Heinrich Schmolze, who had studied art in Munich and fought in the Palatinate, became an illustrator in Philadelphia. Georg Geiwitz, a Saxon revolutionary, painted church murals and stage scenery in Baltimore, and achieved notoriety when he was attacked in the *Turnzeitung* in 1860 for painting figures of angels on church ceilings.[6] Joseph Wissert, who was involved in the Baden Revolution as a lad of seventeen, became a fresco painter in New York and Baltimore.[7] Friedrich Girsch of the Royal Academy in Darmstadt, who was involved in both the French and German Revolutions, did engraving for the *New Yorker Criminal Zeitung und Belletristisches Journal,* engraved the ten-dollar notes issued during the Civil War depicting "De Soto discovering the Mississippi," and designed the liberty head on the fractional currency of the period.[8]

Louis Prang, a close friend and disciple of Heinzen, introduced chromolithographing into the United States—a process of painting in oil colors on canvas-textured paper, and covering the design with a coat of varnish. Prang was born in Breslau of a French Huguenot father and a German mother, and learned to dye and print calico in his father's shop. After traveling as a journeyman in Europe, the young radical fled to America after 1848 and settled in Boston in 1850. In 1856 he started a lithographing business which developed into the prosperous enterprise which he headed for many years. He is remembered for "Prang's Natural History Series," published in 1873, and "Prang's Aids for Objective Teaching," which appeared in 1877, and both had a marked effect on the teaching of art throughout the United States. In 1882 the pioneer of American lithographing organized the Prang Educational Company to publish drawing books for the schools, and Prang's water colors remained standard classroom equipment for many years. Sylvester Koehler, the son of a Leipzig artist, who was brought to the United States as a twelve-year-old boy in 1849, became technical manager of Prang and Company in 1868, one of the founders of the *American Art Review,* and curator of the Boston Museum of Fine Arts.

Ignaz Anton Pilat, trained in landscape gardening at Schönbrunn, Austria, planned a number of estates in Georgia and helped make the botanical surveys for New York's Central Park. Julius Bien, who was educated in Kassel and Frankfurt and arrived in 1848, made the plates for Audubon's *Birds of America,* two of the earliest prints of American baseball, a standard map of the West, and the 175 plates for the *Official Records of the Rebellion,* and made notable contributions to scientific standards in American cartography. He made most of the major geological and geographical maps issued by the government until the end of the century.[9] Richard Petri and Hermann Lungkwitz, who fought in the uprisings in Dresden with young Richard Wagner, and settled on a farm near Fredericksburg, Texas, in 1850, had been students at the Dresden Academy. Petri did portraits and drawings of the American Indian, while Lungkwitz concentrated on Texas landscapes and commercial photography, and opened a studio in San Antonio.[10]

The Forty-eighter immigration included many lawyers trained for the profession in Europe. Others took up the study of law in the United States, by reading with an established firm. Under the prevailing requirements it was not difficult to acquire the small amount of legal information which entitled a man to hang out his shingle. Moreover, there were always minor legal matters of special importance to immigrants, and in this area men who could counsel newcomers in their native tongue had a ready-made clientele.

Where a refugee acquired his legal training seems to have made little difference. Jakob Müller had an unusually successful career in Ohio and read all the law he needed after his arrival in Cleveland. Eduard Salomon, who had studied mathematics and natural science before coming to the United States in 1849, taught school, worked as a surveyor, and became clerk of the court at Manitowoc, Wisconsin, before he moved to Milwaukee to prepare for the bar. He became the Civil War governor of his state.[11] Men like Joseph M. Reichard, who had all their legal training in Europe, were equally successful. He had been a notary in Speyer and a member of the provisional government of the Rhenish Palatinate. Upon his arrival in Philadelphia late in 1849, he tried to make a living as a journalist and a tavernkeeper, but soon returned to the law. By combining his legal work and duties as a notary public with selling insurance, he became one of the most influential and successful members of the German community in Philadelphia.[12] Dr. Aloys Faller, a doctor of law *summa cum laude* from Heidelberg, settled first in St. Clair County, Illinois, as a "Latin farmer," and in 1860 moved to New York

City, to return to the legal practice.[13] Karl T. Ziegler, an associate of Sigel and Mieroslawsky in 1848, practiced in Newark, New Jersey.[14] Rudolf Koch of Hesse, a popular orator and publicist of 1848, studied law in New York.[15] J. Gabriel Woerner, a Württemberger, who was brought to America as a lad in 1833 and educated in St. Louis, went to Germany in 1848 to help the revolutionists and act as correspondent for New York and St. Louis papers. Upon his return to the United States he took up the study of law and became a probate judge. A man of wide intellectual and cultural interests, he was a great admirer of Thomas Hart Benton, wrote novels and plays, and was active in the Philosophical Society of St. Louis with Dr. William T. Harris, who tried to introduce Hegel to the Middle West.[16]

George Hillgärtner, who had spent five years in German universities, practiced law in Chicago and Dubuque in combination with his work as a journalist. Louis Ritter, another refugee who had studied at Würzburg and Heidelberg, was admitted to the American bar in 1854, and became a lawyer and businessman in Cleveland, and associate editor of the *Wächter am Erie*.[17] Hans Reimer Claussen, who represented Schleswig-Holstein in the Frankfurt Parliament, was a distinguished member of the bar in Davenport, Iowa, and served in the state legislature.[18] Otto Friedrich Dresel and Emil Rothe, outstanding Forty-eighters and able lawyers, were active in public affairs as lifelong Democrats. Dresel had studied at Jena before he was charged with treason in the revolution in Lippe-Detmold. Escaping to the United States in 1849, he read law in Massillon, Ohio, while employed as a music teacher and night watchman. He began practicing in Columbus, was a member of the school board and superintendent of schools, and helped establish the Columbus Public Library. Elected to the Ohio Legislature in 1864, he was a storm center of bitter partisan controversy, and was frequently accused of Copperhead sympathies. Rothe practiced law and published a small paper in Watertown, Wisconsin.

The most successful German-American law firm in the early 1850's seems to have been Zitz, Kapp and Fröbel of New York City. All three were prominent refugees. Franz H. Zitz of Mainz had belonged to the Frankfurt Parliament and commanded troops in the Palatinate. Kapp, a friend of the poet Herwegh, had been a private tutor in the home of Alexander Herzen, "the founder of Russian nihilism." Fröbel was a strange combination of revolutionary, publicist, scientist, and scholar, interested in almost everything from law to mineralogy, and in collecting specimens for the Smithsonian Institution in Texas.[19] The law firm of Zitz and Kapp continued to prosper after Fröbel's withdrawal, and much of its business consisted of representing Germans and German commercial houses in the New York area and taking care of the legal business of an immigrant community.[20]

Men trained in German polytechnic institutes readily found employment in an expanding economy where engineering skill and scientific training were at a premium. The Westphalian revolutionist Hermann Ulffers worked as an engineer for several Indiana railroads, helped make geological surveys of Illinois and Missouri, was a member of the engineering corps during the Civil War, and held several federal positions in the postwar years.[21] John G. Gindele, an established architect in Schweinfurth before he joined the rebels in 1848, brought his wife and five children to America. His first efforts to earn a living in Wisconsin ended in failure, and when he moved to Chicago he was practically penniless. Here he became a builder and stonemason contractor and won the recognition he deserved. For twelve years he was chairman of the Illinois Board of Public Works and president of the Michigan-Illinois Canal Board. In that capacity he laid out the plans for Chicago's Lincoln Park, constructed several tunnels, and the first big water line under Lake Michigan for the Chicago Water Works.[22]

Karl Eberhard Salomon, a trained surveyor and a member of the engineer's corps of the Prussian Army, became county surveyor, county engineer, superintendent of streets, and commissioner of water works in St. Louis.[23] Heinrich Flad, a Forty-eighter who fought in Baden in 1848 and 1849, had studied at the polytechnic institute of Karlsruhe. In the United States he became construction engineer for the Erie Railroad, and during the Civil War, colonel of a regiment of engineers. In the postwar years he was assistant engineer for the St. Louis Water Works, a member of the city's Board of Water Commissioners, president of the Board of Public Improvement, and a member of the Mississippi River Commission. During his long career Flad perfected a number of patents, including water meters and filters, pressure gauges, pile drivers, hydraulic elevators, and street sprinkler systems.[24] Rudolf Eickemeyer, a Bavarian who was a revolutionist at the age of seventeen, became a successful inventor in the United States, with approximately 150 patents to his credit. He designed the first electric railway motor for the New York Elevated, and in 1892 consolidated his business with the General Electric,[25] and has the distinction of having been the first employer of Charles P. Steinmetz, the young Socialist refugee from Bismarckian Germany who became the electrical genius of the General Electric Company. He began work in America as a draftsman for Eickemeyer at two dollars a day.[26]

Christian Heinrich Friedrich Peters, a native of Schleswig and educated at Berlin and Göttingen, was engaged in a scientific survey in Sicily and lost his post because of his sympathy for the Italian revolutionaries. After spending some time in France and Turkey, Peters came to America in 1854 to join the United States Coast Survey. He later became a professor of astronomy and director of observatories, and the discoverer of two comets and forty-eight asteroids, as well as the publisher of important researches on the sun.[27] Carl Theodore Mohr, from the polytechnic school of Stuttgart, published nearly a hundred papers in the field of botany, including a report on the forests of Alabama for the Tenth United States Census.[28] Joseph Zentmeyer, an instrument maker in Mannheim who was forced to leave Germany after the Revolution, opened a shop in Philadelphia in 1853. His work was widely known among American scientists, and his microscopes in great demand. In 1865 Zentmeyer invented a photographic lens which revolutionized microscopy and won him the gold medal of the Franklin Institute of Philadelphia and similar honors at the Philadelphia Centennial of 1876 and the Paris Exhibition of 1878.[29]

Members of the clergy were not numerous in the Forty-eighter emigration. Because of the nature of their calling and the close relation of church and state in Catholic and Lutheran Germany, few pastors were likely to be openly sympathetic with the rebels, and many violently disapproved of the rationalism of the leaders of "Young Germany." Among the few exceptions was Karl Auerbach, a pastor in Baden who had written mildly democratic poetry, found it expedient to leave in 1849, and filled regular pulpits in Ohio.[30] Wilhelm Wagner, son of a pastor in Dürkheim, was more deeply involved in the German Revolution. Although he took no part in the actual uprisings, his unorthodox political and social theories led to his suspension from his pastorate in Baden in 1849, and he was sentenced, *in absentia,* to a year and a half in jail. In September 1851 he arrived in New York and proceeded to Wisconsin, where he acquired a farm near Monroe, and lived in a crude blockhouse with a friend. He was later called to a church in Monroe, and at the time of his death in 1877 was a minister in Freeport, Illinois. Wagner was an active member of the *Turnverein,* the Odd Fellows, the local German singing society, and the volunteer fire company, and for a short time published the *Deutsche Anzeiger.*[31] Karl Tuercke, a student of Schleiermacher and Schelling in Berlin, preached the funeral sermons for several victims of the Berlin revolution and thus lost all chance for theological advancement in Germany. In 1857 he came to the United States, and the following year accepted the pastorate of a German Lutheran Church in Cincinnati.[32] Gustav Wilhelm Eisenlohr, a native of Baden who studied theology at Halle and Heidelberg and was accused in 1848 of subversive contributions to the *Oberrheinische Zeitung,* escaped sentence by promising to leave the country. He held pastorates in New Richmond, Ohio, Cincinnati, New Braunfels and Dallas, Texas. His *Protestantische Zeitblätter* definitely indicate his liberal views.[33] Dr. Karl Schramm, a delegate to the Prussian Diet in 1848, was one of New York's ablest German pastors.[34] Franz Schmidt von Löwenberg, another veteran of the Frankfurt Parliament, was the leader of a rationalist movement among the German Catholics of St. Louis, and the founder of the *Freie Blätter.*[35] Isidor Kalisch, a reform rabbi, fled to America in 1849 to escape charges of sedition, and became identified with reformed Judaism. Isidor Löwenthal, on the other hand, became a convert to Christianity. Reared in Germany in the orthodox Jewish faith, he tangled with the authorities and emigrated to avoid arrest. In the United States Löwenthal was befriended by a Protestant minister in Wilmington, Delaware, and secured a position as a teacher at Lafayette College in 1847. He was converted, baptized, received into membership in the Presbyterian church, and admitted to Princeton Theological Seminary, where he was ordained in 1855 and later made an outstanding record as a missionary in India.[36]

In pharmacy, medicine, and to a lesser degree in dentistry, well-trained refugees were able to work in fields still largely undeveloped in the United States. German pharmacists were astonished and horrified that there was no law in America requiring pharmaceutical training or an examination for a license to operate a drugstore, and that no legal safeguards guaranteed the quality of the medical concoctions sold to the public. Apparently anyone could open a pharmacy; and fraudulent diplomas, with the title of "doctor," were conspicuously displayed in American drugstores.[37] The German immigration introduced trained prescription druggists with a basic knowledge of chemistry, and in the 1850's made the *Deutsche Apotheke* a highly regarded institution in American cities. German pharmacists also founded manufacturing houses for pharmaceutical products, and others taught in American schools of pharmacy and helped raise the standards of the profession.

A number of the pharmacists among the Forty-eighters became successful businessmen. Emil Dietzsch, under arrest during the Revolution, prospered in Chicago. Enno Sander, a radical journalist who was Blenker's adjutant at Ludwigshafen in 1848, arrived in New York on a clipper ship, and spent most of his American career in St. Louis, where he was one of the founders of the American Pharmaceutical Society in 1858, and of the St. Louis College of Pharmacy in 1863. Hans Hermann Behr, who had studied medicine in Germany, held a professorship in a school of pharmacy in San Francisco.[38]

Anton Hottinger, a mechanic's son who fled to America after the Revolution, completed his apprenticeship as a druggist in Pittsburgh and Cincinnati and opened his own pharmacy in Guttenberg, Iowa, in 1856, became the town's mayor, and later moved to Chicago.[39] Edmund Märklin of Württemberg, a veteran of the fighting in 1849 and an active Turner in Milwaukee, was the pharmacist for the 34th Wisconsin Volunteers during the Civil War, and upon his return to civilian life operated drugstores in Manitowoc and Milwaukee.[40] Johann Michael Maisch, a young German pharmacist who came to the United States in 1849 to acquire further training, was appointed to the chair of botany and materia medica in the New York College of Pharmacy in 1861. In 1863 he had charge of a United States army laboratory for medical supplies, and after the war had his own business in Philadelphia and taught in the Philadelphia College of Pharmacy.[41] Maisch belonged to several scientific societies, published extensively in his field, and from 1871 to 1893 edited the *American Journal of Pharmacy*.[42]

European dentistry had less to offer American practitioners, and to this day lags behind the profession in the United States. One dentist among the Forty-eighters won a place in the *Dictionary of American Biography*. Adelbert J. Volck, a native of Augsburg and a student in the polytechnic institute of Nürnberg, had played a minor part in the uprisings in Berlin.

In 1849 he joined the gold rush to California. In 1852 he received a degree in dentistry and became an instructor in the Baltimore College of Dental Surgery. A man of varied talents, Volck was also a good cartoonist. His pro-Southern cartoons got him into serious trouble during the Civil War. During a long and active life, Volck produced a volume of *Confederate War Etchings* and *Sketches from the Civil War in North America;* illustrated Emily V. Mason's popular life of Robert E. Lee in 1872; and did the oil painting of the Confederate general which was hung in the Valentine Museum of Richmond. He was a charter member of the Maryland State Dental Association, and one of the founders of the Association of Dental Surgeons.[43] Joseph Deshauer, who studied in Vienna, and helped defend the city against the armies of Windischgrätz in 1848, began a dental practice in Chicago in 1856. He was an enthusiastic member of the *Schützenverein.* His biographers record no prizes for his skill in dentistry, but several for expert marksmanship at *Schützenfeste.*[44]

Immigrants trained in medicine were shocked by the low level of medical practice in the United States. They found that the title of doctor could be obtained in American medical schools by one year's attendance upon lectures, and that Americans swallowed unusual quantities and varieties of medicines without being concerned whether it was the product of quackery and superstition or scientific investigation in a medical laboratory.[45] When Joseph Goldmark, an assistant physician in the Vienna General Hospital before he took to the barricades, arrived in New York, he was horrified to find "not a single eminent physiologist . . . and few biologists."[46] He promptly hung out his shingle in New York as a skin specialist. In addition to his medical practice, he worked on the production of red phosphorus for safety matches, and in 1857 patented a mercury compound for explosives which proved valuable for the manufacture of percussion caps during the Civil War.

By 1854 it was estimated that one-third of the doctors in New York were Germans, and the proportion was substantial in other large cities as well. Many older German doctors bitterly resented the competition of the newcomers after 1848, and the Society of German Doctors urged the refugees either to return to their homeland or be content to "carry stones, sweep the streets, and clean out the sewers."[47] At the same time, American-born doctors resented all German competitors whether earlier or later arrivals, and at a national convention of doctors in 1855, there were but five German physicians in a total attendance of 520 delegates.[48] As a result German doctors organized their own societies in New York, Cincinnati, Buffalo, St. Louis, and Milwaukee,[49] and among the founders and promoters of these new associations were prominent Forty-eighters. In New York, Abraham Jacobi, Goldmark, Tellkampf, and Krackowitzer helped organize the Society of German Physicians and opened a free dispensary for poor German immigrants.[50] In Philadelphia, Dr. Tiedemann and his associates promoted a German hospital largely because German physicians were excluded from many American hospitals.[51]

The number of physicians among the refugees of 1848 was surprisingly large and included men of varying degrees of training and ability, from mediocre general practitioners to outstanding specialists and scholars. Dr. Alfred von Behr, an M.D. and a revolutionist from Anhalt, established a practice in Missouri and Texas. Dr. Louis Bauer, a member of the Prussian Diet, was a surgeon in St. Louis and founded the College of Physicians and Surgeons.[52] Hecker's comrade, Dr. Adam Hammer, opened *Das Humboldt Institut,* a German medical school, in St. Louis in 1859, and from 1869 to 1872 was a professor in the Missouri Medical College. Five years later, tired and disillusioned, he returned, *Amerikamüde,* to die in his native Baden in 1878.[53]

The Tiedemann family, one of the most prominent in the Revolution of 1848, settled in Philadelphia, where several members practiced medicine. Dr. Karl Hartmann, who studied medicine in Bonn and was an active revolutionist, became a practicing physician in Cleveland and an enthusiastic supporter of all the activities of the German community. He died at the age of thirty-six from wounds received at the battle of Chancellorsville.[54] Dr. Philipp F. Weigel, another Forty-eighter, was surgeon general for Missouri during the war. Dr. John Menninger, a doctor in Rhenish Hesse, who clashed with the police and came to the United States in 1849, practiced in New York for thirty-two years, was a gifted linguist, a correspondent of Huxley, and a keen student of natural history.[55] Eduard Morwitz of Danzig, who received his medical degree in 1841, and was busy compiling a history of medicine when his liberal views forced him to emigrate, began his American career as a doctor in Philadelphia, established a dispensary for the poor, and published and edited several papers, including the *Philadelphia Demokrat.* After the Civil War he turned more and more to publishing, and organized the German Press Association of Pennsylvania, printed English-American pocket dictionaries, and founded *Uncle Sam's Almanac* in 1873 and the *Jewish Record* in 1875.[56]

Gustav Brühl, who studied in several German universities, was one of Cincinnati's first throat specialists, and lectured at the Miami Medical College.[57] Eduard Dorsch, surgeon in the revolutionary levies of South Germany late in 1849, began his practice in Monroe, Michigan, where he was a surgeon and general practitioner until his death in 1887. His home in Monroe became the "Dorsch Memorial Library."[58] Gustav Carl Erich Weber, a student companion of Carl Schurz, settled originally on a farm near St. Louis. He returned to study medicine in Europe, and in 1853 began practicing in New York. Three years later he was a professor in the Cleveland Medical College, and in 1859 helped establish the *Cleveland Medical Gazette*. On his return from service as surgeon general of Ohio troops in the Civil War, he founded the Charity Hospital Medical College of Cleveland and organized the staff of St. Vincent's Charity Hospital. From 1870 to 1881, Weber was dean of the medical department at Wooster, Ohio, and from 1881 to 1894, dean of what became the medical department of Western Reserve University.[59]

Friedrich Roessler, with a two-year prison sentence behind him, founded the first private German hospital in New York. Dr. A. W. Rittler, who was accused of harboring refugees from Dresden in his home in Altenburg, established his medical practice in New York and Hoboken. Dr. Alexander Hexamer, a native of Coblenz, who was involved in the Berlin revolution, specialized in gynecology and pediatrics in New York. Dr. Georg Edward Wiss, another Forty-eighter, practiced in Baltimore and published *The Healing and Preventing of Diphtheria* in Berlin in 1879.[60] Johann Philipp Trau, an M.D. from Heidelberg and Munich, who marched with Blenker in 1848, practiced in Philadelphia from 1850 to his death in 1883.[61] Wilhelm Loewe aus Calbe, a student of medicine at Halle and president of the Rump Parliament in Stuttgart in 1849, advertised in the New York papers as "a physician, surgeon and obstetrician,"[62] but apparently devoted most of his time to becoming a successful Republican politician in the pre-Civil War years. Karl Hermann Berendt lost his post as lecturer on obstetrics and surgery at the University of Breslau because he favored a constitutional monarchy at Frankfurt. He came to the United States in 1851, but went on to Nicaragua and Mexico to practice medicine and become an authority on Mayan civilization. In 1866 he made a survey for the Smithsonian Institution in Guatemala, and in 1869 the American Ethnological Society published his "Analytical Alphabet for the Mexican and Central American Languages."[63]

It is important to remember that not all of the German refugee doctors remained in the large Eastern cities. Some went to the smaller towns of the West where medical men were especially needed. Robert Roskoten, a member of the revolutionary student corps at Halle and Jena, for example, became a doctor in Peoria, Illinois. Friedrich Brendel, who lost his post in a Bamberg hospital for political reasons, settled there also, and in addition to his medical practice, published a book on *Flora Peoriana*. Wilhelm Hoffbauer, a member of the left at Frankfurt, practiced in Dubuque, Iowa. Dr. Karl Neubert, who published the liberal *Koburger Tageblatt* in 1848, and was a member of the Landtag, accepted Hecker's advice to come to Belleville.[64] Lorenz Ehrhart, a physician who fled to Strassburg to escape arrest, practiced in Allegheny for thirty-three years.[65] Dr. Hermann Theodore Schultz, a refugee from Tübingen, practiced in several Texas cities and was a doctor in the Confederate Army.[66] Dr. Rudolf Neuhaus, a staff physician in Sigel's corps and at Rastatt; Dr. Emil Haas, a surgeon for Missouri troops; Dr. Adolph Zipperlen, a Suabian who marched with Sherman through Georgia; and Dr. Julius von Hausen, of Vienna, doctor for a brigade in the army of the Potomac,[67] made good records during the Civil War.

In this long list of refugees interested in medicine, five seem to outrank all others as men of unusual caliber, character, and scientific and cultural attainment. Dr. Hermann Kiefer's name is perpetuated in one of the largest hospitals in Detroit. A native of Baden, he had studied from 1844 to 1849 at Freiburg, Heidelberg, Prague, and Vienna. In March 1848 he was chairman of a mass meeting in Freiburg which demanded a constitution and a federal republic, and the following year he attended a *Landeskongress* in Baden. In May 1849 he volunteered as a regimental surgeon, and a month later had the high-sounding title of chairman of the departments of surgery and obstetrics in the "Republic of Baden." Kiefer began his medical practice in Detroit immediately upon his arrival in the United States, and became one of that city's most highly respected citizens. He was a presidential elector in 1872, United States consul in Stettin in the 1880's, a regent of the University of Michigan and a professor in its medical school, and in addition, a poet and orator of outstanding talent.

Dr. Ernst Schmidt, the son of a druggist, was educated for medicine at Würzburg, Heidelberg, Munich, and Zurich. A radical socialist, he escaped a jail sentence in 1849 only because of family influence. When his career as a doctor and teacher at the University of Würzburg seemed hopelessly blocked, he came to the United States and moved to Chicago in 1857, where he immediately identified himself with the radical abolitionists, and made an address in honor of John Brown at a German mass meeting. During the Civil War he was regimental doctor in the 3d Missouri Volunteers. After the war Dr. Schmidt became one of Chicago's most successful physicians and for many years was chief of staff of the Michael Reese Hospital. Never changing the convictions of his youth, he ran for mayor of Chicago in 1879 on the Socialist Labor ticket, and at the time of the Haymarket riots was treasurer for the defense committee for the indicted anarchists.

Hans Kudlich (1823-1917) was a native of Austrian Silesia and the leader in the Vienna Parliament who wished to abolish the feudal burdens that still weighed upon the peasants of the medieval Habsburg state. Kudlich was wounded while fighting with the Vienna student legion, fled to Switzerland, and completed his medical training there. For many years Dr. Kudlich carried on a successful practice in Hoboken and was regarded as one of the more distinguished physicians of the greater New York area. He was an ardent abolitionist, and his three volumes of reminiscences are an important source for both European and American history.[68]

Dr. Ernst Krackowitzer came from a Jewish family in the Steyermark. He studied medicine in Vienna and Padua, and in 1848 was a captain in the Vienna student legion during the October uprising. The young doctor fled to Tübingen and the United States, began practicing in Williamsburg, New York, and in 1857 moved into New York City. Dr. Krackowitzer was the leading surgeon at Mount Sinai and New York Hospital, and a member of the committee which reorganized Bellevue Hospital in 1874. He was a frequent contributor to scientific journals, and president of the Pathological Society of New York. A radical and freethinker, he was one of those rare intellects who can properly be referred to as a universal scholar and an intellectual aristocrat, for he was a student of art, literature, history, philosophy, and languages. He died on his estate outside the city in 1875.[69]

Dr. Abraham Jacobi was one of Krackowitzer's closest friends, and the attending physician at the time of his death. The son of poor Jewish parents in Westphalia, Jacobi received his medical degree from the University of Bonn. During the Revolution, he was prosecuted for *lèse majesté,* and was one of the defendants in the famous communist "red" trial in Cologne. He proudly admitted his leadership of the student *Turnverein* at Bonn and made no effort to hide his socialist principles as a "revolutionary democrat." Although finally acquitted, he spent nearly two years in jail while under investigation. In 1853 he arrived in the United States. He established his medical practice in New York, and here he remained throughout an unusually long and successful career. At a time when his income was still small, this German-Jewish refugee doctor developed a deep interest in children and the problems of the tenement districts, and during his first year in America published a study of children's diseases in which he analyzed the extraordinarily high death rate among the children of New York and stressed, among other factors, matters of housing, ventilation, and milk supply.[70] His first practice was largely in the tenement districts, and his fees were as low as twenty-five and fifty cents. Specializing in what is now called pediatrics, he wrote articles on children's diseases for the *New York Medical Journal,* lectured on the pathology of infancy and childhood at the College of Physicians and Surgeons, and became the first professor of the diseases of children in this country at the New York Medical College in 1860. Two years later he founded the *American Journal of Obstetrics,* and in 1870 he became professor of pediatrics in the New York College of Physicians and Surgeons. Dr. Jacobi published several monographs, was a prominent member of the German Social Scientific Society of New York, and belonged to various German social and cultural organizations. He is also remembered as one of the earliest advocates of birth control. He received honorary degrees from Yale, Harvard, Columbia, and Michigan, and was president of the American Medical Association. His wife, Mary Putnam, was a pioneer woman physician. Jacobi died in 1919 in the home of his old friend Carl Schurz, who had died thirteen years earlier.

Although manufacturing and business frequently have been regarded as the special province of Yankee ingenuity, the history of immigration reveals a number of foreign-born who succeeded in these fields, and thousands of craftsmen, trained in the thorough apprentice system of Europe, who helped speed the economic and industrial progress of the United States after 1850. If foreigners as a class showed less daring than their Yankee contemporaries, many were their superiors in dependable, thorough, and patient workmanship, and many Americans learned their trades from European immigrants. Most of these workers and small businessmen belonged to the rank and file whose names did not appear in the press except in the death notices when their careers were finished, and their story must be culled from fragments of information scattered in many places.

The one notable exception from the business world was the distinguished entrepreneur Henry Villard, and strictly speaking, he was not a Forty-eighter, for he was only thirteen years old when the Revolution occurred. In a sense, however, he belongs to the Forty-eighter tradition, and he always regarded himself as a member of that distinguished group of political refugees. His two uncles were leading supporters of the Revolution, but his father was an extreme and stern conservative. The boy Henry, according to a well-authenticated family tradition, is said to have broken up a class in Zweibrücken by refusing to join in a prayer for the King of Bavaria. Another story relates that the lad saw the Frankfurt Parliament in action, caught a glimpse of its noted leaders, and returned home wearing a red feather in the band of his Hecker hat. The father, an ambitious judge, remained loyal to the King and disciplined his son by sending him to a military school in Alsace and then to the University of Munich where the boy revolted against the study of law, and after an unhappy interval at the University of Würzburg left on a sailing vessel for New York. He changed his name from Heinrich Hillgard to Henry Villard, to thwart any effort that might be made to force him to return to Germany.

Villard arrived in the United States in October 1853, eighteen and a half years old, with twenty dollars in his pocket, no knowledge of English, and no relatives nearer than St. Louis. Somehow he managed to survive until his fortunes suddenly took a turn for the better in 1858 when he became a special correspondent for the *New Yorker Staatszeitung* and reported the Lincoln-Douglas debates in German. Within five years of his arrival he mastered the English language sufficiently to write for leading American papers. In 1860 Villard published *The Past and Present of the Pike's Peak Gold Regions* (Cincinnati), reported the Chicago convention which nominated Lincoln, followed the candidate throughout the campaign, and was on the presidential train for Washington in 1861. As a war correspondent, Villard witnessed many major battles during the Civil War and became a confirmed pacifist. In 1866 he married Fanny Garrison, daughter of the famous abolitionist, and returned to Germany to report the Austro-Prussian War for the *New York Tribune*. Here he met a group of Germans who held defaulted American railroad bonds, and joined their bondholders' protective committee in Frankfurt. He had a remarkable career as a railroad promoter and builder, became president of the Oregon and California Railroad and the Oregon Steamship Company, and a receiver for the Kansas Pacific. His activities as a railroad builder were climaxed in 1881 by the formation of a "blind pool," in which friends loaned him $8,000,000 to acquire the presidency of the Northern Pacific Railway Company. Two and a half years later, his railroad empire collapsed. In 1889 he helped Thomas Edison establish the Edison General Electric Company, and built and equipped the first steamship to be electrically lighted. Its generator is on exhibition in the Ford Museum at Dearborn. Villard, to quote his own words, never ceased to be grateful for "the incomparable advantages arising from the free play of the human faculties enjoyed in this country."[71]

Heinrich Steinweg found opportunity in quite a different field. He too was not directly involved in the Revolution, but his business was adversely affected by it, and financial difficulties hastened his emigration. In the United States the celebrated builder of pianos, who began as a cabinetmaker and manufacturer of zithers and guitars, started making pianos in 1853, with four sons who came with him from Brunswick. By 1859 Steinweg's factory employed eight hundred workmen and produced sixty pianos a week, and the Steinway piano is still the acknowledged leader in the concert field.[72]

Of less distinction in the field of business, but more directly connected with the exodus after 1848, were refugees like Major Franz Backhoff, who refused to order his battery to fire on the people at Rastatt, and fought in the major battle of Waghäusel. He became a successful building contractor in St. Louis and a member of its city council.[73] F. C. König, of the Rhenish Palatinate, who fled to France in 1849, operated a soap and candle factory in Peoria, Illinois.[74] Gottlieb Wanner, a Turner and a veteran of the Revolution in Baden, was a respected member of the large German-American business community of Cincinnati.[75] Rudolf Diepenbeck, trained in Germany for a business career, came to the United States as a refugee in 1850 and developed an insurance business in Michigan,[76] and Dr. Karl Mieding, another Forty-eighter, became secretary of the Mutual Hail Insurance Company of Milwaukee.[77] Wilhelm Frankfurth, who left Germany after the Revolution as a young man of twenty, tried to make a living as a tanner, a grocer, and a bookkeeper for a hardware firm, before he finally organized his own hardware business in Milwaukee. He generously contributed to the support of the free congregation of Milwaukee, the German-English Academy, and the German-American Teachers' Seminary.[78]

Philipp Haimbach of Mannheim, who fought with Sigel in 1848, and helped Struve publish his *Die soziale Republik* in New York, was a well-to-do businessman of Philadelphia and one of the founders of the Philadelphia Opera Association.[79] Karl Friedrich Kirchhof, a skilled German mechanic who served a nine-months' sentence after the Revolution in Saxony, invented a fire-alarm and police telegraph system in New Jersey.[80] J. Helfenstein and G. Rassigh, veterans of the Revolution, operated a soap factory in New York and invented a new cleaning fluid.[81] Charles Adolph Schieren and his father, who ran afoul of the police during the Revolution, operated a tobacco business in America and later manufactured leather belting. The son became the head of Charles A. Schieren and Company, makers of patented machine belting, a founder of the Brooklyn Institute of Arts and Sciences, president of the Brooklyn Academy of Music, and in 1893 served a term as mayor.[82] John Eberhard Faber, who came to the United States after the Revolution interrupted his study of law at Erlangen and Heidelberg, produced the first pencils with erasers in the United States.[83]

In the brewing business Germans not only were pioneers but for years held a virtual monopoly. Lager beer was popular with Americans by the time of the Civil War, and there were lager beer houses in American cities as early as the 1850's. Several Forty-eighters were prominent in the development of the brewing industry in the United States. Joseph Fickler operated a bar and restaurant in the German section of New York City, and the area along William Street, with its many taverns, stores, and beer saloons, was a favorite rendezvous for refugees. C. F. Kiefer, who had a varied career in Germany before the Revolution as a teacher, soldier, manufacturer of calico and bricks, and as a member of the Landtag of Baden and the Parliament of Frankfurt, and commander of the people's guard at Emmendingen in 1849, operated Kiefer's Hotel in Philadelphia, and later, with several associates, established a brewery on Third Street, and operated a wine business. He belonged to many German societies, including a German freethinkers' organization which he helped establish in 1852, but his special interests were the *Schützenverein* and the local German hospital.[84] Johann Schneider, a young Bavarian rebel, was a well-known American brewmaster.[85] C. W. Schmidt, who was sentenced to death and had his property confiscated in the Palatinate in 1849, became one of the founders of the Schmidt and Hoffman Brewery of Cleveland.[86] Meinrad Kleiner became an expert in the chemistry of fermentation in his father's brewery. After the Revolution, the Kleiner family came to America and Meinrad became the owner of a brewery in Cincinnati, and like his brother was one of Cincinnati's wealthy German-Americans.[87] Carl Gehm closed his dyer's shop to volunteer for the Revolution, and left the Palatinate for the United States. His first nine years in America were spent in the dyeing business in Belleville, Illinois, but during the Civil War he moved to Quincy and became a successful brewer.[88] The Lenk brothers from Würzburg arrived in 1849. One developed the Toledo Brewing Company, the other the Lenk Wine Company in the same city.[89] The oldest brewery in Davenport, Iowa, and the largest in the state, was founded by Mathias Frahm, another Forty-eighter. A stubborn freethinker, he left $10,000 for the establishment of a free German school in Davenport[90] and stipulated that his grandson must be educated as a rationalist.

In the 1850's it was not unusual for German tavernkeepers to be closely allied with the brewing business, for much of their profit depended on the sale of beer. German hotelkeepers enjoyed an enviable reputation, and travelers stopping at little German inns about the country invariably commented on their cleanliness and excellent food. Several prominent refugees went into the hotel business in the United States. Karl Göhringer, a friend of Hecker, operated hotels and inns on three continents, and after 1866 managed restaurants in Pittsburgh.[91] Peter Bickel of Baden, after unsuccessful ventures in farming in Illinois, operated hotels in Waukegan, Belleville, and Cincinnati, where he died in 1881.[92] General

Joseph Gerhardt, who fled to Switzerland after the fall of Rastatt and won high military rank in the American Civil War, operated a restaurant in Washington, D. C., in 1851, played the violin in theatre orchestras, and later owned the Germania Hotel.[93] Sixtus Ludwig Kapff, a former law student at Tübingen and a veteran of both the Baden Revolution and the American Civil War, operated the Steuben House in the Bowery in New York for a brief period.[94]

Carl Rietz, trained for a mercantile career, developed a profitable lumber business in Saginaw, Michigan, and in 1877 organized the Charles Rietz and Brothers Lumber Company of Chicago.[95] Christian L. H. Müller of Holstein, who was wounded and imprisoned in 1848, was associated with his father-in-law, Hans Reimer Claussen, in a lumber mill in Davenport, and was active in the lumber trade in Iowa for many years.[96]

A number of Forty-eighters made their living in the jewelry business. Hermann Franz Serodino, a native of Nordhausen, and a skillful manufacturer of jewelry, who escaped from Berlin to St. Petersburg, worked at the jeweler's trade for nearly thirty years in Cincinnati.[97] Anton Brookmann, a goldsmith who belonged to the Vienna National Guard, conducted a nickel-plating and jewelry business in Newark, New Jersey, Saginaw, Michigan, and Chicago, and took an active part in the society of German Veterans of 1848 and 1849.[98] Joseph Rudolph, a Bohemian who studied at Prague and was a member of the academic legion of Vienna, drifted from one job to another in Cincinnati, St. Louis, and Dubuque before settling in Chicago in 1855 to operate a successful jewelry and notions business,[99] and Wilhelm Vogt, a Turner who was arrested for distributing radical literature in Frankfurt, was an expert jeweler in Louisville, and won first prize at a *Turnfest* in Cincinnati.[100]

First in the list of Forty-eighters who were printers and publishers is Heinrich Hoff, the courageous publisher for German liberals and radicals in the fatherland at a time when the censorship laid a heavy hand on authors and printers alike. Hoff died in a New York hospital in 1852.[101] Franz E. Loes, a book dealer who fled after the Saxon revolution, was associated with F. W. Thomas, the Philadelphia publisher.[102] Julius Schieferdecker, publisher of the *Leipziger Illustrierte Monatshefte,* fled in 1848 and worked as a typesetter in Philadelphia, Reading, Baltimore, Cincinnati, St. Louis, and Milwaukee, but died almost penniless in the home of a friend in Milwaukee, at the age of eighty.[103] Carl Friedrich Haussner, a veteran of the Dresden revolution, spent his first weeks in the United States in the hospital on Ward's Island, and after trying various jobs finally became a typesetter for the *Neu England Zeitung* in Boston, and in 1855 opened a bookstore in Chicago.[104]

Johann W. Dietz, whose father published the *Rheinische Zeitung,* and who therefore was nurtured on the liberal tradition of Freiligrath, Becker, and Kinkel, was only thirteen years old at the outbreak of the Revolution, but six years later was sent to the United States to work as a printer. In 1869 he began publishing on a small scale in Chicago.[105] Friedrich Gerhard, of the liberal *Danziger Dampfboot,* operated a bookstore and publishing business in New York, and issued a German-American *Konversations Lexicon*.[106] Karl Rühl had learned the book business in Frankfurt and Breslau. His brother sat with the left at Frankfurt; a nephew married a daughter of Karl Blind; and Rühl himself took part in the revolution in Silesia. Three years after his arrival in New York in 1849 he operated several bookstores in Philadelphia. His later career was devoted to journalism on the *California Demokrat,* the *New Yorker Staatszeitung,* and the *Philadelphia Demokrat*.[107] Johann H. Bieling, a correspondent for the *Kurhessische Zeitung* who set the type for the reports of the Frankfurt Parliament and was wounded and captured with a Turner company in Baden, became a printer and typesetter in New York, and after serving in the Civil War, opened his own printing establishment in New York.[108]

Unfortunately no estimate of the number of workers among the Forty-eighters can be made with any reasonable accuracy, although we know that more of the revolutionary forces were drawn from the rank and file than from among the intellectuals or upper social classes. Among the German-Americans of whose part in the Revolution we can be certain there were carpenters, cabinetmakers, tanners, weavers, bakers, cigar makers, butchers, bookbinders, gardeners, foundrymen, millers, coopers, coppersmiths and blacksmiths, tailors, and representatives of other crafts, as well as men who belonged to the unskilled working class. Many had served prison terms in Germany, or had been wounded in the Revolution, and others managed to leave before the law caught up with them. They too had their difficult and often dramatic struggles to reëstablish themselves and their families in a new environment. They were not articulate or prominent in American affairs, and found their satisfaction in honest work and their recreation in the *Turnverein,* the singing society, the card or bowling club, the numerous German-American lodges, and less often in local associations of "Forty-eighter Battle Comrades." Their names are not recorded in history, alongside of Schurz and Hecker, but their lives blended harmoniously with the great American stream, and they found both freedom and economic opportunity in the Republic which gave them their new start in life.[109]

FOOTNOTES

Chapter 21

1. *New Yorker Staatszeitung,* Nov. 18, 1853.
2. See *New Yorker Staatszeitung,* Nov. 18, Dec. 29, 1853; and A. E. Zucker: "Theodor Kaufmann, Forty-eighter Artist," in *The American-German Review* (Oct. 1950) XVII, No. 1, pp. 17-24.
3. See article by Titus Ulke, in *The American-German Review,* XI, 12-14.
4. See *Dictionary of American Biography.* Hereafter cited as *D.A.B.*
5. Harry B. Weiss: *The Pioneer Century of American Entomology* (New Brunswick, N. J. 1936) p. 259.
6. Cunz: *The Maryland Germans,* p. 273.
7. *Der Deutsche Pionier,* XV (No. 8) Nov. 1883, pp. 336-37.
8. *D.A.B.*
9. See *D. A. B.,* and Martin W. Wiesendanger: "Lithographic Lives," in *The American-German Review,* IX, 7-10.
10. A. J. F. Zieglschmid: "Petri and Lungkwitz—Pioneer Artists in Texas" in *The American-German Review,* IX, 4-6.
11. Koss: *Milwaukee,* pp. 386-87.
12. *Wächter am Erie,* May 18, 1872; *Westbote,* May 18, 1872; and *Mitteilungen des Deutschen Pionier Vereins von Philadelphia,* III (1907) pp. 18-19.
13. *Der Deutsche Pionier,* XIV, No. 7 (Oct. 1882) p. 277.
14. *Ibid.,* XIV, No. 1 (April 1882) p. 36.
15. *New Yorker Staatszeitung,* Sept. 1, 1859.
16. Scharf: *St. Louis,* pp. 695-96.
17. See Jakob E. Mueller: *Cleveland und sein Deutschtum* (Cleveland, n.d.) pp. 477-80.
18. Hildegard Binder Johnson: "Hans Reimer Claussen," in *The American-German Review,* X, 30-32.
19. See also, Julius Fröbel: *Aus Amerika; Erfahrungen, Reisen und Studien*—2 vols. (1857-58).
20. See *Belletristisches Journal,* March 19, 1858; also March 27, April 17, 1852; and *New Yorker Handelszeitung,* May 30, 1855.
21. *Der Deutsche Pionier,* XI, No. 10 (Jan. 1880) p. 395.
22. See Wilhelm Rapp: *Erinnerungen eines Deutsch-Amerikaners an das alte Vaterland* (Chicago 1890) p. 12; and *Westbote,* Feb. 3, 1872.
23. *Der Deutsche Pionier,* XI, No. 5 (Aug. 1879) p. 198; see also Theodore W. Knauth: "Albert Fink, 1829-1897, A Memoir," in *The American-German Review,* XV, No. 3, pp. 12-13, 30.

24. *D.A.B.*
25. *Ibid.*
26. See John W. Hammond: *Charles Proteus Steinmetz* (New York, 1924) pp. 132 *et seq.*
27. *D.A.B.*
28. *Ibid.*
29. *Ibid.*
30. *Der Deutsche Pionier*, XIII, No. 9 (Dec. 1881) pp. 331-39.
31. *Deutsch-Amerikanische Geschichtsblätter*, IV (April 1904) pp. 5-19.
32. *Der Deutsche Pionier*, XVII (No. 3) 1886, pp. 249-51.
33. *Der Deutsche Pionier*, XIII, No. 2 (May 1881) p. 77.
34. *Wächter am Erie*, Sept. 12, 1867.
35. Börnstein: *Memoiren*, II, 105.
36. *D.A.B.*
37. *Atlantische Studien*, III, 67-68.
38. *Der Deutsche Pionier*, X, No. 6 (Sept. 1878) p. 247. For Sander, see Otto Heller: "Aus dem Tagebuch eines Achtundvierzigers" (Dr. Enno Sander) in *Deutsch-Amerikanische Geschichtsblätter*, XIII, 309-40.
39. *Deutsch-Amerikanische Geschichtsblätter*, VIII (1908) p. 30; and Stern and Kressmann: *Chicago's Deutsche Männer*, pp. 113-15.
40. *Jahrbücher der Deutschen Turnerei*, III, 174-76.
41. *D.A.B.*
42. *Mitteilungen des Deutschen Pionier Vereins von Philadelphia*, XIX (1911) pp. 25-28. *New Yorker Staatszeitung*, April 25, 1854. Gustav Christian Dohme, though not a refugee or revolutionist, came to Baltimore during the 1848 migration, and founded the chemical house now known as Sharp and Dohme.
43. *D.A.B.;* and Cunz: *The Maryland Germans*, p. 272.
44. Stern and Kressmann: *Chicago's Deutsche Männer.*
45. *Atlantische Studien*, II, 23; III, 24.
46. Josephine Goldmark: *Pilgrims of '48* (New Haven, 1930) p. 248.
47. See *Belletristisches Journal*, Dec. 21, 1855.
48. *Ibid.*, May 18, 1855.
49. See Scharf: *St. Louis*, p. 1542; Still: *Milwaukee*, pp. 204-5; *Belletristisches Journal*, March 30, 1855.
50. *Belletristisches Journal*, March 30, 1855; Sept. 26, 1856; May 29, 1857.
51. *Ibid.*, Feb. 15, 1856.
52. Heller: "Aus dem Tagebuch eines Achtundvierzigers," in *Deutsch-Amerikanische Geschichtsblätter*, XIII, 316, 319.
53. *Der Deutsche Pionier*, X, No. 6 (Sept. 1878) pp. 242-44.
54. *Wächter am Erie*, May 23, 1863.
55. *Der Deutsche Pionier*, XIII, No. 9 (Dec. 1881) p. 344; and *Deutsch-Amerikanische Apotheker-Zeitung* (New York, Nov. 15, 1881) II, No. 17, p. 377.
56. *D.A.B.*
57. *Ibid.*
58. *Ibid.*
59. Jakob Müller: *Cleveland und sein Deutschtum*, pp. 191-93; and *D.A.B.*
60. Cunz: *The Maryland Germans*, p. 274.
61. *Der Deutsche Pionier*, XV, No. 8 (Nov. 1883) p. 333.
62. *Belletristisches Journal*, Jan. 13, 1854.
63. *Der Deutsche Pionier*, XII, No. 7 (Oct. 1880) pp. 251-56.
64. *Deutsch-Amerikanische Geschichtsblätter*, II (April 1902) p. 71.
65. *Der Deutsche Pionier*, XV, No. 5 (Aug. 1883) p. 213.
66. *Ibid.*, XV, No. 3 (June 1883) p. 132.

67. See Ella Lonn: "The Forty-eighters in the Civil War," in Zucker: *Forty-eighters*, p. 214 *et seq.*

68. *Wächter am Erie*, May 18, 1872.

69. *Wächter am Erie*, Sept. 29, 1875.

70. *New Yorker Staatszeitung*, June 7, 15, 1854.

71. See *D.A.B.*; Heinrich Hilgard-Villard: *Jugend-Erinnerungen* (New York, 1902); *Memoirs of Henry Villard* (Boston, 1904); and Oswald Garrison Villard: *Fighting Years, Memoirs of a Liberal Editor* (New York, 1939) pp. 9-23.

72. A. B. Faust: *The German Element in the United States* (N. Y., 1909) II, 115-16.

73. *Der Deutsche Pionier*, XII, No. 6 (Sept. 1880) pp. 216-17.

74. *Ibid.*, IX, No. 6 (Sept. 1877) p. 252.

75. *Ibid.*, XI, No. 12 (March 1880) p. 505.

76. *Wächter am Erie*, June 11, 1875.

77. *Der Deutsche Pionier*, XV, No. 6 (Sept. 1883) p. 254.

78. Hense-Jensen and Bruncken: *Wisconsin's Deutsch-Amerikaner*, I, 265-66.

79. *Mitteilungen des Deutschen Pionier Vereins von Philadelphia* V (1907) pp. 30-32.

80. *Der Deutsche Pionier*, XIV, No. 11 (Feb. 1883) p. 439.

81. *Belletristisches Journal*, Feb. 5, 1858.

82. *D.A.B.*

83. *Ibid.*

84. *Der Deutsche Pionier*, X, No. 2 (May 1878) pp. 74-75; and *Mitteilungen des Deutschen Pionier Vereins von Philadelphia*, XVI (1910) pp. 38-39.

85. *Wächter am Erie*, Aug. 9, 1902, p. 91.

86. *Der Deutsche Pionier*, XVIII, No. 4 (1887) pp. 335, 346.

87. *Ibid.*, IV, No. 12 (Feb. 1873) pp. 426-28.

88. *Deutsch-Amerikanische Geschichtsblätter*, IX, No. 1 (Jan. 1909) p. 9.

89. *Der Deutsche Pionier*, XVI, No. 4 (July 1884) pp. 144-45.

90. Johnson, M. A. Thesis—"Attitude of the Germans in Minnesota Toward the Republican Party," pp. 50-51.

91. *Der Deutsche Pionier*, XIII, No. 9 (Dec. 1881) p. 374.

92. *Ibid.*, p. 375.

93. *Ibid.*, XIII, No. 7 (Oct. 1881) p. 282.

94. *Ibid.*, VIII, No. 12 (March 1877) p. 515.

95. Stern and Kressmann: *Chicago's Deutsche Männer*, pp. 141-43.

96. Richter: *Geschichte der Stadt Davenport*, pp. 540-43.

97. *Der Deutsche Pionier*, XI, No. 10 (Jan. 1880) p. 404.

98. *Chicago und sein Deutschtum* (Cleveland, 1901-02) pp. 160-61.

99. *Ibid.*, p. 154.

100. *Jahrbücher der deutsch-amerikanischen Turnerei*, I, 181-83.

101. *Westbote*, May 28, 1852.

102. *Der Deutsche Pionier*, XVI, No. 3 (June 1884) p. 118.

103. *Ibid.*, XIII, No. 8 (Nov. 1881) p. 326.

104. Stern and Kressmann: *Chicago's Deutsche Männer*, pp. 229-31.

105. *Chicago und sein Deutschtum* (Cleveland, 1901-2) pp. 379-80.

106. *Wächter am Erie*, July 26, 1875.

107. *Wächter am Erie*, Dec. 30, 1875.

108. *Der Deutsche Pionier*, XVIII, No. 3 (1887) pp. 290-91.

109. For specific cases, see the volumes of *Der Deutsche Pionier*, especially the obituary notices; and such volumes as Stern and Kressmann: *Chicago's Deutsche Männer*; Müller: *Cleveland und sein Deutschtum*; *Chicago und sein Deutschtum*; and the files of the German-language press, especially in the period after 1870.

Chapter 22 · *BISMARCK AND GERMAN UNITY*

I⊤ is characteristic of refugees to cling, to the end of their days, to the memories of a lost fatherland. Memories become sweeter with the passing years, and time has a way of drawing a kindly veil over what was unpleasant. The experiences of the Forty-eighters were no exception. Many attained influence and distinction in the United States, and by 1870 were part of the comfortable, middle-class society which is the backbone of America. Yet the fatherland continued to hold their interest and part of their affections, especially in the stirring decade of the 1860's, when so much was happening in Western Europe. Many never quite overcame a gnawing homesickness for the land of their birth, and though it had spurned their dreams of a united, free Germany as "madness" and "passing intoxication" which delayed the destined march of German history, they continued to think well of their former home. By 1870, time had taken its toll among the Forty-eighters, and few lived long enough, like Schurz and Jacobi, to see the new century. With advancing years and increasing material prosperity, something of their youthful zeal for political and social reform was lost, and in the free atmosphere of America the attitude of many Forty-eighters toward political and social problems at home and abroad became more conservative.

The decade from 1860 to 1870 was momentous in German history. Under the Iron Chancellor's policy of "blood and iron," Prussia fought three wars in less than ten years, and in 1871 a unified Germany emerged from centuries of chaos in the heartland of Europe. It was inevitable that the Bismarck Era should fan into flame a new spirit of "Germanism" among America's German group, for national pride is one of the strongest emotions of every immigrant people. A discussion of the reaction of

Forty-eighters to the Bismarckian Era is therefore important, for 1870 forced the liberals of 1848 to choose between national unity and liberty. If most Forty-eighters decided to support German unification and temporarily forget political reform, their decision merely proved that twenty years in a new country had not extinguished the natural pride which immigrants feel for the land of their origin when, after long years of humiliation, it suddenly wins the respect and approbation of the rest of the world.

The discussion of the tangled diplomacy that started the chain reaction which ended in the Franco-German War of 1870-71 may well begin with the Schleswig-Holstein question, in which many Forty-eighters and members of the Frankfurt Parliament had been deeply involved nearly twenty years earlier. The nub of the controversy was whether these duchies, or certain portions of them, were Danish or German, and how they should be governed, and the issue dragged on without a settlement into the 1860's. At first the question received relatively little attention in the German-language press of the United States. Most readers assumed that Schleswig-Holstein was German. They therefore favored its incorporation with one or more of the German states, but expected this to be accomplished without war, and through a national uprising to complete the unification of Germany.

When Prussia and Austria intervened in the Schleswig-Holstein dispute in 1864 with military force and went to war with little Denmark, the German-language press of the United States, and that portion edited by Forty-eighters in particular, disapproved of such a solution and distrusted the motives of the two reactionary German powers, which were suspected of fomenting war to stop the spread of liberal institutions. Kapp and Solger sponsored a German meeting in New York which raised $2,500 for the Germans in Schleswig-Holstein, but such gestures, insofar as they had any larger purpose beyond mere relief, were made in the interest of the unification of Germany, and not to give moral support to either Prussia or Austria.[1] By the Convention of Gastein, the two duchies were divided between Austria and Prussia, in violation of considerations of ethnic unity, as the German-American press pointed out. When the Baltimore *Turnzeitung* published a favorable appraisal of the character and policies of the King of Prussia, from the pen of Dr. Georg Wiss, his comments provoked such a storm of protests from Adolf

Douai and other radicals that Wiss was forced to resign his editorship.[2]

In 1866 Prussia went to war with Austria. The diplomatic maneuvers preceding this appeal to arms involved much more than the quarrel over the disposition of Schleswig-Holstein, although that issue poisoned the relations between Austria and Prussia from the outset. The future of the German Confederation and its control by Prussia or Austria was the real issue, as well as the hegemony of Germany in all of Central Europe, and both Bismarck and Napoleon III, who played a shifty game of secret diplomacy over this fundamental question, understood what was at stake. Bismarck's fundamental aim in the War of 1866 was to shatter the German Confederation and construct on its ruins a new Empire that would be the creature of a Greater Prussia.

The War of 1866 failed to evoke much enthusiasm in the United States. German-Americans regarded it as a fratricidal struggle in which it was difficult to sympathize with either party. The fact that the German-American population derived from both Prussia and South German States which were friendly to Austria further complicated the question. In general, however, it may be said that the liberal leaders of German-American opinion were hostile to Prussia, or at least suspicious of her motives, and were inclined to regard her as the aggressor, but at the same time showed no strong sympathy for Austria or the German Confederation. Forty-eighters who were vocal in the German-language press distrusted Bismarck's brand of German unification, hated the growing military power of Prussia, and advocated a union of the German states by democratic methods.

Nearly all of Europe expected a long and bloody war, but in reality the fighting between Austria and Prussia was over in less than two months. The Prussian victory at Sadowa was quick and decisive and marked the first great triumph of the new Prussian needle gun and the strategy of the brilliant General Helmuth von Moltke. The reaction to this unexpected turn of events was immediate in German-American circles. Nothing succeeds like success, and there was a remarkably quick shift in American public opinion after the victory at Sadowa. Even Forty-eighters discovered virtues in Bismarck and the Prussian King, and were ready to forgive their sins if they would only complete German unification.

The *Wächter am Erie,* on the eighteenth anniversary of the death of Robert Blum, printed an editorial pointing out that though few remembered the martyr of 1848, his dream of a unified Germany would soon be realized.[3] Forty-eighters, less confident of their earlier plans for reform and revolution, resolved to be practical, accept German unity, and hope that the future would bring freedom to the German people. Their special hatred for Napoleon III, "the murderer of the French Republic," made it easier to condone Bismarck's *Realpolitik* against the French intriguer.

The liberal leaders of Germany also were divided in their attitude toward the sudden turn of events. Herwegh and von Fallersleben were deeply disturbed by the War of 1866; Freiligrath seemed to give approval by his studied silence. Arnold Ruge, in an open letter in 1866 to the *Berliner Nationalzeitung,* called on Germans of every political persuasion to support unification even though Bismarck and the King of Prussia were its instruments. Later he wrote from Brighton, England, to the *Baltimore Wecker* to express delight that so many German-Americans approved the victory at Sadowa. Skeptics like Struve and Blind were brushed aside, and Ruge called attention to Kinkel's acceptance of Bismarck as the "German Cavour," and insisted that Germany could become republican only after it had become a state and that unification was impossible by republican methods.[4] In the United States, Henry Villard, in the *North American Review,* told his fellow German-Americans in 1869, that they must accept Bismarck despite his faults, as "the trenchant instrument of Providence which hewed a way to national unity, and made their fatherland more respected abroad than it had been since the reign of Charles V."[5]

Although the Cleveland *Wächter am Erie* welcomed the elimination of the Habsburgs from German affairs and the victory of a northern Protestant power over Catholic Austria, its editor was unconvinced that unification would be followed by greater liberties for the German people. "We believe," commented the aging Thieme, "that the only result will be the aggrandizement of Prussia . . . but the more of Germany it consumes, the less it will remain Prussian and the more it will become German."[6] From such comments, which were typical, it is clear that German-American liberals would have welcomed the decline of the Hohenzollerns, Bismarck, and the Junker class and an end to Prussian reaction, yet did not desire an Austrian victory which would strengthen the power of the Habsburgs. Hecker, in 1865, was alarmed by the rise of Prussia but impressed by Bismarck's clear-headed program, and in a letter written in September 1866, rejoiced that reactionary Austria had been eliminated from German affairs. He urged Prussia to put economic pressure on the smaller states to force them to join the movement for unification. He was certain that Germany was entering upon an age of enlightened despotism which would increase her self-respect and national pride, and he expected the period of absolutism to be brief.[7] The *New Yorker Abendzeitung* denounced the "particularism" and "state pride" of the German people, and pointed out that disunity among the rank and file must be overcome before ruling princes could be blamed for their reluctance to surrender power to a national sovereign.[8]

Such discussions, the prelude to 1870 and 1871, suggest a gradual acceptance, even by liberal German-Americans, of the march of events, and growing approval of the methods by which unification was being accomplished, although there was sober reflection about what a Bismarckian Germany implied for civil rights in a nation dominated by a Prussian Junker aristocracy.

In 1868 Carl Schurz revisited Germany and was royally received. Bancroft, the American minister, met him in Berlin, and the rebel of 1848 was able to spend more than an hour with Bismarck. The next day, when he was a guest of the Iron Chancellor at a dinner party, the two men talked long after the rest of the company had left. Schurz reported his observations and experiences for the St. Louis *Westliche Post*. Though lionized everywhere by the liberals, he was profoundly impressed by Bismarck as an extraordinary personality. "Perhaps the feudal ideas inculcated in him persist," he wrote his friend Kinkel, but in a modern, industrial age, a "feudal reaction" in Germany would be impossible. Although Schurz was deeply moved by his experiences in his old fatherland, he was happy to return to the United States, and wrote his wife "that this country seems home to me."[9]

Dr. B. Cyriax of Cleveland, who made a similar visit in 1869, was far more critical and severe in his appraisals than Schurz had been, for he found the Germans under the blight of reaction; "freedom of speech and press . . . an empty phrase," and the *Turnvereine* no longer centers of reform. "Germany is a land without republicans," he concluded, and "therefore is not ready for a republic." Although he found the old German sociability unchanged, he could not understand why every liberty-loving German did not emigrate.[10] Jakob Müller, another Cleveland

Forty-eighter, reported from South Germany in 1869 in a similar vein, took sharp issue with German-American papers which accepted Bismarck without reservations, and announced that he was "still a federal republican."[11] His letters referred to the "servility" and "title-sickness" of the Germans, their obsequious attitude toward the nobility, and the latter's predominance in the North German Parliament. Though he conceded the sincerity of Bismarck's efforts to unite Germany, and characterized him as "a Titan among dwarfs" who "looked like Ben Butler," Müller could not rid his mind of misgivings about the future. In one of his last letters he appealed to the United States to prove to Europe "that universal liberty also can mean general welfare," and to export the products of its expanding industry and help nations less richly endowed through a planned program of humanitarianism.[12]

Struve, in his *Diesseits und Jenseits des Ozeans,* made devastating comparisons between Germany and the United States. An American correspondent for the *Cincinnati Volksblatt* pointed out that "the real German Republicans live in voluntary or forced exile, in England, the United States, Australia, Brazil, Switzerland, but not in Germany."[13] Other observers reported that Germany was a police state, without guarantees of individual liberty.[14] A Forty-eighter who had visited Baden after the amnesty wrote as early as 1859 that he was returning to the United States because he was tired of being shadowed by the police and having his mail opened.[15] Restrictions on freedom of the press were especially disturbing to German-language papers in the United States, and the *Baltimore Wecker,* picking up a false rumor that Bismarck planned to spend his vacation in America, urged him to come, for "here he could learn that popular liberties are quite compatible with public order," and improve his "domestic policies," in such regrettable contrast "with his progressive foreign policy."[16]

The editorials of the *Wächter am Erie* from 1866 to 1870 best illustrate the quandary in which honest and intelligent German-American liberals found themselves. In the fall of 1866 Thieme referred to Bismarck as "the Junker of Berlin" and "the sick man of Pomerania," but urged support for the "German Cavour's" plan to unify Germany. In the spring of 1867 the *Wächter* lauded Bismarck's opening address before the North German Parliament and made favorable reference to the speech from the throne. Thieme still believed Prussia would not resort to force and that popular sentiment, as voiced in the Reichstag, would produce a constitution and reforms comparable to 1848. His paper gave additional space to foreign news. In April 1867 the editor rejoiced that "Germany has become a military unit of 40,000,000 souls with an army of 1,200,000," and for the first time speculated on a possible attack on France and the annexation of Alsace-Lorraine. Although Bismarck's policy, "at one stroke," had made Germany a power to be "respected and feared," he refused to believe that war was imminent, for Prussia "still has other things to do," and "the time will come." Two months later, the editor of the *Wächter* was worried by Bismarck's undemocratic procedures and concluded that he "is not the man to carry German unification farther. . . . We need a man in the spirit of Stein, who has faith in the people and their liberties." A little later, in reply to an article by Karl Grün in the *New Yorker Demokrat* which criticized German-Americans for supporting Bismarck, the Cleveland paper pleaded for a more charitable attitude "because Germany is growing in the estimation of the world" and democratic forces were still too feeble to be effective. German-Americans followed Bismarck's diplomatic victories with pride, and on the eve of the Franco-German War the liberal Thieme wrote in praise of King William of Prussia, though admitting that he "would not do for the cause of liberty."[17]

In 1870 the devious diplomacy of Bismarck and Napoleon III, and the clash of interests between the emerging German *Reich* and the French Empire, led to war. Neither side was wholly without fault, and the causes of the Franco-German War go back farther than the immediate crisis over the succession to the Spanish throne and the famous Ems telegram. Our present concern is solely with the reaction of the Germans in the United States, and more specifically with the impact of the war upon the Forty-eighters.

It was only human for German-Americans to feel a mounting pride as they followed, with breathless expectation, the victories of their blood-brothers, as the German war machine swept toward Paris. After centuries of disunion when Germany had been the battleground of Europe, the fatherland was about to assume the rôle of a first-class power in an important key position of Europe. It seemed of little consequence whether Germans were led by a king or a popular democrat, and it has never been difficult to represent wars as purely defensive. The Franco-German

War was no exception, and before long German-Americans were talking about an "unjust war," forced upon the fatherland by Napoleon III.[18] The German-language press pointed out that Germany had sympathized with the Union in the dark hours of the Civil War, whereas Napoleon had sent an army to Mexico to challenge the Monroe Doctrine, and when American newspapers expressed sympathy for the French and reminded their readers of Lafayette in the American Revolution, their comments were dismissed as cheap attempts to win the Irish Catholic vote.[19] The German element became as united in America during the Franco-German War as did Germany itself. The war was not regarded as a war of dynasties, but as a war between the Romance and the Teutonic peoples. France, after four years of diplomatic sparring, had "impudently broken the peace," and forced peaceful Germans to take up arms.[20]

By 1870 many Forty-eighters were approaching the twilight of their careers on two continents. On some issues, as preceding chapters have shown, they had been a group apart from the total German immigration. But now, with few exceptions, they joined the great majority of German-Americans in blessing the German army and the new Germany under Prussia, Bismarck, and the Hohenzollerns. They had envisaged the unification of the German states along quite different lines, but their disappointment was largely forgotten in the universal rejoicing that hailed the final achievement of a united fatherland.

Franz Sigel never revisited Germany and stubbornly refused to participate in birthday celebrations of a German Emperor who as King of Prussia had shot down his comrades at Rastatt in 1848. But even Sigel welcomed unification when it came, and the *Baltimore Wecker* in 1870 proposed sending him as a spokesman for the Germans of the United States to the German army, but Sigel tactfully suggested that German-Americans could be more helpful in other ways.[21] Wilhelm Rapp, once imprisoned for high treason, and a lifelong exponent of Turner ideals, defended Prussia's leadership with enthusiasm in 1871 in an address in Chicago to the veterans of 1848, arguing that liberals must yield their "former ideals" in this "sternly realistic age," and abandon their hopes for a "universal brotherhood" "like a beautiful and foolish dream." He approved the methods of German unification and concluded that popular liberties could only be achieved gradually.[22] Friedrich Hecker, in the main address at a victory celebration in St. Louis in 1871, described the

French as "insolent and untrustworthy," inveterate enemies who had bullied the Kaiser and his Chancellor into war. He rejoiced that Alsace-Lorraine had "been brought home again," and attributed German success to education and universal military training. He eulogized the true *egalité* of the German army, and the Teuton warrior whom he pictured as a perfect union of mind and physical strength. Yet Hecker could not overlook the absence of a German bill of rights altogether, and he was unhappy about a "parliament without authority" provided in the German Constitution. Always a republican at heart, he urged his German-American friends to help Germany secure a more liberal government by stressing the example of the United States.[23]

August Willich, former proletarian, offered to fight for the King of Prussia in 1870, but when his military aid was declined, studied philosophy at the University of Berlin instead. August Becker, another erstwhile leftist, wrote poems celebrating German victories. Fritz Anneke concluded that "History wishes it otherwise, it says too plainly: Through unity to freedom." His wife, somewhat more distrustful of the Hohenzollerns, nevertheless "hoped conditions of peace will be dictated to the proud Frenchman."[24] Philipp Wagner, another Forty-eighter with a radical's instinctive love for France, nevertheless concluded that Germany had "the higher culture," and the defeat of France was a blessing for all Europe. When he returned to Europe for a visit after the War, he found Paris a second-rate city in comparison with New York, and concluded that the sacrifices of the German people in 1870-71 were futile, for "what does it profit to have unity without liberty?"[25]

Friedrich Kapp, who had visited Germany in 1863 and reported great material but no significant political progress,[26] returned to his native land in the spring of 1870, to stay. The number of Forty-eighters who returned to Germany after 1871 was conspicuously small, although Karl Dänzer of the *Westliche Post* and Theodor Olshausen of the *Davenport Demokrat* were among them. Three hundred friends gathered at a dinner at the Apollo Hall in New York to bid Kapp farewell. Never completely at home in the United States, he had written his friend Heinrich Bernhard Oppenheim in March 1866 that he intended to spend his last days in Germany on the savings accumulated in America. "Better a glass of beer in Germany," he observed, "than champagne in America." "Whoever wants to be a German," he wrote on another occasion, "let him remain at home, or return to his fatherland," for emigration means "national death."[27] Before the end of the summer of 1870, Kapp was reporting an interview with Bismarck, "the man of peace," for the *Illinois Staatszeitung*. He felt at home in the new Germany from the outset, and referred to himself as "a citizen of two worlds." His servility to the new regime and his obvious bids for favor provoked sharp criticism in the United States. By 1875 Kapp was seriously contending that German-Americans who returned to the fatherland and had not had military training before their emigration should be forced into the army.[28]

Carl Schurz had written his friend Theodore Petrasch in August 1866, "Peace came a little too quickly to suit me. I had hoped for an embroilment between Prussia and France, out of which Germany would certainly have emerged as a unity. I now fear that victorious Prussia will be too Prussian and too little German."[29] By 1870, however, he celebrated the victories of the German army and the unification of the fatherland as eagerly as any of his fellow countrymen. In 1875 he visited Germany a second time. The Germans gave him a farewell dinner at Delmonico's in New York, and he was honored at a banquet arranged by Americans in Berlin, and attended by leading scholars such as Mommsen and Gneist, and Friedrich Kapp, his fellow Forty-eighter. On these and other occasions Schurz gave no indication that he was particularly disturbed by the turn of events in Germany. In 1881, in a memorial address in New York for Kaiser Wilhelm I, he weighed the deceased monarch's shortcomings against his good qualities, and concluded that the unification of Germany was the one great act which "illumined all his past" and guaranteed the Kaiser a place in German history comparable only with that of Friedrich Barbarossa.[30] Still later, in 1898, the distinguished Forty-eighter spoke at memorial exercises for Bismarck. In a laudatory address, he confessed the inherent weaknesses and the futility of the rebellion of 1848 and described the Chancellor as "one who realized the dreams of the Forty-eighters." Apparently he believed that the Bismarckian system eventually would give way "to the power of free ideas and a higher popular self-respect."[31]

Such statements by leading Forty-eighters were natural manifestations of the filial devotion refugees instinctively feel for their native land. They are to be judged by the standards of 1870 and 1871, not by what has happened since. Further, it is a sociological phenomenon that an increase in the prestige of the fatherland enables the immigrant to shed whatever inferiority he still may feel as an adopted citizen among the native-born; to emerge from his political and social isolation; and to proclaim the "mission" of his people in the world. Forty-eighters were no exception to this universal phenomenon in the history of immigration, and their earlier devotion to a republican Germany evaporated in the emotional heat of the victory celebrations of 1871. Some became offensive and boastful; almost all were proud of their blood-brothers across the sea, and felt drawn closely together by a strong class consciousness. Germany had ceased being "the Cinderella among the nations," and German-Americans who had been called "Dutchmen" long enough now demanded recognition in the United States as equals.[32]

The number of Forty-eighters who refused all compromise with the New Germany was small indeed. Adolf Douai condemned the war of 1870, and a few papers, like the *New Yorker Demokrat,* expressed disgust over the wild enthusiasm of Germans who showered telegrams of congratulation upon the King of Prussia and his military machine. "As republicans," wrote the editor, "we should have nothing to do with demonstrations which give the appearance of subservience, and glorify personalities."[33] In greater New York a few workers' organizations, such as the German Workingmen's Union, the Productive Coöperative Association of cabinet workers, upholsterers, varnishers, and gilders, and the German tailors of Williamsburg, still under the influence of the earlier labor movement led by Weitling and his associates, opposed the German cause in 1870,[34] but such groups had little influence. The cosmopolitanism which had characterized most liberal German groups in 1848 and made them especially friendly toward France, the mother of revolutions, had almost completely disappeared by 1870.

Of the small group of dissenters from the universal acclaim of the new Germany, none was so outspoken as Karl Heinzen, long a lone wolf in the German-American world, and now practically cast off by his fellow Germans. He remained true to his convictions of a lifetime even though it meant sacrificing what little support he still had among the readers of his *Pionier.* Heinzen had not forgotten his unhappy experiences with the Prussian bureaucracy, and as early as the 1850's had become convinced that the menacing shadow of Prussia hung over the rest of the German states. As his fellow Forty-eighters waxed enthusiastic about

Bismarck's progress to power, he became more alarmed over the prospects of a Germany unified by Junkers, bureaucrats, the police, and the military, and in 1866 he advocated the forceful assimilation of Prussia into the rest of Germany. The war with Austria he regarded as a defeat for progress, culture, and freedom, and Bismarck's North German Confederation as an alliance "between a tiger and a dozen lap-dogs." He would not support "the Bismarck comedy and the Hohenzollern swindle."

In 1870, though he denounced French mobilization and admitted that Napoleon III deserved to be chastised, Heinzen bemoaned the fate of the German and the French people now that war had come. He predicted that Germany would win; he contributed his bit to the relief of German wounded, widows and orphans, and he was ready to sanction certain annexations at the expense of France, but he hoped that the war would result in more democracy for both powers. When a French Republic emerged from Napoleon's defeat, Heinzen wrote vigorously in its favor, and when France capitulated in 1871, "the year of disaster," he published a moving tribute to the French people and their historic rôle in western Europe. Gambetta became one of his heroes, and Bismarck the arch enemy when the latter seemed determined to bleed France white to rid Europe of "the poison of republicanism." "I can congratulate Germany for having chastened French chauvinism," Heinzen wrote to a friend in Germany in 1872, "but German chauvinism is even more disgusting to me than French, because it is fed by servility and insolence." Heinzen continued to belabor German megalomania and to expound republican principles until he was practically excommunicated by the German-Americans and the circulation of his paper dropped to the vanishing point. He accused Schurz and other Forty-eighters of "sentimental servility," and Kapp of betraying the cause of liberalism. In the eyes of his critics Heinzen had become a "Francophile" and a "traitor," and when he suggested that American friends of European monarchs should be deprived of their American citizenship, the *Wächter am Erie* denounced him as a megalomaniac and a fool.[35] After the war, when Heinzen returned to Europe for a short visit, he refused to set foot upon soil ruled by a Hohenzollern despot, though his heart yearned for one more glimpse of his beloved homeland. In 1878, in one of the last issues of the dying *Pionier,* he published an editorial entitled "Homesickness, by a Man Who Has No Home."[36]

Heinzen and his little group of devoted disciples were regarded as irresponsible mavericks by German-Americans, including most Forty-eighters. Regardless of whether they had been "Grays" or "Greens," Germans were united into a solid front by the glorious victories of 1870 and 1871. Gustav Körner recounted in his diary how Germans of the old "Latin" settlement around Belleville, Illinois, rushed into the streets to hail each new German victory, singing and embracing out of sheer joy, and described how "Rhine wine and champagne flowed in streams." Suddenly Frenchmen had become less attractive to German liberals, and Germans had a mission to lead the western world into a new "Hellas of art and science." Even unorthodox radicals detected the hand of God in the recent march of events.

Huge crowds in the larger cities cheered the progress of the war. Turner and singers paraded in America while German troops moved on Paris. In the spring of 1870, the King of Prussia contributed $250 in gold to the treasury of the *Deutsche Gesellschaft* of New York, and the *New Yorker Handelszeitung* expressed the thanks of the whole German community for such royal beneficence.[37] Flags decorated homes in the German sections of the larger cities. Signatures for a patriotic resolution to the North German Bund were collected in the offices of all the New York German-language newspapers. Dr. Kudlich presided at a mass meeting in Hoboken, and Butz in Chicago, and cables congratulating the King of Prussia, and extending good wishes for a speedy victory, were sent from many cities.[38] Cleveland Germans telegraphed his Prussian Majesty—"To-night we fired a hundred cannon salute in honor of the glorious victory of the German army." In Madison, Wisconsin, and Louisville, cannonades summoned the Germans to mass meetings. The San Francisco Germans paraded with torchlights. In Chicago, buglers rode through the streets to announce the declaration of war and summon Germans to the Turner Hall, to sing *Die Wacht am Rhein,* and listen to speeches by Butz, Dr. Ernst Schmidt, and Hermann Raster. Telegrams drafted on such occasions frequently sounded the significant note: "We know a victory for the German arms across the sea would also raise the respect for the German-Americans."[39]

In Baltimore, the Germans assembled in Monument Square to hear Wilhelm Rapp, and Schurz helped draft resolutions of felicitation to the North German Parliament.[40] August Thieme told the Germans of Cleveland that their countrymen were not conquerors or oppressors, but true cosmopolitans, "who understand the meaning of freedom better than anyone else."[41] Louisville Germans, their houses bedecked with American and German flags, marked the capitulation of Sedan with a "Fraternal Festival" *(Verbrüderungsfest)* and a parade,[42] and the Republican state convention of Ohio adopted resolutions of sympathy for the German people in their heroic war for national unity.[43]

Exciting and thrilling as these celebrations were, they hardly compared with the "Victory Celebrations" in 1871. In New York, the German-language press demanded a parade, "to show Anglo-Americans and Celtic citizens the stuff of which German immigration is made." The procession, as finally constituted, represented the arts, sciences, trades, agriculture, and industry, and German militia companies and veterans of the Civil War marched in the first division. German gardeners carried bouquets of flowers; six hundred butchers turned out on horseback; two thousand carpenters marched with axes over their shoulders, and every trade carried its appropriate insignia. A reception and review followed at the City Hall, with a mass meeting in Tompkins Square and a German theatre performance the following day. Oswald Ottendörfer of the *New Yorker Staatszeitung* and other prominent Forty-eighters helped plan the celebration, and proposed a national society to foster better relations between America and Germany, increase the political influence of the German-American group, and preserve German culture and the German language in America.[44]

In a peace parade in Milwaukee, said to have been five miles long, the marchers carried transparencies reminding "Brother Jonathan" of the achievements of "the German Michel." Ernst Lasche's *The Soldier's Bequest* was performed in the German Theatre, and an address was sent to the German *Reichstag* pointing out that Germany's victories were won "for the Germans in the United States also."[45] German-Americans staged similar demonstrations in Pittsburgh, Detroit, Madison, Columbus, Philadelphia, Washington, Baltimore, Wheeling, Wilmington, North Carolina, Nashville, Rochester, Terre Haute, and Indianapolis. In Cleveland, a huge "Germania," eight feet high and mounted on a pedestal to add another five feet, was hauled through a triumphal arch on the Public Square, in a parade consisting of six divisions and floats representing various crafts and societies. Bakers distributed pretzels; another float dispensed confections; the Swiss float represented Wilhelm Tell shooting the apple from his son's head; and other entries depicted episodes from German history, or were intended to be humorous. The Negroes of Cleveland had a float with the motto "Peace unto all Nations." In the Public Square, the crowd was addressed by Dr. Jacob Mayer and August Thieme, who made every effort to make the occasion something more than boastful gloating over a vanquished enemy.[46]

It has been asserted that Chicago spent $200,000 on its victory celebrations, which featured a parade of many divisions and a float with stout Arminius, forty Teuton riders and sixty foot soldiers, dressed in bearskins and carrying lances and clubs. The shoemakers marched three hundred strong, with white gloves and high hats, behind a figure of Hans Sachs. Busts of Händel, Haydn, Beethoven, Schiller, Goethe, and Humboldt stressed Germany's contributions to world civilization, and various floats depicted episodes from German history from the Peasants War, the Liberation, and Father Jahn to the birth of the German Empire in the Hall of Mirrors at Versailles, in a garish display of the "German spirit" in history.[47]

Through all these celebrations ran the note that they were necessary "to show Americans what Germans could do when they are united." The *Louisville Volksblatt,* published in a city where Germans had been driven through the streets by a nativist mob sixteen years earlier, referred to its peace celebration "as a day of honor which fully compensates for all the dishonor and misrepresentation endured until now."[48] A correspondent of the Columbus *Westbote* maintained that the Franco-German War had improved the status of German-Americans by fifty per cent, "so that one can have a little hope that before long the name 'Dutchman' may be changed into German."[49]

The popular excitement produced new outbursts of sentimental poetry. E. A. Zündt, a radical Turner poet who had written voluminously about the need for social revolution in America, now wrote a poem of homesickness and filial devotion for Germany, and pride in her achievements. Friedrich Lexow, a Forty-eighter who had been in the United States since 1852, wrote "Germania" on a similar theme, and Caspar Butz hailed the rebirth of the fatherland in a poem entitled "Greetings from the Germans in America."[50] August Becker composed a "Drinking Song" positively gloating over the fall of France. Freiligrath's "Hurrah, Germania," written for the *Rhein Zeitung,* was reprinted in many German-language newspapers in this country.[51]

Of more tangible benefit to the fatherland than verse of doubtful literary merit was the relief work for German widows, orphans, and wounded. By the fall of 1870, $35,000 was collected in Chicago, and at one meeting addressed by Butz, Raster, and Edmund Jüssen, the proceeds amounted to $3,000. Fairs, bazaars, and other benefits were organized in many cities. A fair in Akron yielded $2,000; in Louisville, $3,150 was collected in July 1870, at a single meeting, and in Washington, $2,700. The Germans of St. Louis pledged $50,000. Steinweg, at a gathering in New York addressed by Schurz and Sigel, led the subscription list with $2,000, and by August 1870, the New York total reached $64,000. A concert by the Concordia Singing Society of Chicago netted $2,000. The North American *Turnerbund* urged its members "to remember the fatherland" in this "battle of scientific humanism against barbarians," between "the moral man" and "the ruffian." In Cleveland, Turner and singers joined in a concert and gymnastic exhibition for the benefit of the wounded "in Germany's army of liberation." Evansville, Indiana, sponsored a concert and *Turnfest,* and in Omaha the Germans collected $1,000 at one meeting. In Milwaukee, Anneke exhorted his fellow Germans to give generously, and the *Illinois Staatszeitung* offered $200 to the German soldier who captured the first French flag.[52] Efforts to consolidate German-American relief into a national organization had the enthusiastic support of leading Forty-eighters such as Sigel and Ottendörfer, and a national convention of "Patriotic Relief Societies" held in Chicago, designated Friedrich Kapp as its Berlin representative. How much was actually raised in the United States is difficult to estimate. According to one report, three million marks were sent to Berlin in 1871. Körner estimated that more than a million dollars were dispatched to Berlin in six months.[53]

The peace treaty which ended the war satisfied most German-Americans, including the Forty-eighters. Heinzen railed against its harsh terms to no avail. Arnold Ruge argued that the war helped France to get rid of Napoleon and brought the better elements into control of her government. The *Wächter am Erie* approved the transfer of Alsace to Germany, but dissented on most of Lorraine and insisted that the boundary follow ethnic lines. Yet the same paper rejected a plebiscite, condemned the counterfeit republic of Gambetta, and defended the principle that in war might becomes right. Its liberal editor severely criticized German radicals who objected to a "Kaiser by divine right," predicted there would be no "Caesarism" in Germany, and refused to consider Gambetta's "red revolution" in the same category as the Revolution of 1848.[54]

The years which followed the sudden birth of the new German Empire provided German-Americans with many satisfactions as they followed the phenomenal progress of their native land in industry, commerce, the arts and sciences, social legislation, and national prestige. More than forty years of peace followed the war with France and, like other German-Americans, the Forty-eighters basked in the reflected glory of Germany's rise to power.

In May 1871, Hecker had the courage to point out, in a letter addressed to a gathering of Forty-eighters in New York, that Bismarck would not be able to resist the implications of universal suffrage for the *Reichstag,* and that property qualifications for voting and office-holding could not be defended indefinitely.[55] The New Jersey *Freie Zeitung* predicted a victory for the *Reichstag* in the conflict "between the rights of the people and the powers of the sovereign." The *Wächter am Erie* hoped for a "victory of liberty" which would reflect glory for Germany as the victory over France had brought prestige to the fatherland in international affairs.[56] But when Kapp, in his *Frederick the Great and the United States,* made derogatory references to this country, the editor of the Cleveland paper took him to task "for quickly exchanging his Republican toga for the frock-coat of a lackey," attacked his "one-sided, unjust and untrue" judgments concerning the United States, and accused the erstwhile Forty-eighter of ingratitude toward a nation which had supported him for twenty years and enabled him to retire to Germany on his savings.[57]

In 1873 Hecker revisited Germany to see for himself what the new order was like. Mannheim gave its most famous Forty-eighter a rousing welcome and ten thousand people lined the streets as the great Revolutionary made his triumphal entry to the cheers of the crowds and the singing of the old *Hecker Lied* of 1848. The *Mannheimer Familienblätter* greeted the city's illustrious son with a poem about the "Man of the West," come home "to the free Rhine in his German Fatherland," and the *Mannheimer Tageblatt* published flattering accounts of his career.[58]

Hecker was deeply moved, lauded the enterprise and phenomenal progress of the German people, expressed his preference for some of the things he saw in Germany, but also his dislike for "so many uniforms."[59]

But joy soon turned to disappointment, and within a few weeks Hecker was convinced that he never again could be happy in Germany. In Frankfurt the police confiscated the torches which the German People's Party had collected for a procession in his honor, and prohibited Hecker from speaking from his hotel to a crowd gathered beneath his window. At a banquet in Leipzig he gave due credit to Germany's phenomenal progress, but also expressed the fervent hope that the fatherland might become "strong in the liberties of the citizen," and like the United States, a symbol of freedom for the world.[60] In Stuttgart, on the Fourth of July, Hecker lauded the United States as the land of freedom and equality, and described three American miracles which he had seen with his own eyes—the abolition of slavery, the return of a huge military establishment to peaceful pursuits, and the decision not to bestow military decorations on the victorious generals of the Civil War. He referred to Germany's title sickness and hunger for medals; he defended Americans against the charge that they were "dollar mad," and insisted that Europeans were as bad or worse; and he pointed with pride to the many philanthropies of American men of wealth, whose counterpart could not be found in all of Europe. But above all, he spoke in praise of the American bill of rights, freedom of the press, and jury trial, and frankly stated that German immigrants had made a wise decision when they left their native land for the free republic across the Atlantic.[61] In reports to the St. Louis *Westliche Post,* the *Illinois Staatszeitung* and other papers, Hecker referred to his displeasure about compulsory military training and the billeting of soldiers on German civilians during maneuvers, and to the impotence of the *Reichstag.*[62]

Such frank statements did not ingratiate the old Forty-eighter with the new regime in Germany. His Stuttgart address was regarded as especially tactless and offensive, and papers like the *Weser Zeitung* took violent exception to Hecker's contrast of the repressive atmosphere of Germany with the free air of Switzerland and the United States. In Frankfurt the police dispersed a crowd which had gathered to say farewell. Speaking once more to his Mannheimer friends at a banquet in honor of the distinguished republican, Hecker took pains, in a long speech widely circulated in the United States, to make it clear that, culturally speaking, he was still a German, but in all other respects he was an American and a republican.

One more observation of Hecker's is significant, because he never supported equal rights for women. Though he found many German women charming, and in some respects superior to their American sisters, he was outraged to learn of the hard manual labor which they had to perform, especially in rural areas. He saw women walking alongside of ox-carts while husbands and sons slept on top of the load, and in the cities he found them carrying mortar as high as the third and fourth stories. He reported to the *Illinois Staatszeitung* that he had seen a man guiding a plow pulled by a cow and his wife in double harness, and his wrath did not cool when he was told that the "son was in the army" and therefore the mother had to help with the farm work.[63]

When Hecker's ship docked in Baltimore in October 1873, almost his first words to the reception committee were, "Thank God, I am again on free soil and can say what is in my heart, without the gag of imperial penal statutes," and in a land where "no gendarmes dare interfere with the right of free assembly." He described the German Empire as "more autocratic than the old Roman imperium," and contended that there had been more freedom under Marcus Aurelius and Hadrian than under Bismarck.[64] He had always deplored political corruption in the United States, but in contrast he found Germany in a state of "chronic, incurable corruption." When Hecker spoke again to his Baltimore friends, after the customary parading and serenading, he predicted that Bismarck would eventually be forgotten, and hoped he might live long enough to witness the birth of a true German Republic.[65] In 1876 he appealed for support for the widow of Georg Herwegh, who had died in poverty, and for a monument over the grave of "the poet of freedom."[66]

Few were as courageous and outspoken as Hecker and Heinzen, but many had to admit that Bismarck was a reactionary. It could not be denied that real freedom of speech and assembly and responsible government did not exist in Germany, although it was not clear whether the German people were completely satisfied with the existing state of affairs, not interested, or simply indolent. In a major address in Chicago in 1874, Wilhelm Rapp admitted that the new German national state "does not conform to our ideals" and years would be required to produce full liberty for the German people.[67] Hermann Raster was irritated by the obsequiousness of German journalists whom he met while touring in Germany. Thieme's devotion to his beloved Saxony could not overcome his depression in 1873 when he discovered not only that the Germans had few civil liberties, but seemed to accept the situation without complaint.[68] The old revolutionist, Amand Gögg, lecturing to a small audience in Cleveland, painted a gloomy picture of a police state without a constitution, in which laboring men had few rights and public education was deplorable.[69] Dr. Kiefer of Detroit discussed unification in a public address without a single reference to Bismarck and the Kaiser, and quoted von Stein to the effect that Germany could well do without an Emperor. When the power of the German Socialists began to grow in the 1880's, Kiefer welcomed their influence and hoped they would help Germany fulfill her rôle in Europe, not by the sword, but in the spirit of liberty and humanity, and through science and freedom of thought and inquiry.[70] He was outraged when Prussia refused to permit the erection of a simple monument to the patriots of 1848 on the fiftieth anniversary of the Revolution. The venerable Forty-eighter, Dr. Hans Kudlich, as late as 1898, in an address in Chicago, denounced the stupid arrogance of the German minister of war who referred to the Revolution of 1848 as "the saddest page in German history," and predicted that the battle between popular sovereignty and divine right would go on.[71] Such isolated protests were the last manifestations of the old liberal spirit of 1848. They made no impression on Germany, and almost none upon the Germans in the United States.

FOOTNOTES

CHAPTER 22

1. *Wächter am Erie*, Jan. 13, 1864.
2. Cunz: *The Maryland Germans*, p. 375.
3. Nov. 15, 1866.
4. See *Wächter am Erie*, July 28, Dec. 13, 1866.
5. Quoted in John G. Gazley: *American Opinion of German Unification, 1848-1871*, in Columbia University Studies (New York, 1926) CXXI, pp. 483. This is an excellent study which I have summarized in part here. See especially Ch. IX, pp. 425-508.
6. See July 28, Aug. 4, 1866.
7. *Wächter am Erie*, Nov. 22, 1866.
8. Quoted in *Wächter am Erie*, Dec. 20, 1866.
9. March 29, 1868, in *Intimate Letters*, p. 430; and Schurz to Kinkel, Feb. 24, 1868; *Ibid.*, p. 426; also *Wächter am Erie*, Feb. 12, 24, 1868.

10. *Wächter am Erie,* July 2, 10, Aug. 4, Sept. 16, 1869.

11. *Ibid.,* Sept. 9, 1869.

12. *Wächter am Erie,* April 30, May 9, 20, June 8, July 2, 1870.

13. Quoted in *Wächter am Erie,* March 7, 1867.

14. *Ibid.,* May 3, 1865.

15. *Westbote,* May 26, 1859.

16. *Wächter am Erie,* May 31, 1870.

17. See *Wächter am Erie,* Oct. 25, 1866; March 21, April 11, June 6, Nov. 21, 27, Dec. 12, 1867; July 22, 1870.

18. *Wächter am Erie,* July 18, 1870.

19. *Wächter am Erie,* July 29, 1870. On Bismarck's attitude during the Civil War, see Ralph Lutz: *Die Beziehungen zwischen Deutschland und die Vereinigten Staaten während des Sezessionskrieges* (1911).

20. *Wächter am Erie,* July 16, 1870.

21. *Ibid.,* July 29, 1870.

22. Wilhelm Rapp: *Erinnerungen eines Deutsch-Amerikaners an das alte Vaterland* (Chicago, 1890) pp. 8-12.

23. See *Deutsch-Amerikanische Geschichtsblätter,* XXXIII, p. 126 and "Hecker's Festrede zur St. Louis Friedensfeier" (1871) in *Friedrich Hecker und sein Antheil an der Geschichte Deutschlands und Amerikas* (Cincinnati, 1881) pp. 49-62.

24. Quoted in Wittke: *Heinzen,* p. 276.

25. See Philipp Wagner: *Ein Achtundvierziger* (Brooklyn 1882) pp. 234-45; 386-89; 394.

26. *Wächter am Erie,* Jan. 21, 1863.

27. Kapp: *Aus und über Amerika,* I, 343-44.

28. See *Wächter am Erie,* Aug. 12, 1870; June 12, 1875; and article signed "R" (probably Heinrich Rattermann) in *Der Deutsche Pionier,* VII (No. 4) (June 1875) pp. 162-65.

29. *Intimate Letters,* p. 365.

30. Joseph Schafer: *Carl Schurz, Militant Liberal* (Evansville, Wisconsin, 1930) pp. 246-47.

31. See *Deutsch-Amerikanische Geschichtsblätter,* XXIX (1929) pp. 137-49.

32. *Liberty Writings,* pp. 464-65, for a speech by Dr. Hermann Kiefer.

33. Quoted in *Wächter am Erie,* July 23, 1870.

34. See Gazley: *op. cit.,* p. 508.

35. *Wächter am Erie,* March 31, 1871.

36. Wittke, *Heinzen,* pp. 268-281.

37. See *Wächter am Erie,* April 24, 1870.

38. *Ibid.,* July 19, 29, 1870.

39. Max Stern and Fred Kressmann: *Chicago's Deutsche Männer* (Chicago, 1885) p. 67. See also *Sixty Years in Chicago, Autobiography of August Lueders* (Chicago, 1929) p. 24.

40. Wilhelm Rapp: *Erinnerungen eines Deutsch-Amerikaners an das alte Vaterland* (Chicago, 1890) p. 7.

41. *Wächter am Erie,* July 21, 1870.

42. Stierlin: *Kentucky,* pp. 226-27.

43. Roseboom: *The Civil War Era,* p. 474.

44. See *Wächter am Erie,* March 30, May 4, 1871.

45. Hense-Jensen and Bruncken: *Wisconsin's Deutsch-Amerikaner,* I, 227-31.

46. See *Wächter am Erie,* April 4, 11, 1871. In New York, the butchers carried a huge sausage, with the couplet,

"Diese Wurst ist unter Würsten
Was Kaiser Wilhelm ist unter den Fürsten."

Ibid., April 12, 1871.

47. *Wächter am Erie,* June 1, 1871.

48. Stierlin: *Kentucky,* pp. 228-29.

49. *Westbote,* Jan. 3, 1872; Jan. 6, Feb. 8, 1873.

50. See B. A. Uhlendorff: "German-American Poetry," in *Deutsch-Amerikanische Geschichtsblätter*, XXII-XXIII, pp. 258-62; and Caspar Butz: *Gedichte eines Deutsch-Amerikaners* (Chicago, 1879) p. 154.

51. See also *Wächter am Erie*, Aug. 20, 1870; and Karl Knortz: *Das Deutschtum der Vereinigten Staaten* (Hamburg, 1898) p. 48.

52. For these items, see *Wächter am Erie*, July 20, 21, 23, 25, Aug. 1, 4, 1870; and Still: *Milwaukee*, p. 129.

53. See Oscar Canstatt: *Die Deutsche Auswanderung* (Berlin 1901) p. 193; Kapp: *Aus und über Amerika*, I, 187.

54. *Wächter am Erie*, Sept. 6, 1870, March 21, 28, 1871. The *Philadelphia Demokrat* took the same position.

55. *Wächter am Erie*, May 25, 1871.

56. *Ibid.*, May 30, June 17, 1871.

57. *Ibid.*, June 19, 1871.

58. See *Wächter am Erie*, June 27, 1873.

59. See *Westbote*, June 25, July 2, 1873.

60. *Westbote*, Aug. 6, 1873.

61. *Wächter am Erie*, July 25, 1873.

62. *Ibid.*, July 5, 15, 1873.

63. *Westbote*, Aug. 27, 1873. See also a letter by another disillusioned Forty-eighter to the *Westliche Post*, in *Westbote*, Oct. 4, 1873.

64. *Westbote*, Oct. 25, 1873.

65. *Baltimore Wecker*, cited in *Wächter am Erie*, Oct. 27, 1873. It is not without importance to note that Hecker's speeches were interrupted in Baltimore with shouts of "Hoch, Bismarck!" and that his remarks stirred up a violent controversy in the German newspapers and among the Germans of the city.

66. *Wächter am Erie*, Jan. 24, 1876.

67. *Aus grosser Zeit. Beiträge zur Geschichte der Achtundvierziger in Amerika* (Chicago, 1900) p. 50. Cited hereafter *Aus grosser Zeit*.

68. *Wächter am Erie*, June 13, July 23, Aug. 15, Sept. 16, Dec. 1, 1873.

69. *Ibid.*, May 17, 1872.

70. *Liberty Writings*, pp. 74-89; 464-65; 120-35.

71. *Aus grosser Zeit*.

Chapter 23 · *THE END OF AN ERA*

THE EVENTS of 1870 and 1871 unified the German-Americans as nothing else had ever done before. The rivalries between "Grays" and "Greens," greatly mitigated by the common experiences of the Civil War, disappeared completely during the Franco-German War. Enthusiastic young "stormers of the heavens" accepted the new order, and "Greens" became "Grays." The radical idealism for which political refugees fought in the 1850's had mellowed with the years, and been heavily diluted with practical Americanism. The star-gazing period was over. Satisfied with German unification, not too concerned about the methods which brought it about, and deeply absorbed in their American experiences, many Forty-eighters now were convinced that they had tried to accomplish the impossible in 1848.

As men grow older they seem to derive increasing pleasure from their reminiscences. Their ranks thinning rapidly after 1870, the Forty-eighters formed organizations, like the veterans' organizations of other wars, to preserve the comradeship and memories of days long past when young rebels risked their necks for reform. It became a mark of distinction to be known as a Forty-eighter, and the veterans of the Revolution pressed their claims to fame as eagerly as the Sons and Daughters of the American Revolution emphasize the deeds of their ancestors. Forty-eighters bought canes and pipes, decorated with the names of their comrades in arms, or depicting in color events of the Revolution, and handed them on as heirlooms to their children and grandchildren. In 1907 a medal was issued in Germany, commemorating the hundredth anniversary of the birth of Robert Blum. In the larger cities the veterans of 1848 and 1849 formed organizations and sponsored programs of varied activities. Occasionally they responded to appeals from abroad to help erect a monument to the martyrs of the Revolution in a particular locality.[1] In Davenport,

Iowa, the veterans of the Schleswig-Holstein crisis met in the local Turner Hall in 1872 to form an organization which for many years assembled the Forty-eighters annually at the banquet table, to live again, in speeches and poems, the exciting days when they had fought in Schleswig-Holstein.[2] In Cincinnati, in 1875, Hassaurek reviewed the history of the Forty-eighters at the seventh anniversary meeting of the Society of German Pioneers, and spoke as a conservative, looking back upon the romantic dreams of a youthful band of world reformers with impracticable ideals.[3] In Chicago and other cities Forty-eighters held annual reunions.

In 1873 the twenty-fifth anniversary of the Revolution was observed in a number of American cities. In Chicago, where the celebration was postponed until the spring of 1874, the veterans of 1848 were welcomed in a hall decorated with the colors of the new German *Reich* hanging alongside the black-red-gold of the Revolution. On a tablet were inscribed the names of those executed for treason in 1848 and 1849. Thirty-five bona fide veterans were present, including such prominent Chicagoans as Rapp, Balatka, and Butz. Their records were read in full, with special stress upon the time spent in jail, and each honored guest received a black-red-gold rosette for his coat lapel. In a poem for the occasion, inspired by a line from Ulrich von Hutten, Butz celebrated the new German Empire as a popular government, built on the cornerstone of 1848, and destined to evolve from the present "barracks state" into a land of freedom. Hecker, too ill to attend, sent a letter urging a more practical approach to the German problem and pleading for patience, for he seemed convinced that popular liberties would come through a slow process of evolution. Wilhelm Rapp made the principal address; the Chicago Turner sent greetings; letters were read from prominent Germans in other cities; the Germania *Männerchor* sang German songs, and at the close of the program, toasts were drunk to the free republics of Switzerland and the United States.[4]

The twenty-fifth anniversary celebration in Davenport was attended by 337 members of the veterans' organization, although some were honorary members only. In New York, the "Society of German Patriots" which met annually from 1870 to the end of the century, and veterans of the Revolution in Baden residing in New York City, established the tradition of marching each year from the Germania Assembly Hall to Jones's Woods for an outing. At the head of the parade they carried the American colors, the flags of 1848, and the imperial flag of the new German Empire. General Sigel made the principal address in 1870, and on that occasion letters were read from Schurz, Rapp, and other Forty-eighters, and from the son of Robert Blum.[5]

In 1881 Friedrich Hecker, in many respects the most typical Forty-eighter, died on his farm in Illinois. More than any other German of his time, Hecker was the popular, romantic incarnation of the Revolution, a cosmopolitan, warm-blooded "man of the people," and a symbol of liberty and republicanism in Europe, and among the Germans of the United States. When he died, nearly all the German-language papers printed glowing obituary notices. The Illinois legislature adopted memorial resolutions, and the *Nordamerikanische Turnerbund* and other German societies sent messages of condolence. Delegations came from many cities for the funeral, and the burial rites took on the characteristics of a solemn state occasion, with a flood of oratory at the funeral exercises and at the grave. Emil Praetorius of St. Louis and Caspar Butz of Chicago paid tribute to their old comrade in revolution. George Schneider compared Hecker with Ulrich von Hutten and America's John Brown. Carl Lüdeking spoke for the freethinkers of St. Louis, and a Hungarian judge for his nationality group. Dr. Hugo Starkloff represented the *Turnerbund*. A minister laid a laurel wreath on Hecker's coffin for the Swiss; flowers came from all parts of the country, from French and Italian Republicans, Forty-eighters, Hecker's comrades of the Civil War, *Turnvereine* and German societies of every variety. One speaker spoke for the French Republicans in the United States, and the venerable Gustav Körner finally brought these extraordinary tributes to a close. Shortly after the funeral, the German-American Hecker Monument Society of Cincinnati published a brochure describing the great liberal's contributions to the republican cause on two continents, and committees were organized to raise funds for an appropriate monument.[6] Though Schurz, Sigel, Jacobi, and several other prominent Forty-eighters lived on into the twentieth century and died rich in public honors, no other occasion so completely symbolized the original spirit of 1848 as the tributes paid to Hecker at the time of his death in 1881.

The year 1898 marked the fiftieth anniversary of the Revolution, but relatively few actual veterans were left to celebrate the occasion, and its significance was either forgotten or belittled in both Germany and the United States. In Chicago the Germania *Männerchor* sponsored an anniversary celebration. The walls of the banquet hall were decorated with garlands of evergreen, the American flag, and the colors of the German Revolution, and pictures of Hecker, Schurz, Sigel, Krez, and other well-known Forty-eighters. Over the main entrance hung a likeness of the martyred Robert Blum, with the inscription "Through Darkness to Light." The Forty-eighters occupied places of honor on the stage, and were flanked on their right and left by an honor guard in the uniforms of 1848. The audience greeted their entrance with three resounding cheers; two ladies representing "Germania" recited a poem by Johann W. Dietz entitled "The Greetings of Spring to the Forty-eighters," and the *Männerchor* sang "Lützow's Wilde Jagd." Joseph Rudolph made an address stressing the contributions of his group to American liberty, especially during the slavery controversy and the Civil War. Dr. Emil G. Hirsch, the main speaker, reviewed the ideals of 1848, with their emphasis on civil rights, legal equality, public education, and the brotherhood of man, and appealed to "Young Germans" in the fatherland to work for their realization in the new Empire. With great emotion he spoke of Forty-eighters "who escaped the mass grave of Rastatt," only to fall in the service of their adopted country "on the battlefields of the Potomac and Tennessee." He ended his oration with felicitations to the new Germany and a pledge of undivided loyalty to the United States. Portraits of Hecker, Brentano, Butz, and several other refugees were unveiled and presented to the Germania *Männerchor*. The festivities concluded with an address in English by a Chicago judge, a speech in German by Wilhelm Rapp, several choruses, and the singing by the entire company of *Die Wacht am Rhein* and "Columbia, the Gem of the Ocean."[7]

The following year, sixteen white-haired veterans met in Schmuckert's Garden in Chicago to commemorate the fiftieth anniversary of the battle of Waghäusel, perhaps the bloodiest engagement of the Revolution, and Anton Hottinger, president of the Society of Forty-eighters, gave a detailed account of the famous battle. A professor from Northwestern University read an editorial which Rapp had written for the *Illinois Staatszeitung,* and Joseph Rudolph and Johann W. Dietz made addresses. A nephew of Karl Schapper, a prominent German refugee who had settled in London, and the son of Brentano were among the distinguished visitors and were introduced with great ceremony.[8]

In New York, ten members of the Society of German Patriots of 1848, ranging in age from seventy-eight to eighty-six, were still living in 1909. After a brief ceremony attended by Bernhard Kröger, Philipp F. Körner, F. J. Schlott, David Mayer, Franz Dambacher, and Leopold Maisch, they solemnly decreed that after the death of their last member the property of the organization should go to the New York *Turnverein,* whose leader was the son of a Forty-eighter.[9]

Thus ends a notable chapter in the history of American immigration. Among all the newcomers to the United States, the Forty-eighters were unique. Not their number, but their extraordinary ability, spirit, and influence made them significant. They sent a spark into the inert German-American masses and helped transform them into one of the most important groups in the American population during one of the most critical periods in American history. The intellectual contributions of the Forty-eighters represent the transit of civilization from an old to a new world. The men and women of 1848 were convinced of their mission on two continents. Sincere and devoted republicans in Europe and in America, they were determined to awaken their contemporaries to an understanding of true democracy and German culture. If they were tactless, impatient, and impractical, and rejected halfway measures, it may be said that their zeal sprang from a genuine devotion to a fixed set of principles for which they were ready to scale the heavens.

No group quite like the German Forty-eighters and their kindred spirits from neighboring lands ever appeared again in the history of American immigration, although refugees from Hitler's Germany suggest certain similarities in cultural and political interests. In general, the refugees of 1848 were an honorable lot, though not without their small quota of pure adventurers and vagabonds, and they meant well by their adopted country even though in their early years they clung tenaciously to their hopes for a new European Revolution. The German-language press of the United States profited enormously by their presence, and their political leadership was important, if not decisive, during the shifting party allegiances of the 1850's.

These men knew how to speak and how to write, and some were among the best-educated Americans of their time. They were not indifferent to the cultural and political values which they found in the United States, as so many immigrants have been before or after their time, but they were determined to rebuild America to conform to their theories. Some expected too much in too short a time and used methods that were neither wise nor effective. Yet much of what was best in the German community in the United States—its press, societies, theatres, schools, and other cultural and social institutions—stemmed from the Forty-eighters, or took on new life from their insistence on higher standards of excellence.[10]

By 1870 much of the fire of youth had burned itself out, and material success had made radicals more conservative. After 1870, though the German immigration remained large, its character changed markedly. It included more industrial workers and artisans, and fewer with the intellectual and cultural attainments of the Forty-eighters. Immigration statistics fluctuated sharply after the Franco-German War with conditions in Germany; reached a new peak in 1882, but declined again in the 1890's, largely because of Germany's phenomenal progress as a growing industrial and commercial power.

There was much less criticism of the German government after 1871, and fewer political liberals among later arrivals. The German-language press was no longer as interested in political reforms abroad as it had been in the 1850's, when many papers were edited by refugees. There was general satisfaction with German progress after 1870, and genuine pride in her achievements. Many editors of the German-language press were imported from Germany in this later period simply because men with sufficient training and experience were unavailable here, and it was natural for the newcomers to write with approbation of the country whose phenomenal progress they had witnessed. Unification, national progress, and increasing power, not republicanism and civil liberties, were the new *motifs* of the German-American press, whose readers became more and more absorbed in domestic matters. A few Forty-eighters, still active in journalism, deplored the lower cultural level of the more recent German immigration, were shocked by the indifference of the newer arrivals toward the finer things of German culture, and concluded that the German element in the United States had entered upon a period of retrogression and decay.[11]

In Germany significant changes were taking place also, especially in the realm of moral and spiritual values, and in the field of politics. The new generation, to use again the words of Ricarda Huch, looked back upon the year 1848 "as a childish comedy with a shot of sentimentality."

The failure of the Frankfurt Parliament had discredited professors and intellectuals as practical political leaders, and they were ridiculed for their talkativeness and their theories. The new Germany worshiped Bismarck. Liberals like von Stein were forgotten. Absolute monarchy, with its military trappings and its gospel of discipline, law, and order, became a protecting cloak for modern capitalism and industrialism, and in turn received its powerful support. Though Junkers hated both the proletariat and the new aristocracy of capital, they concurred in revering the monarchy as the visible symbol of Germany's greatness.

Germany became less the land of poets and thinkers and free spirits, and more a nation whose faith was in material things, discipline, and physical strength. Respect for power, law, and order triumphed over the old ideals of humanitarianism, cosmopolitanism, liberty, and justice, so fervently advanced in 1848. "The spirit of 1848" had had its day in Europe as well as in the United States. Although not all Forty-eighters were intellectuals and ardent reformers, there were among them the literal heirs of the liberal traditions of Kant, Fichte, Schiller, Lessing, Feuerbach, and Germany's golden age of liberalism and rationalism. With the decline of their influence the flowering time of German culture in America reached its end.

FOOTNOTES

CHAPTER 23

1. See *Wächter am Erie*, June 17, 1872.
2. Richter: *Geschichte der Stadt Davenport*, pp. 602-18.
3. *Wächter am Erie*, May 28, 1875.
4. *Aus grosser Zeit* (Chicago, 1900) pp. 38-54.
5. *Wächter am Erie*, May 16, 1870; also Feb. 10, May 12, 1874.
6. *Friedrich Hecker und sein Antheil an der Geschichte Deutschlands und Amerikas* (Cincinnati, 1881).
7. *Aus grosser Zeit*, pp. 55-82.
8. *Aus grosser Zeit*, pp. 83-96. By 1900, the roster of the Chicago organization still contained the names of the following veterans of 1848-49: Anton Brockmann, Louis Kurz, Johann Latas, and Joseph Rudolph of Austria; C. H. Gottig and Heinrich W. Heuermann of Schleswig-Holstein; Friedrich Hanke of Hesse-Nassau; Eugen Hepp and Georg Schneider of the Rhenish-Palatinate; Anton Hottinger, Karl Jais, Heinrich Keller, Franz S. Kapp, Gustav May, and Julius Rosenthal of Baden; Johann Krissler and Wilhelm Rapp of Württemberg; and Franz Schuberth of Bavaria. H. W. Heuermann acted as secretary, and Johann W. Dietz was carried on the rolls as an honorary member. *Ibid.*, p. 113.
9. *Deutsch-Amerikanische Geschichtsblätter*, IX (July 1909) No. 3, p. 97.
10. See also, T. S. Baker: "Young Germany in America," in *Americana Germanica* (New York, 1897) I, No. 2, pp. 72, *et seq.*
11. See *Wächter am Erie*, Feb. 9, 1875.

INDEX

71
72
74
75
76
77
79
81
83
85
88